D1595338

MOSBY's
FIGHTING PARSON

The life and times of
Sam Chapman

Peter A. Brown

Willow Bend Books
Westminster, Maryland
2001

On Sam Chapman:

> "His character as a soldier was more on the model of the Hebrew prophets than the Evangelist or the Baptist in whom he was so devout a believer. He was generally in front of everybody in a fight."

> "One of the noblest and most heroic soldiers in the Southern army."
>
> Col. John S. Mosby
> Commander, 43rd Battalion
> Virginia Cavalry, C. S. A.

> "He was the bravest man I ever knew."
>
> Pvt. Ludlow Lake, Jr.
> Company A, 43rd Battalion
> Virginia Cavalry, C. S. A.

MOSBY'S FIGHTING PARSON

THE LIFE AND TIMES OF SAM CHAPMAN

PETER A. BROWN

Willow Bend Books

65 East Main Street
Westminster, Maryland 21157-5026
1-800-876-6103

WB2839

Source books, early maps, CDs — Worldwide

For our listing of thousands of titles offered

by hundreds of publishers see our website

www.WillowBendBooks.com

Visit our retail store

International Standard Book Number: 1-58549-668-5

Printed in the United States of America

For
JACKIE AND STEPHEN

and in memory of
JAMES MAHLON MOYER
1935-1999

MOSBY'S FIGHTING PARSON
THE LIFE AND TIMES OF SAM CHAPMAN

CONTENTS

ACKNOWLEDGEMENTS

When attempting to record the life story of another, utmost attention must be given to the accuracy of the information used; likewise, the sources must be both dependable and objective. I was fortunate to find such sources in my search for this story—this life—that is Sam Chapman's. It was not always an easy task, for Chapman was an extremely modest man and he became more so as his years passed.

Here, I want to introduce the reader to those people who contributed of their time and knowledge so that I might bring you the story of an extraordinary man and the times, places, and persons who were so much a part of his life. To these people I am, and always will be, most graciously indebted.

Without the late Jim Moyer this book may have never been possible. I first met Jim in 1991, when he and Tom Evans spoke to our Civil War Round Table in Lexington. They had just completed their *Mosby's Confederacy: a Guide to the Roads and Sites of Colonel John Singleton Mosby*. Virgil Carrington "Pat" Jones, renowned author of *Ranger Mosby* accompanied them and in talking with Pat that evening my long-held wish to tell Sam Chapman's story was given its impetus. However, several years would pass before time and opportunity would allow me to begin the task in earnest. When I did, Jim Moyer was among the first persons I contacted, and over the next few years he shared with me his friendship and his vast knowledge of Colonel Mosby and his men and unselfishly provided me with the personal contacts that would prove so crucial to my work. He led me to such people as John K. Gott, the gentlemanly historian of Fauquier County, who shared his unending knowledge of so many things, from Mosby to the churches of Fauquier. Jim also led me to Carolyn and Chris Russell from whom I obtained personal wartime correspondence of Lieutenant Colonel William Chapman. This material was vital within itself, but it also provided me with other trails to follow in my quest. I am thankful to John Gott and to the Russells for their undying patience when I repeatedly intruded with what must have seemed endless questions.

Horace Mewborn shared with me his files based on the vast research that he and Hugh Keen did for their Virginia Regimental History Series volume *43rd Battalion/Virginia Cavalry/Mosby's Command*. It was Horace who led me to the 1864 Baltimore newspaper article containing excerpts from the diary of the British soldier-of-fortune Bradford Hoskins, mortally wounded while in the service of Mosby.

Without Charlie and Jeanne Lewis much of the information pertaining to Reverend Sam Chapman's children would have been incomplete. Through the unselfish act of making personal family correspondence and papers available to me, would-be gaps in the postwar life of Chapman were avoided. Likewise, my thanks must go to Howard Revercomb Hammond who not only directed me to the Lewises' but also provided numerous amounts of genealogical data from his own records.

Several people provided me with either originals or copies of many of the hundreds of letters that passed between Colonel Mosby and Captain Chapman, beginning shortly after the end of the war and continuing until a few days before Mosby's death in 1916. Primary in this regard was George Revercomb Hudnall, who also provided family correspondence from the years following the war. John Kincheloe, Hugh Keen, Duane Miller, Bob Daly, Jackie Lee of The Fauquier Historical Society in Warrenton, Oliver "Chillie" Wood and Milton Cockrell furnished copies of Mosby-Chapman letters. My thanks also to Lewis Leigh of Leesburg, Bob Lurate of Lexington, and Bill Turner of La Plata, Maryland, for their assistance in my search for this correspondence. "Chillie" Wood and Jere Mac Willis, Jr. provided assistance in gathering information on their kinsman, Albert Gallatin Willis, hanged by Union cavalrymen in Rappahannock County for being "one of Mosby's gang." Fred Anderson, Executive Director, and Darlene Slater, Research Assistant, of The Virginia Baptist Historical Society at the University of Richmond, were most helpful in having requested records available for my perusal and in running down information from my numerous inquiries. John Coski, Archivist at the Museum of the Confederacy, Richmond, searched for and produced several valuable records including the James Thomas Petty diary and the reunion ledgers for the 43rd Battalion. The staff at The Library of Virginia, Richmond, were most helpful, especially in bringing to me records of the State Auditor, consisting of large, heavy-bound ledgers of city and county tax records, covered with the dust of a hundred years; and to Phyllis M. Young of the Special Collections branch a special "thank you" for searching the *Special Orders of the Adjutant and Inspector General, C. S. A.* for some never-located Orders, but who made my day when she did locate others believed to have been long lost!

The staff of many of the repositories were especially helpful and made my work one of pleasure and anticipation—Graham Dozier, Archivist, Virginia Historical Society, Richmond; Janie C. Morris, Research Services Librarian, Duke University Library, Durham, North Carolina; Vickie Cyphert, Page Public Library, Luray; Kitty Fitzgerald, Sarah Rice Pryor Chapter, United Daughters of the Confederacy, Covington; Dr. Richard Sommers, United States Military History Institute, Carlisle Barracks, Pennsylvania; the staff in the Special Collections Branch, University of Virginia Alderman Library, Charlottesville; the reference staff of Preston Library, Virginia Military Institute, Lexington, and Carol Tuckwiller, librarian in the Virginia Room of the Roanoke Public Library. Particularly memorable is the reference staff of the Rockbridge Public Library, Lexington, for continually honoring my many requests, for volumes obtained through the Inter-Library Loan system, with patience and dispatch.

The churches that Reverend Chapman served during his ministry were a great source of information, supplying me with minutes books and other materials so pertinent to my research. Much appreciation goes to – Rev. Kenneth Schmidt, Woodlawn Baptist Church, Alexandria; Mary Bunch and Catherine Blevins, Main Street Baptist Church, Luray; Ellen Snead, Sharon Baptist Church, Clifton Forge; Benton Stull, Rich Patch Union Church; Joan Macky, Healing Springs Baptist Church; Ernest and Lucille Huntington, Clifton Forge Baptist Church; Teenie Hodges, Teresa Craighead, and Rev. Jeffery Gibby, Covington Baptist Church. My good friend Jim Mead of Low Moor provided valuable information and leads to follow pertaining to the Low Moor Union (now Presbyterian) Church, and Gracie McCoy Jackson of Staunton was helpful with information on the old Rich Patch Mines Church.

Many of the people I have mentioned invited me into their homes and they will always remain close, not just for the valuable information and insights pertaining to Sam Chapman's story, but for who they are and how they made me feel—not as a stranger but as a welcomed friend! Nancy Chappelear Baird was a friendly and knowledgeable hostess, entertaining my wife and me with her stories of the people of Fauquier and of her work on the journals of "Tee" Edmunds. Paul and Gertrude Lacy, owners of the farm that once belonged to Sam's son, Willie, shared anecdotes and some of Sam's belongings including a spur and a copy of the 1895 painting, *The Fight at Miskel's*, by James E. Taylor.

Mrs. David R. Chapman and Mrs. Samuel Chapman Stephenson, had photos and family material. Horace A. Revercomb, III surprised me with a photograph of the commissioned officers of the 4th Immune Regiment taken at the close of the war with Spain. Merrill Mays graciously loaned me several items from Sam Chapman's days as Covington postmaster, including Chapman's own copy of his appointment. Archer Hanson invited me to view material and personal items belonging to Sam's brother, William, while Mary and Max Roha shared a large quantity of genealogical material. William Pollard, Archivist at Mary Baldwin College, Staunton, obtained pertinent information on the long-defunct Staunton Female Seminary. My thanks also to Pat Loving of Covington for searching old hand-written funeral records.

Howard Crawford made the long trip from North Carolina to Lexington to show me first-hand the little revolver given during the war by Sam Chapman to his future wife Rebecca. With it was the "Miss Beck" letter, penned by Sam in June 1863 while he was recovering from his near fatal wound following the disastrous fight near Greenwich. The letter and pistol were discovered in a secret compartment of a family trunk over 130 years later.

My sincere thanks to Robert Ballou of Sterling for his excellent work on the maps and to authors and historians Bob Driver, Brownsburg, John Heatwole, Bridgewater, Bill Miller, Churchville, Harold Woodward, Rochelle, Ed Hagerty, Glasgow, Bob Krick, Fredericksburg, and Peter Carmichael, Cullowhee, North Carolina for their assistance and encouragement.

Finally, my eternal love and gratitude to my wife, Kitty, for the many hours she spent hovering over library microfilm readers, reading and re-reading drafts of the manuscript (even those "bloody war descriptions"), making suggestions and correcting errors. She instilled in me the confidence and kept the faith that I would finish what I had set out to do!

P.A.B.
Lexington, Virginia

PART I

"THAT FELLOW MOSBY"

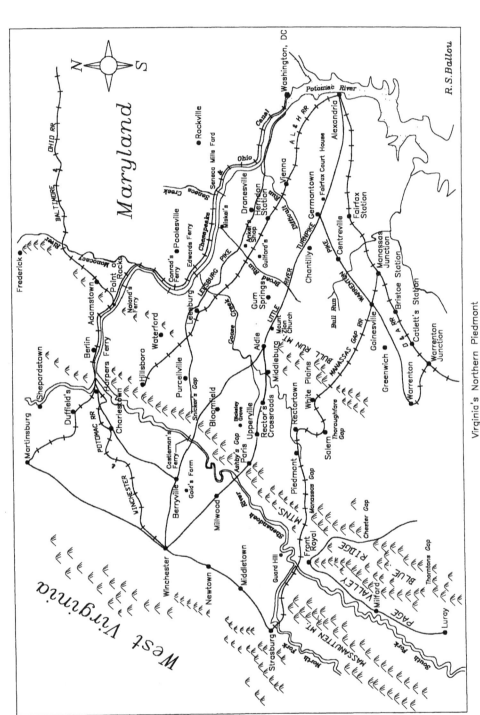

Virginia's Northern Piedmont

Primary location of Mosby's operations from January 1863 to April 1865.

R.S. Ballou

1. Courthouse Pleadings to Partisan Plans

January 15, 1863 dawned cold and overcast in Warrenton, the small but bustling county seat of Fauquier County, Virginia. Sam Chapman was up early and his attention was drawn to the slight figure riding out from the Warren-Green Hotel toward the Marsh Road. His gray uniform was splattered with mud, almost obscuring the yellow trimmings that denoted a cavalryman. The rider's presence would have probably gone unnoticed in the town of some 1200 residents, augmented by a few dozen Southern troops, mostly the wounded and some conscripts awaiting assignment. But recent happenings in nearby Fairfax County had stirred up talk among the locals. "If that fellow Mosby attempts that 'caper' again, he will be caught," Chapman had heard the hotel-keeper remark,[1] summing up the general feeling among the citizens in a region whose northern and eastern reaches, after nearly two years of war, were infested with enemy patrols. "It was the first time I ever saw Mosby," Sam later recalled, "and I remember how youthful he looked and how thin he was from the active service he had seen."[2] Wiry, yet muscular, with a slight stoop, that was not ungraceful, and keen, piercing blue eyes that flashed from beneath the brown felt hat, his five foot, eight inch, 125 pound [3] frame belied a restless, almost impatient, urgency to duty.

"That fellow Mosby" was twenty-nine-year-old John Singleton Mosby. The imprudent nature of his younger days—like the blustery winds of a late winter—had been replaced with a spring-like tranquility that bespoke the life of a husband, father and inveterate attorney. But nothing in his settled life could foretell the role Mosby was yet to play, following the nation's headlong fall into the fiery darkness of civil war. Winter winds would return.

Born on December 6, 1833, at the home of his mother's parents in Powhatan County, Virginia, forty miles west of Richmond, John was the second child of Alfred Daniel and Virginia McLaurine Mosby, the first having died in infancy. Soon after his birth, the family returned to their home in Nelson County, but in 1840 they relocated to a farm in adjoining Albemarle County, just four miles from Charlottesville and the University of Virginia. Only a few weeks shy of his seventeenth birthday, young John enrolled at the University. Though he was small of stature and frail, a dominant trait in his makeup was a tendency to fight, whether his adversary was his own size or one towering above him. He was a battler by instinct, and it was an easy evolution from fists to firearms,[4] an evolution that was soon to play itself out at Mr. Jefferson's university.

Young Mosby's first year at the school was, from an academic view, a good one. However, it was marred by his involvement in a melee in town during which he leapt on—and soundly thrashed—a clumsy town policeman, resulting in a court fine. And chronic illnesses often kept him from his classes. He passed the next two years, hard at his studies but still finding time to engage in the social life of the school and community. But his final year at the college would prove to be tragically disruptive. Bad talk and even stronger ill feelings with a fellow student, by the name of Turpin, resulted in a face to face confrontation on March 29, 1853. Feeling threatened by the much larger and robust town bully, and with an aggressive nature that invited his antagonist to a showdown, Mosby armed himself and awaited the tavernkeeper's son at the top of the stairs of the Brock Boarding House. As the enraged Turpin advanced, the thin nineteen-year-old student took aim—with a small caliber pepperbox pistol—and sent a bullet into his would-be attacker's neck. The wound proved to be slight and Turpin would fully recover. However, a subsequent trial brought a one-year jail sentence and a $500 fine to the now expelled Mosby and, though he would later receive a full pardon, the next seven months would be spent in the local jail. [5]

During Mosby's confinement, in a fateful, albeit ironic, reversal of fortune, the young prisoner found a friend and tutor in his former prosecutor, William J. Robertson, who would later serve on the state's hightest court and become the first president of the Virginia Bar Association. Mosby had told Robertson of his intention to study the law. "The law has made a great deal out of me," he had remarked, "I am now going to make something out of the law."[6] Impressed by the former student's intelligence, affability and good humor, Robertson offered him the use of his library and, upon his release from jail, the use of his office for his continued studies. Applying the tenacity and singleness of purpose that would be hallmarks of his life, Mosby set his course and, on September 4, 1855, the Commonwealth of Virginia licensed him to practice law. Within a short time he had opened up his first law practice in Howardsville, a rural village situated on the James River, in southern Albemarle County. It was here that he would meet and fall in love with the visiting Pauline Clarke, a spirited and devout Kentucky girl and daughter of a former United States Congressman. John Mosby and Pauline Clarke were married in Nashville, Tennessee, not far from her home in Franklin, Kentucky, on December 30, 1857. The following year the newlyweds relocated to Bristol, Virginia on the Tennessee border, where Mosby would become the town's first lawyer to open a practice to the public. [7]

In the summer of 1860, with the rumble of discord growing louder and the threat of civil war racing toward reality, the young attorney, to oblige a former University classmate, allowed his name to be put on the muster roll of a local militia company. Named the Washington Mounted Rifles, the company was led by a peculiar, profane, cantankerous, but warm-hearted former West Pointer by the name of William Edmondson "Grumble" Jones. Mosby was so indifferent about the whole affair that he was not present when the company was organized some months later. He did attend, however, the first drill, held in the nearby county seat of Abingdon, in January of 1861.[8]

From both a political and a military standpoint the spring of 1861 would turn out to be hot as any summer. On April 24, Virginia entered into a military alliance with the new Confederacy. This action was preceded by the firing on Fort Sumter by South Carolina shore batteries, April 12-13, and by Virginia's passing of a secession ordinance four days later. On May 14, "Grumble" Jones' company enlisted in the service of the Commonwealth; less than two months later, the Washington Mounted Rifles was integrated as Company L (later to be Company D) in the 1st Regiment Virginia Cavalry. The 1st Virginia was commanded by a twenty-eight-year-old lieutenant colonel who had spent most of the previous eight years as a lieutenant in the U.S. Cavalry assigned to the Kansas frontier. This caped, plumed, and sashed cavalry leader, with the large curved mustache and reddish-brown beard, had been nicked-named "Beaut" by his West Point classmates. His name: James Ewell Brown Stuart, better known now by the sobriquet "Jeb."[9]

Private Mosby would now begin his soldiering in earnest. The regiment was at First Manassas on July 21. Although Captain Jones' company would experience limited service, mostly in reserve, Mosby would write to his wife: "There was a great battle yesterday...I was in the fight...We stood ...under a perfect storm of shot and shell—it was a miracle that none of our company was killed...We were placed in the most trying position in which troops can be placed, to be exposed to a fire which you cannot return...." The remainder of the summer was spent primarily on picket duty in and around Fairfax. In August, there were a few encounters with Union cavalry patrols that intruded too near the regiment's picket posts.[10]

On September 11 Colonel Stuart rounded up 305 men—infantrymen, a section of artillery, and two companies of cavalry, including "Grumble Jones'—and left camp, heading northwest, to look for a large number of Yankees, reported to be near Lewinsville. Several miles out, Stuart picked Mosby and three others and rode forward to reconnoiter the enemy. The five riders spotted a force across a field about 100 yards off. Mosby quickly dropped from his horse and took aim with a "...splendid Sharp's carbine which will kill (at) a thousand yards...Their Colonel was gaily dressed. I was in the act of shooting him...when Colonel Stuart told me not to shoot, fearing they were our men." The Southerners soon realized it was a Union regiment, and fell back until artillery could be brought up to scatter the bluecoats.[11]

"Grumble" Jones had taken a liking to Mosby soon after the lawyer began active service with the company. And Mosby grew to like the rough veteran also. Even though Jones hounded him because of his small size and the stoop to his shoulders Mosby would later say: "Jones was always very kind to me." When it became time for the company to leave Bristol, "Captain Jones allowed me to remain for some time to close up the business...and to provide for my family." On September 17, while the regiment was still in Fairfax, Mosby wrote to his sister Liz: "Although Captain Jones is a strict officer he is very indulgent to me and never refuses me any favor I ask him. I think he will be made a Colonel soon." The prophetic private was right; Captain Jones was promoted eleven days later. But the respect these two soldiers, one the young recruit and the other the gritty veteran, had for each other would not change.[12]

Following his promotion to colonel on September 28, Jones was placed in command of the 1st Virginia Cavalry. At the same time, his superior, Colonel Stuart, was promoted to brigadier general. The older, eccentric Jones would feud bitterly with his younger, flamboyant superior. Lieutenant Colonel W.W. Blackford, a future aide-de-camp on Stuart's staff and former classmate of Mosby at the University of Virginia, would later say: "He (Jones) regarded (Stuart) with intense jealousy when placed under his command, a feeling that ripened afterwards into as genuine hatred as I ever remember to have seen in my experience in life." [13]

(Although antagonists for the entire three years before their deaths in the spring of 1864, both Jones and Stuart would each, in his own way, come to have an enormous influence on the military life and career of John S. Mosby.)

By November 18 the headquarters of the 1st Virginia Cavalry had been moved to about three miles below Centreville. That morning John Mosby was one of eighty men from the regiment sent with Lieutenant Colonel Fitzhugh Lee on a scout in search of a company of Yankees who had approached close to the Confederate outer line. "They were concealed in a pine thicket... We charged right into them and they poured a raking fire into our ranks," Mosby would write to his wife three days later; " (Another man) and myself in the ardor of pursuit, had gotten separated ... from our main body." Mosby and his companion and a third trooper killed two Yankees, members of the Brooklyn Zouaves. "I jumped down from my horse (and) rested my carbine against a tree and shot him dead" Mosby would tell Pauline. [14]

Mosby requested a furlough on January 21, 1862 because of sickness in his family, now back in Nelson County. The request was granted, primarily because of the endorsement of Jones: "Private Mosby left home a lawyer in good practice as a private in the ranks and has always been ready in the most active and dangerous duty, rendering brilliant service. If any is entitled to consideration, surely he is." Less than a month later, on February 14, the gruff commander summoned the private to his tent and, without ceremony, offered him the position of adjutant which, if approved, carried with it the rank of first lieutenant. That same day John wrote to Pauline: "The rank and pay is next to that of a captain's... The duties are very light...no picket or guard duty...(the office)... is a good stepping stone for future promotions and it is no small credit to me to be promoted from the ranks over the heads of those under whom I started." [15] And, as he had with Jones, Mosby was soon to find favor with Stuart, and before long was performing valuable service as a scout and gatherer of intelligence. [16]

In March, the Confederate army had withdrawn from its positions around Centreville, north of the Manassas battlefield, and headed southwest toward the Rappahannock River. Near Bealeton Station Stuart had observed a large column of Federals coming up on the army's rear and wondered aloud: "General Johnston wants to know if McClellan's army is following us, or if this is only a feint he is making..." [17] Mosby, who was standing nearby with Colonel Jones, "...saw the opportunity for which I had longed." [18] If Stuart would give him a guide Mosby would find out. Stuart agreed to do so, and with three companions, Mosby immediately started out on a trek that would take him around the flank of the hostile column and into its rear. As he got behind the enemy, he soon discovered that only an isolated body was following the Southern army and that it kept up no line of communication with its headquarters. When Mosby reported this information to Stuart, the cavalry leader sent "Grumble" Jones on a flying pursuit that soon dispersed the column. The following day, in his report to General Joseph E. Johnston, commander of the Confederate army in Virginia, Stuart had high praise for his new scout: "Adjutant Mosby...volunteered to perform the most hazardous service, and accomplished it in the most satisfactory and creditable manner. (He is) worthy of promotion and should be so rewarded." [19]

Mosby's promotion to lieutenant, as recommended by Jones in February, was confirmed on April 2, 1862, to take effect from February 17. But just as things looked promising for the lawyer-turned-soldier an inane practice, carried over from the Regular U.S. Army, was inserted in a military bill enacted by the Confederate Congress the previous January. It would have a profound effect on the new lieutenant's career. The legislation allowed for the election of lower officers, to determine just who would command the company or regiment, and permitted the rank-and-file to canvass the post seeking votes for their candidates. Indeed, the candidate himself would often conduct full-fledged campaigns, shaking hands, and backslapping, even speech making in the purest political sense. Popularity, rather than ability, was the primary factor in deciding who would command. [20] It was during this process that, on April 23, Fitzhugh Lee was elevated to colonel, replacing Jones as commander of the 1st Regiment. Jones would leave the regiment but, soon after, assume leadership of the 7th Virginia Cavalry. Promoted to brigadier general, he would be killed at the battle of Piedmont, Virginia on June 5, 1864, only three weeks after Stuart was to be mortally wounded in a clash with Union cavalry at Yellow Tavern outside Richmond. [21]

The popular, but humorless, Fitzhugh Lee, a nephew of Robert E. Lee, was an able soldier and officer. Eventually rising to the rank of major general, he would command a division, suffering a serious wound at Third Winchester in September 1864 that would curtail his active service until just before the end of the war. After the war he would serve as governor of Virginia and later as a major general and commander of the U.S.Volunteer's VII Corps in the Spanish-American War. [22] However, Mosby, for reasons he never made entirely clear, had an intense dislike for his new colonel; this feeling would grow over the next three years into almost an obsession. In his memoirs, written a half-century after the war, Mosby alluded to the "indifference" shown to him by Fitz Lee, and to an instance in March 1863 when he felt Lee was trying to deprive him of forming his own command. These instances occurred well after Lee's election to be the new leader of the regiment, but Mosby wrote to Pauline on April 25, 1862: "Our regiment was reorganized day before yesterday. Col. Lee was elected over Col. Jones... Immediately after the election I handed in my resignation of my commission. The President had commissioned me for the war, but I would not be adjutant of a Colonel against his wishes or if I were not his first choice." [23]

The former lieutenant was not without a job for long. When Mosby resigned his commission in the regiment, Stuart quickly made him an aide on his own staff. The general did not want to loose the services of this frail, but staunchly resolute, cavalryman whose coolness and flair for scouting he had come to know and respect. As for Mosby, he welcomed the opportunity to more fully serve his friend and mentor. "He made me all that I was in the war. But for his friendship I would never have been heard of," Mosby was to write years later.[24] "...my friendship for Stuart...lasted as long as he lived."[25] Although Mosby now had no commission, Stuart still referred to him as lieutenant,[26] and would waste little time in taking advantage of his new aide's talents.

By early June, the Union Army of the Potomac, nearly 105,000 strong, under the command of Major General George B. McClellan, had advanced up the Virginia peninsula and was poised before Richmond. The previous March, as he readied his huge army to set sail for Fortress Monroe, on the Virginia coast, "Little Mac" had confidently declared: "I shall soon leave (Alexandria) on the wing for Richmond—which you may be sure I will take." Opposing this host of blue-clad invaders was General Robert E. Lee, with the newly organized Army of Northern Virginia. Lee's forces numbered about 74,000 and General T. J. "Stonewall" Jackson's 18,500 infantrymen would not arrive on the scene, from the Shenandoah Valley, for another three weeks. Less than two weeks before, on May 31, the two giants had gone toe-to-toe at a Virginia crossroads, in a bloody, error-laden fight that would end in a stalemate, with no winner but enough blame to go around for leaders on both sides. The crossroads, aptly named Seven Pines for the seven large pine trees standing there, was only a half-dozen miles from the Confederate capitol.[27] The fight would be a fearsome prelude for what was to come, during a fateful seven days less than a month away.

Mosby was at breakfast with General Stuart at the cavalry leader's headquarters a couple of miles from Richmond near the York River Railroad. [28] The sun was already up and the still air brought the promise of another hot day in the low, marshy bottomland between the Chickahominy and James Rivers. It was June 10, and Stuart had just returned from an early meeting with General Lee. McClellan's army, following the fight at Seven Pines, was divided; the bulk of his forces, some 70,000 soldiers, was spread out along the south bank of the Chickahominy, while one reinforced corps of nearly 30,000 was encamped on the north side. [29] The enterprising Lee had told Stuart of his design for an offensive on the north side of the river against the reticent McClellan. The ever cautious Union commander was busy preparing fortifications and bringing up his heavy guns for a siege-like bombardment of the Confederate capitol—"an active defense" his West Point instructors called it—a tactic for advancing against an opponent from behind one's own fortifications.[30] The irresolute-to-a-fault McClellan wanted no room for failure in this, his grand scheme, one that would surely take him through the gates of Richmond! But Lee had other plans for the Federal commander.

As Stuart sat down beside Mosby, he related his conversation with Lee: if Lee's strategy against McClellan was to succeed, the Confederate commander must know how well, if at all, the Union right was protected. This flank, comprised of Major General Fitz John Porter's V Corps, was northeast of Richmond on the north bank of the Chickahominy. Nearby, and below a ridge of trees, ran Totopotomoy Creek, meandering southeast into the Pamunkey River; further down river at White House Landing, was McClellan's vast supply depot. If the wing of the Union army was unprotected, Lee surmised, he could bring Stonewall Jackson's "foot cavalry," soon to be on its way from the Valley, pouncing down on Porter from behind, while the main Confederate force attacked his front and flank. But to do this, Lee needed to better know the position of the Union troops, and, in particular, if the ridge along Totopotomoy Creek was fortified, thus presenting an obstacle to Jackson. [31] Could Mosby ascertain this, Stuart asked. The scout jumped at this chance and with three men started out. The following day he was back. He had been unable to get through the Union lines, he reported to Stuart, but he had made a surprising discovery—McClellan had only cavalry pickets guarding his line of communication with his base on the Pamunkey. Using his finger as a pencil, Mosby sketched roads and landmarks on the ground. Stuart watched and listened in silence but a plan was already formating in his mind—from Richmond north, astride the Richmond,

Fredericksburg and Potomac Railroad, to the South Anna River above Ashland; east, behind Porter's V Corps, to Hanover Court House; south, paralleling the Pamunkey River and behind the main Federal army spread out on the Chickahominy near Seven Pines; then across the York River Railroad at Tunstall's Station and above the Federal supply depot at White House Landing; on to Forge Bridge, crossing the Chickahominy and into Charles City Court House, wheeling north at Harrison's Landing on the James and back into Richmond—a route that would take them entirely around McClellan's huge army! When Mosby had finished, Stuart told him to write a repport of his findings for General Lee; then the cavalry leader was up and off to Lee's tent. [32]

At 2:00 a. m. on June 12, Stuart assembled 1200 of the best troopers in the brigade, along with two light cannons, and—with John Mosby in the forefront—set out on what General Lee was to call "an expedition." It was to last nearly four days and cover over 100 miles, completely encircling an enemy force exceeding 100,00 men. Stuart accomplished his primary objective, finding that McClellan's right flank was indeed unsecured and that there was no Federal force of any consequence on the watershed of the Pamunkey, north of Totopotomoy Creek. The mission was not entirely uneventful, however. Captain William Latane, a twenty-eight-year-old physician from the 9th Virginia Cavalry, was shot dead, while leading a charge near Old Church, on the second day out from Richmond He was the raid's only fatality. (Tragically, Latane's younger brother, John, a lieutenant in the same regiment, would be accidentally, but mortally, wounded by his own men less than a year later). There were other exchanges with Union pickets and outposts and, at Tunstall's Station on the York River Railroad, the column routed one or two companies of Federal infantry and tore up the track. In the process, they narrowly missed derailing a locomotive pulling a string of flatcars loaded with blue-coated infantry, heading for McClellan's supply base barely four miles away at White House Landing.[33] Overall, the raid resulted in vast quantities of stores being captured or destroyed, including thousands of pounds of bacon and forage, sugar, coffee, rice, and even whiskey. Pistols, cavalry saddles, and bridles were turned over to the quartermaster department, together with several hundred horses and mules; a large number of prisoners (various reports put the number anywhere from 165 to over 200) were surrendered to the provost marshal.[34]

Mosby, writing to Pauline the day after he was back in camp, could hardly contain himself: "I returned yesterday with General Stuart from the grandest scout of the war. I not only helped execute it, but was the first one who conceived and demonstrated that it was practical," he triumphantly wrote. A few days later, and for the first time, he was mentioned in general orders; Lee named him among privates who had received special commendation.[35]

By July 2, McClellan had withdrawn his army from its positions east of Richmond to his new base at Harrison's Landing on the James River, effectively ending his Peninsula Campaign. In human terms, the Seven Days Battles had been excruciatingly costly, especially for Lee—20,204 dead, wounded or missing. Union losses were put at 15,855.[36] During the lull that followed the fighting, Mosby had time to further contemplate his long sought-after goal of leading his own command, to operate behind the enemy's lines, to "...make the harvest where the laborers were few..." On more than one occasion, he had discussed the possibilities with Stuart. To this end, less than a week after his return from the now celebrated "Ride around McClellan," Mosby was in the office of Secretary of War George W. Randolph with a note from Stuart: "Permit me to present to you John S. Mosby, who for months past has rendered time and again services of the most important and valuable nature, exposing himself regardless of danger, and in my estimation, fairly won promotion. I am anxious that he should get the Captaincy of a Company of Sharpshooters in my brigade...I commend him to your notice." [37] But, despite this strong endorsement from the South's newest hero, for the time being, it was not to be. Mosby would resume his duties as aide to General Stuart.

The next few weeks were relatively calm for Mosby. He continued to talk with Stuart about the prospect of having his own command, particularly in light of the Partisan Ranger Law passed by the Confederate Congress on April 21, 1862. This act authorized any officer, deemed appropriate by the President, to raise a unit of partisans—infantry, cavalry, or artillery—to be subject to the same regulations as other soldiers, receiving the same pay and allowances, but operating primarily behind the enemy's lines. They would be allowed to range widely, detached from the regular army. The law also permitted the partisans to be paid for any captured military equipment that was delivered to the quartermaster; conversely, any non-military items captured could be retained by the partisans as "spoils."[38] Although opposition from within the regular military commands would later cause the law, with some exceptions, to be repealed, John Mosby was ready to seize the moment.

During the afternoon of Sunday, July 13, after attending morning church services, Stonewall Jackson led his columns from their camps around Richmond towards the town of Gordonsville where the Virginia Central Railroad rail-headed with the tracks of the Orange and Alexandria.[39] The following Saturday, Mosby set out, from the cavalry camp at Hanover Court House, for Beaver Dam Station to catch the cars for Gordonsville. In his haversack he had a letter from Stuart to Jackson. Stuart had listened anew to Mosby's pleadings for a command and the cavalry leader now felt that his scout's best bet to obtain the dozen or so men he wanted would be from Jackson's infantry ranks. Stuart was recruiting for an active cavalry campaign and was unwilling to detach the men from his force. In his letter, Stuart informed Jackson that Mosby "...is bold, daring, intelligent and discreet. The information he may obtain and transmit to you may be relied upon, and I have no doubt that he will soon give additional proofs of his value."[40]

On the morning of July 20, Mosby arrived at Beaver Dam depot. He took off his pistols and haversack and stretched out in the warm morning sun to await the train. No sooner had he done so, than a regiment of Union cavalry suddenly came up. The surprised passenger-to-be began to run, but was soon ridden down. His captors, the Harris Light Cavalry, a New York outfit, emptied his haversack, read Stuart's letter to Jackson, and promptly threw it away. As for Mosby, he was sent to Old Capitol Prison in Washington, D. C., but in less than two weeks would be exchanged. But the experienced scout did not idle his time while awaiting the completion of the process.

After Mosby was removed from the prison he was transported with other prisoners to Fort Monroe. While waiting for the vessel that was to carry the prisoners up the James River to Richmond for exchanging, Mosby took note of a large number of transports, with troops, lying near by. He soon learned that the troops were part of the 10,000-man army of Brigadier General Ambrose P. Burnside, recently arrived from a successful campaign in North Carolina. But where were they destined for now, Mosby wondered. Aware that McClellan still had his massive army at Harrison's Landing farther up the James, could these troops be going to join up with "Little Mac" for another push on Richmond? If not, then they must be going to join Major General John Pope, whose Union Army of Virginia was somewhere in the northeastern part of the state and believed to be making preparations to advance southward toward Jackson or the Confederate capitol.

Mosby had made friends with the captain of the steamer that had brought the prisoners down from Washington, finding him to be a Southern sympathizer. Learning the captain was going ashore for his orders, Mosby asked him to try and find out where the transports were going. He soon had his answer— Aquia Creek, near the mouth of the Potomac, north of Fredericksburg. They were going to join Pope! This would mean, thought Mosby, that the threat on Richmond would be relieved and reinforcements could now be sent to Stonewall Jackson, who was near Gordonsville, to defend against Pope. When the exchange boat docked at Richmond, an excited John Mosby, partly by foot and partly on horseback, hurried the twelve miles to General Lee's headquarters, "…bringing information of vital importance…." and leaving the Confederate commander with a dozen lemons he had acquired while in Washington. [41]

By the middle of August, after going home to get a horse, Mosby was back with Stuart. While his aide was waiting to be exchanged, Stuart had been promoted to major general, and would shortly be placed in command of all cavalry in the Army of Northern Virginia. As for Mosby, the former prisoner was still smarting from the New York cavalry's interference with his attempt to meet up with Stonewall Jackson a month earlier; by this time he might very well have had his own command. Now, on the 17th, he, Stuart, and four others of Stuart's staff were riding toward Raccoon Ford on the Rapidan River. They were to meet Fitz Lee, coming with his brigade from Hanover Court House to join up with the rest of Lee's army. Pope's Union army was heading this way and the Confederate command had devised a plan to bottle it up in the narrow V formed by the confluence of the Rapidan and Rappahannock Rivers. But Fitz Lee had not yet arrived, so Stuart's small group settled in for the night at a small hamlet a few miles from Orange Court House. About dawn, the sound of approaching cavalry could be heard, possibly that of Colonel Lee, Stuart thought. He sent Mosby and a Lieutenant Gibson to investigate. Soon shots were heard and Mosby and Gibson suddenly appeared around a curve in the road, riding hard and shouting. A Yankee detail was hot on their heels. Stuart and the rest quickly scattered. Afterwards, Mosby doubled back to see what had happened to his companions and there found his general—bareheaded—watching as a disappearing column of Pope's Federal cavalry triumphantly rode away with Stuart's famed plumed hat, red-lined clock, and yellow sash!

Three days later, the cavalry chief galloped past Mosby, shouting "I am going to get my hat!" He was on his way to raid Pope's headquarters at Catlett's Station. Stuart subsequently came away with the Yankee commander's wagons containing his papers and his army treasure chest with $50,000 in greenbacks and $20,000 in gold. But the biggest treasure of all, at least for Stuart, was Pope's personal baggage. In it were Pope's hat, military cloak, and one of his uniform frock coats. The frock coat was made of fine, black broadcloth, with a velvet collar bearing the insignia of a major general and with the front and sleeves resplendent with brass buttons. [42]   Stuart felt avenged.

Mosby continued his campaigning with Stuart and returned to Manassas in late August, a little over a year since the first fight there, to be a part of the second battle. Afterwards, he would write to Pauline: "I have escaped unhurt, though I got my horse slightly shot…and had a bullet through the top of my hat, which slightly grazed my head…." In the same letter, he mentioned the possibility of a Maryland invasion: "Our Army is now marching on towards Leesburg and we all suppose it will cross into Maryland." [43]

On September 17, the Confederate army was at Sharpsburg, in Maryland, to fight a bloody battle along Antietam Creek. The terrible carnage that began at dawn and lasted until darkness, along a once tranquil stream would stay with Mosby for a lifetime. His vivid description of a scene after the fighting, written some fifty years later, revealed a seldom seen sensitive and benevolent nature. The cavalryman rarely expressed such emotions during the war, unless it was in letters to his "dearest Pauline". "…the killed and wounded were strewn on the ground 'like leaves of the forest when autumn hath blown', and I had to be careful not to ride over them. Whole ranks seemed to have been struck down by a volley. Although hundreds were lying all around me, my attention was drawn to a wounded officer… lying in an uncomfortable position…suffering great agony. I dismounted, fixed him more comfortably, and rolled up a blanket on which he rested his head, and then got a canteen of water for him from the body of a dead soldier lying near him." [44]

Sharpsburg proved to be the war's bloodiest day thus far. By September 19, Lee's exhausted army was back across the Potomac, in Virginia. McClellan's Union forces just didn't have enough left to pursue them.

By mid-October, General Lee had just about completed his reorganization of the Army of Northern Virginia. The dispirited and disorganized troops that had staggered and straggled into Virginia a month earlier had been transformed and confidence prevailed throughout as the warriors renewed themselves in the peaceful, secure shadow of the Blue Ridge. Rest, food, refitting, and discipline would be Lee's prescription. Consolidation of the artillery units, division of the cavalry into four brigades, and the division of the army itself into two corps, were basic ingredients in the commander's scheme of things. A scarce item in Lee's prescription, however, was—horses. To help remedy the shortage, Stuart's cavalry had returned from a raid into Pennsylvania with 1200 mounts; but this was a nearly infinitesimal number considering the overall shortage. However, Stuart had been in Pennsylvania for a larger, more vital, purpose. [45]

On October 8, Stuart received written orders from Lee: undertake a cavalry raid into Maryland and Pennsylvania, destroying the bridge over the Concocheaque River at Chambersburg. In addition to any other hostile action he might take, Stuart was to ascertain the disposition and probable movements of the Union army. Lee believed that McClellan, following the Antietam fight, was planning on moving his Union forces against the Virginia Central Railroad.[46] The tracks ran north out of Richmond to Hanover Junction, and then proceeded northwest to Gordonsville, where they ran headlong into the north-south tracks of the Orange and Alexandria Railroad. The Virginia Central was an indispensable link in the Army of Northern Virginia's supply routes, from Richmond and Petersburg in the east to the Shenandoah Valley and beyond in the west.

Mosby was with Stuart from October 8-12, on a raid into Chambersburg, Pennsylvania. The information Stuart and his scouts brought back to Lee, together with subsequent intelligence—and changes in the Federal command—would lead to considerable movement and positioning by both armies. They would finally clash at Fredericksburg, fifty miles northeast of Gordonsville on December 13. But McClellan would not be there.

November and December of 1862 saw an increase in both the frequency and results of Mosby's scouting. Around mid-November, he watched as McClellan departed Catlett's Station, enroute to Washington, after being relieved of command of the Union Army of the Potomac; Catlett's Station was some 40 miles in the rear of the Yankee lines. Later in the month, "General Stuart sent me with nine men to reconnoitre in the vicinity of Manassas. (We came upon ten members of a Yankee regiment and) we charged them with a yell. (They) ran and stampeded their whole regiment, thinking all of Stuart's cavalry was upon them." And on yet another venture, he and a companion captured seven Federal cavalrymen and two infantrymen. Mosby came away with a good Yankee horse, a fine saddle, and two pistols. [47]

The integrative nature of John Mosby allowed him, at times, to make room for things other than those war-like. On December 9 he wrote to Pauline, asking her to send him "... some books to read. Send Plutarch, Macaulay's 'History' and 'Essays', 'Encyclopedia of Anecdotes', Scotts Works, Shakespeare, Byron, Scott's Poems, Hazlitt's 'Life of Napoleon', ...also 'Corinne' and 'Sketchbook.'" [48] Such was the mind of this thin, stooped Rebel, with the low voice and pleasant, sometimes satirical, smile—an enigmatic warrior that his foes, try as they might, would never quite be able to figure out.

For Christmas, Stuart gave Mosby a long-wished-for, long-awaited present. Following the bloody and disastrous defeat of the Union army under Burnside at Fredericksburg on December 13, Stuart gathered 1800 troopers from his three brigades. The day after Christmas, the column started on a northern raid into Prince William and Fairfax Counties, south of Washington, D.C. Known as the "Christmas Raid"—or the "Dumfries Raid" for the town that was one of its objectives—the column struck at Union supplies and communications along Telegraph Road, venturing deep into enemy lines. After reaching Burke's Station, only nine miles from the Washington defenses, the force went southeast toward Fairfax Court House. Finding the enemy there too strong to attack, they turned west, into Loudoun County, ending up in Middleburg on the 30th. It was during this stopover that Mosby again approached Stuart: this time, he asked, could he stay behind when the command returned to its winter camp near Fredericksburg. Stuart's friend and favorite scout believed that, with only a handful of good men, he could be effective behind the enemy's lines in and around the Fairfax County area of northern Virginia. He could prey on the Federal outposts and pickets when they were most vulnerable, during the winter months, while the armies were quartered and awaiting the resumption of major activities in the spring. Stuart thought quietly for a few moments and then, in a voice that seemed to resonate with both fervor and quiet assurance, granted Mosby his request. [49]

There could have been any one of several reasons—or maybe all of them—to cause Stuart to finally give Mosby what he had wanted and asked for all these months. Perhaps it was the delight Stuart felt at the success of his Christmas excursion—200 prisoners, an equal number of horses, twenty wagons, 100 or more arms, and much miscellaneous loot. Additionally,

Stuart was able to report that he had destroyed Burnside's direct line of communication with Washington, scattered the Union cavalry on the Occoquan River, necessitated the detachment of a large Federal force to patrol the country between Aquia Creek and Vienna, and created the impression that the Confederates were going into Maryland, requiring the Federals to send off large forces of cavalry, breaking down many of their horses in the process. [50] Or maybe it was because the cavalry chief now felt that his protégé was ready—he had watched as Mosby gained the skills to go with the resourcefulness and determination he already possessed. Then again, maybe it was the season of the year…or above all, maybe it was—well—just time. It had been eight months since Mosby had gone on his first scout for Stuart, near the small depot of Bealeton Station on the Orange and Alexandria Railroad. And since then, respect, trust, and friendship had flourished between the pupil and the mentor, and the jaunty, gallant cavalry chief had finally come " …to repose unlimited confidence in his (Mosby's) resources and relied implicitly upon him." [51] Yes, perhaps it was time.

As the divided country entered the third year of what some had predicted would be only a Sunday morning fight and afternoon picnic, Stuart's cavalry returned to winter quarters, minus one "lieutenant" and nine troopers.

On January 10, 1863, and again, two nights later, Mosby's small band of detached raiders struck at outposts of the 5th New York and 1st Vermont Cavalries in Fairfax County, coming away with twenty-two prisoners, their horses, equipment, and even their playing cards and clothing. Striking swiftly, under cover of darkness, the unsuspecting Yankees were little match for Mosby's skillful lot. The first bluecoats to be victimized by these gray guerrillas were at a post far removed from the closest Southern army and snugly settled down with their usual game of euchre when the attackers came. Likewise, the others were confidently asleep only a few miles distant, in a thin weather-boarded house, which soon became target practice for the raiders. [52] These unfortunate Yankees had no way of knowing that they had just been introduced to a daring new brand of warfare and to a man who would haunt and taunt them and their comrades for the next two years in a land that was soon to become "Mosby's Confederacy."

Now, on this cold January morning, as the sun struggled to pierce the ashen sky, Sam Chapman watched Mosby leave Warrenton, to head south and east on the narrow, muddy Virginia road. He was going to report to General Stuart, in camp, sixteen miles west of Fredericksburg, on the results of his recent "caper." The General would be greatly pleased with his scout's success and would listen with excited admiration and growing interest while the young raider made a new proposal: give him a detail of fifteen picked men and he would undertake, in two months time, to compel the enemy in Fairfax to abandon their advance line of outposts and give up ten miles of country. An ambitious plan to be sure, but after only a moment of hesitation, Stuart would reply: "Very well, you shall have them; and let it be so; we will destroy them in detail!" [53]

For Mosby, it was, finally, to be; this time he would not return as a scout and aide on Stuart's staff. On January 18, the scout-turned-raider, with fifteen handpicked troopers, left the new camp of the 1st Virginia at King William Court House. The small command rode toward upper Fauquier County and, upon reaching Warrenton, Mosby dispersed them. Their orders: to scatter throughout the region, concealing themselves in the farms and villages with those they could trust—just as a tree blends into the forest, or a sheep into the flock—then meet again in ten days.

During the next twenty-seven months, until Lee's surrender at Appomattox Court House on April 9, 1865, Mosby and his sundry collection of raiders would grow to number, at various times, in the hundreds. Though the command would increase in size to that of a regiment, this—the 43rd Battalion, Virginia Cavalry, Army of Northern Virginia—would forever be "Mosby's Rangers." Through the farmlands and in the hamlets, between the mountains and in the valleys, through the passes and along the rivers, they would ride to the enemy. Wagon trains and rail trains, outposts and encampments, stragglers and patrols, privates and even generals—all would come to fear these strange new warriors, who appeared without warning, did their deed, and then "dissolved like the midst."[54] Tam O'Shanter Rebels, their leader called them.[55] They would write the history of partisan warfare throughout the countryside of northern Virginia—and Sam Chapman was about to become one of the authors.

PART II

MAKING OF THE MAN

2. Bloodlines

The summer of 1838 had been unusually hot in Virginia's Page Valley. [56] Lying along the South Fork of the Shenandoah River, between the Blue Ridge and Massanutten Mountains, the narrow valley had seen too little rain and too much heat. The season's harshness had stunted crops just reaching their prime and transformed the once full, green pastures into short, distressed carpets with rust-like hues. But now, in the last week of August, a succession of day-long thunderstorms and night-time rains had left in their wake a cooling, cordial kind of breeze. More like a zephyr, it seemed, wandering out of the western foothills to refresh the land—nature's repast, come to green the pastures, revive the crops, and make the Valley want to come awake once again and take on a new life!

So it was for Elizabeth Forrer Chapman. She had come home, to the place of her birth, to bring a new life into the resurrected land. With her husband William, she had made the uncomfortable journey from adjoining Madison County, passing through the Blue Ridge Mountains at Fisher's Gap and dropping down into the Valley. The farm of her parents, the late Samuel Forrer and his widow Catherine, lay sprawled over 700 acres along Hawksbill Creek, near a settlement called Mundellsville, named for the German, Mr. Mundell, who ran the store there. The Forrers had built a spacious brick house in 1825 to replace the log house occupied by the previous owner, and by Samuel and his family; it was in the log house that Elizabeth was born. The newer home sat on the north bank of Little Hawksbill near the fork of the East and West Branches and commanded a vast view of the homestead. Fourteen large rooms and fourteen fireplaces filled the two stories; a large basement contained the kitchen, a dining room, and rooms for storing fruits and vegetables and other foodstuffs, plus a wine cellar. One large room, some forty-eight feet long, occupied the entire south side of the house on the first floor. The early Forrers were members of the Dunkers or German Baptist church, so named for their practice of immersion. This large room was often used for services with a folding partition employed to divide the men and women. [57]

The baby was born on August 27, bringing, at once, feelings of exceptional joy and melancholy-like sadness to the new mother. In fact, it seemed the last two years had been a mixture of sorrow and happiness for Samuel and Catherine's youngest child. Her father had died barely two years before, while a short year ago, she had married the prosperous William Allen

Chapman of neighboring Madison County. Samuel had not been with her on her wedding day and now he was not here to share this, the most blessed of events in her life.[58]

Elizabeth's first born was named Samuel Forrer Chapman for her father. As he grew, young Sam would have his grandfather's features—the intense eyes, the high forehead, and the strong, but at the same time, friendly look to the mouth and jaw.

Sam Chapman's great-grandfather, on his mother's side, was Christian Forrer. Along with his brother Daniel and sister Christina, he had come to the American Colonies from Langnau, Switzerland, arriving in the port at Philadelphia on October 1, 1754. Christian was the youngest of the three and Christina, at twenty-five, the oldest. Their father, Daniel had died in 1740 and mother, Anna, in 1747. The three siblings had disembarked at Philadelphia with some money and later received considerable more upon the disposition of the estate in Langnau. Upon their arrival they settled seventy-five miles west in Lancaster County. [59]

Although only seventeen, Christian, to his good fortune had brought with him from his homeland, a trade: he was an indentured clockmaker—a good clockmaker—with papers testifying to his training and capabilities. Christian plied his trade well, and on September 16, 1760 married Elizabeth Kendrick, and settled into family life in his adopted country. Christian and Elizabeth would have four sons while in Lancaster: Henry, Daniel and Christian were born between 1761 and 1765, and the youngest, Samuel, Sam Chapman's grandfather, on November 16, 1773.[60]

Elizabeth's father, Henry Kendrick, had died in 1756, and left some land in Lancaster County to Elizabeth and her sister, Mary. Christian bought Mary's half of the land and then sold both portions for a profit. In addition, he sold fifteen acres where he and Elizabeth had their home and in 1772 moved farther south to York. On March 23, 1774, the enterprising immigrant purchased a 212-acre farm in York County, together with a river ferry and fifteen acres on an island in the Susquehanna River. The ferry was a profitable business, operating across the Susquehanna midway, and on the main road, between Lancaster and York. [61]

The Swiss clockmaker was but forty-six when he died in 1783, and after six years the widow Elizabeth married again, to Jacob Erisman, a next door neighbor and a widower. This second marriage was not popular with her sons. Because Christian had left a large estate to Elizabeth and, with Samuel not yet twenty-one, a pre-nuptial agreement was entered into. This prevented any of Christian's estate from going to Jacob or his family in the event of Elizabeth's death. All of this became a moot issue, however, when Jacob died three years later.[62]

By 1795, Elizabeth Forrer and three of her sons—Christian, Henry, and Samuel—had joined thousands of other immigrant families traversing the Great Road south and into the Great Valley of Virginia—the Shenandoah—spread out like a huge blanket between the Allegheny and Blue Ridge Mountains.[63]

Like a stepchild of the Great Valley, Page Valley lies midway of the Shenandoah, but snuggled in between the Blue Ridge to the east and the Massanutten, a fifty-mile-long range bisecting the Shenandoah Valley, to the west. It was here that Samuel Forrer and the next youngest of his three brothers—their father's namesake, Christian—obtained a deed in 1795 for 1400 acres, on Hawksbill Creek and Dry Run, near Mundellsville. Belonging to Joseph Ruffner, 400 of the acres were part of an original patent, dated January 27, 1774, from King George II.[64]

Several years after the two brothers, as co-tenants, had purchased the Ruffner place, Christian and Samuel decided it was time to divide the farm and work the parts separately. Samuel was the better businessman, excelling in operating his large portion, and became quite wealthy for those days. His crops of wheat, corn, oats, rye, and barley would abound. Livestock, including sheep and hogs, as well as poultry, were commonly raised on the farm and dairy products were routinely produced.[65]

On March 12, 1799, Samuel married Catherine Ebersole, daughter of Christian and Mary Ebersole. The Ebersoles lived in Washington County, Maryland, near Hagerstown. Catherine would recall in her later years that George Washington, while on his tour to select a site for the seat of the government, was a guest of her father. Catherine was six years older than her husband, but she would outlive him by twenty-three years, dying in 1859 at the age of ninety-two. There were six children born of the union; Sam Chapman's mother, Elizabeth, born on June 16, 1811, was the youngest.[66] Sam Chapman's grandfather seems to have been as enterprising a businessman as his father, Christian, had been before him. In addition to the running of the large farming operation, he owned or operated a mill, a tan yard, a distillery and a saw mill, all situated on about five and one-half acres at Mundellsville. On May 27, 1833 and again a year later, Samuel was granted a license by the court to "…keep a house of private entertainment." In granting these hotel licenses, the court always was satisfied that the owners and operators were men of good character, not addicted to drunkenness or gambling.[67]

Sam Chapman's paternal ancestors are known to have been in Virginia since before 1729. On March 23rd of that year, Sam's great-great-grandfather, John Chapman of King and Queen County bought 295 acres and 3540 pounds of tobacco in Spotsylvania County. On March 5, 1753, he and his wife, Ann, were deeded 200 acres more in Spotsylvania County. Sometime prior to this he had acquired 364 acres in Orange County. After his death, at a sale of his estate on November 19, 1776, in addition to land holdings…"14 very fine Virginia born Slaves, considerable stock of all kinds, the household furniture and crop of corn, wheat and fodder…." was offered.[68]

Sam's great-grandfather, William Chapman, was born in 1739. He was among the first justices appointed following the formation of Madison County on May 1, 1793. The same year, William was appointed, by the Court, as one of the Overseers of the various roads in the county. Twice married, with two sons by his first wife, William Chapman's second wife, the former Mary Buford of neighboring Culpeper County, would bear him six children.[69] When William's will was probated in 1832, he owned more than 1,000 acres in Madison County.[70]

William Allen Chapman, Sam's grandfather, was born on March 29, 1777, from the uniting of William Chapman and Mary Buford. On April 30, 1799, William Allen married Caty Gaines, daughter of Edmund and Tabitha Gains. When the county's Superior Court was established in 1809, he was on the first jury; the first hearing was a murder trial.[71]

The third William Chapman in as many generations was Sam's father, born on January 14, 1808; he married Elizabeth Forrer on November 27, 1837. From this union, there was Sam and William Henry (the fourth successive William), five other boys and three girls.[72]

After Sam's birth in 1838, William and Elizabeth Chapman, with the baby, crossed the Blue Ridge once more, returning to their home on Quaker Run,

26

near Criglersville. Here, on April 17, 1840, William Henry Chapman arrived, named for his father and for his mother's brother. Endowed with a strong and loving family of some means, the brothers, separated by only twenty months in age, would grow to be as close as any siblings could hope to be. Little could they realize, in their young years, to what ends the closeness of their relationship would bring them.

In 1848, the elder William Chapman purchased a large farm and manor house from the Ruffner family, the same family that had owned the property bought by the Forrers in 1795. It was located in Page County only a short way from the Forrers and about one-half mile north of the town of Luray. William had purchased a smaller adjoining tract six years earlier from the same family. Following the birth of their second son and the subsequent purchase of the Ruffner house and farm, the Chapmans sold their Madison County farm and traveled the road through Fisher's Gap and down the mountain into Page Valley one last time. [73]

When the Chapmans moved into their new home, they were continuing to live in a manner that befitted both sides of the family. The Forrers were already well established among the wealthier and actively involved citizens of the county. The Chapmans were among the most prosperous of Madison. The 1840 census for that county showed Sam's father and grandfather owning twenty slaves - eleven males and nine females.

The Ruffner house was a grand building. It was constructed of brick, two and one-half stories, with four chimneys and eight fireplaces. Its large rooms had ceilings of ten feet, and its floors were made of five and six-inch-wide pine boards. There was a five-room English basement, containing a kitchen, dining room and three rooms for servants quarters.

The Chapman home was noted the county over for its hospitality. One of the neighbors, David Coffman, ran a boarding school in his home. Fire practically destroyed the home and during the rebuilding the school was moved into the Chapman home. John, a later son of William and Elizabeth, married Jennie, a daughter of Mr. and Mrs. Coffman. [74]

After settling in at their new home, a third child—and another son—was born to William and Elizabeth on February 1, 1842. Christened Edmund Gaines for his great-grandparents on his father's side, he would be the third and last of the Chapman siblings to serve the Confederacy as a soldier when war would rend the country some nineteen years hence.

Hannah Catherine (Kate) Chapman was the first daughter of the couple, born on December 12, 1843, and was followed by two more of Sam Chapman's sisters, Mary Elizabeth (Bettie) on May 2, 1845 and Margaret Ann (Annie) on January 29, 1847. Mary Elizabeth would later marry a veteran of the War, Joseph Milton Carter, who would see service with two of his future brothers-in-law, Sam and William, in Colonel Mosby's command of Partisan Rangers. Four more sons were to follow, rounding out the large family— John Newton was born on January 24, 1849; James Harvey would come into the world on May 17, 1850 but would live only thirteen months; George Thomas, was born on Christmas eve 1851; Andrew Jackson was the youngest, born May 2, 1854.

3. Preparation for a Calling

The first ironworks in the sprawling Virginia Colony was founded at Germanna, on the Rappahannock River, in 1714 by the Swiss Baron de Graffenried. The Massachusetts Bay Colony had established an ironworks several years before and now the fledging industry was finding its way into the remaining colonies. Spreading throughout the states following the Revolution, Virginia was able to claim its share in the mining of ore and the production of pig and bar iron. The Forrers of Page County would not be bystanders, but become major participants in the venture begun by their fellow Swiss countryman. [75]

On February 13, 1836, an event took place that would serve to set the course for the future of two of Elizabeth Forrer Chapman's brothers—Daniel and Henry Forrer entered into a partnership with Samuel Gibbons to manufacture iron. Gibbons owned the land and each of the three partners had a one-third interest in the business. Just over four months later, on June 27, the three petitioned the Page County Court "...to permit them to raise their present mill dam three feet to enable them to propel the necessary machinery for a furnace, forge, sawmill and other machinery on the South Branch of the Shenandoah River." [76]

Gibbons sold his interest in what was now the Shenandoah Ironworks to the Forrers on October 2, 1837 and conveyed to them over 1,000 acres around the site, near the Rockingham County line in southern Page County. Although there had been a furnace at the site since at least 1812, [77] this initial endeavor by the two brothers and Samuel Gibbons marked the beginning of an ironworks industry that would become synonymous with the name Forrer in the middle part of the century.

In addition to the furnace at Shenandoah, the Forrers would own or operate many other such enterprises. By the late 1850's, they were operating Catherine Furnace, fourteen miles from Luray at the foot of Massanutten Mountain, Shenandoah Number 1, twenty miles south of Luray, and the newest, Shenandoah Number 2, built in 1857 on Naked Creek, five miles from her sister furnace. In 1861 all three furnaces would be refitted to help satisfy the growing needs of the Confederate war effort. [78]

Twenty-six-year-old Daniel Forrer and Elizabeth Keneagy, the twenty-three-year-old daughter of John and Mary Keneagy of Lancaster County, Pennsylvania were married on August 18, 1828. The first seven and one-half years of their marriage were spent in Lancaster, but in 1836 they and their four young children moved to Shenandoah where Daniel and his brother, Henry had begun the ironworks. Elizabeth's late father had owned and operated an ironworks at Mossy Creek, in Augusta County, Virginia, and upon his death, his only daughter had inherited a large interest in it. [79]

In 1843, Daniel again moved, this time from his home at the Shenandoah Ironworks up the Valley to the northern part of Augusta County. There, at Mossy Creek, midway between Bridgewater and Churchville, his family, along with his brother Henry, made their new home. Only about thirty-five miles from Shenandoah as the crow flies, Mossy Creek was a considerably longer journey in a wagon on the roads of that day. The reason for the move was part of the continuing saga of the Forrer's affair with the iron industry.

Four years after the Forrers settled in at Mossy Creek, a tall, thin youth of seventeen came walking into their lives and things would never be quite the same. Not for the Forrer family and not for Daniel and Henry's nephew, Sam Chapman, in the Page Valley.

Jedediah Hotchkiss had left his home in southern New York State in the autumn of 1846. His intellect and intense yearning to learn, coupled with an unending curiosity and passion for things unseen, had brought the accomplished teenager to a juncture in his life. With the blessing of his parents, Jed set out. Traveling by canal boat when he could, but largely by foot, he made his way into central Pennsylvania. Here the necessities of life required him to find work, so he spent the winter teaching in a small immigrant community near Harrisburg. By spring he was off again, and in a few weeks had crossed the Potomac River at Harper's Ferry, and thence into Virginia's Shenandoah Valley. [80] He would have no desire to leave.

When Jed Hotchkiss strode into Staunton that summer of 1847 he met Henry Forrer. [81] Although forty-three and still a bachelor, Henry was keenly aware of the need for instruction in those things not normally available in the home. The parents could instill the moral values so essential to the development of the character of their children. But what else was needed—and what was not available to them—was proper instruction in the sciences and the languages and in those things a young person would need in the rapidly changing world of the mid-nineteenth century. Henry's nephews and nieces, confined to the limited environment around the Mossy Creek Ironworks, needed just what Jedediah Hotchkiss could offer them.

Daniel and Elizabeth Forrer now had six children—three boys and three girls—ranging in age from eight to fifteen. In addition, they had taken in a nephew and niece—Judah, twelve and Henrietta, nearly fourteen—after the youngsters' father, Christian Forrer, had died the year before.[82] Daniel was impressed with the young adventurer, just as Henry had been. He offered Jed Hotchkiss the job of teacher to the children of the Forrer household. Hotchkiss accepted and instruction started that November of 1847 with Daniel and Elizabeth's six, and Christian's two children, making up the class.[83] Instruction took place in the Forrer home, and the Forrers gave young Hotchkiss a generously free rein in planning and carrying out the methods and means of teaching and learning.

In 1850, a new pupil arrived in Mossy Creek. He was the son of Daniel Forrer's younger sister, Elizabeth. Sam Chapman was nearly twelve years old when his parents decided to send him to stay with his aunt and uncle at Mossy Creek in order to further his schooling with the young teacher they had heard so much about. And it appears young Sam was an extraordinarily serious student. For the five-month session that ran from January to June 1850, he would be enrolled in no less than fourteen courses of instruction. The report sent to his parents on December 6 of that year by Jedediah Hotchkiss revealed a student who was "even with anyone in school and, if he continues to study, as he does at this time, he will, undoubtedly, be foremost by the close of the session." [84]

Apparently Mr. and Mrs. Chapman had a career already in mind for their eldest child. In his letter accompanying the report, Hotchkiss said that Sam "did not seem inclined to like the study of Medicine, when I first said something to him about it, but since he has been studying Physiology, he has become more interested in matters relating to it, and it may be that he will become sufficiently interested in the profession you think of choosing for him, to desire, of his own inclination, to follow it." [85]

The year 1854 would see the proud opening of the new Mossy Creek Academy. The success of the home school had so impressed the community that Daniel Forrer was able to persuade some of the local men to invest in a new building. [86] "This Institution is located on Mossy Creek, in the Northern part of Augusta County, Virginia", the broadside read. "The second half of the

Session of 1853 and '54 commences on the Sixth of February, 1854, in the commodious building lately erected for the accommodation of the School." Courses were offered in three Departments, and included the basics such as spelling, reading and writing, as well as arithmetic and geography. Advanced classes were taught in geometry, surveying, Latin, Greek and French, along with other sciences and languages. The faculty was made up of Hotchkiss, principal, and professor of Natural Science, two additional professors for languages, mathematics, and elocution, and an assistant in the Primary Department. Charges for one ten-month session ran from ten to thirty dollars. [87]

For the youngster Sam Chapman, his stay at Mossy Creek was like nothing he had ever experienced. Although he had completed his schooling before the opening of the new academy building, he had attained a higher level of maturity under the tutorage of Jed Hotchkiss. In the Forrer home, without the larger enrollment and other distractions of the academy, the personal relationship with the professor created an added incentive for the inquiring teen-ager.

Although Sam did not occupy a desk at the new academy, his brother William was enrolled for the 1856-57 term, which ran from September to June. He would take classes in Mathematics, Natural Science, Modern Languages, and Common English. The academy stressed involvement by each pupil in all activities related to it and William was no exception. For the semi-annual Exhibition, held on December 19, 1856, he recited, to musical accompaniment, Daniel Webster's "Liberty and Union". He also played the part of the showman, P. T. Barnum, in a dramatic presentation.[88] William later attempted to further his education at the University of Virginia. It was to be cut short, just as Sam's would be, by the events in April 1861.

There was another significant difference in the Chapman brother's experience at Mossy Creek. William would not have the personal influence of Jedediah Hotchkiss. Citing severe financial difficulties, Hotchkiss had requested—and received—his release from the contract with the trustees to run the academy, effective June 20, 1856, three months prior to William's enrollment.[89]

But the success of Professor Hotchkiss at Mossy Creek, and his growing reputation as an educator, would not be the zenith in his life. Just as Sam Chapman would find a calling outside of Mossy Creek and Page Valley, so too would Jed Hotchkiss. Each would have his calling put to the test in a far different world than the serene one at Mossy Creek in the mid-1850s. This world was just now being created beyond the dark clouds that had settled over the nation's horizon.

Upon the completion of his studies at Mossy Creek, Sam entered Columbian College in Washington, D. C. Columbian had gotten its start in 1819 when a group of Baptist ministers and laymen came forward with the idea for establishing such a school in the nation's capital. On February 9, 1821, President Monroe signed the Act which created the college, with the provision that "...persons of every religious denomination shall be capable of being elected Trustees...nor shall any (person) be refused admission or denied privileges...on account of his sentiments in matters of religion." The new college was situated a short walk from the Capitol building, on slightly over forty-six acres. The central building could board 100 students, and there were three smaller buildings for housing professors and others associated with the school. [90] Major support for the establishment of Columbian College had come from Virginia Baptists. In 1819-20, the planned college received approximately 625 gifts toward the purchase price of the site for the college and 50 percent of the offerings came from Virginia citizens. And with only one exception, all contributions to the original fund were from Virginia. It was no surprise then that a major portion of the student enrollment would be made up of Virginians. [91]

While Sam was growing in years and knowledge, he was also beginning to take an active part in the life of Main Street Baptist Church in Luray. The church had its beginning on September 17, 1844, when twelve faithful brothers and sisters set about to organize a "Regular Baptist Church of Christ." The little congregation built a humble frame building on a rocky slope two blocks off Main Street and christened it Luray Baptist Church. It was about this time that a division of Baptists was taking place throughout the country over the question of missions. Early in the century, the question of strong support for foreign, as well as home missions, had been a heated one. The New School or Missionary Baptists supported the new concept in missions. On the other side was the faction that opposed an increased mission program, particularly in foreign missions. They were known as the Old School Baptists. Ironically, the little church had been organized during the middle of the controversy and both factions worshiped in the new building albeit on different days. [92]

The debate on missions would go on for several decades. The Missionary Baptists had a very rapid growth and was the larger of the two factions by far. In 1851 Daniel Flinn conveyed a lot on which to construct a new building for worship. With the help of the money received as their portion from sale of the church building on the rocky slope, by 1853 the Missionary Baptists were worshiping in a new one-story brick building on Main Street; they named it, logically enough, Main Street Baptist Church. It was into this church that Sam returned. He and his brother, William, were immersed in the waters of the Baptist faith on "the second Lord's Day in May", 1858. On the same Sunday and "At the same time, Phoebe, a colored woman of John Booten and Fanny, a woman of color of Charles Flinn, were baptized." [93]

On June 5, 1858, Sam was appointed one of the delegates to represent the church in the regional association of Baptist Churches; his father was appointed an alternate delegate. At the same business meeting, his father and "…Brother Baker were appointed to purchase lamps for the church." The following day the minutes of the church recorded "Evelina, a woman of color of Chapman was baptized" into the fellowship of Main Street Baptist Church. [94]

October 26, 1858 would be a salient day in the life of twenty-year-old Sam Chapman. It was recorded in the minutes of the church. "At a call meeting of the church on Motion it was unanimously resolved that it is the opinion of this church that Bro. Samuel F. Chapman has gifts for usefulness in the Kingdom of Jesus. Wherefore on Motion it was Resolved that this body grant him a license to exercise his gifts in preaching & exhortation to his fellow men, whereas in the Providence of God his lot may be cast." [95]

Sam Chapman had heard the calling and had submitted to it. But it would not be long before he would race headlong into a test of its genuineness.

No records can be found to establish exactly when Sam entered and when he left Columbian College. But his appetite for knowledge had been whet. Shortly after his twentieth birthday he enrolled at Richmond College for the Session of 1858-59. [96]

Richmond College had begun as Virginia Baptist Seminary and opened its doors in 1832, on a property of 220 acres known as Spring Farm, about five miles from the city of Richmond. Complaints about the remoteness of the site were almost immediate, prompting the trustees to give consideration to moving. Less than three years after its opening at Spring Farm, the seminary had moved to a new location about one mile west of the city limits and only a half-mile more to the State capitol. In 1840 the seminary was chartered as Richmond College.[97]

Richmond College, unlike its predecessor, the seminary, was a much more mainstream liberal arts institution. The former had been Baptist, not only in name but also in fact. The Theological Department was central in the program of instruction and the chief objective was the preparation of young men for the ministry. The college on the other hand had no theological department and it welcomed, not only to its student body but also to its faculty and the Board of Trustees, persons of various religious affiliations.[98]

Just prior to Sam's arrival the trustees had reorganized the institution and successfully petitioned the General Assembly to allow amendments to its charter. Chief among these was the removal of the prohibition against theological instruction.[99] This prohibition had been installed at the time of the original charter in 1840, which dissolved Virginia Baptist Seminary and created Richmond College as primarily a preparatory school for students wishing to further their education at a degree conferring college. Additionally, in what was apparently an attempt to bring the school back to its roots, the board instituted compulsory chapel attendance by students and faculty.[100]

When Sam enrolled at Richmond College for the 1858-59 session, one of 119 students, he decided to take up his studies where he left off at Mossy Creek. He signed up to take Greek, Mathematics, and Chemistry in his first year. Added to these courses were Latin, and Natural Philosophy.[101] The college had, within the last few years, abolished the standard curriculum and instituted in its stead a system of classification and advancement in each study according to a student's ability and attainment.[102] This major change in how the school perceived its mission resulted in the opening of additional courses to lift the curriculum to collegiate level. Chapman was confident that he could attain whatever goal he set for himself, but earthly enough to know that it would not be accomplished solely through his wants but through hard work and study. This determination to learn had been instilled in him by his friend and professor at Mossy Creek, Jedediah Hotchkiss.

As Sam began the 1859-60 second session there was a net loss of 5 students, putting the enrollment at 114 students, including 30 ministerials,[103] and just as in the previous session, he was the only student from Page County. He continued his studies of the languages, taking another year of Latin and Greek. These courses were important in two ways; first, a student who received a certificate in these courses, along with mathematics, natural science, and moral science, was entitled to a B.A. degree, [104] and second, the courses in the languages would prepare him for his future studies of the Scriptures. Sam's schedule was filled with all the required courses.

In November 1859, soon after Sam began his second year at Richmond College, a large number of the students organized themselves into a military company to be known as " The Richmond College Minute Men." Several students " made eloquent and patriotic addresses, expressing their devotion to Southern Rights...and (to) maintain the independence of their native land" [105] The students further resolved "that in view of the present aspect of affairs, we organize ourselves into a military company." In this atmosphere a student from Portsmouth, J. M. Binford, had announced himself captain of this new military company and the faculty had given its approval. In fact, Governor Wise had agreed to furnish requisite arms to the members. [106]

Whether Sam Chapman was a member of the Minute Men is not known but arguments can be made that he was. His younger brother, William, a student at the University of Virginia, had joined a military company that had formed there. In any regard, nothing seems to have come of the Minute Men. With the advent of hostilities the following year, Captain Thomas H. Carter was stationed at Richmond College—now known as the Artillery Barracks—with three companies of men. This seems to have been a temporary command, calling itself the Baptist College Battalion, Virginia Artillery. [107] Sam was gone by then and was not involved.

(Following the war, an unknown acquaintance would offer this assessment of Sam Chapman, the student: "During my student life at Richmond College, I, a non-resident student, was assigned to a room occupied by two ministerial students, Samuel F. Chapman and (another student.) Chapman was a good student, a decided brunette, rather taciturn, a faithful plodder, phlegmatic, a pious devotee to his work, never neglecting it even for an opportunity to try his talent on any of the country churches. He gave no promise of the magnificent military career which is buried under the cloud of his excessive modesty...He shrank from notice and, of course, as time passed he was allowed to have his way.") [108]

Now, in April of 1861, heated rhetoric became armed conflict and Sam returned home to Page County, as did William from the University in Charlottesville. In slightly over a month Sam, William, and younger brother Edmund would all be in the military service of the new Confederacy.

In June, Jedediah Hotchkiss left his home to become a teamster with the Confederate army. He was driving a team carrying supplies to the troops in the mountains of western Virginia, not far from his home and family in Churchville. Unlike Sam, who was serving as a private, with a private's pay, Hotchkiss wasn't even officially in the army. He was a civilian without rank or pay—a volunteer, doing his part for the war effort while hoping for a chance to use his self-taught talents of engineering and cartography. [109] Perseverance would be his ally.

PART III

A DIFFERENT CALLING

4. A Call to Arms

News of the bombardment of Fort Sumter by South Carolina batteries caused pandemonium to break loose in Virginia's capitol city. Three thousand citizens quickly formed, marched to the Tredegar Iron Works and watched as a Confederate flag was run up and listened as speech-makers informed the Tredegar workers that it was cannon which they had made that had breached the walls of Sumter. From the state arsenal they seized artillery pieces, dragged them to Capitol Square and fired a salute of a hundred guns. This was followed by the hoisting of a Confederate flag atop the capitol. That night torchlight processions wound their way through the streets of Richmond amidst burning tar barrels, whirling rockets, and illuminated buildings.[110]

After Fort Sumter, an avalanche of troops descended upon the Confederate War Department, fearing that the army might be filled before they could get there. The Secretary of War declared that he was forced to refuse 200,000 troops because of a lack of arms.[111]

It was in this atmosphere of Southern fervor and patriotism that Sam Chapman, less than three weeks after his return home from Richmond College, made the thirty-mile journey to Front Royal in neighboring Warren County. Here, on May 3,1861, he enlisted as a private in the Warren Rifles, listing as his occupation, "Minister."[112]

The Warren Rifles was a volunteer militia company, organized in 1860 by Captain Robert H. Simpson, a schoolteacher and graduate of the Virginia Military Institute. On April 18, the company enlisted for active service in the Confederate States Army. On May 26, the Rifles were mustered, along with several other companies, as part of the 6th Battalion, Virginia Volunteers (Alexandria Battalion).[113]

Sam Chapman's initial call to arms—and that of the Warren Rifles—was something less than heroic. On May 23, the city of Alexandria had ratified the ordinance of secession by an overwhelming margin. By 2:00 a.m. the next day, the Union navy had dispatched a gunboat down the Potomac River and, when challenged by the sentinel on the wharf, fired a harmless volley. This was followed by a flag of truce and consultations began for the surrender of the city and the promised withdrawal of the Confederate troops. Federal forces started crossing the bridge, entering the city, however, before the consultations were concluded. [114]

By 3:00 a. m. Captain Simpson had aroused his company: "Wake up boys. They are coming! By George they are across the bridge!" [115] The battalion then began a hasty withdrawal, retreating westward, out of the city, where they commandeered several trains which took them twenty-seven miles further west, to Manassas Junction. [116]

A few days after its arrival at the Junction, the Alexandria Battalion moved seven miles to Camp Pickens. Troops were arriving almost daily at the camp, from various parts of Virginia and from the states further south. The soldiers begin building wooden quarters to replace the tents; the initial attempt of the Alexandria group in this endeavor was several plank buildings, big enough to hold about eighty men, or one company, with bunks stacked in fours. However, pouring rains went through the roofs and drove the men from their bunks; there were no floors and the occupants waded through water between the bunks. Fires were lit to try to dry out the building and clothing but the smoke ran nearly everybody out. [117]

On June 10, the Alexandria Battalion was reorganized into the 17th Regiment of Virginia Infantry; the Warren Rifles was designated Company B. Ten days later, the army organized all troops at Manassas into the First Corps, Army of the Potomac. The 17th Regiment was assigned, along with the 1st and 19th Virginia Regiments, to the Fourth Brigade. On July 2, Brigadier General James Longstreet became brigade commander. [118]

Around the first of July, General P. G. T. Beauregard's adjutant, Lieutenant Colonel Thomas Jordan, was looking for a detail to serve in the Adjutant General's office. Being from Luray, Jordan sought out the Warren Rifles and Sam Chapman was one of those chosen. After a couple of weeks, Chapman asked to be returned to his unit and the request was granted just in time for the fighting that was soon to begin. [119]

For several weeks, the men of the 17th Virginia had been busy building large earthworks and erecting field fortifications. The regiments in the camp had different details digging and ditching, wielding spade and axe, as rifle pits and infantry works sprang up on all sides. It was generally known that the Union forces were moving toward the Confederate lines so every effort was made to prepare the troops; extra details were made to strengthen the

works around Manassas. The 16th and 17th of July were truly busy days—
and nights.[120]

On the 18th, Private Chapman and his comrades in the regiment found themselves along the south bank of Blackburn's Ford, on Bull Run. Union troops
were within one-half mile of the Confederate positions and on the move.
The 17th Virginia was actually deployed as a reserve, in the thick under-
growth back from the stream and was disposed in depth to fill a gap between
the right flank and Ewell's brigade on the left. When the first attack came,
this position left them susceptible to heavy enemy artillery fire that burst
overhead, raining fragments down upon them. This was followed by musketry from the Union infantry, situated on a high bluff across the stream.[121]

Despite the enemy's favorable position and intensive fire, the Confederate
forces were able to withstand the assault and in the afternoon, three companies of the regiment crossed the stream and drove the enemy off the bank
and back to their main body, returning with seven prisoners in the process.
When the fighting ended on that first day, the 17th Regiment counted one
killed and seventeen wounded; the Warren Rifles, and Company F, the
Prince William Rifles, were the only ones to have no casualties, out of the
nine companies that comprised the regiment.[122] The next day and the day
following saw a lull in the fighting. A cool rain made for miserable attempts
at sleeping on the cold, wet ground with no cover and ever-present thoughts
of a deadly foe just across the ford.

A bright sunny morning broke over the battlefield on Sunday, July 21, and
Sam's company was ordered from its reserve position to the bank along
Blackburn's Ford. The enemy's movements foretold another, more sangui-
nary fight was on the way. Shortly after daybreak, Company H, the Old
Dominion Rifles, was ordered across the stream and it soon ran into Yankee
skirmishers, several hundred yards inland.[123] About this time, Federal artillery broke the stillness of the Sabbath morning and Yankee troops began
massing upstream, preparing to attack the left flank of the Confederate line.
The cannonading continued for some four hours, but the only real effect was
to cause the Confederates to bring more troops into the line on the left.[124]
Meanwhile, the Union force opposite Longstreet's Fourth Brigade at Blackburn's Ford begin their own symphony of shot and shell, followed by a rain-
storm of grape and canister. This localized artillery blitz lasted for half-an-
hour, wounding some in the regiment. But one of the Old Dominion Rifles

on the opposite shore was not so lucky, becoming the second and last member of the regiment to be killed in the First Battle of Manassas.[125]

Meanwhile, the sounds of the battle raging upstream could be clearly heard and late in the afternoon cheers and shouts broadcast the news that the enemy was being routed. At sunset, the Fourth Brigade crossed at the ford and joined in the pursuit for about two miles. They stopped, rested for an hour in the hot evening and then returned to their positions along Bull Run.[126] Later recalling the events of that July, Sam Chapman mused: "Our fate was to be under the fire of infantry and artillery for two days, with scarcely a sight of the enemy, so dense was the foliage in our front."[127]

Sam had received his second baptism in just over three years, but this time it was one of fire, not water. His regiment had lost two killed and suffered several wounded during the four days spent on the field at Manassas. Now, he gave thanks for the safe return of the remainder of the regiment and, on the morning of July 24, the brigade marched to Centreville and went into camp just below the village.[128]

James Thomas Petty was a twenty-five-year-old native Virginian, born near Fredericksburg, but who had been living in Washington, D. C. since 1851. He was working as a bookkeeper when the war started and, six days after the firing on Fort Sumter, he was in Winchester where he enlisted in the Warren Rifles.[129] Petty soon became a fast friend with his fellow private, Sam Chapman.

On August 7, the regiment's campsite was moved about 400 yards to the top of a hill, which afforded a splendid view of the countryside. That evening, Chapman and Petty walked and talked for a long while before winding up on the steps of a little church "...that the Yankees had defaced so badly." Here, they sat and listened as the band from the 1st Virginia Regiment serenaded General Longstreet. [130]

Tom Petty made a handsome soldier, at five-foot, eight inches tall, with a dark complexion, dark hair, and hazel eyes.[131] He was much a favorite of the ladies and he returned their geniality in kind. A month or so after the two soldiers had listened to the band concert, they relaxed one evening in Sam's tent and "...had an exchange of 'confidentials' and a very pleasant chat generally." [132]

People from nearby, and from some outlying communities, such as Warrenton and Leesburg—homes to members of the regiment—were frequent visitors to Centreville and Fairfax Court House, coming mostly on weekends and spending a night or two at the local hotel. Private Petty had his share of these visitors. Once he, Sam, and four comrades serenaded several young ladies at their hotel and afterward were invited in. Tom and Sam and two others accepted the invitation, enjoying refreshments and, as Tom recalled, "a very pleasant chat with the ladies" [133] away from the war they knew would soon return to them.

On September 21, Sam reported for duty at the Signal Station near Fairfax Court House. When he returned, he tried to get his friend Petty interested in joining the Signal Corps, but abandoned the idea. "I urged him to get the place for Walter E. Franklin. He promised to do so," Petty recorded.[134] Franklin was a friend from Washington, and a member of Company K of the 17th Infantry. There is no record of Franklin being in the Signal Corps, but he and Chapman would cross paths again, in entirely new roles, as members of Mosby's Rangers less than two years later.

On the 23rd of the month, visitors from Front Royal were in the camp. Sam's younger brother, Edmund, a private with the 10th Virginia Infantry, was there as well—his regiment was encamped nearby—and Sam introduced him to his friend, Petty. [135]

Privates Chapman and Petty spent another month together in the 17th, then went their separate ways, soldiering for the South. Before war's end, Petty would be wounded and captured, sent to a Northern prison, exchanged, and then wounded a second time, ten days before Lee's surrender. Following the war, he would return to Washington, D. C. and spend fifty-four years in the service of the country he had once fought against and been imprisoned by.[136]

But for now, the brief sojourn of August and September of 1861 was coming to an end. War was returning to the young warriors.

The regiment broke camp on September 24 and marched, together with a South Carolina regiment and three pieces of the Washington Artillery, up the Alexandria and Leesburg Turnpike toward Lewinsville. Here they engaged a column of Yankee infantry, with artillery, forcing it into a retreat until darkness brought a halt to the skirmish. One of the South Carolinians was killed and one wounded by an artillery shell.[137]

A number of organizational changes took place in October. Early in the month, Longstreet received a promotion to major general and, on the 12th, was reassigned as a division commander; on October 22, he took command of the Third Division in the reorganized First Corps.[138]

Private Chapman had been involved in his own reorganization. On October 19, he transferred out of the infantry company to Captain John K. Booton's Company, Virginia Light Artillery. The battery was from Sam's home county of Page. Lieutenant William Chapman was one of its officers.[139]

William Chapman was still at the University in Charlottesville prior to the firing on Fort Sumter. On April 17, he was among a company of infantry, comprised of University students and called the Southern Guards, enroute to Harper's Ferry. The abandoned Federal arsenal had been selected to be a place of training for militia companies that were being mustered into service from throughout the state. A Virginia Military Institute professor by the name of Thomas J. Jackson, was the colonel in charge and the training was to be conducted by cadets from the Institute. After about two weeks, however, the Southern Guards were ordered back to the University and there disbanded. By June 1, William was at home in Page County. Here, along with John Kaylor Booton, the captain of a disbanded artillery company of sorts, he helped raise a new company of artillery. Resurrecting two old iron cannon from the disbanded unit and what little equipment remained, Booton and Chapman were successful in recruiting eighty-two men for the battery, which would eventually be known as the Dixie Artillery.[140]

Low on funds and with limited training, the company nevertheless enlisted in the army on June 21, for a period of one year. William Chapman was appointed second lieutenant, the third ranked man, below Captain Booton and an Englishman, First Lieutenant William H. Crisp. Now the company, without equipment or the means to obtain it, sat back and anxiously awaited orders to report for active duty.[141]

Booton's battery finally received orders to move to Winchester on July 19. They remained in the inactivity of that city until August 26, at which time they received orders to proceed to Manassas—five weeks late for the battle there. The next two weeks were spent in drilling until, on September 11, the company moved again to a spot east of the railroad.[142] It was here that Sam Chapman found it on October 21, following his departure from the 17th Virginia.

Whether due to his experience, familiarity, or his kinship to William, Sam's transformation in the service of the Confederacy was rapid indeed. Upon his arrival in the battery, Booton appointed Sam second lieutenant. In November, Booton was elected to the Virginia legislature and resigned his commission. First Lieutenant Crisp called for an election and William Chapman was picked to be the new captain. Sam Chapman was elected first lieutenant, while Lieutenant Crisp retained his position and rank. In less than one month's time, Sam had gone from a mere private in an infantry company to an officer in an artillery battery commanded by his brother. On November 21, the unit officially became Captain William Henry Chapman's Company, Virginia Light Artillery, but retained its nom de guerre of Dixie Artillery.[143]

When Sam found the battery near Manassas, he also found his cousin and former classmate at Mossy Creek, Judah Forrer. Married less than a year when he enlisted in August 1861, Forrer would be discharged the following January and return home to his wife.[144] But, just like Walter Franklin, Sam and Judah would be brought together again, in just over two years, when the conflict was entering its third winter.

When Judah Forrer received his discharge from the army on January 28, 1862, he was not alone. His first cousins, Samuel and John Keneagy Forrer, sons of Daniel Forrer of Mossy Creek, were discharged at the same time. Samuel had served in Captain Edward M. Dabney's Company (Letcher Guard), of the Virginia Volunteers. The company became Company C of the 52nd Virginia Infantry and was mustered into service on July 30, 1861, at Staunton. His brother, John, enlisted in Company F of the 52nd at Staunton and was mustered in at the same time.[145]

In addition to the Mossy Creek Ironworks in northern Augusta County, Daniel and Henry Forrer operated Elizabeth Furnace at Buffalo Gap in the southern part of the county. When the war began, their blast furnaces became vital to the Confederacy's military supply; Elizabeth was turning out about thirty tons of iron a week.[146] Daniel Forrer, who had no small influence in the region, felt that he needed his sons and nephew back home to ensure the increased production demanded by the new government. To this end, he saw that all three received discharges from the service by order of the Secretary of War.[147]

Before Samuel Forrer joined the 52nd, he was involved in an operation at the beginning of the war that proved to have far-reaching results. The latest load of iron produced at Elizabeth Furnace had been floated down the river, destined for the Federal arsenal at Harper's Ferry. The Forrers were quite anxious to retrieve this shipment before it got into Union hands. Samuel went to Harper's Ferry and saw the iron was on the opposite side of the river from some Federal troops stationed there. The railroad that operated between there and Winchester was on his side of the river. After much haranguing and some bribery, he persuaded the soldiers to load the iron onto the cars and hauled it to Winchester. From Winchester he carried it by horse teams back to the ironworks. It is said that this iron, like that from numerous other Southern furnaces, was subsequently used to make armor plates for the South's ironclad ship, the CSS Virginia. [148]

5. Musketeer to Cannoneer
(A Year in the Artillery)

Following the election of officers in the Dixie Artillery, the battery went into winter quarters with the rest of the army not far from the battlefield at Manassas. Early March brought the first real break in the late winter and General Longstreet was selected to command an expeditionary force. With the combined division of Major General Gustavus W. Smith, and reinforced with light artillery of which the Dixie Battery was a part, the command headed south on March 5, 1862. Moving along the Warrenton Pike to Centreville, they reached their objective, the Rappahannock River, on March 9. General Joseph E. Johnston's orders to Longstreet and Smith were to reconnoiter a defense line along the Rappahannock and Rapidan Rivers. The reconnaissance was soon made and, prior to the middle of March, the remainder of the Confederate forces were withdrawn from their camps and started south to the new positions.[149] This move south was part of Johnston's "retreat" from the battleground of northern Virginia, ever fearful that the enemy was about to launch an attack on his scattered forces.

Lieutenant Chapman may have quit the infantry, but as the Dixie Artillery and the rest of Longstreet's command trudged south, he found himself over his ankles in mud. The wagons, horses, and especially the heavy artillery pieces became mired down in the muddle caused by poorly disciplined troops and the March quagmire.

About the time Longstreet's southward-bound army was reaching the Rappahannock, Jedediah Hotchkiss was making his way north on the Valley Turnpike. From his home in Churchville, west of Staunton, the professor was on his way to the headquarters of the hero of Manassas, Stonewall Jackson, in Winchester.

Hotchkiss' initial venture in the Southern army had proved to be one of frustration, fatigue, and depression. After a disastrous defeat at Rich Mountain and the abandonment of Camp Garnett in the northwestern mountains of Virginia, Jed had returned home the third week in September, broken in spirit, seriously ill, and exhausted emotionally. In his state of mind, his seventy-nine-day campaign, as a volunteer in the Confederate

Army had been a dismal failure. But through his skill and resourcefulness he had led a column of seventy men of the 25th Infantry and the Augusta Lee Rifles thirty miles to safety through a dense tangle of evergreen and laurel, swampy land, and craggy cliffs, across both Rich Mountain and Cheat Mountain, after Camp Garnett was given up to the Federals.

Now, having rested and regained his health and self-confidence, he was ready to try again. Encouraged by his friend, William S. H. Baylor, a fellow Augusta County resident who happened to be on Jackson's staff, he started out with renewed energy, hoping to see Jackson and to ask him directly if he could use a topographical engineer. To get to Winchester, Hotchkiss decided to accompany a group of local militiamen, the 160th Regiment, Virginia Militia, which had recently been called up by Governor J. B. Letcher, and was on its way to join up with Jackson's army.[150]

The day before Hotchkiss left Churchville, Jackson's Army of the Valley left Winchester. Union General Nathaniel P. Banks was less than seven miles east at Berryville, while McClellan's Army of the Potomac was occupying the abandoned works at Manassas, less than fifty miles away. Jackson's small force of 4,500 was, for the most part, totally alone in the northwestern Virginia town; Johnston's army was now beyond the Rappahannock, too far to be of any help should Banks move.

Jackson had devised a plan. He would march out of Winchester to the southern limits, secure food, rest, and then slip back around to the north of the town and surprise Banks in the dark. However, things immediately fell apart when Jackson's supply trains went more than eight miles beyond the proposed location, causing the troops to have to march that much farther for their rations. An all night march of twelve miles would be required to bring them back into position for the attack. A disappointed and frustrated Jackson marched his army forty-five miles farther up the valley to near Mt. Jackson, where he went into camp.[151] (Note: In the parlance of the Shenandoah Valley, the southern most part of the valley is the upper valley; likewise, the lower valley is the northern portion. In the geographical context, the valley is more narrow in its upper or southern most end and broadens as it proceeds north, being at its widest in the lower valley. The Shenandoah River runs in a northerly direction, from the upper, toward the lower valley. Staunton and Lexington, for example, are in the upper most part of the valley, while Winchester and Harper's Ferry are in the lower part.)

On March 20, Hotchkiss rode into Jackson's headquarters. However, his petition to the general for an engineering position would have to be put on hold. Jackson's eyes and ears, cavalry Colonel Turner Ashby, brought news that the Yankees, who had advanced as far south as Strasburg, nearly half the way to Jackson's camp at Mt. Jackson, had turned and were on their way back to Winchester. Jackson immediately broke camp and started down the Valley Pike once more. By the afternoon of the 23rd he was at Kernstown, just four miles from Winchester. He believed, based primarily on Ashby's reports, that only a small contingent of Federal infantry and cavalry, a brigade at the most, remained in Winchester. He was ready to dispose of any such resistance and re-enter the town.

When Jackson ordered the attack, on what he thought was only a rear guard of the Union forces that had abandoned Winchester that afternoon, he quickly found out that his and Ashby's assessment of the situation around Winchester was dangerously flawed. The Federal contingent, the "brigade" still in the town, turned out to be three times that many and by nightfall his exhausted, bewildered, and beaten army marched in a different direction on the Valley Pike for the third time in just over two weeks. [152]

Jed Hotchkiss had not been in the fight; his small group of unarmed and unorganized militiamen had been waiting a day's march further south and joined in the flight up the Valley as the main body passed by them.

The Army of the Valley retreated slowly south until they arrived at their camp just south of Mt. Jackson. Jackson had been thinking about the former schoolmaster and his abilities; three days after the fighting at Kernstown, the general summoned Hotchkiss to his headquarters. The two men were discussing Hotchkiss' topographical work the previous summer in northwestern Virginia, when suddenly, as if satisfied of any doubts, Jackson abruptly said: "I want you to make me a map of the Valley, from Harper's Ferry to Lexington, showing all the points of offense and defense in those places. Mr. Pendleton will give you orders for whatever outfit you want. Good morning, sir." [153]

Jackson's gruffness did not bother Hotchkiss. The request that the celebrated general had made—words that someday would echo in the annals of the conflict—was music to Jed's ears. He immediately went to work as a mapmaker for the soldier whose tactics, and knowledge of terrain, would allow him to dictate the course of the war in the Shenandoah Valley. This knowledge, thanks to Hotchkiss, would give the Confederates great advantage over the enemy, an advantage that could not be overcome as long as Jackson was in the Valley. Such an achievement would not have been possible without the work of the newest member of the general's staff.

Meanwhile, the Dixie Artillery, with Longstreet's division, departed its camp along the Rappahannock on March 28 and started south in the direction of the Confederate capital. By April 9, "Old Pete" Longstreet had established his headquarters at Louisa Court House, about fifty miles northwest of Richmond. By April 18, he was on the lower Peninsula, between Yorktown and Williamsburg. Lieutenant Chapman and his brother's battery were not there, however; they went into a reserve position, just a few miles east of Richmond, on the Chickahominy River. Here, the famed Washington Artillery of New Orleans would join them.[154]

McClellan's huge Army of the Potomac had disembarked at Fort Monroe, on the Virginia coast, and was making its way slowly up the Peninsula toward Richmond. During the night of May 3, the 56,000-man Army of Northern Virginia had stolen out of its defenses around Yorktown, unbeknown to the Federals. On May 4, McClellan's cavalry caught up with the rear guard, comprised of Longstreet's division, in the nearly knee-deep east Virginia mud. The next day a pitched battle was joined at Williamsburg. But the Southerners were able to extricate themselves from McClellan's grasp.

During the late afternoon of May 5, Union Brigadier General William B. Franklin began to bring ashore his 11,000 man division at Eltham's Landing, on the south bank of the York River. He would not complete this operation until two o'clock the following morning. His intention was to cut off the retreat of Johnston's army from Williamsburg. But, as was so often the case with McClellan's Army of the Potomac, the timing was off—off by a full forty-eight hours. If Franklin had landed his division on May 4 or even early on May 5, he could have gotten on the main road at Barhamsville, five miles away, and with his infantry and artillery, possibly been successful in blocking Johnston's escape route. But on this morning, Franklin's only thought was to hold his landing ground and wait for the three other Yankee divisions at Yorktown to join him. In doing so, Franklin clashed with General John Bell Hood's Texans, who drove the Federals to the rear, clearing the way for Johnston's army to continue its retreat toward Richmond. On May 9, the Southern army was safely within its fortifications, along the Chickahominy River, east of the Confederate capital.[155]

On May 23, while Sam and William Chapman and the rest of the Dixie Artillery were encamped along the south bank of the Chickahominy, an addition was made to the battery. Like Sam, this newest member was a transfer from an infantry regiment, the 10th Virginia. Private Edmund Chapman, the twenty-year-old younger brother of the Chapmans, had enlisted in Company K at Luray on the second day of June 1861, and his company, the Page Volunteers, had joined the regiment near Winchester three weeks later. Moving to Manassas, the regiment came under heavy fire on July 21, while fighting on the Confederate left, suffering seven killed and eleven wounded. Following the battle, the unit moved to various camps throughout Fairfax County with the men on picket duty a good bit of the time. A week before Christmas, the 10th Virginia went into permanent winter quarters near Culpeper Court House.[156]

In early March, the 10th Virginia took part in General Johnston's "retreat" to the Rappahannock River. Then, in a general reorganization about the middle of April, the regiment was officially detached from Colonel Arnold Elzey's Fourth Brigade and transferred to the Third Brigade, which, together with the Second and the First (Stonewall) Brigades, made up the 6,000 man Army of the Valley under Jackson.

Almost immediately, Edmund and the other members of the regiment were initiated into Jackson's "foot cavalry." The regiment left Culpeper Court House on the 17th and marched north into Madison County. From here they turned west, across the Rapidan River, crossing the Blue Ridge through Swift Run Gap. Five days after leaving Culpeper Court House, the regiment was in Jackson's camps in Elk Run Valley at the southern tip of the Massanutten Mountain range. On April 29, the troops were on the move again. By foot and in railroad cars, in the rain and mud of Virginia's springtime, they made their way west, by way of Staunton, into the rugged Allegheny Mountains. On May 7, Jackson's army was atop Shenandoah Mountain. Their march culminated the next day in Highland County, near the small village of McDowell [157].

The Battle of McDowell was fought on May 8. The combined forces of Jackson and General Edward "Allegheny Ed" Johnson, numbering 10,000, faced the combined forces of General Robert Schenck and General Robert H. Milroy, totaling about 6,000. [158] In the ensuing fight, Jackson forced the Federals to turn back, thus ensuring the safety of the huge Confederate stores located at the army's supply depot in Staunton. Just as important, it also kept the enemy from entering the upper Shenandoah Valley.

By May 17, Jackson's army was encamped at Mossy Creek, in Augusta County. Leaving here on the 19th, the army continued down the Valley to New Market, where it turned east, crossed the Massanutten range through the gap there, and proceded down into the Page Valley, encamping near Luray on May 22. [159] From here, Jackson turned north again in the direction of Front Royal.

The Page Valley was home to most of the men of Company K, and many took advantage of it, just as their comrades in the other companies had done when they passed through Rockingham and Shenandoah Counties. Slipping out of ranks, they made hasty visits to their homes. Some returned in a few hours and some did not come back until the next day. [160] One, at least, did not return at all. Instead, he requested and was granted a transfer to the Dixie Artillery. Just like his brother Sam, Edmund had enough of "foot soldiering". With two brothers in the Dixie Battery, one its commanding officer, it wasn't hard to persuade both his family and his superiors that this is where he should be. The young private had spent nearly a year—a rough year—in the ranks of the infantry and now, he surmised, he would see better times. But times would not be all that easy in the artillery either. [161]

June, 1862, would find the Chapman brothers with the rest of the Dixie Artillery on the right wing of the Richmond defense line, east of the city, along the Chickahominy River. Most of the seventy-five men in the battery—six were absent—had been in the service of the Confederacy for a year now, but had yet to fire their first round, as a unit, against an enemy. During the Battle of Seven Pines, May 31- June 1, they had been relegated, along with the Washington Artillery, to General John B. Magruder's Reserve Division, under Colonel James B. Walton, at Blakely's Mill Pond. At Mechanicsville, on June 26, they were still with Colonel Walton but were now in Brigadier General W. S. Featherston's brigade, with the Washington Artillery and Dearing's Lynchburg battery. [162]

At Gaines' Mill, on June 27, the Dixie Battery was as close to a battle as it had ever been. Longstreet's division was on the right flank of the Confederate line, anchored on a sluggish bog of a stream called, aptly, Boatswain's Swamp. To get to the Federals and have any hope of breaking their line, the attackers would have to cross a quarter-mile of open ground, sloping down

54

to the swamp, with the first line of Yankee field works just on the other side. In doing this, they would be within range of Union batteries both there and on the Chickahominy to the south. On the hillside behind the swamp were two additional lines of defenders.

The charge into the guns of the Union cannon and musketry was indescribably brutal; one Louisiana company lost twenty-nine of its forty-five men. On the right and in the center of the Confederate line, one man in four would be lost in the battle, two-thirds of them in the final charge alone. Between the two of them, the opposing forces had a total of 96,100 men on the field. One Yankee regiment incurred 220 casualties while another had 173, a third of its number. And the 4th New Jersey had the inglorious distinction of having 1,072 men captured. But the Federal line was broken, and Longstreet's division, with the two brigades of Hood's Texans and Laws' Mississippians, from Chase Whiting's division, stormed through. With bayonets fixed and screaming the Rebel yell, they sounded like "forty thousand wild cats", according to one of Longstreet's men.

The breakthrough was complete and before nightfall the Federals had been driven from the field. But still the Dixie Artillery, although as close as they were to the fighting, had been held in reserve—again.

Perhaps the Dixie Battery was lucky after all. According to veterans on both sides, who would fight for the entire four years of the war, the volume of fire at Gaines' Mill was unparalleled in all their wartime experience. Between the two armies, 15, 223 men were casualties in less than nine hours of grueling fighting.[163]

The next day, Lee's army rested. Unable to ascertain just where McClellan was going next—and with Federal guns along the south bank of the Chickahominy controlling the crossing points—Lee had to cool his heels and wait. Additionally, Gaines' Mill had been the bloodiest of the Seven Days campaign so far, and there was little incentive for the commanders on either side to start up again so soon.

By first light on the 28th, Union engineers were busy constructing crossings in White Oak Swamp. The swamp lay primarily between Charles City Road and the Williamsburg Road, southwest of the Chickahominy. In order for McClellan to extricate himself from his positions along the north side of the Chickahominy, and get safely back to his base at White House on the Pamunkey River, or to a new base on the James, he would have to cross through the swamp.

By five o'clock on the afternoon of June 28, the engineers had finished two bridges, a mile-and-a-half apart, across White Oak Swamp. At noon of the same day the troops started across the first bridge. Soon reports began to reach Lee that told him in no uncertain terms that McClellan was abandoning his base at White House on the Pamunkey and heading for Harrison's Landing on the James. In other words, Little Mac was giving up the fight for Richmond and trying to get off the Virginia peninsula. When Jeb Stuart's troopers finally reached White House, they found it evacuated and its great stores in flames.

Following Gaines' Mill, McClellan had established his new headquarters at Savage Station on the Richmond and York River Railroad. He would have three of his corps, still holding the lines in front of Richmond, to pull back down the railroad, constituting a rear guard—a rear guard of half the army— to protect the White Oak Swamp crossings.[164]

In the meantime, Chapman's Dixie Artillery was reassigned again; this time it was part of Anderson's brigade of South Carolinians, presently under the command of Colonel Micah Jenkins, and still in Longstreet's division. And on this day, it was on Nine Mile Road heading for Darbytown Road and thence to Long Bridge Road, leading them to Glendale, just south of White Oak Swamp. Longstreet's division would comprise the southern most arm of Lee's plan to trap McClellan before he could make it across the swamp.[165]

The Dixie Battery was too far away to take part in the fight of June 29 at Savage Station, where the Yankee rear guard went up against less than three full brigades of Magruder's division. When night ended the conflict, casualties were 919 for the Northerners against 444 for the Southerners; these casualties did not include a fight earlier that day, in which the Union loss was twenty-nine men and MaGruder's thirty.[166] In spite of the disproportionate casualties, McClellan had accomplished his objective—keeping Lee at bay while he withdrew the remainder of his army toward the James River. The rear guard slipped out during the night and now all of McClellan's army was safely across White Oak Swamp. Due to the failures of his commanders, Lee had been unable to take the advantage when it was handed to him.

The chase was now on. McClellan, after safely crossing White Oak Swamp with his huge army, was headed for the James by the shortest route possible. Lee, with the Army of Northern Virginia, was hard on his heels. On June 30, at a little settlement called Glendale, or Riddell's Shop, the fox would catch up with the rabbit.

Glendale sat quietly at the intersection of three roads—Quaker Road, coming up from the James River to the south; Charles City Road, beginning outside Richmond, going southeastwardly, past Mr. Riddell's blacksmith shop, directly through Glendale; and Long Bridge Road, coming from the Chickahominy, in a southwest slant, intersecting the other two to form the center of the hamlet. The largest property in the neighborhood was known as Frayser's Farm and would become another name for the coming battle.

Longstreet's division was advancing on either side of the Long Bridge Road toward Glendale; Branch's brigade of Hill's division was on Longstreets's immediate right, Kemper's brigade of Longstreet's division was on it's left. Then came Anderson's brigade of South Carolinians commanded by Colonel Micah Jenkins. Captain Chapman's Dixie Artillery was with Jenkins. Shouldering Jenkins, and astride the Long Bridge Road, was Cadmus Wilcox's brigade of Alabamians.

Jenkins' brigade, with Chapman's battery in support, was dead center of the Confederate line on the afternoon of June 30. With two brigades, Kemper's and Wilcox's, hard on either side of Jenkins' and each with a battery of light artillery, they numbered 4,700 men. When the assault began, it was nearly five o'clock in the afternoon. Chapman's guns opened on the enemy across a small stream called Western Run and were immediately answered by the enemy's artillery. Jenkins was the first brigade off, followed by Kemper and then Branch. Finding that the Federals had retired their guns on the Confederate left, Jenkins ordered the 5th South Carolina to shoot the horses. For some unexplained reason, Jenkins gained little ground at first, as did Branch. Kemper on the other hand, pushed aside the enemy skirmishers, double-timed it through the woods, across a small field, through another boggy wood, thick with underbrush, and broke out into another field. Branch's men stormed a lightly constructed breastwork of fence rails, around a small house, capturing six guns, before running into heavier artillery from the Union center. Finally, Kemper's brigade reached the center Union defenses, on the far side of Western Run, directly in front of and along the Quaker Road.

After Jenkins had ordered the shooting of the enemy's artillery horses on his left, he was met with a severe fire from the Union breastworks 300 yards in his front. Caught in an enfilade of grape and shell, with no support on the left of the line, the Confederates were suffering heavy casualties. But on they came. Facing the Confederate charge beyond Western Run was General George McCall's division of Pennsylvanians with Brigadier General Truman Seymour's brigade just left of the center, protected by two batteries of the German Light Artillery. When Kemper struck the Union defenses, his troops were in a ragged, disorderly line; letting loose with the Rebel yell, they stormed through the German batteries, with the frightened gunners abandoning all four guns. In the meantime, the natural obstacles on either side of the Long Bridge Road had divided Wilcox's brigade. The right side of the brigade, along with Kemper's Virginians, finally stormed up and over the Union left center, driving back the Pennsylvanians, until they had to abandon the field. [167]

The success of Jenkins' courageous assault was tempered by the actions of Branch's brigade. In a report of the fight, Jenkin's was highly critical of Branch: "I had gained command of the Quaker Road and their reinforcing masses could not advance but in direct fire of our men…but here occurred a painful and disastrous event. Branch's brigade came up on our right in great disorder (and)…commenced firing through our lines They threw my right regiment into confusion by massing upon it and firing through it and then withdrew in great disorder, leaving my few to hold the ground. The enemy having advanced beyond our flank, we were compelled to retire from this position and joined Wilcox's brigade in their advance… to our left…in the attack upon and capture of the enemy's guns." [168]

Jenkins' South Carolinians and the Dixie Battery had been under heavy fire from the six 10-pound Parrott rifles of Captain James H. Cooper's Pennsylvania Light Artillery. Unlike their German counterparts, Cooper's gunners stuck by their guns, despite the head-on assault from Jenkins' brigade. Without room to maneuver, the brigade, supported by the fire from the Dixie Battery, charged straight into the mouth of the Yankee guns. Although reinforced by a reserve brigade, Cooper, in sometimes hand-to-hand fighting, was unable to fend off the Southerner's assault, falling back toward the Quaker Road. There he found help, with a regiment of infantry, and was able to retake his guns. But Jenkins would not be denied this day. Finally breaking the Yankee defenders, causing mass confusion, Jenkins men overran the guns for a second and final time.

The South Carolinians paid dearly for their victory. The brigade suffered the highest number of casualties of any Confederate brigade on the day—532. The men of the Dixie Battery " suffered considerably," according to its commanding officer. [169] And Issac Hite detailed the sad news in a letter to his younger brother, Daniel, at home: "Ambrose Rothgeb had his left hand blown off and Daniel Brubaker was wounded along his right side from head to foot. His right eye is thought to be out. Besides these there were several others that were bruised slightly by fragments of shells. John Keyser (was badly wounded and) died the same night." Not less than six batteries faced the oncoming Confederate center that day.[170]

Despite the heroics of men like those in Jenkins' brigade, Lee's plan to converge on McClellan and cut off his escape route to the James was the all-too-familiar story of good planning but poor execution. The plan was aggressive and required excellent coordination of troop movements. But it all came down to the individual commanders, particularly Longstreet, Jackson, Magruder, and Huger, being able to first, understand what they were to do, and second, to do it. If everything had fallen into place, Lee would have finally been able to stop McClellan, not merely beat him up and then let him go—again. If he had been able to converge his forces on the Federal army at the Glendale crossroads, he could have cut it off from its escape routes and its supply base—and then chopped its head off.

It is difficult to appraise Lee's state of mind on the morning after Glendale. The magnanimous side of his character would never permit him to rebuke or reproach, but the feelings of disappointment must have been overwhelming. Twice now in two days—first at Savage Station and now at Glendale—he had the opportunity not merely to defeat the enemy but to envelop him. Total and complete victory, the kind that brings the foe to the bar for terms, was within his grasp. But it was not to be and would never be again.

Lee had been ready but his army had not. The opportunity at Savage Station, just the day before, to pursue and attack an enemy in full retreat, without his base, only came once in a war. At Glendale he had a good plan but was unable to execute it. The opportunity to trap McClellan's army was now gone. Why? How? Magruder's continued confusion, Jackson's unexplained delay, and, once there, his failure to attack, and General Benjamin Huger's mysterious silence. Anyone of these lapses could have been the one that permitted McClellan to escape the snare. Taken together, they all but guaranteed the rabbit would get away while the fox still looked for the hole.

Malvern Hill overlooked the James. And it overlooked the approach of the Army of Northern Virginia. Not being familiar with the terrain, Lee had unwisely decided to take the battle to the enemy in a region that offered him no advantage whatsoever.

The Dixie Artillery did not take part in the heavy artillery duel that took place the first day of July at Malvern Hill. Battle-weary from the previous day's fighting, it was kept in reserve along with the rest of Longstreet's division. There was a time in that long afternoon when the request was made for Longstreet's batteries to be brought up.[171] But the outcome had already been determined. The Federal artillery, elevated as much as fifty yards above the valley through which Lee's troops would have to come, showered down a virtual hailstorm.

The blows delivered to the men and guns of Lee's army were savage. Several hours of trying to shell the Federals on the hill, while being pummeled in return, nearly decimated the Confederate artillery. Battery after battery fell like so much wheat before the scythe. By three o'clock it had become obvious that " the long arm of Lee" [172] would come up far short this day.

Following the failure of his artillery, Lee turned to his infantry. At 5:30 p.m. several brigades set out to storm the hill or to try to turn the enemy's flanks. But these repeated attempts resulted in repeated bloodbaths, as shell and canister and musketry cut them down. The Federal guns continued to bellow until well after dark, covering the summer landscape with an eerie, surrealistic glow, while the earth shook as if a giant wave was moving just beneath the soil. At ten o'clock that night the guns fell silent. By ten o'clock the next morning McClellan was gone, his Army of the Potomac in a safe haven at Harrison's Landing on the James River.[173]

This last day of the Seven Days would cost the Confederacy 869 dead, 4,224 wounded and 540 missing, most of who would eventually be counted among the dead. Major General D. H. Hill summed it up: "It was not war—it was murder." [174]

Of all the "what ifs" and "should haves" that came in the aftermath of the debacle at Malvern Hill, the lack of order, and ineffective command structure, of the artillery in the Army of Northern Virginia in the summer of 1862 was poignantly clear. D. H. Hill again: "The battle of Malvern Hill might have been a complete and glorious success had not our artillery and infantry been fought in detail. My...batteries...had exhausted all their ammunition and been sent back for a fresh supply. If I had ...a good supply of ammunition ...we could have beaten the force immediately in front of us. The want of concert with the infantry divisions was most painful." [175] Overly optimistic perhaps, but on the 5th of July, General Lee's assistant adjutant general wrote Porter Alexander, chief of ordnance for the Army of Northern Virginia: "General Lee directs me to say that General Pendleton is absent, and he (does) not know who is in charge of the Reserve Artillery; he therefore desires that you will go at once and ascertain the condition of the Reserve Artillery, and have it put in condition to move to Malvern hill..."[176] And from General Pendleton himself: "Too little was (in) action at once, too much was left in the rear unused...." [177] Ninety Confederate guns, including those of the Dixie Artillery, remained idle, in the woods north of Malvern Hill, on that hot July day in 1862.

The failures of the Confederate artillery at Malvern Hill would play a big part, in just over three months time, in determining Sam Chapman's future. Maybe the luck of the Dixie Battery—and of Sam Chapman—was still there.

Following the brutal fighting of the Seven Days, both armies withdrew into non-combative positions, to rest, lick their wounds, and evaluate their respective options. McClellan, with his 90,000-man army, was encamped at Harrison's Landing, in the low country along the James River. In an area four miles long and one mile wide, the men were crowded in with 27,000 horses and mules, 2,000 beef cattle, 288 guns, and 3,000 wagons. The intense heat of the Tidewater summer, coupled with poor sanitary conditions would account for almost 43,000 reported cases of illness during July.

On July 8, President Lincoln arrived at McClellan's headquarters. When he returned to Washington several days later, he recalled Henry Wager Halleck from the Western theatre and made him the new general-in-chief of the army, the same position McClellan had held before being fired by Lincoln the previous March. Halleck's views on the conduct of the war were 180 degrees south of McClellan's. A month later, much to his chagrin, Little

Mac's grand army was on its way down the peninsula to Fort Monroe. Where it had landed five months before to begin the grand adventure that was to take it to the gates of Richmond—or at least to Seven Pines—the Army of the Potomac was now embarking to return north. Left behind were nearly 8,000 dead and missing comrades, at least forty pieces of artillery, and 31,000 stands of small arms. The Army of Northern Virginia would re-equip itself, courtesy of the Union quartermasters. The Peninsula Campaign was officially ended. [178]

While McClellan, with his portable printing press, was declaring the events of the Seven Days as not a defeat or retreat but as "changing (his) base of operations by a flank movement," after being attacked by a Confederate "army of 200,000," [179] Lee was busy, refitting and reinforcing the Army of Northern Virginia. With captured and imported arms and new uniforms, regiments were matched as they should be and morale was quickly restored in the rank and file.

It was a far different story for the command structure in the days and weeks following the Seven Days. General Daniel Hill was challenged to a duel by General Toombs. Longstreet feuded publicly in the Richmond papers with A.P. Hill, even going as far as to put Hill under arrest and giving command of his division to General Joseph R. Anderson. And General's Huger and Magruder were relieved of their commands, and transferred, for their conduct during the campaign.

For the Dixie Artillery though, things seemed to go along as usual. For most of the men in the battery, the Seven Days had provided their first exposure to a shooting war. They had experienced military life to its fullest in the previous fifteen months—camp, drill, march, wait, and wait some more—but life at war was something totally different indeed. And they had survived—at least most of them had. Official records, such as they are, contain no mention of casualties in the Dixie Artillery up through the Seven Days battles, so only personal reminiscences are available for this purpose.

Some of the men in the battery—Lieutenant Chapman for instance—had previously experienced the shooting side of war. But, for Chapman, it also presented him with a problem, or so it would appear. Paradoxical would probably best describe Sam's situation. Just thirty months prior to his enlistment in the Warren Rifles, he was in Main Street Baptist Church at Luray being recognized—licensed as it were—to exercise "his gifts in preaching &

exhortation to his fellow men, whereas in the Providence of God his lot may be cast." Well, Sam's lot was cast in troubled waters to be sure and in April 1861 the young private/minister, carried a rifle and a sundry supply of other weapons of war in addition to his Bible.

Chapman was, of course, not the only person who would find himself in such a situation. Most prominent was probably William Nelson Pendleton, a fifty-one-year-old graduate of West Point and minister of the Gospel in Lexington, Virginia, when the war began. He had spent three years in the U.S. Artillery and in 1837 had resigned his commission to teach; in 1838 he was ordained, and moved into the rectory of the small Episcopal Church in Lexington. For whatever reason, in 1860 he accepted an offer to drill some young men in the community who had organized a battery. When war broke out, he asked for, and was elected, captain of the Rockbridge Artillery, naming his cannons Matthew, Mark, Luke, and John. To add to Pendleton's seemingly antinomic principals, at the Battle of Falling Waters on July 2, 1861, he is reported to have loaded his gun and then raised his hand in prayer: "May the Lord have mercy on their poor souls—fire. " Eventually Pendleton would win promotion to brigadier general and become Lee's chief of artillery, [180] leading his men into war while, at the same time, preaching the message of repentance and salvation—and good works.

(Perhaps the tenets of another noted cannoneer best explain the mind-set of a 19th century Sam Chapman and others like him during this time in the history of the country. Raised in an aristocratic, deeply religious Virginia home, William J. "Willy" Pegram would rise to the rank of colonel, commanding an artillery brigade at the age of twenty-three. He would die a hero's death, five days before the surrender at Appomattox, from wounds received at nearby Five Forks. Several times in his short life he expressed himself, particularly during the early days of the war, on matters religious and moral— and nationalistic. Biographer Peter S. Carmichael offers these views: "(Pegram) saw the South as engaged in a war to preserve the home of Christian civilization from the ungodly North. He was neither a zealot nor a fanatic; he articulated a view that almost certainly reflected the basic assumptions of many men of his class and generation. Religion and nationalism were (intertwined); God had assigned men and women specific stations in life. Tampering with this delicate arrangement constituted a direct challenge to God's preordained world. God had ordained his country's 'war for political independence', (thereby making it) a crusade. Pegram and all men of the South were obligated to do everything in their power to defeat (its) enemy. It was a religion of action, not just prayer and this was a holy war. And although religion did not make all Southerners uniformly nationalistic, it (did) introduce the possibility that they interpreted their world through a (common) religious prism—one that gave them just cause and comfort for dying." Carmichael goes on to suggest that Southern officers fought aggressively, even recklessly, repeatedly exposing themselves under fire, without the slightest concern for personal safety, because Southern independence must be achieved at any cost; surrender was worse than defeat.) [181]

Things settled down for the Dixie Artillery for most of the rest of July and into the second week of August. Lee had deduced that McClellan was no longer a threat to Richmond. Burnside, with 10,000 men newly arrived on the coast of Virginia from North Carolina, was enroute to join Pope north of Fredericksburg. The next move against the Confederacy, Lee thought, would come from the north, involving attempts to cut the vital Virginia Central Railroad and to once again try to enter Richmond, only this time from a different direction.

On August 13, Lee ordered Longstreet's division to Gordonsville; he had previously sent Jackson there, after the Seven Days. John Bell Hood, with his command was also departing the camps around Richmond, heading north. The Dixie Artillery had its moving orders too. Being a part of Longstreet's division it was attached, along with the Washington Artillery, to the artillery brigade under the command of General Featherston of Mississippi. On August 20, they were moving with the rest of the division toward Kelly's Ford on the Rappahannock. On the opposite bank were General Pope and the Federal army. [182]

On August 22, preacher-turned-soldier Sam Chapman was in command of a two-gun section of the Dixie Battery consisting of one 3-inch rifle and one 12-pound Napoleon light gun. He was positioned on the right of a line, near Rappahannock Station, having moved as Pope's forces had moved, cat-and-mouse fashion, on the other side of the stream. His guns were part of a contingent of nineteen guns forming a line on the south bank of the river at a crossing known as Beverly Ford. Immediately to Chapman's right were two guns from Captain Victor Maurin's Louisiana battery. To his left were four cannon of Captain R. M. Stribling's battery, and four 3-inch rifle guns from Captain Squires' battery of Washington Artillery. On the left side, one 10-pound Parrott gun from Captain Anderson's Alabama battery, two more Parrotts under Captain A. L. Rogers, and four guns from the Washington Artillery, commanded by Captain M. B. Miller, completed the line.[183]

Soon after six o'clock in the morning, the fog lifted and so did the silence of Longstreet's batteries. The firing was intense, with the Union cannon, primarily long-range guns, firing from a thousand yards away, returning a rapid and vigorous fire. After a short while, the guns of Rogers and Anderson were withdrawn to cover beneath a hill. By shortly after seven, all the Confederate batteries on the left had been withdrawn from the field, leaving the four batteries on the right, including Sam's section, to receive the concentrated fire of the enemy's guns. Stribling's section of four guns was forced to retire after running out of ammunition. On the day, Stribling's battery expended 354 rounds, while suffering two men wounded and four horses killed.

Around eleven o'clock, the remaining Confederate cannoneers received notice that the infantry was preparing to engage the enemy. Soon after, the firing ceased. By nightfall, all the Union batteries had pulled back.

In two official reports of the fight, written by on-the-scene commanders, Sam was commended; one report said "Lieutenant Chapman, with his section of the Dixie Artillery, behaved with great coolness and handled his guns with effect." In the other report, he was included, along with other batteries on the right with "Too much praise cannot be awarded...for the stubborn and unflinching manner in which they fought the enemy's batteries...." In the fight at Beverly Ford on the Rappahannock River, the Dixie Artillery suffered it's first *official* casualties—four men wounded and one horse killed. Out of a total of 1182 rounds fired, Chapman's section of only two guns accounted for 299, or 25 per cent. [184]

The next day, August 25, Longstreet's command continued up the Rappahannock and the following afternoon crossed over at Hinson's Mill. Old Pete continued moving around the enemy's right flank, following Jackson's line of march the day before. After fighting skirmishes on August 27 and 28, the troops passed through the Bull Run Mountains, west-to-east, at Thoroughfare Gap. The division finally joined Jackson's Army of the Valley on the Manassas Plain around noon of August 29. [185]

Jackson was already engaged with Pope's army and had it pinned to the ground when Longstreet arrived. Longstreet took his army, now comprised of three divisions and 30,000 men, and late that afternoon began to feel his way down the Groveton (or Gainesville and Centreville) Pike. Suddenly, he ran into a Union division making a similar movement in the opposite direction. After a furious fight, which lasted until nine o'clock, without gain to either side, Longstreet withdrew his line to a position on Jackson's right astride the turnpike. Together, the two armies formed a set of jaws that opened wide to the southeast. Would Pope be reckless enough to thrust his infantry into those jaws? [186]

When the hot August sun rose on August 30, Longstreet's and Jackson's combined armies numbered 50,000 as they faced a Union army of 60,000. But Pope's Federals were massed in a northerly and easterly facing direction and, suprisingly, no pressure was being brought to bear against Longstreet's right wing. It was as though Longstreet was not even included in Pope's calculations. [187] This would be a fatal blunder on the Union commander's part and Chapman's Dixie Artillery was destined to capitalize on it to such a degree that the outcome of the battle very possibly might have depended upon its action.

All morning and well into the afternoon, of that still, hot day, the Southern high command—Jackson, Lee, Longstreet, Stuart—watched and waited. The Yankees seemed to not want to move against the Confederate lines and Lee was pondering how he might stir Pope into action as the day passed. Then around three o'clock Pope's forces hit—and hit hard. Infantry, with artillery shaking the ground, charged against Jackson's right. Three lines of bluecoats were advancing through the woods and a similar attack was getting up steam on the center and the left. The attack became sterner, more violent and the enemy was growing increasingly more numerous. [188]

Featherston's Mississippi brigade had been posted since early morning about half-a-mile west of the Groveton Turnpike with its right shouldering Pryor's brigade, which in turn had its right astride the turnpike. Featherston's left was in contact with Jackson's extreme right. The Dixie Artillery, which had been assigned to the Mississippi brigade since departing the lines around Richmond, was placed to the left of the turnpike, nearer the village itself. For most of the day two batteries of the Washington Artillery, on a hill in the rear of Featherston's brigade, kept up a duel, at times severe, with Union batteries positioned in the woods across a field directly in their front. [189] Pope referred to the Washington Artillery as "...an annoying battery...." [190]

Between two and three o'clock that afternoon, Captain Chapman rode from his battery's position over to where Featherston's brigade was assigned. Chapman later wrote: "While at the highest point occupied by (Featherston) we could see the enemy infantry about a mile distant, moving in large bodies to the left and disappear in a body of woods in front of Jackson's left wing." What Chapman was observing were troops of Union Major General Fitz John Porter's V Corps. The firing of a single cannon was the signal for 12,000 infantrymen—thirty seven regiments—to advance 600 yards, across an open field toward an unfinished railroad cut and on to the right, and right-center, of Jackson's line above the cut. Chapman rode hastily back to his command where he saw Longstreet and some of his staff passing on the turnpike, going toward the front. Five minutes after they had passed, Colonel Manning, of Longstreet's staff, hurried back, saying Longstreet needed batteries right away.[191]

Sam Chapman had been waiting with the rest of the battery for his brother's return. As soon as William had the word from Colonel Manning, the battery was off at a gallop, going into position in the front of Whiting's (Laws') brigade, on the left of, and about fifty or a hundred yards off, the turnpike. "We... commenced firing at a heavily massed body of infantry on our left not more than 400 yards distant. I fired from this position until their ranks were broken and driven back...." recalled Captain Chapman.[192]

The initial shots from the Dixie Battery had nearly disastrous results as they ricocheted into Jackson's lines. For this reason, Captain Chapman remembered, it was some six or seven minutes before the Union batteries responded, probably thinking that the ricocheting fire was from one of their own batteries and not a Confederate one. But then Chapman's guns found their mark as they broke the ranks of the enemy with grapeshot as well as shell, driving them back toward the reserve lines in the woods.[193] Sam Chapman recalled the terrible cannon fire decimating the blue-coated troops: "The order to fire upon them was given, and as the guns were on their left flank, a most destructive enfilade fire was given. Behind this line of battle came another and still another. The first had halted under the fire that ploughed their ranks. The second and third line was soon mixed with the first and the work of destruction went on more fiercely as shot and shell tore to pieces all formation of this body of men—Morell' s division of Fitz John Porter's corps." The artillery lieutenant observed: "As they gave way, Jackson's men sprang out of the R. R. cut in pursuit and their faded uniforms were in striking contrast to the blue of those retiring." [194]

"They were on the hill sloping toward us...we could not miss them," Captain Chapman recalled. "We could see each shot as they (sic) went thro' their massed troops." As the Federals threatening Jackson's right and center fell back, Chapman's battery limbered up and quickly moved back down the pike toward Groveton. The captain continued: "I...took a position in an old apple orchard from which we fired at the retreating infantry for about thirty minutes." By now the Union gunners had zeroed in on Chapman's position and "...the firing from their batteries at us while in the orchard was terrific. While there, the horse I was riding had both hind legs carried away by a cannon ball and while at Groveton the second one was killed by a shell which exploded in front of me." [195]

At the same time the Dixie Battery was pouring enfilading fire down on the assault of the Federal infantry, Colonel Stephen Lee's battalion of eighteen guns, was positioned between Hood's extreme left and Jackson's extreme right, just in front of the railroad cut. This location, some several hundred yards to the northwest of Chapman, allowed Lee to also place enfilading fire into the advancing Yankees, which he did with deadly precision. [196]

After the repulse of Porter's assault against Jackson's lines, the Confederate forces readied for a charge of their own. Longstreet swung the right of his line around to face in a northeastwardly direction while the left of his line, with Hood's brigades, charged due east. Jackson, in turn, would advance east and southeast. The converging lines quickly overran and swallowed up the ranks of the confused enemy. Finally, it became a rout, and so continued, until darkness overcame the battlefield. After more than a mile and a half, the victorious Southerner's were weak and scattered, and becoming confused themselves by strange ground and poor visibility. That night, in a hard thunderstorm, followed by a steady rain, they bivouaced along a concave line that stretched from near Sudley Church, just south of where Cat Harpin Run converges with Bull Run, southeast to where the Manassas-Sudley Road crosses Old Warrenton-Alexandria-Washington Road, a distance of nearly four miles.

This had been the Dixie Artillery's finest hour. However, when the histories and reports of the Second Battle of Manassas were written, the batteries sending forth the deadly enfilading fire that saved the day for Jackson were identified only as those of Colonel Stephen D. Lee, opening on the advancing Federal infantry, [197] and the batteries of Captain Robert Boyce and Captain James Reilly. Reilly's guns were concerned mainly with silencing the

Federal batteries adjacent to the northwest side of the pike.[198] No mention was made of Chapman's battery or the part it played—only a mention in some reports of an "unidentified battery."

The exhibition of a painting, after the war, illustrating the Second Battle of Manassas, as seen in the Panorama of the same name, offended William Chapman. The Dixie Artillery had received no recognition for its role in turning the assault against Jackson, and was not depicted in the painting. On August 27, 1887, the twenty-fifth anniversary of the battle, the former captain wrote a letter to Longstreet, stating his case for the Dixie Artillery. Chapman contended that the placement of the batteries of Stephen Lee, as depicted in the painting, was not where the guns that sent forth the enfilading fire on the assaulting troops were located. He supported his view by reminding Longstreet of his (Longstreet's) and General C. M. Wilcox's reports. In their reports, an unnamed battery is referred to as the one which first opened fire in front of Whiting's (Laws') brigade of Hood's division, on the left of the Gainesville and Alexandria (Groveton) Turnpike, at 3:30 p.m. on the 30th of August. [199]

From the various reports, both Union and Confederate, and maps made of the battleground and placement of the troops on August 30, it appears there is merit in what Chapman says, and the following scenario seems likely:

1) The location of the Dixie Battery was some 300-500 yards southeast of the Lee batteries, nearer to Groveton and closer to the pike. There is every reason to believe that, at one point in the afternoon, both batteries were firing at the same time.[200]

2) At the time Jackson sent word to Longstreet for help, Lee's batteries had been firing for thirty minutes or so. What Chapman was firing at was most likely the second or third wave, or battle line, or possibly the combination of the three lines that the Federals had started across the field. Lee's guns had fired on the first and possibly the second waves. [201]

3) Longstreet, in his report of the battle, says that he ordered two batteries up and that one was ready and was placed in position and immediately opened. In his letter, Chapman states that after he returned to his position from visiting Featherston's brigade, he "...directed his men and drivers to be ready to move." [202]

4) General Wilcox, in his report of the battle, says "...a battery was directed by (Longstreet) to fire (on the advancing troops), this battery being near the turnpike." He added: "This artillery fire, *alone*, broke regiment after regiment and drove them back into the woods." [203]

It seems quite possible that Colonel Lee's batteries opened first, followed by Chapman's battery some thirty minutes later. It is clear that one of the batteries ordered up by Longstreet, in response to Jackson's request for help, was the Dixie Battery. (The reports show that Captain Reilly's battery was also ordered up at three o'clock that afternoon.) It is clear that two different commands were firing from two different emplacements. The only fault that can be found with Chapman's complaint is that his battery alone did not save the day for Jackson; whether or not his battery initiated the fire is specutive. However, his request for recognition of the critical role his battery played in turning back the assault appears valid. [204]

For Major General Porter, things only got worse, following his disastrous assault that August day. General Pope, an old foe who dispised Porter and whom Porter dispised in return—and openly told him so—took advantage of the situation. He relieved Porter of command that November and brought charges of disloyalty, disobedience, and misconduct in the face of the enemy. Porter, a good friend of General McClellan, was court-martialed, by a court presided over by foes of McClellan, found guilty, and on January 21, 1863 cashiered from the army. Fifteen years later, in 1878, he won a new hearing and was exonerated. However, politics again got in the way and it was not until 1886 that President Cleveland signed a bill restoring Porter to the rank of colonel—without any back pay. He was to feel the fire from the Dixie Artillery's guns the rest of his life. [205]

Sam Chapman's old friend and mentor from Mossy Creek, Jed Hotchkiss, did not accompany Jackson on his march from Gordonsville to the Manassas Plain; he had stayed behind working on much needed maps for Lee's planned Northern invasion. He would draw all day and then pack up each night and follow in the wake of the army. Gradually gaining on the troops, he joined Jackson by the close of fighting on August 30.

Jackson told Hotchkiss to map the battlefield, but the mapmaker was unprepared for what he saw. In a letter to his wife he wrote of the Federal dead, "(laying) in thousands over the battlefield, rotting and enriching the soil they vainly boasted as their own. Never have I seen such horrors. I thought I had seen war and bloodshed in its worse shape...but that was nothing...their dead were strewn over a space of five miles long and three wide, piled up in many places, sometimes in long lines as they stood in the ranks, and upon one another as they attempted, seven times to break Jackson's line and were as many times repulsed." One of the dead was Jed's good friend from Staunton, Colonel Will Baylor, who, only five months earlier, had persuaded the mapmaker to approach General Jackson for the position he now held.[206]

Casualties at Second Manassas were large, particularly as they impacted individual units. Two small divisions in Fitz John Porter's corps sustained a loss of 331 killed, 1,362 wounded, and 456 missing, for a total of 2,151 out of about 6,500 engaged—a 33 per cent casualty rate. Most of these occurred during the ill-fated charge on August 30 in which the Dixie Artillery and Colonel Stephen Lee's artillery enfiladed Porter's infantry In terms of officers killed or wounded, the Union lost 699 and the Confederatcy a like number. Total numbers in killed, wounded, and missing were 14,462 Federals and 9,474 Confederates; 4,000 of the Federal losses were prisoners.[207]

The word would not get to Sam until much later, but the casualties at Second Manassas would be much more personal—with an ironic sort of duplicity—than he could know at the time.

Christian "Chrisley" Forrer, was the name-sake of the first Christian Forrer, who had stepped ashore in Pennsylvania, from Switzerland, in 1754. Chrisley and Sam were first cousins, Sam's mother and Chrisley's father being brother and sister. Chrisley's two brothers, Samuel and Judah had enlisted in 1861. When Jackson's army arrived at Mt. Jackson following the fight at Kernstown in March of 1862, Chrisley was waiting. He enlisted there in Company G of the 33rd Regiment on March 24. The 33rd had been one of the original five regiments that made up Jackson's First Brigade, forerunner of the famous Stonewall Brigade. On August 30, the 33rd was in the center of Jackson's line, at the railroad cut, against which Porter's V Corps would lead the massive Union assault. It was during this assault that Chapman's Dixie Artillery laid down the brutal enfilading fire that helped break the Union charge and sent it reeling back, saving the day for Jackson. But Sam's cannons could not help his cousin that day. The young private received wounds from which he would not recover. Crisley Forrer was nineteen years old when he died. [208]

Rain. And more rain. The day following the rout of Pope's army by Jackson and Longstreet the downpour that had begun the evening before had deluged the countryside making any movement by the infantry and artillery impossible. Stuart's cavalry was on the move, however, and he soon discovered that Pope had slipped away during the night to a strong position near Centreville. Stuart reported this to his commander, but Lee knew there was no use in trying to bring Pope out of his defenses this day. His wet, tired, and famished brigades would be hard pressed to go up against Pope's guns again so soon. Besides, Pope's legions must be poor shape also, so there was no hurry. Lee would wait and rest a day.

The next day, September 1, Jackson caught up with Pope at Ox Hill, near the Chantilly mansion. With Hill's division setting the pace, Jackson's army had swung around hard to the left from Groveton and caught the Little River Turnpike west of Chantilly, hoping to get behind Pope. But even with the forced march, the going was too slow and the Union commander had evaded the flanking move. As Jackson's weary foot soldiers sloshed down the turnpike, Pope was waiting. In fact, waiting was the wrong word; Pope took Jackson completely by surprise and attacked. Though brief, the fight was anything but ordinary. It was more like a series of deadly, disorderly, skirmishes in the mud and rain. Darkness and a heavy downpour from black, sullen skies brought an end to the fight. But the end had come earlier for two of the Union's better known commanders; Isaac I. Stevens, a former governor, and decorated veteran of the Mexican War, and the popular veteran, Major General Philip Kearny, had both been killed. Stevens was leading a charge and Kearny inadvertently rode his horse into the Confederate lines. When daylight came, Pope was gone, finding his haven at last in the shelter of the Washington defenses. The pursuit was over.[209]

Sam Chapman was glad to see the rain. It meant at least one day of rest and a time to take stock. The horses were hungry—as were the cannoneers—and bridles, limbers and guns all needed attention. But it would not last—the rain or the rest. Orders were given to move on the third day of September,

Lee had made up his mind. He was going north, into Maryland and then into Pennsylvania, As he looked around on the once fertile land of northern and central Virginia, he felt an overwhelming sadness. What he saw had once been a "horn of plenty," but now was empty and bare. The constant tramp, tramp, tramp, of the armies, their cannons booming and their shells falling to the earth to destroy it and the seed within, the minie balls slashing through the grain and the ears, all brought an early yield of waste. The rich, lush landscape of Maryland, bursting with the soon-to-be harvest, was calling to him, as a maiden beckons her lover. The General was listening.

Lee's soldiers and his horses were hungry. His civilians were weary of the war and scared of what was to come if and when it ended. A successful expedition into the land of the enemy would awaken France and England, would bring pressure to bear on Washington, both from a military standpoint and from a domestic one, and would give relief to his people, now suffering under the oppressor's boot.

By September 7, the Army of Northern Virginia was across the Potomac and in Frederick, Maryland. Already, Washington was nervous. The feared Rebel army was only thirty-five miles away. George McClellan had returned as chief of all the Union armies in the East. And he knew he had to do something—this time. It was not Richmond that was being threatened now.

The Dixie Artillery was once again assigned to the Reserve Brigade, this time under the command of General William Pendleton, Lee's chief of artillery. Back in the good graces of Lee, following his strange absence at Malvern Hill, the Episcopal clergyman would go on the Maryland campaign with perhaps his largest direct field command to date—twenty-four batteries with forty-four guns. [210]

Lee was not overly concerned about the cautious McClellan. After all, he had run him and his 105,000-man army off the Virginia peninsula, less than five months before. What he was concerned about was Harper's Ferry. Lee believed that the garrison at Harper's Ferry would evacuate when he approached Frederick. It didn't. Instead, four days after the Confederates entered Frederick, a 2500-man Union detachment from Martinsburg, in advance of Jackson's troops, made the fifteen mile trek to Harper's Ferry and joined the 12,000 men already there. [211]

Lee entered Maryland with scarcely 50,000 men. Stragglers and deserters amounted for the loss of an astounding 15,000, and only reinforcements from Richmond could make up the difference. For the most part, the Southerners appeared to the Marylanders to be a bedraggled collection of rag-tailed and barefoot soldiers at best, with only the cavalry and artillery bearing any resemblance to an invading army. But after four days of rest, with good food and a bath, morale was much improved and spirits were high as the army once again picked up its march.[212]

The morning of September 10, the Army of Northern Virginia was on the road north to Hagerstown. Jackson, was in the lead, followed by McLaws' and Dick Anderson's divisions; these three would go as far as Middletown, where Jackson would turn west to Martinsburg, with the intention of capturing the garrison there and cutting off any retreat of the Harper's Ferry contingent. McLaws and Anderson would proceed south to Harper's Ferry. At the time everyone else was leaving Frederick heading north, Brigadier General J. G. Walker with his two brigades was turning back south, for the Potomac, by way of the Monocacy aqueduct, to come onto Loudoun Heights on the south side of Harper's Ferry. When everything was in hand at Harper's Ferry, they would all rejoin the rest at either Boonsboro or Hagerstown.

In the meantime, Longstreet's division, followed by D. H. Hill as the rear guard, was proceeding on to Boonsboro. In between Longstreet and Hill were the remainder of the wagon trains and the Reserve Artillery, [213] but the Dixie Battery was not in this column. It had been reassigned once more, this time to Brigadier General Joseph B. Kershaw's brigade of South Carolinians in Lafayette McLaws' division, already on their way south towards Harper's Ferry. The Dixie Artillery was ordered to join up with Kershaw's brigade there.[214]

General McLaws had been given a formidable task. He was to take his division and proceed south from Middletown and occupy the Maryland Heights, high above Harper's Ferry and the Potomac River. Once he had accomplished this he was make every effort to capture the arsenal and its complement of enemy troops.

But there was to be a fly in Lee's ointment. Or four flies were more like it. First, a written copy of Lee's plans for dividing his army as he left Frederick had fallen into McClellan's hands. The other three flies were the gaps at South Mountain. South Mountain is a fifty-mile-long range running from near the Potomac River on the south, northward into Pennsylvania, and can be likened to the Massanutten range in Virginia. It divides Frederick and Middletown on the east from Boonsboro, Sharpsburg, and Martinsburg, on the west, and Harper's Ferry to the south. The main road from Frederick to Boonsboro and thence to Hagerstown goes through Turner's Gap; not over a mile south is the smaller Fox's Gap. Approximately six miles further south Crampton's Gap allows a back way into Harper's Ferry.[215]

With the information gleaned from Lee's infamous "Lost Order," McClellan dispatched the largest part of his Army of the Potomac, some 70,000 men, up the Boonsboro Road toward Turner's Gap; he incorrectly believed that the majority of the Confederate army was at Boonsboro. The remainder of about 20,000 he sent toward Crampton's Gap, to cut off Lee's forces at Harper's Ferry. McClellan, with characteristically innate reasoning, still believed Lee had brought 120,000 men north of the Potomac. Lee, in the meantime, had received some alarming reports on the movements by McClellan—alarming enough that he sent two messages on the 14th and another on the 15th to McLaws, to hurry with the task at Harper's Ferry and to then get out of harm's way. He feared the Federals, by advancing on the road through South Mountain from Frederick, might cut McLaws off. Lee also felt a full defense of Turner's Gap was vital, sending orders to D. H. Hill at Boonsboro to prepare to do so.[216]

The attack came at Fox's Gap, not Turner's. By early on the morning of the 14th, the Federals had turned the Confederate right and were advancing along the ridge of the mountain toward the Hagerstown Road at Turner's Gap. To add to the already precarious circumstances of Lee's force on the mountain, McClellan was massing reinforcements in the valley below. But Lee was also sending, or rather bringing, help as he appeared with Longstreet, after a nineteen-hour march over rugged terrain from Boonsboro. With Hood's Texans in the forefront, the hole in the line at Fox's Gap was plugged, relieving the pressure on the out-numbered men on the ridge between Fox's and Turner's Gaps. [217]

While the stalemate south of Turner's Gap continued, McClellan decided to try to flank the Gap from another direction. Late in the afternoon, with all but one brigade of Joe Hooker's I Corps, he started a long flanking movement around to the north, while the remaining brigade made a head-on charge straight up the Hagerstown Road toward the Gap. By nine o'clock that night, newly promoted Brigadier General Alfred Colquitt's Georgia brigade still held the Gap on the Hagerstown Road. But on the north end, Robert Rodes' brigade of Alabamians was losing the battle against Hooker's two divisions in his front and a division each on his right and left flanks. With help from three small brigades of Longstreet's division, Rodes was able to lessen the ground he had to give up, before nightfall brought an end to the struggle. The coming of dawn would reveal the horrid intensity of the fight. Lying wounded or dead were 1800 Confederates; a like number of Union casualties lay on the ridges. Rodes alone lost 422 men, fully one-third of his brigade. [218]

After things had settled down on the night of September 14, General Lee held a council with Longstreet, D. H. Hill, and Hood. The news was all bad; the three subordinates agreed that South Mountain must be abandoned and the army retreat back across the Potomac. But Lee held his own council and did not tell the generals that he too felt that the invasion had been lost. He only instructed them to march to Centreville, on the road to Sharpsburg, in order to give some bit of protection to McLaws' rear. [219] Neither did he tell them that he had earlier sent a courier to McLaws, advising him that "The day has gone against us and...you(must) abandon your position tonight (and) retire by Sharpsburg." [220]

As if the news wasn't bad enough, soon after the council had ended and the others had left, Lee received news that Generals Munford and Hampton, with their cavalry and horse artillery, totaling about 1,000 men, had been overrun by nearly two full divisions. The Yankees were pouring through Crampton's Gap, directly in McLaws' rear. [221] Lee was now in a worse situation than he could possibly have imagined only a few hours earlier. With the Federals having a direct road to Sharpsburg from the west side of Crampton's Gap, not only was McLaws in immediate danger of being cut off, but his own line of retreat, past Sharpsburg, was in danger of being eliminated.

But maybe all was not lost; along with the bad news about Crampton's Gap, Lee got some news from Jackson—finally. Although non-specific, it offered hope: "Through God's blessings the advance has been successful thus far, and I look to Him for complete success tomorrow." [222] What Lee did not know—and what Jackson had only hinted at—was that he and McLaws had the garrison at Harper's Ferry surrounded, except for one road to the north; that night, the 1300-man cavalry command inside the ferry rode out the road, undetected. But by dawn the next morning, the remaining garrison could see what was all about them. The menacing guns of Jackson's artillery began blasting away at the enclosure from heights that a gunner would never, in all his dreams, believe he would command, over a target. By 11:00 a. m. of the 15th, Jackson was inside the garrison. He would receive the surrender of over 11,000 troops (some authorities put the number at 12,500), 1300 small arms, 73 pieces of artillery, and 200 wagons. It would be the largest capitulation of Union forces in the entire war. [223]

Chapman's guns finally reached the vicinity of Harper's Ferry but too late to take part in any of the brief fighting. Writing to his brother Sam after the war, William recalled the situation vividly: "You will remember too that our Battery was engaged in the capture of Harper's Ferry, as we were assigned there to join Kershaw's Division (sic), and marched from Frederick City west through Crampton's Gap and through by Burketsville (sic) on to the little village on the north side of the Potomac before reaching Harper's Ferry." (William Chapman mentioned that he was unable to recall the name of the village. In all probability it was Sandy Hook or Weverton, both just due east of Harper's Ferry. Part of McLaws' division was here, under the east edge of Maryland Heights, while Kershaw's brigade was on the Heights.) "We were there with our guns ready for action, but General (sic) Miles capitulated before we had occasion to use them. We were among the first Confederate troops to cross the Potomac Bridge at Harper's Ferry," William added. [224]

Following the surrender of the Union garrison at Harper's Ferry the Dixie Artillery was on the road to Shepherdstown, crossing the Potomac near there early the next morning, and then marching on to Sharpsburg. The battery, though ready and waiting, would not be called upon, though the battle raged throughout the day of September 17 along the banks of Antietam Creek. The following day the two armies rested; that evening, William Chapman moved his men and guns back of the lines where his quartermaster had located some much-needed hay. They fed their horses and stayed in that position until daylight of the 19th. [225]

Sam Chapman could hear the reports of the big guns, four miles away at Sharpsburg. He had been hearing them since the afternoon of the 16th. They started small that first day, but on the following morning it seemed the whole earth shook, without ceasing. The sky back to the north was a mixture of black and gray, although the sun was shining through, in an eerie, part day, part night sort of way. Sam couldn't help but remember how it was at Malvern Hill, less than three months before; although the battery had not been engaged, he was so close to that thundering cannonade that the guns still sounded in the recesses of his consciousness when things got too still. And before that, there was Glendale—and Second Manassas just six weeks ago—where he was both participant and witness to the carnage wrought by the cannon—his cannon.

While the Dixie Artillery had been waiting, expecting at any moment to be called into the fray, Lee gathered the scattered divisions and brigades of the Army of Northern Virginia along the range of hills, between the town of Sharpsburg and Antietam Creek. Although his original plan was to use the small village as a gathering place for his army's retreat to the south side of the Potomac, several things had come into play in a short period of time to change Lee's mind. Foremost was the word from Jackson that Harper's Ferry had fallen; added to this was the belief that McLaws could escape McClellan and proceed on to Sharpsburg. With A. P. Hill's and Jackson's troops on the way, he would essentially have all his army intact in one place. Then there was McClellan himself. Overly cautious, reticent, languid McClellan, quick to boast, slow to move. So confident was Lee of his assessment of his foe that he did not hesitate to express the opinion that the next day (16th) would pass without a battle. Last, but certainly not least, was the terrain. Even though he had the Potomac at his back and with narrow Boteler's Ford a mile and a half below Shepherdstown, as his only escape route, Lee felt that the lay of the land he had chosen offered a moderately favorable offensive and defensive position.[226]

The battle began in earnest the morning of September 17, with heavy artillery fire from the Union's long-range guns, followed up by an infantry attack on Jackson's troops on the Confederate left. This in turn was followed by attacks upon the center and right. Heavily out-numbered, with McClellan sending in fresh reinforcements, the left and then the center gave way. But reinforcements by McLaws, Walker, and Hood sent the Federals reeling and the line was reformed. Finally, on the left, the assaults by the Union infantry stopped, after being repulsed repeatedly, and were replaced by concentrated artillery fire.[227]

Having abandoned the attacks on the left of the Confederate line, the Federals once again took aim at the center. They were turned back there also, and retired beyond the crest of a hill. But a crucial mistake in orders caused Rodes' brigade to withdraw from its position in the line and Yankee infantry poured through the gap en masse. Effective fire by the Dixie Artillery's old battery-mate, the Washington Artillery, and by Boyce's South Carolina battery checked the progress of the enemy, and in about an hour and a half, the offense against the center ceased.[228]

Over on the right it was a different story. Assaults were made against two regiments of General Toombs' Georgia brigade, at Rohrbach's Bridge (later called Burnside's Bridge) by the brigades of General Ambrose Burnside. With the help of General D. R. Jones' artillery, Burnside was repulsed five times. But when the Federal line was extended, Toombs was forced to withdraw to protect his flank and Jones was overpowered and gave way. The Georgians' perseverance had cost Burnside 500 casualties, while the Georgians lost 100.

After Burnside had broken the resistance at the bridge, McClellan was ready to roll. He now had the entire IX Corps across Antietam Creek and ready to advance against Lee's right and center, pushing the Southerners back into Sharpsburg and closing off their retreat to Shepherdstown. He had 8,000 men and twenty-two cannon to do the job. But once again, McClellan hesitated. And A. P. Hill arrived on the field after a forced march of seventeen miles in seven hours from Harper's Ferry. Wearing his flannel red shirt that he always wore when going into battle, Hill pushed off against Burnside with 2,000 yelling infantryman. Archer's brigade, on Hill's left, was the first off, hurling against a Federal column that had overrun a battery. Recovering the lost guns, Archer pressed on. Gregg's South Carolinians, together with Branch's North Carolinians, were on Archer's right, quickly repulsing a Federal advance and forcing the enemy to quit the field. Before Pender could be brought up on Hill's extreme right, the entire Union force was in confused retreat, through the town and toward the protection of the Federal batteries on the opposite side of the creek. It was nearing nightfall when the exhausted Confederates halted the pursuit. It had been exactly one and a half hours since A. P. Hill had put his three brigades on the field.[229]

Lee's success would be costly. Three of his general officers would die. Branch and William Starke were killed and G. B. Anderson was mortally wounded. Lee suffered 10,000 casualties out of the 36,000 or so that saw action on the day. For the expedition to date, 13,609 were casualties, while Federal losses were put at 27,767, with nearly half accounted for in the surrender at Harper's Ferry. Although the ratio of Union to Confederate losses was two to one, that was more than the South could afford to pay.[230]

The following day saw no action on the part of either army. Lee held the same positions as he had on the 17th, with the exception of the center, which was drawn in about 200 yards. McClellan was expecting reinforcements and would not make another offensive until they arrived. It had been the bloodiest day in American history and Lee was ready to go back home. The Army of Northern Virginia ended its invasion and crossed into Virginia the night of September 18. [231]

William Chapman, hearing the rumbling of wagons and gun carriages throughout the night and early morning of September 18-19 could not sleep. Little did he know that the sounds that were keeping him awake were from Lee's army, withdrawing from the battle lines of Sharpsburg toward the Potomac and Virginia. "I persuaded myself to believe that Jackson was making one of his flank movement (sic), and just about daylight two cavalrymen came across the fields from the front, asking what Battery our (sic) was." Chapman identified his unit and the cavalrymen's response sent shivers through the battery commander. "They said there was nothing between us and the advancing Federal army except a few cavalry pickets and that they were advancing and that Lee's Army had crossed the Potomac River." It didn't take the men of the Dixie Artillery but a few minutes to harness their horses and hitch up the guns. Traveling down a ravine and through the woods, off the public road until they were nearly to the river, the command made its escape. And while crossing the stream, Federal batteries and sharpshooters situated on the hill behind them, opened up on the retreating Confederates already on the opposite side. [232] While Sam Chapman and the Dixie Battery were in the river, Jackson's transportation wagons were there also. And whom should Sam spy, amongst the escort, urging the drivers to all possible speed in crossing, but "Old Jack" himself! Out of great respect "but with a tinge of curiosity to know whether the celebrity would recognize a subordinate under such circumstances," Chapman saluted Jackson. "The General returned the salute," Sam recalled. [233]

Early the next morning, Chapman's guns were stationed on the bluff overlooking the river, in order to defer the enemy from crossing to the south side. Pendleton's artillery was already in place at Boteler's Ford. The enemy's long range rifles opened on Pendleton's emplacements, with the Confederate batteries responding. While Lee moved his army out of range, he left about 600 infantry under Pendleton's command to help ensure the safety of the ford, ordering him to hold it the night of the 19th-20th. The cavalries of Fitz Lee and Jeb Stuart covered the withdrawal of Lee's troops on the morning of the 19th, keeping the enemy at bay at both Shepherdstown and Williamsport. That night however, Pendleton received word that Union forces were preparing to cross the river and there was not sufficient cavalry available to prevent it, even with the help of his 600 infantrymen. During the dark, he ordered the withdrawal of certain batteries further inland, while others covered them. In the darkness and confusion of the ensuing fight, Pendleton lost four pieces of artillery, their horses having been killed and the men too weary to drag the guns to safety. They spiked the cannon and left them. The next morning when help arrived they found the Yankees had thrown the guns over the cliff. When Pendleton withdrew from the ford for good at noon on the 20th he recorded three men killed, four wounded, the four guns lost, and twenty-six horses killed or disabled. The Dixie Artillery listed one casualty from an exploding shell, in which the man lost an eye and permanently disabled a leg.[234] Luck—or Providence—had again been with the Chapmans and the Dixie Artillery.

The Reserve Artillery of Pendleton's command, which now included the Dixie Battery, caught up with the rest of the army on Opequon Creek, below Martinsburg, the evening of September 20. There they went into camp for several days before removing to the Bunker Hill/Winchester area. While here, on October 4, Lee began the reorganization of his army. One of the key areas to be addressed by Lee was the artillery. Another major problem area was that of stragglers. These two seemingly unrelated concerns would find a common ground in the person of Lieutenant Samuel Chapman and his future in the service of the Confederacy.

Lee's desire to overhaul the artillery arm would come to fruition quickly. He called on his wordy, but highly efficient organizer, William Pendleton and, on October 2, Pendleton gave Lee his plan for the restructuring of the artillery of the Army of Northern Virginia. It was to be accomplished by "...reducing the number and yet increasing the efficiency of the (artillery)...and in case of a company much reduced below the service standard, it would seem right to merge it in some others." [235] Pendleton's plan inquired into each battery in the army, giving an analysis and recommending a disposition. Item 7(2) of his report to Lee read: "Captain Chapman's (General Featherston's brigade) is... greatly below the service standard, having only 32 men present for duty...." [236]

Pendleton's plan was endorsed by Lee and forwarded to Secretary of War Randolph. On October 4, while Captain Chapman was back in Page County recruiting men and purchasing horses for the battery, Special Order No. 209, calling for the reorganization of the artillery, was issued; Article IX read: "The officers of Captain Chapman's battery, of General Featherston's brigade, are relieved from duty with their company. The men and horses will be assigned to Captain Pegram's battery." [237]

William Chapman made a personal trip to General Lee's headquarters, making his case for retaining the Dixie Artillery intact. The Confederate commander patiently explained the necessity of disbanding the batteries and carrying out the reorganization, and gave Chapman his personal regrets for having to do so. [238]

The Dixie Artillery was no more.

6. Sojourner Behind the Lines

The reorganization of the Army of Northern Virginia, in October 1862, brought to an end the artillery career of Sam Chapman. Lacking a couple of weeks, it had been twelve months since Sam had left the muskets of the infantry for the cannons of the artillery. Now he was an artilleryman in name only. He was still, officially, a first lieutenant of artillery in the Army of the Confederate States, and he would draw his $100 monthly pay as such but just where was his army? [239]

When The Dixie Artillery and other batteries like it were being disbanded, Lee was hoping to remedy the command and organizational deficiencies that were prevalent in that arm of the service, with the broad swipe of Pendleton's restructuring brush. But there was another problem that so frustrated the commander that he was heard to remark to then Colonel Porter Alexander, his ordnance chief, "My army is being ruined by stragglers." [240]

In Lee's report to President Davis on September 21, relating to the Maryland invasion, he wrote: " (The army's) present efficiency is greatly paralyzed by the loss to its ranks of the numerous stragglers. A great many men belonging to the army never entered Maryland at all; many returned after getting there, while others who crossed the river kept aloof. It ought to be construed (as) desertion in the face of the enemy..." [241]

On September 3, while the army was still at Chantilly, following Second Manassas, Lee had written to Secretary Randolph: "...there are many conscripts in the counties recently vacated by the enemy that can now be had. In Fauquier ... the number (exceeds) 400." Lee suggested to the Secretary that "...measures be taken at once to get these conscripts and those in adjoining counties (and) that they be taken to Richmond for future distribution, under the law." He went on, "There are also in all these counties men who have left the service and gone home...They should be apprehended as soon as possible." [242]

Just as Lee's artillery problem, and the subsequent steps taken to alleviate it, had brought Sam's career in "Lee's Long Arm" to an end, the straggler and deserter problem and the enactment of a conscription act would present him with a new career; and this one offered a pleasant respite from the din and horror that was war.

After receiving his pay at Winchester on October 1, Lieutenant Chapman reported for duty to Lieutenant Colonel John C. Shields, at the Camp of Instruction near Richmond.[243] The forty-two-year-old Shields was a former artilleryman and was one of the organizers of the First Company, Richmond Howitzers, before the war. He was serving as captain of the company in June, 1862, when he was appointed a lieutenant colonel in the Provisional Army of the Confederate States and put in command of the newly established Camp of Instruction. [244]

On April 21, 1862, the Confederate Congress had passed *"An Act to Provide for the Public Defense,"* commonly know as the Conscription Act. The stated purpose for the legislation was in the preamble: *"In view of the exigencies of the country, and the absolute necessity of keeping in the service our gallant Army, and of placing in the field a large additional force to meet the advancing columns of the enemy now invading our soil..."* The act constituted the first national law in American history providing for the conscription of troops. It required all white males between the ages of eighteen and thirty-five, not legally exempt, to be members of the army of the Confederacy for a term of three years, unless the war ended sooner. The term "conscript", although never actually appearing in the Act, was the common term used to refer to the eligible men. In actuality, the law was one of selective service rather than a draft because it, and legislation that followed, established elaborate exemption procedures.[245]

The same Act that made conscription the law of the land also called for the establishment of "camps of instruction", where the recruits would be collected, drilled and otherwise prepared for the field. This preparation included "...(vaccination) and (passing) through the usual camp diseases" [246]

In response to Lee's strongly worded letter of September 3 to the Secretary of War, Colonel Shields was informed that immediate action would be taken to get the conscripts and deserters out of the counties evacuated by the Northern troops. Shields' report on the execution of the conscript law for the months of September and October 1862 showed that a total of 4,459 conscripts were enrolled (registered), but nearly one-half or 2,183 were either exempt or discharged for cause, leaving a net of 2,276. The number of these sent to the Camp of Instruction near Richmond was 765, or only about one-third of those still lawfully under conscription. [247]

On October 8, Lee again wrote to the Secretary of War, advising that there were about 4,500 sick conscripts and recruits in the Valley, from Staunton to Winchester, who had been sent to the army since his return from Maryland on September 20. Lee stated that they were afflicted with measles, camp fever, etc and that his medical director "...thinks that all the conscripts we have received are thus afflicted ...and have become a burden." These sick were in addition to a like number of sick and wounded from the Maryland Campaign. Lee requested that no more conscripts be sent to him from the Camp of Instruction, but instead " remain there ... so that they may pass through these inevitable diseases, and become a little inured to camp life." The Secretary directed Shields "...to suspend the sending forward of conscripts who have not had the measles or mumps"[248]

To enforce the Conscription Act, officers of the state or of the Confederate army were assigned as enrollment officers. These officers were authorized, in addition to enrolling conscripts or otherwise legal recruits, to arrest deserters and those absent without leave. On November 6, Shields reported to the Adjutant and Inspector General (A&IG), Samuel Cooper, that "The counties of the Valley have been nearly drained of conscripts by officers sent for the purpose, (however), the men are never accounted for to me." Shields went on to explain that the discrepancy between the "total number enrolled" and the total number actually received into the camp of instruction was due to a great number deserting en route or failing to report as directed. The enrolling officers, in this instance, were men of Stonewall Jackson's command. [249] At that time there was no central structure for enrollment officers; each command or each civilian jurisdiction could authorize its own.

To solve or at least lessen the problem, Shields proposed to the A&IG that he (Shields)"...assign a superior officer to each Congressional district, who will have entire charge of the business in his district, and...forwarding the conscripts as enrolled to the nearest camp of instruction...." General Order No. 82 from the A&IGO carried out this recommendation. [250]

By the beginning of the new year, Sam Chapman was the enrollment officer for the Ninth District of Virginia, centered in Warrenton. This would prove to be a fateful transfer for the lieutenant. His " pleasant respite" was about to come to an end. [251]

PART IV

PARTISAN

7. Joining That Fellow Mosby

Sam Chapman was glad to be out of Richmond. The capital city was one great hubbub and not much to his liking. The peaceful—or as peaceful as the Yankees would allow—countryside of northern Virginia was much more suitable to his disposition. He had been able to get back home, to Luray, in time for Christmas. But that once joyful time for the Chapman and Forrer clans was greatly subdued in 1862. There was the loss of Crisley Forrer at Second Manassas, that brought so much sadness this first Christmas without him. Other families in the Valley were hurting also. The Hite boy, David, had been wounded at Second Manassas, fighting along side Crisley. He survived but would be killed two years later at Winchester. The Hites had four sons in the 33rd Infantry. Only one would come home from the war. Ambrose Shenk, who became a captain in company H of the same regiment, was killed in March at Kernstown. And Judah Forrer had witnessed the killing of Charles Wheat, a nineteen-year-old trooper in Ashby's cavalry, on April 19, just outside Luray. They buried him in the Forrer cemetery, the first soldier killed in the county. No, this second Christmas of the war was not a happy time for a lot of folks in the Page Valley. [252]

Bad enough it was that her sons were being killed, but the Yankees had been pestering the civilians of the Valley also. The previous July, four regiments of the Second Brigade, Second Division of the I Army Corps, with a section of artillery and some mountain howitzers, took possession of, and occupied Luray. The provost marshal sat up quarters in the courthouse and a residence in town was taken over for a hospital. Three weeks before, a cavalry column of two battalions of the 1st Michigan and eight companies from the 1st Vermont and the 1st Maine made a three-day reconnaissance through the Valley. [253] It was hard to figure why such a force would be needed in the little town or even in the entire Page Valley. One citizen remarked as how it reminded him of "a swarm of locusts come to devour everything in sight." A worker at the foundry said it was like "taking a drop hammer to an ant killing."

Sam's brother, William, was home for Christmas also. He too had accepted duty as an enrollment officer in the Ninth District. In fact, William had been in Fauquier County ever since the break-up of the Dixie Artillery, unlike Sam who had spent the major part of that time in Richmond. Now they were both back, doing conscript duty. William was busy lately paroling Union prisoners, but prior to that he was gathering conscripts. The job involved locating men who were subject to the new conscription law, enrolling them and then arranging for their movement to a camp of instruction. But the brother's duties also included finding those soldiers who had left their units voluntarily, whether through desertion or simply by being absent without leave. In many instances it required them to deal with, and even arrest, men they had known all their lives. There wasn't much discussion between the two veteran artillerists of changing things, only the mutual voicing of their frustration at being removed from the war. [254]

Sam returned to Warrenton soon after the first of January, 1863. Just a couple of weeks later, he began to hear talk of an ex-scout from Stuart's cavalry named Mosby who had recently made things uncomfortable for some Yankees over in Fairfax. Toward the end of the month the tales and rumors increased, but Sam didn't put a lot of credence in loose talk and rumors. That is, not until some of the conscripts he was enrolling began asking him about joining up with "that fellow Mosby", when required to do their service. Then there was the news from up in Middleburg about how the Yankee, Colonel Wyndham, from down in Fairfax had come up and threatened to burn the town and destroy all the property if the raids against his outposts didn't stop. And how the good citizens of that village had written to this Mosby asking him to cease his attacks so the Yankees wouldn't take it out on them and their town. Mosby had reportedly written to the town fathers and, in no uncertain terms, told them he would have nothing to do with such a "...degrading compromise with the Yankees." [255]

It was along about this time that Sam started to give serious consideration to getting back into the war. He was intrigued by these later stories he was hearing about Mosby and his bunch and so what if they might be embellished some in the telling. It was a different way of fighting the invaders, one that did not involve drilling men and marching to battle, or lying in a trench or manning a battery. No, this sounded as if it were something entirely different, something that would get him out from under his increasingly unpleasant conscription duties. The nearly three months at the camp of instruction near Richmond and almost two months in the enrollment district had given him his fill of the business, and "...finding it not at all to my taste, I asked to be relieved (of) gathering men who were very unwilling to leave their homes to become soldiers." [256]

John Mosby had put the time, before he began harassing the Federals again, in latter January to good use. Constantly riding about the countryside, he familiarized himself with the geography of the area in which he was to spend the next two years and three months. He found the best places to rendezvous his men, located safe-houses and available forage, mentally noted the trails and little used pathways that could help a man or a group of men quickly vanish. And probably most importantly of all, he familiarized himself with the military lay of the land—where were the enemy's outposts and pickets, what were the most probable places that a force would ford a stream or river, make a bivouac, establish a signal station, cross a ridge or pass through a mountain. The former scout had also gathered information that told him the Yankees were keeping a large number of troops—infantry, artillery, cavalry—at Fairfax Court House, and from there the outposts were being served. It was these outposts that interested him.[257]

Mosby's activities in the weeks preceding the first of March had greatly annoyed the Yankees, especially Colonel Wyndham. Sir Percy Wyndham was a British soldier-of-fortune who had fought with the Italian patriot and general, Garibaldi, in Italy. He commanded the cavalry brigade at Fairfax Court House and was in charge of the outposts. Being familiar with the old rules of warfare, he was unable to counteract the forays and surprises that kept his men in the saddle all the time. Loss of sleep and trying to combat an invisible foe frustrated the Colonel to such a degree that he called Mosby and his men "horse thieves". To this, Mosby offered no denial, except to say "... that all the horses (we) had stolen had riders, and that the riders had sabres, carbines, and pistols."[258]

Sam Chapman had made up his mind. When he finally caught up with Mosby, around the end of February, he told the guerrilla leader that he had been relieved of his conscription assignment in order to join his command. Mosby's response was plain and direct: Have a good horse, at least one, preferably two or more, revolvers, a place to hide away between raids, and a good story to explain why you aren't in the army should Union sympathizers or Yankee soldiers get inquisitive.

Mosby received another recruit into the command about this time. Walter Frankland had been in the 17th Infantry with Sam, although not in the same company. Frankland was a friend of Sam's best friend in that regiment, Tom Petty. Sam had promised Petty that he would try to get Frankland an assignment in the Signal Corps while the regiment was encamped at Centrevile in September of 1861, but nothing seemed to come of it. It was about the same time that these recruits were joining with Mosby that the leader sent a report to General Stuart in which he talked of increasing his small force: "My men (are) mostly raw recruits. I had only twenty-seven men with me. I am still receiving additions to my numbers. If you would let me have some of the dismounted men of the 1st Cavalry, I would undertake to mount them." [259]

Sam Chapman, first lieutenant of artillery, was now a recruit in a command that had no official name and whose commander had no rank other than private in the cavalry. Despite this, Sam would not have to wait long for his first action in this "different way of fighting." Just after midnight on March 2, 1863, Major Joseph Gilmer, with 200 men of the 18th Pennsylvania Cavalry, was directed to conduct a reconnaissance from Fairfax Court House in the direction of Aldie, about twenty miles west on the Little River Turnpike. From there he would proceed to Middleburg in search of Mosby and his followers. He was given two specific orders: (1) proceed carefully and send back couriers through the night with information on whether he saw any enemy or not, and (2) do not cross Cub Run until daylight, and then try to gain all the information possible by flankers and small detached scouting parties.

Major Gilmer, for whatever reason, took it upon himself to ignore both these orders. Without sending back any couriers or dispatching any scouts he proceeded on to Middleburg, four miles beyond Aldie and well past Cub Run, arriving in the town before daybreak. Throwing a net around the village, the cavalrymen proceeded to call out every man and boy. There was no one connected with Mosby to be found; in fact, Mosby had never stayed in the village, only passed through it on occasion. The result of the Yankee shakedown was a street full of old men and cripples.[260] Angered by his failure to entrap anyone of consequence, much less Mosby, the major made several of the men mark time in the street before ordering them into a march through the town. In the meantime, some whiskey had turned up and by the time the column started back toward Fairfax with its "prisoners", several of the troopers, Gilmer included, were very much fortified against the cold night air. [261]

That morning, while Gilmer and his consocation of weaving troopers and waddling citizens departed Middleburg, Mosby was four miles away at Rector's Cross Roads, awaiting a gathering of his men. When word reached him that Middleburg was occupied by Federal troops, he collected seventeen of his companions and set out for the village. When he arrived, a mob of wailing women and crying children greeted him. They told him that the

Yankees had ridden out at daybreak in the direction of Aldie with the men folk now perched on the horses behind the troopers. What Mosby didn't know was that Gilmer and most of his command had turned off the turnpike just past Aldie, when Gilmer spotted, through his dilated pupils, a fifty-man detachment of Vermont cavalry ahead of him. Thinking it was the enemy he had not been able to find in Middleburg, Gilmer took his command off the turnpike and struck out in the direction of Groveton, hoping to gain Centreville and safety. Some of his column, however, proceeded on down the pike and met the Vermonters.

Mosby, in the meantime, had arrived at the western end of the village and, in a charge, scattered several horsemen and captured nineteen troopers who were busy feeding their mounts at the door of a mill. He then spotted some cavalrymen on the other end of the town and presumed he had caught up with the rear guard of Gilmer's column and that the entire command would soon turn on him. In Sam Chapman's words, "There were less than a dozen of us and we were attempting to follow up a raiding party of the enemy (at Middleburg). We set out to pick up their stragglers, but came up too near, and the whole command turned on us, and we fled in regular Tam'O'Shanter style. This was kept up for a mile or two, with no other loss to us than uniforms bespattered with mud and a weary lot of horses." Mosby, still under the impression he had come upon Gilmer's rear guard, had ordered the men to return to Middleburg, while he lingered behind in Aldie; it was then that he learned it was not Gilmer's men but the Vermont detachment that he had fought. [262]

Major Gilmer, when he returned to Fairfax, was unable to make a report of what had happened. After the effects of the whiskey had worn off, he was placed under arrest, charged with drunkenness and cowardliness and, shortly thereafter, cashiered from the army. [263]

Sam Chapman was no longer a recruit in a command with no name, under a leader with no rank. In less than three weeks, Private Mosby of Stuart's cavalry would become Captain Mosby of the Provisional Army of the Confederate States, with his own command of Partisan Rangers. [264] As for Sam, just like his introduction to warfare at Alexandria back in 1861, he had experienced another rather innocuous beginning to a career change.

8. Of Recruits and Generals and Such

When Walter Frankland showed up at Mosby's camp on February 11, 1863, he was accompanied by three other men—Frank Williams, on foot, and two riders, George Whitescarver and Joseph Nelson. Frankland had been with Whitescarver for a time in Richmond when they decided to travel to northern Virginia in an attempt to join Elijah White's cavalry. Both men had been discharged from the army and were now anxious to get back in, especially into a partisan-type command. White's was one such command, operating in the border service generally. They had spent some time with relatives in Fauquier County and at Salem they were joined by Nelson, a relative of Whitescarver's. Nelson, too, had been discharged after being wounded at Second Manassas. The fourth member of the group, Williams, joined them when they stopped at the home of James Hathaway near White Plains, not far from Salem.[265]

Nelson and Williams had horses, Frankland and Whitescarver did not. After Hathaway, a Mosby confidant, told them about the scout who had been bothering the Yankees in Fairfax, they decided against seeking out White. Instead, with directions from Hathaway, the four men set out for Rector's Cross Roads, where Mosby was gathering his men. Mosby accepted Williams and Nelson since they were mounted. Frankland and Whitescarver were promised mounts from the raid Mosby was preparing to set upon—a Federal picket post near Herndon Station. Williams and Nelson were invited to go along.

When the raiding party returned to the camp, there were no horses for Frankland and Whitescarver; they had been divvied up among the raiders. Whitescarver was able to borrow a horse and, and on February 25, went along with the next raiding party. This time the objective was a Federal outpost near Germantown on the Ox Road where it intersects with the road from Chantilly Church.[266]

Just before Mosby left on the Ox Road raid, a Union sergeant in full uniform, but without sidearms or a horse, strode into the camp. With legs slightly bowed, he walked with the swing of a man who had spent some time on the sea. Large of frame, with deep dark eyes, James F. Ames was a deserter from the 5th New York Cavalry in Fairfax. He had walked from the cavalry camp at Germantown to Rector's Cross Roads. He gave no reason for his desertion except to say that Lincoln's Emancipation Proclamation changed the purpose for the war. Mosby never inquired further. He was satisfied with his story, after questions put to him, regarding the distribution of troops and the gaps in the picket lines, coincided with what Mosby already knew. The men were not convinced, however, thinking the big Yankee had been sent to lure Mosby into a trap. Since he had come without a horse, he proposed to Mosby that he go back to his camp and secure one. Mosby agreed to this and suggested Frankland go with him since he was in need of a mount also. And this would be a good test of Ames' sincerity. [267]

The two horseless cavalrymen started out, the day after the raiders returned from Ox Road, on the thirty-mile trek to Ames' old camp at Germantown. It had been snowing and the roads were nothing but thick, putty-like mud. After nearly three days in the snow, mud, and a soaking rain, the two would-be riders reached the camp of the 5th New York. They waited for the camp to quieten-down and turn in, but a couple of hours after "Taps" they heard the bugler blow "Boots and Saddles." It was Gilmer's troopers setting out for Middleburg. As soon as the column had cleared the camp, Frankland and Ames talked briefly with the sentinel, walked into the officers' stable and came out with two fine horses. Without any ado, they rode out of the camp. They tried to get to Mosby, fearing he was going to be caught in a trap, but before they could get back to the Cross Roads, Mosby had already heard of the Yankee's visit to Middleburg and was on his way there. [268]

One of Mosby's first recruits—probably the first outside the original nine he had borrowed from Stuart's 1st Virginia—was a burly, muscular thirty-year-old woodcutter appropriately named John Underwood. A native of Maryland but a long-time resident of the thick piney forests around the Frying Pan section of northwestern Fairfax County, Underwood became a faithful member of Mosby's command on the raider's first excursion. Mosby picked Underwood up as the small band of ten riders passed his isolated house the night of January 10, 1863. The intricate forests and tangled underbrush were still somewhat alien to Mosby. Using his extraordinary skills of persuasion, which the sternest of men found hard to resist, he soon convinced the woodsman to guide him that night and the next as well when Mosby raided his first two Union picket posts. Underwood's uncomely appearance belied his true nature and intelligence; pleasant, but with eyes constantly in motion, he had a shock of white hair growing straight up from his forehead. He would prove to be invaluable to Mosby with his prowess as a scout and guide. [269]

Because of the success of Ames, now known as "Big Yankee" to the partisans, and Frankland, in violating the integrity of the Yankee lines around Fairfax Court House, and with the information Ames and some captured Federals were able to give him, Mosby put into motion a plan that had been developing in his mind for several weeks. [270]

On the evening of March 8, Mosby set out from Aldie, on the Little River Turnpike, with twenty-nine men. The weather was cold, with a melting snow, and soon thereafter it began to rain. Mosby was headed for Fairfax Court House, the heart of the Yankee presence in northern Virginia. Only two of the men with him knew his destination—Ames, and John Underwood. Mosby would need their skill and knowledge if he hoped to have any chance of getting into, and safely out of, the Union lines. Pulling away from the turnpike, Underwood guided the band until they reached a point about three miles from Chantilly. At Centreville, a few miles to the south, were several thousand enemy troops. Here, Ames led the band through a break in the picket line. Proceeding south, they came onto the Warrenton Pike, east of Centreville and about four miles from Fairfax Court House. Staying on the pike until they were about a mile and a half from the courthouse, they again left the main road and came into the town from the direction of the railroad station. The few guards stationed around the town were easily taken. The plan had been to be in the village around midnight but it was now after two o'clock in the morning. [271]

Edwin Henry Stoughton was not yet twenty-five years old. He had promise—or it was said he did. He had graduated seventeenth, in the first five-year class at West Point, two years before. He was on garrison duty in New York City when the governor of his home state of Vermont appointed him colonel of that state's 4th Infantry regiment. With war breaking out, Stoughton re-entered the army, taking his regiment to the Virginia peninsula for that campaign in the spring and summer of 1862. On November 5, 1862 he was promoted to brigadier general, at that time the youngest brigadier in the Union army. Throughout the winter he had served on garrison duty around the capitol before settling in at Fairfax Court House. [272]

When Mosby and five of his men went to Stoughton's quarters, the general and his staff were asleep. There was evidence about the room that some revelry had taken place the previous night. Mosby awoke Stoughton by lifting the bedcovers, hoisting his nightshirt and delivering a sharp slap to the sleeping general's now bare posterior. [273]

While Mosby was attending to Stoughton, Ames was off looking for his former commander, Colonel Wyndham. This time the luck was with Wyndham; the evening before, he had taken the train into Washington. Ames brought back his former captain, however, and another staff officer, plus Wyndham's uniform and his horses. "Big Yankee" seemed to take great pride in his catch, despite missing Wyndham. Meanwhile, a third party went to the quarters of Lieutenant Colonel Robert Johnstone, the brigade commander of the 5th New York Cavalry. One of the few who had been alerted of the presence of enemy cavalry in the town, Johnstone hurried from his bed and out the back entrance while his wife clawed and scraped the Rangers at the door. The Colonel left in such a fright that he failed to put on a stitch of clothes. Making his way from the house, he hid in a privy, shaking from both fright and the cold. He would not emerge until daylight. [274]

When it came time for the different elements of the raiding party to rendezvous in the courtyard, the captives outnumbered their captors. There were thirty prisoners, not including the general and two captains, fifty-eight fine officers' horses, and a considerable number of guns. The raiders had been inside the enemy headquarters for one and one-half hours. Now it appeared that their leaving would be much more difficult then their arrival. They had the horses and thirty-three prisoners to be concerned with, not to mention the thousands of troops in and around the courthouse and only a short time until sun-up. Within one mile there were three regiments of Union cavalry. Two infantry regiments were encamped within a few hundred yards of the town, another brigade of infantry was in the vicinity of Fairfax Station, and finally, another infantry brigade, with artillery and cavalry was at Centreville.

Again Mosby relied heavily on Underwood and Ames to bring him out from within the enemy lines. No easy task this. When the raiders left the courtyard, they headed off in one direction until they had cleared the town, and then, to confuse any pursuers, turned in another direction. Flanking Federal cavalry posts and camps they were soon on the pike for Centreville. As they approached within a half-mile of the town, they could see the thousands of campfires burning as far as the night allowed. The raiders turned north, off the turnpike, and soon reached the banks of Cub Run. In the darkness, and with the raiding party having to keep as quiet as possible so as not to alert the enemy pickets, one of the captured lieutenants, along with several men and horses, made his escape.

Cub Run was more like a bear that morning as Mosby surveyed the scene. The melting snow and heavy rains of the winter had turned the placid stream into a torrent. Unable to go back now, Mosby tighened the grip on his horse's reins and plunged into the water. William Hunter, who had been one of the original fifteen raiders from the 1st Virginia, had hold of Stoughton's horse's bridle and the two were the next to go in. The rest of the command, with their prisoners, followed and all arrived safely on the other bank. They had cleared the Union lines. Mosby turned and looked behind him. It was beginning to get light on the eastern horizon. [275]

Hard feelings between John Mosby and Fitz Lee went back to their days in the 1st Virginia Cavalry. The cause is open to conjecture. But when, on the morning following the raid, Mosby went to Culpeper Court House to deliver Stoughton and the other captured officers, old wounds of egotism, jealousy, and vanity were reopened. It had been a cold rain all the way to Culpeper. Mosby was soaked and shivering when he entered the house in which Lee had his headquarters. "(Lee) was very polite to his old classmate (Stoughton) and to the officers, when I introduced them, but he treated me with indifference, did not ask me to take a seat by the fire, nor seem impressed with what I had done." [276]

Fitzhugh Lee's snub of Mosby wasn't the last offense he would give to the guerrilla leader. A few days afterwards Mosby received a letter from him. Lee wanted the fifteen men from the brigade, who had been assigned to Mosby by Stuart in January, returned to their regiment. Mosby perceived this as another attempt to deprive him of his own command. Stuart stepped in and ordered the men to stay with Mosby until he, Stuart, recalled them. When the spring offensive began in April, the men went back to their regiment. By this time however, a considerable number of recruits had joined Mosby and his attacks against Union facilities in northern Virginia continued. [277]

The reports, Union and Confederate, best tell the extent of the astonishing Fairfax raid. From Lieutenant Lawrence L. Conner, the Union provost marshal: "March 9, 1863, 3:30 a.m. Captain Mosby, with his command, entered this town this morning at 2:00 a.m. They captured my patrols, horses, etc. They took Brigadier-General Stoughton and horses, and all men detached from his brigade. They took every horse that could be found, public and private, and the commanding officer of the post, Colonel Johnston (sic) of the Fifth New York Cavalry, made his escape from them in a nude state by accident."[278]

Stuart's report of March 12, 1863 said in part: "(Mosby's) last brilliant exploit—the capture of Brigadier-General Stoughton, U.S.A., two captains, and thirty other prisoners, together with their arms, equipments, and fifty-eight horses justifies this recognition in General Orders. This feat, unparalleled in the war, was performed in the midst of the enemy's troops, at Fairfax Court House, without loss or injury."[279]

The fall-out from the Fairfax raid was severely felt within the Union command. Stoughton, the vain, but promising, young brigadier, was exchanged in May, but when he returned he found he had no assignment. Leaving the army, he went to New York City and established a law practice with an uncle. He would die in 1868 at the age of thirty.[280]

Colonel Johnstone did not survive the fall-out either. The ridicule heaped upon him for his hiding place and for appearing at headquarters that morning totally out of uniform—and everything else—never left him. After having arrested Major Gilmer for making a fool of himself a week before, he now followed him into oblivion. Wyndham, who was away in Washington, but who, nevertheless, received his comeuppance for not filling the gaps in his lines, was relieved of his command and reassigned.[281]

President Lincoln, upon hearing of the affair, said " Well, I am sorry for that; I can make brigadier generals, but I can't make horses."[282]

Mosby was not one to rest on his laurels. Just over a week after his Fairfax handiwork, he was gathering forty men for an expedition against a reserve union picket post at Herndon Station on the Alexandria, Loudoun, and Hampshire Railroad. Again led by Underwood, the raiders took a route toward Dranesville that many in the band felt was meant to confuse them rather than the enemy. As was his custom, especially during the early months of his career, Mosby kept his own counsel. No one except Underwood knew the destination or the objective of the raid. Mosby had become aware of a fairly large picket of the 1st Vermont Cavalry at the station and believed he could bring the ultimate surprise upon it by going in during the day instead of at night. After gaining the Dranesville Road, the group turned south toward Herndon Station, three miles distant. The surprise was complete and when it was over, the entire picket, comprised of twenty-one troopers who made up the garrison and four officers, three of whom were visitors to the post, were prisoners. Additionally, twenty-six fully equipped horses, were added to the Rangers' stable.[283]

Upon the recommendation of Lee and Stuart, President Davis promoted Private Mosby, on March 23, 1863, to captain. At the same time, the new captain received a directive from General Lee to "proceed at once to organize your company...to be placed on a footing with all troops of the line, and to be mustered unconditionally into the Confederate service for and during the war. Though you are to be their captain, the men will have the privilege of electing the lieutenants." Stuart, in a letter to Mosby on March 25, cautioned him against using the term "Partisan Ranger" but instead to use "Mosby's Regulars," stating that the former was "in bad repute."[284]

As pleased as Mosby was with the promotion and the official blessing to form his own command, three things in the two communications bothered him a great deal. The first was Lee's directive that his men be identified with, and on the same footing as, regular troops of the service; the second was the part about election of lieutenants. The third matter was Stuart's admonishment concerning use of the term "Partisan Ranger". To this end, Mosby hitched his galluses a little higher and fired back, sending a missive to Stuart who forwarded it on to Lee. "The letter...says they are to be organized... on the same footing with other cavalry. The men who have joined me have done so under the impression they are to be entitled to the privileges allowed in the Partisan Ranger Act. If they are to be denied them I can not accept the (promotion)."[285] It was probably the first time—the only time—a subordinate officer had written such a letter in which he set forth conditions for accepting or refusing a commission offered to him by Robert E. Lee. But then it was the only time the country would experience a man such as Mosby.

When Lee received Mosby's letter, he replied: " No authority has been given to (Mosby) to raise partisan troops, nor has it been intended. He was commissioned (so that) he could organize companies that could be mustered into the regular service". The fat was in the fire and Mosby tightened his galluses a little more and appealed Lee's decision to the Secretary of War, who determined that his commission did entitle him to recruit a partisan command. Lee and Stuart accepted the decision without malice. There was enough character amongst these three strong-willed warriors to go around.[286]

Captain Mosby did not broach the matter of what name to use for his command. He simply went on the presumption that it was his command to name and the issue never arose again. As far as the election of the officers was concerned, Mosby was diametrically opposed to such a practice. His experience with it while in the 1st Virginia had set him dead against it. In fact, when Fitz Lee won command of the regiment over Grumble Jones in that election, Mosby had resigned his commission as a lieutenant and became a scout—a private-in-rank scout—with Stuart. However, this would not be a problem. Mosby knew how to hold an election. He simply would nominate his personal choice, close the nominations, and open the voting. Needless to say, votes were unanimous. [287]

After the Fairfax raid, the reputation of Mosby and his men, and the feats they had accomplished, spread across northern Virginia, into the Valley and even northward into Maryland. Recruiting took on a whole new life, with the young and the old and the lame, all trying to gain a place on Mosby's muster rolls. Some came with crutches, some with discharge papers, others on furlough, and of course the deserters. To combat the problem of men of conscript age, i.e., eighteen to thirty-five, avoiding the regular army by enlisting in the partisan units, the War Department had put out an order the previous July to the enrollment officers; the order specifically prohibited such persons from being enrolled as Partisan Rangers. [288]

The guerrilla chieftain had some hard and fast rules about just who could and could not be a Mosby Ranger. Deserters had best forget it. Fugitives from military or civil authority were usually automatically rejected if Mosby was aware of their status. On the other hand, officers from the other services who resigned their commissions to ride for private's pay with Mosby were usually welcome, much to the chagrin of the regular army commanders. The Captain was especially fond of the youth and enlisted several boys in their early or middle teens. Charles Conrad, of Company G, was only fourteen when he was paroled at Winchester in 1865, if the records are accurate; Samuel Keen has his age shown as seventeen at the same time. Sympathizers from a divided Maryland were another source of manpower for Mosby. Foreigners who championed the Southern cause or who were simply soldiers-of-fortune came to the command. The "older element" was there also. "Dick" Moran was born in 1814, "Major" Hibbs in 1817. These two were part of the three or four who comprised the nucleus of the command as it was being organized in early 1863.[289]

Sam Chapman had not been selected to go on the Fairfax raid but he was ready to get back to soldiering when Mosby called. And call he did. Mosby and Underwood had gone down to Fairfax to locate the Federal picket posts in the direction of Fairfax Court House. What they found was a large picket of 70-100 men from the 5th New York Cavalry near Chantilly with other cavalry within supporting distance. On March 23, Mosby assembled about fifty-five men at Rector's Cross Roads. Included in this group were some visitors who would ride along that day. Sergeant James William "Willie" Foster, a native of Fauquier County was in the area on horse detail with twelve troopers from the 7th Virginia Cavalry. When he learned of Mosby's plans, Foster requested, and was granted permission, to bring his troopers along. After all, he was looking for horses and what better way to "requisition" some good Union mounts. Also going was William Kennon, a former captain with the now-disbanded Wheat's Louisiana Tigers. And there was Captain Bradford Smith Hoskins, a veteran of the British 44th Royal Infantry regiment, who had fought with distinction in the Crimea War and with Garibaldi in Sicily. [290]

Hoskins had come to Mosby by way of Baltimore and Richmond. Apparently he was nearly destitute, having sold his watch, clothing, valise and other items to support himself while in Baltimore. He then entered into arrangements to "convoy goods', suggesting some contraband activities, before arriving in the Confederate capitol on the afternoon of March 11, 1863. Hoskins slept his first night at Ballard's Hotel, paying nine dollars, before moving to the home of a local Main Street attorney. His diary suggests a socially active individual, savvy in the art of meeting the right people. Hoskins would use these contacts to gain letters to first, the Secretary of War and, second, to General Stuart and on March 16, he was ordered to report to Mosby. But first, a "St. Patrick's night...(with) whiskey punch and sentiment" resulted in his "(missing) the train in the morning in consequence." But by March 20, he was spending the night at Fitz Lee's headquarters at Culpeper Court House and would report to Mosby in time for the Chantilly raid. [291]

The group started down the Little River Turnpike. The day was raw and chilly and the roads were bad anywhere off the turnpike. "What a happy, go-lucky band it was!", Sam Chapman thought. Up near the front of the column was Captain Kennon, "and oh what yarns he could spin. And Moran and Hibbs rode in the rear to keep the column closed up. Moran had been dubbed 'Brigadier' and Hibbs 'Major', and they spoke to the younger soldiers with as much authority as if their rank had been real, and not fanciful. Good soldiers they were, though," Sam mused as he rode along. [292]

As the Rangers neared Saunders' Tollgate, they left the turnpike, and headed in a southerly direction for a short piece, and then resumed their easterly route, parallel to the turnpike. The idea was to get into the pickets' rear, but the post was too widespread for that. Suddenly, they came into sight of the vedettes, who were hardly looking for raiders in broad daylight. Sam, with four or five others, charged after the New Yorkers and caught five of them. However, the reserve, hearing the commotion, mounted about seventy men and came upon the raiders. Mosby gave the order to fall back up the turnpike. Between the tollgate and Cub Run, trees had been felled along the road in two places, to inhibit an attacking force coming from that direction. The Southerners rode around the first barricade and, when they had gotten past the second, Mosby called out, "Left about, men, we'll fight 'em here." Some of the riders dismounted and took positions behind the fallen trees, while the others continued on a few yards. "Most of us obeyed promptly," Sam recalled. "Some few did not seem to approve of (Mosby's order) and kept on in their retreat. I met two and said: 'Aren't you going to charge with us?' They shook their heads and said they were not going to be caught in such a snap as that. With this trifling exception, the men rushed most gallantly at the foe in mid-career. They broke and we were soon mingled with them, shooting and striking, and taking prisoners every few rods. The pursuit was kept up for about two miles, " according to Chapman. With darkness coming on and fresh Yankee cavalry on the way, Mosby gathered his spoils and retired. [293]

The Union report of the fight stated its losses were one killed, two mortally wounded, and two taken prisoner. Mosby's report of the Union losses was much more severe, however: five killed, a considerable number wounded, and one lieutenant and thirty-five troopers captured. The only loss to the command was "Major" Hibbs' boot heel, which was shot off. [294]

Sam Chapman had been in his first real fight as a Ranger. Earlier that day he had asked a veteran cavalryman what was likely to happen to a man in a cavalry charge. "Oh", he said, "beside the possibility of a sabre stroke or a pistol shot, you have a good chance of being knocked from side to side by friend or foe, or knocked down, horse and rider, and being run over."[295] Fortunately for Sam he wasn't knocked down or run over this day. But his luck—and that of the command—was hanging on a short, thin string.

9. The String Breaks

When Captain Mosby telegraphed his report of the Chantilly fight to General Stuart the following day, he received a reply from Stuart on March 27: "Your telegram, announcing your brilliant achievements near Chantilly, was duly received and forwarded to General Lee. He exclaimed upon reading it, 'Hurrah for Mosby! I wish I had a hundred like him!' " [296]

Sam Chapman was at the Warren-Green Hotel in Warrenton, with his brother, the day after the Chantilly fight. Like Sam, William had taken leave from his enrollment duties and accompanied Mosby. And like Sam, he found it difficult to think about returning to conscription work. Sam was still finding it hard to settle down from the excitement of the day before. Expressing to William his feelings of his first cavalry charge, he exclaimed, "It was a thrilling sensation!" The two veterans talked about the Dixie Artillery and Sam recalled Second Manassas: "We enfiladed Morrel's and King's divisions and cut down more than a thousand of their men in ten minutes; but (yesterday) at Chantilly, was more exciting, if possible!" William had similar thoughts, although he did not share them as intimately as his older brother. That was a difference in the siblings; Sam, impulsive, even reckless at times, knowing no fear, and William, quieter, brave, and more inclined to reflect inwardly. William knew his days in the enrollment service were numbered. He was planning on asking for permanent reassignment, just as Sam had done. [297]

Following Chantilly, Mosby enjoyed a brief interlude at the home of his friend and loyal Confederate, James Hathaway. The Hathaway house, located in an isolated area of middle Fauquier County a few miles from White Plains and Salem, was a favorite of Mosby. His wife, Pauline, and the children had arrived there between the Herndon and Chantilly fights just after mid-March. He had been urging Pauline to visit and was happy to be able to spend the better part of the week after Chantilly with the family. [298]

But the call of battle would not be stilled. On March 31, Mosby mustered sixty-nine men at Rector's Cross Roads. The day was a typical day for March in that part of Virginia—cold, windy, overcast. Snow was still on the ground and ice was frozen in the wagon wheel ruts on the turnpike. Sam had ridden up from Warrenton that morning; William had come with him. [299]

Before mid-morning the riders were on the pike heading for Herndon Station. Several regular Confederate cavalrymen were in the group, home on furlough before the armies began the spring offensives. One of these was Harry Hatcher, a Sergeant Major from the 7th Virginia; Hatcher had probably saved the life of General Turner Ashby the previous April by killing a Yankee trooper, one of four who had surrounded Ashby. Also present were members of the famed Black Horse Cavalry of Fauquier County. And there were a few "walking wounded" from the convalescent hospital in Midddleburg who would ride along today. The problem Mosby had with this particular conglomerate was that not more than a dozen of the men were familiar to him.

The objective of this day's raid was an outpost of the 1st Vermont Cavalry, with about 300 men, at Dranesville, just north of Herndon. Mosby had written Stuart about this post back in February: "The most of the infantry have left Fairfax and gone toward Fredericksburg. In Fairfax there are five or six regiments of cavalry; there are about 300 at Dranesville. They are so isolated from the rest of the command that nothing would be easier than their capture. I have harassed them so much that they do not keep their pickets over a half a mile from camp. There is no artillery there." However, Mosby received no response.[300]

Sam Chapman's thoughts wandered as he rode. "If it should be difficult to understand how soldiers without a camp could be efficient, it would certainly not be easier to comprehend how a body without organization could accomplish anything", he told himself. "But Mosby's men had done it. Not a single subordinate officer, commissioned or non-commissioned, had yet been appointed," he noted. Sam couldn't help but be amazed at all this and concluded "the cohesion of this strange band was love of adventure and confidence in their leader." [301]

The party passed through Middleburg and, a bit past Aldie, left the turnpike and started across country, through snow and mud. Finally they reached Herndon Station. Finding no Federals here, Mosby led the band toward Dranesville. Arriving there in the late afternoon, the guerrilla leader was disappointed to find that the post had been broken up and moved several miles inland, nearer Fairfax. In fact, after Chantillly, the Federal commander had decided to move the post beyond Difficult Run. The stream was narrow and deep, with steep banks and skirted with forests. It would provide the troops posted there an excellent defensive position against the ever-present Mosby.

So, Mosby had kept his promise to Stuart. When he had asked for the fifteen men, a little over two months ago, he said he could cause the Federals to constrict their lines. They had.

Darkness was fast approaching and forage was needed for the horses. When the locals told them there was none to be had, the Rangers rode up the Leesburg Turnpike. A few miles west of Dranesville they stopped, a short ways off the turnpike, at the home of Henry Green, a friend of Dick Moran, the forty-nine-year-old "elder" of the Rangers. Green said there might be forage, and a place to stay the night, up the way a short piece at the Miskel farm. Moran stayed to visit and spend the night with his friend, while the rest of the band rode on to the Miskel place. [302]

The partisans soon reached the southeastern boundary of the Miskel farm at a point where a considerable wooded area shaded both sides of a narrow road as it left the pike. Bisecting the wood on its way to the dwelling house and barn, the road passed through a gated fence that separated the wood from a large cultivated field. Leaving the wood and entering the field, the narrow road, or lane, was closed in on the side opposite the field by a large wooden fence that bordered it all the way to the buildings at the top of a rise. The lane terminated at the barnyard where another gate allowed entry into the yard, while the tall fence encircled both the barn and house lot. Thus, the only ingress and egress for the house and barn area was by way of the narrow road and the two gates at either end of the lane. From the rear of the buildings, the Chesapeake and Ohio Canal was visible, hugging the north shore of the river. So too, were the Union soldiers guarding it and the signal station that was situated on the high ground further back. [303]

The Rangers' long ride that day had not gone unnoticed. When they passed through Herndon Station, a Union loyalist had observed them and had even counted the number of riders. This information had made its way to Major Charles Taggart, in charge of the cavalry detachment at Difficult Run. From the information on the direction Mosby was traveling, Taggart felt he had a once in a lifetime opportunity to trap the guerrilla's entire command. Mosby would have the Potomac River on his north and the railroad to the south, with swollen Broad Run hindering him to the west and Taggart's cavalry and Difficult Run now at his rear. All avenues of escape would be covered. The major summoned Captain Henry C. Flint of the 1st Vermont, and directed him to immediately set out on Mosby's trail. Flint, who was known for his courage and ability, chose 148 of his best and bravest men. When they reached Dranesville, the cavalrymen began a house to house search. Although unable to locate any guerrillas, Flint did have the information they had left the village, heading northwest on the turnpike. The captain ordered his men into a canter up the pike, stopping at each house along the way. When they arrived in front of the Thornton residence, they were able to pick up the tracks of the raiders in the snow and mud and followed them to the Miskel farm.[304]

Meanwhile, Sam Chapman had unsaddled and fed his horse. He put the animal in the barn with a few of the other mounts, while the rest of the horsemen turned theirs loose in the barnyard. The men were completed tuckered out; they had been in the saddle for over twelve hours and most had not eaten since leaving Rector's that morning. Mosby, not thinking any Federals were within close proximity, did not post any pickets, only some sentinels to watch the horses in the barnyard. Most of the men were strangers to him, anyway, and he was reluctant to issue any orders at this particular time, being unsure of his authority or the reception from the exhausted would-be raiders. He and a few others went into the house and lay down on the floor in front of the fireplace. William Chapman was with him. They were asleep in minutes.[305]

Sam and the rest of the riders stayed outside. Being without supper, corn cakes and rashers of bacon had been cooked in the kitchen and were eaten with great hardiness. Someone had noticed a cider press in the yard, apparently having been recently used, as the juice had not been completely removed. A couple of the men pressed out the cider, which by this time had become hard. "It had some stimulating effect and we soon needed it. Dutch courage, you might say, but," according to Sam, "it was not to be despised." Sam bedded down in the barn. It was cold and he burrowed into the hay best he could for warmth. [306]

Sam was up at sunrise. The rest of the barn residents had started to stir, when suddenly, the stentorian voice of Dick Moran broke open the ear of every man, awake and asleep: "Mount up! Mount up! The Yankees are coming!" Flint's command had passed the Green place just before sunup. Moran was in the kitchen and waited until the horsemen had gotten nearly out of sight, saddled his horse and, riding on their flank, arrived at the farm just ahead of the column. At the alarm, Mosby was out of the house; the sleepy raiders didn't need anything else to bring them awake. Confusion seemed to be the order of the morning, however, with men struggling to bridle their horses, while at the same time knowing not where to go. Captain Flint had divided his command into two sections, a rear squadron, led by Captain George H. Bean, armed with carbines and sabres, and the forward squadron, carrying revolvers. As he started up the lane toward the barnyard, he was elated with the prospect: "At last we have Mosby where we want him. This time he can't get away!"[307]

Flint's lead squadron passed though the first gate and started up the lane. Soon, some of the troopers swung off the lane and into the field. They formed into a rough semicircle, a fan, designed to prevent anyone from riding past them. Following Flint and the first squadron through, the second group of Vermonters closed the gate and placed rails against it, as soon as all were on the inside of the fence. "Now let them try to get out," Flint thought, as he advanced. "April Fool to you Rebels!" [308]

Sam had finished feeding his horse and had placed the saddle over its back, with the girths still loosened and no bridle. He heard Dick Moran's call at the same moment he saw the blue-coated horsemen coming up the road. Their lead section was soon rounding the corner of the barn, in order to encircle those within the yard. Banking heavily on the maxim that "the boldest front oftenest wins the fight, " [309] the Rangers within the barn lot fired into the horsemen advancing up the lane; the Vermonters immediately returned the fire. "What a nervous business it was getting these horses ready amid the whizzing of bullets! Then there was mounting in hot haste," Sam later recalled. "But where to go was the problem. The river was at our back, the enemy in front, and high fences all around." William Chapman, who had slept in the house, had gotten up at daybreak and gone to the stable to feed and curry his horse; he then saddled and bridled him, leaving the bit out of his mouth so the animal could eat the corn in the trough. Returning to the kitchen, he was cooking a piece of middling on a stick in the fireplace when "I noticed a commotion among the men in the yard, and heard someone exclaim, "the Yankees are coming." [310]

Looking out the door Chapman saw the Federals "bearing down on us through a field and road leading up to (the) house." He rushed to the stable and, through the openings in the up-right siding on the building, saw the cavalrymen passing the corner of the barn lot: "I could easily have shot them through the cracks of the weather boarding, but I knew that our only hope of escape was to fight, so putting the bit in my horse's mouth, I mounted him in the stable and went directly toward the gate." At the same instance, Sam pulled the saddle girths tight on his horse, fitted the bridle as fast as he could, and in almost the same movement was up on the horse's back. By now, Flint's column, squeezed in two abreast, was almost entirely up the lane, following on the heels of those already around the barn. When the shooting began in the barnyard and down the lane, the Rangers, in the confusion, acted more on reflex and instinct than on calculated firing. The air was instantly filled with a crescendo of horses' whinnying and neighing and snorting, men shouting and cursing, pistols cracking, and the thud, thump of bullets, indiscriminately finding targets in barn siding, fence, horse and man. [311]

Mosby, still afoot in the barnyard, threw open the gate and not more than fifteen of the partisans charged through. By this time the remainder of Flint's men, the ones still in the lane who had not broken off to encircle the house and barnyard, were no more than thirty yards from the now-open gate. Flint turned and rode back toward Bean, calling for him to come up with his men. "As I came up on the right of Captain Flint with drawn sabers (I had but twenty-five men), his men came rushing back in confusion. Finding it impossible to rally the men I fell back into the wood." Flint bravely started back toward the open barnyard gate, when he suddenly fell from his horse, his body pierced by six pistol balls. He was dead before he landed in the lane. [312]

Back inside the barnyard, Harry Hatcher of the 7th Virginia Cavalry—the same trooper who had come to Ashby's aid—jumped off his horse and gave the reins to Mosby. Panic was setting in on the Yankee horsemen, as they tried to turn and gallop back down the road. But there was too little room to maneuver as they began to be squeezed against the high board fences just outside the barnyard. The few Rangers who had sabres were swinging wildly. Those who had revolvers, and ammunition to fire, were holding a gun in each hand with nothing but their knees in their horses' sides—and some with the reins clinched tightly between their teeth—to control their mounts. As William Chapman charged through the barnyard gate, he immediately met one of Flint's men. "A fierce wind was blowing from the west, and the brim of my Confederate cloth hat flapped down over my eyes. I knocked my hat from my head with my left hand, still holding my pistol in my right hand." The Yankee fired his Remington pistol only a foot away from Chapman's head. Nothing but the snap of the hammer striking was heard. No firing of the bullet, no deadly thud as it struck its target. The Yankee did not have time to contemplate the misfiring of his gun; Chapman's

Colt did not misfire. During the next several minutes—minutes that passed like seconds for some and like hours for others—the former artillery captain fired six times and emptied five saddles. [313]

The Federals were turning and retreating now as hard as they could go, down the narrow road toward the first gate, the same gate that they had closed and reinforced with rails to prevent its being opened by escaping Rebels. As the Yankees got to the gate, it soon became jammed and blocked with members of the first squadron who had managed to turn and flee from the barn area and, with the second squadron, some of who never made it much past the gate. The pursuing Southerners, now with increasing numbers, poured a murderous fire into the teeming mesh of men and horses. In this maddening setting, the gate finally gave way under the pressure against it.[314]

One of the few Rangers to carry a sword, Sam Chapman came through the barnyard gate and plunged directly into the midst of the now leaderless Vermont horsemen. Mosby later recalled the fight and Sam Chapman: "Before he got to the gate, Sam had already exhausted every barrel of his two pistols and drawn his sabre…He was just in front of me—he was generally in front of everybody in a fight—at the gate. It was no fault of the Union cavalry that they did not get through faster than they did, but Sam seemed to think it was. Even at that supreme moment in my life, when I just stood on the brink of ruin and had barely escaped, I could not restrain a propensity to laugh. Sam, to give more vigor to his blows, was standing straight up in his stirrups dealing them right and left." [315] It was nearly forty years later, when a nostalgic Mosby would recall the moment, in a letter to Sam, from Santa Cruz, California: "I just wish you could be here with me. I would feel as young as I was at Miskel's gate when I burst out laughing in the midst of the fight when I saw you standing in your stirrups whaling the Yankees with your sabre." [316]

But Sam was soon to find himself in trouble. Some of Mosby's men chased the Federals down the pike, and Sam, with five others, went two miles below Dranesville in the chase. Here, Chapman caught up with two bluecoats, rode in between them and called on them to surrender. "I never felt like shooting at a man that was running." But surrender was not what they had in mind. "They fell upon me with their sabres, and one fellow gave me a blow on the head (my hat had blown off) that seemed to drive it into my shoulders. His blade turned in the stroke and I received it flatwise rather than the edge or my soldiering would have ended there. I was completely stunned, and it might have been worse for me had not a comrade (Sergeant William Lyle Hunter) come up and knocked one of the men off his horse, and the other gave up." [317]

William Chapman found himself in trouble also. When the gate gave way, he was among the pursuers down the pike. After chasing the routed Federals for about a mile or more, Chapman's horse gave out. Transferring his saddle and equipment to a captured horse, he spotted a small group of Yankee cavalry in a field to his left. " This was evidently a portion of the squadron that had passed around the barn lot and had been cut off. They seemed at first bewildered at finding that the Confederates had reached this point." Chapman and another Ranger started toward them, but upon getting close, Chapman's pistol—a captured Remington six-shooter—misfired. A Federal trooper closed in on him, firing his pistol six times at close range, but five of his shots misfired also, while the other missed its mark. Captured, Chapman was taken about 400 yards from the pike to another group of Yankee cavalrymen. But after a few minutes, help arrived and he was set free; the captors then became the captives. [318]

In speaking of the fight after the war, William Chapman attributed a good deal of the success of the Rangers, and the loss of the Federals, to two things: (1) "Our men were fresh from having had a night (sic) rest and had warmed themselves at the fire in the house, while Capt. Flint's men had been in the saddle most of the night, and had faced a bitter cold," and (2) "We were armed with Colt's pistols while they were armed with Remington pistols. A great many of their pistols failed to go off, and I never heard of a single instance when a Colt pistol snapped when the trigger was pulled. Some of the prisoners stated that they had been out the day before and had gotten their pistols wet, which they gave for the failure of the Remington pistols to go off." [319]

Chapman also takes issue with the Federal report of the affair by Major General Julius Stahel, who alluded to Flint's men firing first, while a distance from the house, and then ordering a sabre charge. [320] "I had heard no shots fired when I came out of the house and the Federal cavalry was then nearing the house. I don't think a sabre charge was made, because the first men we met after we passed through the gate had their pistols drawn and were still making the movement to encircle us and not make a charge directly on us. Capt. Flint's plan was to encircle us to prevent any of us from escaping...he knew he had nearly four times as many men as we had and might easily have taken it for granted that we would surrender…so that the attack upon him was a surprise to his men. Our men really made the attack and it was sudden and unexpected." [321]

In Mosby's report of April 7 on the Miskel Farm (or Broad Run) fight, he reported the enemy casualties as nine killed, fifteen too badly wounded to be removed, and eighty-two prisoners taken. He also reported taking about 100 horses, with all the arms and equipment of the men and animals. Mosby put the losses of his command at four wounded, one mortally. Mosby also accepted blame for leaving his command in a position to be surprised and set upon by enemy forces: "I confess that on this occasion I had not taken sufficient precautions to guard against surprise." He attributed this to the long ride of the command that day, the lateness of the hour when he arrived at Miskel's, and the knowledge that the Federals had removed their posts some eighteen miles further in.

General Stuart forwarded Mosby's report up the chain of command with this endorsement: "Recommended for promotion." When it reached the desk of the Secretary of War, it was sent back to the Adjutant General with this notation: "Nominate as major if it has not been previously done." Mosby's promotion would become effective on April 16, 1863. Three weeks had elapsed since his promotion to captain.

Sam Chapman and eight others were officially recognized in Mosby's report for their "promptitude and boldness in closing in with the enemy." [322]

The Union report of the affair told a different story than Mosby's. "I regret to be obliged to inform the commanding general that the forces sent out by Major Taggart missed so good an opportunity of capturing the rebel guerrilla. It is only to be ascribed to the bad management on the part of the officers and the cowardice of the men. (Those) who are guilty will be stricken from the rolls." This was the report of Stahel to Major General S. P. Heintzelman. Flint had died in the fight, unable to offer any defense, if he had one; Bean was subsequently dismissed from the service for cowardice, although he would later be reinstated. [323]

The fight at Miskel's farm was one of the Rangers finest hours when it came to pure courage. These men were completely boxed in with all the favorable elements—surprise, number of fighters, the ability to decide where and when to engage—clearly on the Union side of the ledger. Mosby had none of these tangibles to assist him. But he did have something intangible—the reactive mind that instinctively told him what to do and when to do it. And he had fearless men—like Sam and William Chapman, Harry Hatcher, William Lyle Hunter—who would do whatever was required of them, regardless of the risk. The two brothers from Page County had clearly exhibited the mettle that would carry them through the many battles yet to be fought. Years after the war, Sam Chapman, reflecting on acts that had taken place that defied logic, remarked: "Things often happen in war that are unaccountable." [324] He could very well have been thinking of Miskel's.

Activity started to pick-up in the Union camps following the affair at Miskel's farm. Union patrols were increased, going through northern Virginia looking for Mosby. In the process, the arresting of the citizens of the countryside was stepped up. Stahel's report of April 11, 1863, to Heintzelman, is typical: "Brig. Gen. J. F. Copeland...left this place on (April 3) and returned here early on the morning of (April 6); it proceeded as far as Middleburg, and searched diligently (for Mosby) During the expedition there were captured and arrested 61 prisoners, citizens and soldiers...." [325]

On April 21, 1863, Major James Dearing, commanding the 38th Battalion, Virginia Light Artillery, wrote to Lee's artillery chief, General Pendleton: "I have received both of the papers recommending officers for Caskie's battery. He has one vacancy for a lieutenant, and I should much prefer Lieut. (S. F.) Chapman to (L.) Booker." Captain William H. Caskie was at that time commanding Company C of the Hampden Artillery. This company and three others made up Dearing's battalion. [326] Sam was still officially a lieutenant of artillery in the regular army, detached to the Adjutant and Inspector General's Office as an enrollment officer, and further detached to Mosby's command. This latter detachment carried no official authority at the time. No action would be taken on the request until the following month.

On April 25, Major Price, adjutant to General Stuart, sent a dispatch to Mosby: " ...your expedition into Fairfax is exactly what (Stuart) wishes. He is extremely anxious to know what is going on behind Centreville, and whether Hooker is moving any troops up in that vicinity." This communication was followed the next day by another from General Stuart: "There is now a splendid opportunity to strike the enemy in rear of Warrenton Junction...Capture a train and interrupt the operation of the railroad." [327] Behind Stuart's suggestion were the changes that were taking place in the Union command. Following Burnside's debacle at Fredericksburg the previous December, General "Fighting Joe" Hooker had assumed command of the Army of the Potomac. He had sent Major General George Stoneman's cavalry corps to Warrenton Junction in preparation for a general movement of the Union army against Lee's flank on the Rappahannock. Stoneman's mission was to disrupt supply and communication lines particularly on the Orange and Alexandria Railroad. His raid turned out to be ineffective, due in large part to the failure of Brigadier General William Averell to move as directed against the railroad near Gordonsville. For his inaction, Averell was subsequently relieved of his command and transferred to West Virginia.[328]

Stoneman was at Warrenton Junction on April 27, with his cavalry corps camped along the tracks of the Orange and Alexandria Railroad. He received a telegram directing him to be at Hooker's headquarters at Morrisville the next day, with all his commanders. When he arrived, he learned that the Union army was to cross the Rappahannock River at Kelly's Ford that same day and he had to prepare to gather his pickets, scouting parties, etc., and move.[329]

Sam Chapman was at Salem on April 28 when he received word that Mosby was assembling the command at Upperville the following day. The guerrilla chieftain had learned that Stoneman had all but abandoned Warrenton Junction and he now had the perfect opportunity to carry out Stuart's request "to strike the enemy in rear of Warrenton Junction." Eighty men gathered at Upperville in response to Mosby's call. Before setting out for the Junction, however, he learned that General Stahel, who had been in "Mosby's Confederacy" since April 27, was marching toward Hopewell Gap. This gap in the Bull Run Mountains is situated a little north of Thoroughfare Gap. Stahel erroneously believed that Stuarts's cavalry had been stalking him and was prepared to attack him at Thoroughfare Gap. Although he had two brigades and a battery of four guns, he had come looking for Mosby and was not ready to tangle with Stuart. All he wanted now was to return to his base within the defensive perimeter around Washington.

Mosby decided to forego his plans to hit Warrenton Junction and instead pounce on Stahel at Hopewell Gap. Heading north, he ran into Stahel's advance party, charged it and drove it back to the main body. Now Stahel was really bothered. He believed that Stuart had found him and was in the initial phase of an all-out attack against him. He took position on a hill near White Plains and waited. Mosby watched and decided that it would be prudent to wait and attack the column as it moved the following day. But during the night, Stahel managed to slip out of his positions and head for Middleburg, tearing up the bridges and blocking the roads with felled trees to protect his rear from attack. Mosby could not gather his men before Stahel was safely out of range and marching at a double time for Fairfax. Mosby dismissed the men, telling them to meet again on May 2.[330]

The partisans gathered early that May morning—ninety-eight in all—near Upperville and began the long ride south and east. Their destination was Falmouth and the rear of Hooker's lines. This time Mosby had a mixed band for sure. There were the members of the Black Horse Cavalry, on furlough, but itching for a fight. About twenty members of the 2nd South Carolina were there; known as the Iron Scouts, they were in the area around Upperville looking for horses. And there were a goodly number of furloughed soldiers from the regular army who saddled up for a chance to ride with Mosby. The group rode to near Warrenton where they went into bivouac. It was getting on toward evening and their leader wanted the men and horses fresh for the morrow.

If Sam Chapman had any doubts about how the people of Warrenton felt when it came to Mosby and his men, those doubts vanished like the morning's dew that sunny afternoon of May 2, 1863. Mosby had asked Chapman and two others to go into the town and arrange for dinner for the command and forage for the horses. Sam describes the reaction: "The request was responded to with heartiness by the citizens at their homes. The reception was an ovation. How gay we were going out of town that afternoon to our bivouac, a few miles distant." It was the first time the command had been in Warrenton in two months; not since the Fairfax raid when they had returned with no less than a Yankee general.[331]

Mosby's plan was to attack Hooker's wagon train at United States Ford, on the Rappahannock. If he could do that, and burn the wagons loaded with rations and forage, the morale effect upon the Federal army would be considerable. At daylight the next morning, the command set out on the road leading to Fredericksburg. At Chancellorsville, twenty-five miles to the southeast, General Stuart, with Jackson's corps of some 26,000 men, was hitting the right wing of Hookers army at Hazel Grove, along the Chancellorsville Turnpike. Stuart had taken command after Jackson, who had rolled up Hookers flank the evening before, had been accidentally wounded by North Carolina troops. The roar of the guns was plainly heard up in Warrenton and Mosby knew that the two giants were once again in a deadly embrace.[332]

When the partisans were a couple of miles from a point where the road crosses the tracks south of Warrenton Junction, the sound of a cavalry bugle splintered the quiet of the spring dawn. There must still be cavalry left from Stoneman's exodus, Mosby thought. The temptation was too much for the fighter in him to resist; he could sweep through the camp and still make his way toward the Rappahannock fords. The raiders had only gone a short distance through a wood when they came upon a Union infantryman, whom they caught and who told them that they were marching right into the camp of an infantry brigade. Not desiring to hook up with that sort of adversary right now, Mosby turned his men in another direction; the captive soldier had told him some Union cavalry was encamped, a short way off, along the railroad. Continuing on through the wood, the Southerners soon came upon them. "You can have a fight now in short order," Mosby said, directing his remark to the Black Horse troopers.[333]

The cavalry was a detachment of the Union 1st Virginia, which had encamped the night before while returning from a scout. The remainder of their regiment was scattered in different directions between the railroad and the Rappahannock. Mosby's men were about 300 yards away when the Yankees were spotted. Sam, riding in the front of the column near Mosby, was able to get a good first look: "Men lounging around in the sunshine, and horses, tied and loose, all around. They gazed at us, but mistook us for a relief picket. We were allowed to ride quietly to within 250 yards of them. A charge was ordered, and a genuine 'rebel yell' was raised. What a scattering among them ensued! To mount their horses was impossible; so they took refuge in some buildings."[334]

The buildings were the depot and some railroad outbuildings. The Rangers centered their attention—and their fire—on the two smaller buildings, ignoring the depot. Although the Federals inside were armed with carbines for the most part, they found it hard to aim and fire at the attackers, the fusillade from the Rangers' revolvers being so intense. After about fifteen minutes or so, a white handkerchief was seen poking out from one of the buildings; this was followed by a like signal from the other. After collecting the prisoners, the raider's attention was directed to the depot. Inside, packed like sardines in a can, were Major Steele and the rest of the command, about 100 men in all. Sam picks up the story: "The approach to this house was perilous, as they were shooting out of the windows and doors. My brother (William) had his horse killed. Some of us assaulted the house on foot. I sheltered myself

117

as well as I could under the window-sill, and struck with my sabre overhead at those, who, in a window, were shooting from it."

While Sam was busy swinging at gun barrels with his sabre, others of the Rangers had mounted and were riding around the building circus style— hanging off the far side of their horses and firing through openings as they passed. But the cost in Rebel blood was rising by the minute. Madison Monroe Templeman, a hero at Sharpsburg as a courier with Hood's Texans, lay on his back, mouth open and eyes staring wildly at the trees, killed in his first ride with Mosby. John Glandell of the 1st Virginia Cavalry, shot through the stomach and captured, would die a painful and agonizing death two days later; Private Gillespie Thornewell, one of the Iron Scouts, likewise would suffer and die from a similar wound.

After about half-an-hour, Mosby had seen enough of his men lying wounded or worse around the station. He was about to order the building be set afire when Sam, along with Rangers Montjoy, DeButts, and Sweeting, burst through the door. Once inside, a room door was forced open and the four raiders were enveloped with gunpowder. About this time, Mosby set fire to the hay and brush that had been piled against, and inside, the building. Sam remembered: "A staircase ran from the room we were in and the men above shouted: 'We surrender. Don't burn us.' I called out to them to come down which they did with promptness. I came out of the house with an armful of pistols and was so loaded I could hardly walk." Sam had just made prisoners of twenty of the enemy. While this was going on, the men in a room on the right side of the building surrendered to the others inside. But those in the room across the hallway would not come out. DeButts fired through the closed door, killing a man leaning against it. Sweeting and Montjoy burst into the smoke-filled room and in the ensuing fight a number of Yankees were killed and wounded. When an officer upstairs realized the uselessness of the situation, he hung a white cloth out of the upper window. [335]

While the smoke was clearing Mosby tallied the spoils. Three hundred officers and men of the 1st (West) Virginia Cavalry Regiment were captives, along with their horses, arms, accoutrements, camp equipment, and an ambulance wagon. The Rangers were getting their prisoners mounted and trying to get organized when John Wild, who had chased a horse down along the tracks, came running back, shouting that a large column of enemy cavalry was coming up. [336]

"We were scattered," said Sam, "a good many catching horses and in no condition to engage them. Down went my pistols on the ground, and I remember passing a Federal soldier—an Irishman—who, encouraged by the approach of help, shook his fist at me and gritted his teeth most maliciously. I had no time to attend to his salutation, but mounted my horse and rode off with all the others." What the Rangers were running from was a large contingent of the 5th New York Cavalry and some troopers from the 1st Vermont, who had been posted in the rear, some distance away, but within earshot of the guns. "Our prisoners dropped away from us fast enough, their friends being right on us," recalled Sam; "a fine looking captain came on in their lead with uplifted sabre, ready to hew down the rebels. He and I exchanged blows, but Montjoy shot him and got his fine bay horse. The pursuit was so hot that I left the road and broke through the pines, getting my face dreadfully scratched. That was better than getting killed, however." Chapman's pursuers passed him by, and despite the urgency of getting away from danger, he still managed to catch two Federal horses that had been turned loose by the Rangers in their hasty flight. The Yankees pursued the Southerners nearly back to Warrenton; Sam, by a roundabout way, made it safely to Salem. [337]

The cost to Mosby was high—the highest he had paid yet. Dead, or mortally wounded, were Templeman, Thornewell and Glandell. Included among the captured were Dick Moran, who had given the alarm at Miskel's; "Major" Hibbs, of whom Sam thought fondly; Sam Underwood, a personal favorite of Mosby's; Jasper Jones, a cousin of Mosby's old commander, "Grumble" Jones and one of the "original fifteen" from the 1st Virginia Cavalry; "Willie" Martin, who would be accidentally killed by a fellow Ranger fifteen months later; Samuel Dushane, the former captain with the disbanded Wheat's Louisiana Tigers; A. J. Brown, assistant surgeon with the 1st Virginia, detailed to Mosby's command; Tom Richards, who, like Sam,was a former student at Columbian College. [338]

According to the Union report of the fight, over thirty of the Rangers were prisoners, sixteen of them badly wounded; forty horses were lost. The same report put the Union losses at two killed, fifteen wounded. Major Steele, who had taken refuge in the depot, was killed, before the building was taken by Sam and the others. [339]

Mosby accepted blame for taking on the Yankees in the first place, even if he had been successful. By his actions he was unable to carry out his plan to attack Hooker's wagon train. However, he also was quick to say that the make-up of his command at tghe time did not lend itself favorably to the kind of operations in which he was engaged. "They were a mere aggregation of men casually gathered, belonging to many different regiments, who happened to be in the country. Of course such a body has none of the cohesion and discipline that springs from organization, no matter how brave the men may be individually. And I had no subordinate officer to help me in command." [340]

The Rangers returned to Warrenton once again and, according to Sam, "How differently we came back—badly routed! But there was no reproach from those true-hearted people, but rather praise for the splendid success before disaster came." [341]

However, for John Mosby and his men...the string had broken.

10. Paroled on the Field

The quick reversal of fortune that was Warrenton Junction had a sobering effect on some of those who had ridden with Mosby. This was especially true of the first-time Rangers. Here, they had found that it was not always a daring adventure with quick rewards but instead a stark, no holds barred war, where kill or be killed was the watchword and the crying of the wounded and dying was real. This reality was such that, less than a week later, only thirty-seven men answered the call to meet at Upperville. Sam Chapman was among the missing—not because of the experience at Warrenton Junction, for he had performed as bravely as any man there—but because he had no clothes to wear. Three months before, while on conscript duty, Federal cavalry had broken into his quarters at Warrenton, and "...had to content themselves, as they could not get me, with my (wardrobe)...." He had gone home to Page County to be refitted.[342]

General Stahel had dispersed large detachments of cavalry from his compliment of 6,000 in the Washington defense command, to protect and keep clear the Orange and Alexandria Railroad from Fairfax to the Rappahannock River. Since these detachments were too strong for Mosby's small bands to attack, the guerrilla chieftain reasoned he must compel Stahel to divide them up into smaller bodies that he, Mosby, could then contend with. General Stuart had said, "...to interrupt the operation of the railroad...." To accomplish this end, Mosby figured he could break up the unprotected portions of track and destroy the unguarded bridges, thus stretching the Yankee patrols even further.

On May 9, Mosby and the thirty-seven struck the railroad between Catlett's and Bristoe Stations, tearing up the track and setting fire to the bridge over Broad Run. They were quickly back in their saddles and heading for the span over Kettle Run. After firing this bridge and then cutting some telegraph wires the raiders returned home. The damage caused one train to derail and ceased operations on the line for two days.

On May 17, Mosby took twenty-five men as far as Dumfries, in eastern Prince William County, but was stymied in his efforts to interrupt transportation on Telegraph Road due to the strong presence of Union infantrymen. Being a long way from home, the men were tired and the horses hungry. Although aware that they were far inside the enemy's lines, they decided to stop for awhile to rest at the home of a farmer named Lynn; here they unbitted the horses and Mosby lay down in the grass. Soon afterwards the cry of "Yankees coming!" aroused the major. Barely getting their horses bridled, the Rangers watched as a long line of cavalry came at a fast gallop toward them. Using the same tactic that was so successful at Miskel's, Mosby opened a gate across the road, between them and the on-coming enemy, and the men dashed through, straight at the Federals. The Northerners were carrying sabres and the Rangers were using their pistols, so the fight was over quickly. The bluecoats were put to flight, leaving behind two dead, five badly wounded, four prisoners, and eight horses.[343]

Sam was back with the command by the last week in May. Major Mosby had been turning some things over in his mind. Taking a few of his closest companions, like Sam and Fount Beattie, into his confidence, he expressed his concern for being able to keep the command together in its present state. His operations might satisfy Stuart and Lee, and tend to keep the enemy in a state of readiness, but the men would not be content with such results. "In order for me to retain them it was necessary to stimulate their enthusiasm with something more tangible. War to them was not an abstraction; it meant prisoners, arms, horses and sutler's stores. Remote consequences were not much considered." [344] With these thoughts in mind, Mosby started the wheels in motion, which would have a significant and lasting effect on Lieutenant Chapman.

In Mosby's report to Stuart, relative to the operations of the command during May, he added a request and had Beattie personally carry the report to Stuart: "If you would let me have a mountain howitzer, I think I could use it to great effect, especially on the railroad trains. I have several experienced artillerists with me. The effect of such annoyance is to force the enemy to make heavy details to guard their communication. I have not attacked any of their railroad trains because I have no ammunition for my carbines, and they are pretty strongly guarded with infantry." [345]

Ten days after Beattie had been sent to Stuart with the request, he made a second trip to cavalry headquarters. This time the Ranger returned to Mosby with the howitzer. The artillery piece was actually a bronze barrel, two and one-fourth inch bore, mountain rifle that carried a twelve-pound shell. It had been manufactured at the Tredegar Iron Works in Richmond in the summer of 1862. The gun was received with some skepticism by the men. "It's a bit too large to be carried in a holster, but not big enough to be called a cannon," said one. Despite Mosby's assertion that he had "several experienced artillerists," according to Private John Munson: "Sam Chapman was one of the few men in the command who knew the difference between a howitzer and a saw-log." If Chapman thought he had left the artillery behind when the Dixie Battery was disbanded, he was mistaken. He was now the officer in charge of Mosby's Light Artillery battery; in addition, he was the command's instructor in artillery tactics. [346] Mosby was now ready to begin disrupting the Federal's train schedules.

Two days later, on May 29, forty partisans met at Patterson's farm, about four miles from Middleburg, on the Little River. Mosby selected a crew and Sam took a couple of hours to teach them the rudiments of handling and firing an artillery piece. The crew was comprised of Chapman, who was to be the gunner, Beattie, Montjoy, and the teen-ager, George Tuberville, picked to be the driver. There was no caisson so the fifteen rounds of ammunition were carried in the limber-chest.

Spring had arrived in the blue grass of northern Virginia as the raiders proceeded south past Plains Station and through Thoroughfare Gap. By nightfall they were close to Greenwich, where they stopped to eat. Several miles further the tired but eager Rangers went into bivouac. They could hear the bugles and drums of the nearby Union camps, interspersed with the melodic sounds of the spring evening. Spirits were on the rise, infected by the potency of nature, like the tree and bush coming to full leaf. Sam had a good feeling about the mission and looked to tomorrow with excitement and anticipation. [347]

Mosby had feelings of reservation on the one hand, but felt commitment and obligation on the other, concerning this particular operation. These were feelings he had not experienced before and which he could not—and would not—share with any of his men, not even Fount Beattie, his closest confidant, who had been with him since their Washington Mounted Rifles days. He realized he could not attack the train without alarming the Union camps, some as near as a mile or so and scattered on either side of the tracks, all the way from the Rappahannock to Manassas. This would of course make retreat very difficult, if not impossible. But, then again, he believed the end justified the risk. Lee's army was on the south side of the Rappahannock, beginning the push north that would lead to Gettysburg in less than five weeks. Hooker's Army of the Potomac was shadowing him on the north side of the river. If Mosby could create a diversion of some magnitude, and draw the Union cavalry off the Confederate's flank, it might help Lee; then the loss of the gun or even his whole command, would be but little compared to the advantage it might give to his commander-in-chief. [348]

The next morning, May 30, the partisans were awakened by the sound of reveille in the Union camps. They proceeded to a point a little bit north of Catlett's Station and there cut the telegraph wires. The railroad was very heavily guarded, with patrols moving up and down so often, that the tracks were hard to get to. Next, just after a patrol had passed, some of the Rangers slipped down and displaced a rail; not a whole lot, so as to be noticed, but enough to ensure derailing the engine.

The locomotive, pulling eleven cars, had started from Alexandria, stopped at Union Mills in western Fairfax County to board a twenty-five man guard of the 15th Vermont Infantry, and resumed an uneventful journey. Its destination was Rappahannock Station, where General Alfred Pleasonton was encamped with his huge cavalry command. The cars were laden with a regular hodge-podge of goods for man and beast: luxuries such as genuine coffee and sugar; delicacies, like fresh shad; fresh fruit—oranges, lemons and pineapples; there was hay and corn for the horses and flour, hardtack and salt pork for the troops, as well as sides of leather for shoe soles, and bags full of U. S. Mail. [349]

On the edge of a piney wood Sam had positioned the gun, at a point opposite the displaced rail, so that he would have a straight-on shot at the locomotive and the first couple of cars. Mosby told nineteen-year-old Willie Foster to be on the lookout and to hold the men in readiness until the time was right. Sam, standing by the gun, saw the train approach and observed: "The cautious engineer saw something was wrong as he drew near and stopped. Our men rushed up. The infantry guard on the train fired one ineffectual volley. A shot from the howitzer sent them to the woods." The Rangers were on top of the cars like bees on a honeycomb, plundering to their hearts content. Mosby, ever aware of the enemy's close proximity, tried to hurry them along.

Wishing to disable the engine, Chapman, Beattie and Turberville rolled the gun to within thirty feet of the locomotive, totally ignorant of the destructive capacity of steam. "(The gun) was loaded; but Montjoy, who had the lanyard and primer wound around his neck, was off watching the railroad," Sam remembered. "The gun could not be fired till he came up." Montjoy finally returned and, when he saw where they had moved the gun, he was flabbergasted. "You will all be scalded to death! Move back seventy-five yards at least!" Sam recalled him shouting. "We moved back and put a shot through the dome, and such a noise and such a spray of steam...!" [350]

Colonel William D. Mann of the 7th Michigan Cavalry was commanding officer of Stahel's cavalry force at Bristoe Station; a patrol from his command was three miles away, and was the same one that had passed through just before the Rangers had displaced the rail. Hearing the report from the howitzer and thinking Stuart's cavalry was near, Mann quickly collected a sizable force of the 1st Vermont and 5th New York Cavalries, along with a detachment of his own 7th Michigan. He ordered Captain Hasbrouck to take the 5th New York across country, toward the Burwell Road, that runs from Catlett's northwest to Haymarket, to cut off any enemy force; Mann took the rest of the command and started down the tracks toward the sound of the firing. In the meantime, Mosby's group had struck the Burwell Road and was galloping in the direction of Haymarket.

Suddenly, on a slight rise, ahead and off to the right, was the advance guard of the 5th New York. Mosby halted the command, called the gun crew forward, and had them send a shell into the New Yorkers midst, killing an officer's horse and stampeding the troopers. As soon as Chapman was able to limber up, the running Rebels continued on for another mile, but the retreating troopers had gathered themselves and were again blocking the route. Behind them, Mann and his cavalry were coming on fast. Mosby told Chapman to unlimber once again. Ordering Willie Foster and some others to act as a rear guard, and try to slow up Mann and his bunch, he instructed Sam to send another shell into the New Yorkers, while he led a charge with the remainder of his command. [351]

Chapman, standing by the howitzer, was put off with some of the Rangers whom he thought were holding back. "Some of our men were quite new to warfare, and lingered near the howitzer, sitting on their horses, quite satisfied with contemplating quietly what their leader and a few followers were doing." Threatened at the point of a pistol by Chapman and Montjoy, the shirkers joined the charge. [352]

Mosby, well aware that he could abandon the gun and have his men skedaddle, had decided to sell it to his pursuers at as high a price as he could exact. "I was fighting on a point of honor," he would say years later. He sent Chapman ahead to look for a good place to put the howitzer for a last stand.

Limbering up one more time, the hounded raiders turned right, off of the Burwell Road about two miles from Greenwich, onto a narrow lane with high banks and an equally high fence on either side. Sam had decided that the Yankee cavalry could purchase his gun right here. The lane led up a slight incline, about a hundred yards from Grapewood Farm, home of Warren Fitzhugh and his family. Nearby was the "The Lawn", an estate belonging to Charles Green, an Englishman who flew the Union Jack to express his neutrality in the American conflict. [353]

While Sam and the gun crew went ahead, Mosby stayed behind with six men as a rear guard to cover his retreating command. "As the enemy came near we slowly withdrew," Mosby recalled. "Their advance guard of 12 or 15 men suddenly dashed upon us as we were retiring through the woods. We…had a fierce hand-to-hand fight…several of their dead and wounded were left on the ground." Captain Bradford Hoskins, the veteran of the 44th Royal Infantry, who had come to Mosby by way of General Stuart in time for the Chantilly raid, was alongside Mosby. Using a sabre, as Englishmen were prone to do, he was giving a thrust when a revolver bullet cut him down. [354]

Chapman had positioned the gun some eighty yards up the narrow lane on a slight rise. On foot, manning the piece with Sam, were Beattie and Montjoy. When Mann's troopers were a couple of hundred yards off, Sam sent a shell exploding into them. This was followed by a charge from Mosby and his men, causing the Yankees to fall back to the woods in confusion. Soon, they reformed again, and instead of deploying in the fields, on the right and left of the lane, they formed in columns of four and charged up the hill. The gunners loaded grapeshot and sent it crashing into the mass of men and horses. Again Mosby's men charged at them, driving them back. And again the Federals formed and started back up the lane, into the mouth of the little rifle, and once more grape and canister decimated the columns, and the Rangers charged through them. This scene was repeated one more time until Chapman was down to his last shell. For the final round, Sam permitted the column, charging four abreast with sabres, to get within fifty yards of him before he raked it with canister. Then the gun was quiet. [355]

When the last round had been rammed home, Beattie found his horse and managed to get to safety. George Turberville, the driver, went off at full speed, saving his two horses and the limber-chest. Chapman's horse, as well as Montjoy's had run off, so the two were left afoot. Montjoy stayed by the gun, emptying both his revolvers before being overrun and captured, while Chapman wielded the rammer, like a Samson wielding a jawbone to slay a thousand Philistines. It was then that the ball tore into Sam's thigh, ripping through and knocking him to the ground. The numbing effect of the wound had not yet given way to the searing pain that was to follow but Sam was totally defenseless when a Yankee cavalryman rode up to the gun and looked down at him: "... with a face black with anger, (he) called to me to turn my back. 'I'm going to finish you,' he said." The fallen Ranger asked why, since he was now a prisoner. "You shot me here in the shoulder," the trooper responded, indicating with his carbine and then pointing it at the prostrate Ranger. "Well, I suppose I had a right to" Sam managed to reply, "as we had not ceased firing then." Some of the cavalryman's comrades stepped in at that point and persuaded the would-be executioner to turn away. "He came to my bedside that afternoon and begged my pardon, which was readily granted. "I would not have talked so," he told Chapman, "but I was confounded mad. You shot me as I rode past you, after some of your men."[356]

Second Lieutenant Barker of the 5th New York, who had a horse killed under him by a shot at close range from Chapman's little rifle, described the final fight for the howitzer. "We got very near to the gun, probably within twenty feet, when it fired, killing ...Corporal Drake...a grape shot passing through his head. Two others were also killed and a number wounded. Two grapes entered my left thigh, another carried off my stirrup and the sole of my boot, and four or five entered my horse. At this time (men from the 1st Vermont Cavalry) came in and we took the gun, the brave Lieutenant Chapman fighting to the last, though mortally wounded." [357]

Lieutenant Barker was wrong. Sam was very badly wounded but not mortally so. In the aftermath of the fight he and the wounded Hoskins were taken by some of the very men they had, just an hour before, been trying to kill—or be killed in return—to the nearby Fitzhugh home. No sooner had they been put inside the house, than Chapman, from loss of blood and exhaustion, began to lose consciousness. "The sensation was rather pleasant as consciousness was leaving me," Sam recalled, "I have wondered often since if I should die as easy as that." A Union officer grabbed a canteen from a passing trooper and dashed water into the wounded prisoner's face. When he began to come around moments later, Sam opened his eyes and saw the officer standing over him, canteen in hand. It was Colonel Mann.[358]

"Poor Hoskins would call out to me during the night to know how I was. We tried to cheer each other up," Sam remembered. The next day, the Englishman, Mr. Green, showed up at Fitzhugh's home with a small horse-pulled cart. With the help of the Union soldiers, he placed Chapman and Hoskins in the conveyance and took them to his neighboring estate. That same day, Hoskins, lying next to Sam, "died before my eyes." [359] Aware of the end that was rapidly approaching, the gallant Englishman was heard to cry out: "Oh! Has it come to this, that I must die in this way? No, No! It can't be! Oh! That I should ever have come to this!" [360] To have to die in this manner, rather than on the field of battle, must have been of great distress to the young soldier-of-fortune. The following morning, Chapman sadly watched from the window as Green, and a few others, took Hoskins' remains and buried them in the churchyard nearby.

"I was the recipient of much kindness from Mr. Fitzhugh, Mr. Green and family, and from the Federal soldiers," Sam said. "At Mr. Green's a Federal soldier also lay wounded. He had been brought over from the same fight. Dr. Edson, a surgeon in the First Vermont, attended him, and he kindly dressed my wound until the neighborhood physician, Dr. Hunton, came. I had every attention, surgical and other," the seriously wounded partisan would graciously recall. "I remained in the Union lines for ten days, 'till I could bear removal." [361]

Mosby, who would later call Chapman, "One of the noblest and most heroic soldiers in the Southern army," characterized his wounding: "Sam had passed through so many fights unscathed that the men had a superstition that he was invulnerable....His hour had come at last, and a bullet pierced the celestial armor of the soldier-priest." Ludwell Lake, a fellow Ranger said that Sam "was the bravest man I ever knew." [362]

The final Union report on the Grapewood Farm fight, from General Stahel to the adjutant-general in Washington, was dated June 3, 1863: "Our loss was 4 killed and 15 wounded. We lost 11 horses killed and several wounded. The loss of the enemy was 6 killed and 20 wounded, besides many others severely wounded, who escaped in the woods. We have 10 prisoners...." General Stahel's report was based on reports sent to him by Colonel Mann, who had included in his own reports: "Our captures of the day are 10 prisoners, including Captain Haskins (sic)...and Lieutenant Chapman, who had charge of the artillery. Both these officers so severely wounded could not be removed and were paroled (on the field)". [363]

128

11. "Miss Beck"

Sam Chapman's recovery from the wound received at Greenwich was going well. He had remained in the Union lines for ten days until he had recovered sufficiently to be removed. From Grapewood Farm he was taken to Salem, where he stayed with his friends, the Murrays. [364]

Eliza Rebecca Elgin lived with her mother, Catherine, and stepfather, William Murray, in Salem. She was five months shy of her nineteenth birthday the summer Sam came to recuperate from his wounds. Rebecca had met the handsome Ranger several months earlier and counted him as one of her more preferred suitors.

Rebecca didn't remember her real father, Gustavus Elgin, who died when she was three months old. But her roots in the area went back one hundred years when her great-great-grandfather, also named Gustavus, moved to Loudoun County from Maryland. He was a captain in the Virginia Militia and present at the surrender of the British at Yorktown in 1783. Rebecca's grandfather, Robert Elgin, had moved to Fairfax and her father was born there in 1820. He had married the former Catherine Lewis Smith around 1842. After her father's death in 1845, Rebecca and her mother went to live with her mother's brother, Withers Smith, and his family.

Rebecca's father willed her some funds for her schooling, and a dower of $1250. She was sent to the prestigious Strawberry Vale Seminary for Young Ladies, where, for fifty dollars per five-month session, she was taught piano and the languages, as well as drawing and painting. Then, in 1855, her mother married William Murray and the family moved from Fairfax to Fauquier County. Murray, who had never been married, was a stock dealer, eleven years Catherine's senior, and showed a real and personal worth in 1860 of $10,000. [365]

Several of the soldiers, particularly some of the partisans of Mosby's command were familiar figures around the Murray place. A good meal could always be had and Rebecca and her parents were fine hosts. Refined, learned, and pretty, most surely Rebecca did not lack for admirers and would-be suitors, dressed in blue as well as gray.

Sam was totally smitten with Rebecca and the irony of war made his gift to her seem entirely appropriate—a little Root pocket revolver and holster that he had confiscated on one of Mosby's recent raids.[366] And oh, she thought well enough of the handsome Ranger. After all, he could be considered a "catch," what with all the young men gone off to war and only a few convalescing soldiers and conscript dodgers left to choose from—that is, if one were choosing. Standing nearly six feet tall, with a fair complexion, dark hair and mustache, and deep-set hazel eyes, the lieutenant struck a fine figure in his uniform. And how he could talk! Such beautiful words that she could sit and listen for hours. But he was, perhaps, just a little too serious-minded. [367]

When they were alone, Rebecca believed him sincere, but then, he had been through so much. And only ten days after he had come back wounded, Sam had asked her to marry him. Perhaps she had doted too much over him, leaving the wrong impression. Was it pity or was it something else she had felt? Still, she convinced herself, he would not feel the same by the morrow, so why should she succumb to her feelings only to be left alone after he had time to think through what he had said. He appeared to be so very hurt when she refused him, though Rebecca had long thought that Sam wore his feelings on his sleeve. Cooler heads must prevail she told herself. So, her wounded suitor had left Salem, to further recouperate at his home in Luray. To her own surprise, she cried after he was gone.

Frank Yager brought the letter when he and and Ben Grove returned to Salem. They had accompanied Sam the day before as far as Yorkdale, the home of the Templemans, who had a mill down on Thumb Run. They knew Sam from Page County and Grove had been in the Dixie Battery with him. Yager and Grove had come to Salem looking to join up with Mosby.[368]

Rebecca had not expected the letter. At least not so soon. No, in truth, she had not expected it at all. Sam had written from Yorkdale and when she began reading she realized just how deeply he really felt and how truly hurt he was....

> *"Miss Beck – Having stopped a short time to rest,*
> *I thought I would drop you a line—pardon the liberty.*
> *Here I leave Messrs. Yager and Grove—May their stay*
> *in S be as pleasant as mine, but without the same regret*
> *with which I left. Regret because I never can feel towards*
> *Salem the same interest, because the principal object of*
> *its interest must, whether I desire it or not, fade from my*

memory forever. Yes 'twas no idle speech that I made
Amo Te, I was fully prepared to abide by all its
consequences. But your happiness would not permit it
and so I forgive and forget."

Rebecca's tears blurred the lines, so she put the letter down. "Could it be Sam had been sincere in his feelings after all?" she asked herself. She had thought the emotion of the moment had caused him to blurt out the words. Could she have misjudged him so? She picked up the paper and continued to read:

"You say you could not love me—I am not surprised
—was only pained. I told you you would continue to
have admirers—but be not too unpleasant. Trust not
too much, the flattery of men. Keep the little pistol,
not as a souvenir of the giver, as once requested, but
of the Great War for Southern Independence. I have
but one request; if you speak of me at all do not call
me fickle though I was impulsive. Speak of me as
honorable in all my intentions, and as one that
loved not wisely but too well.

Very Respectfully Yours, S.F.C. " [369]

"Now he was gone" was her only thought.

Chapman, Yager and Grove had left Salem early the morning of June 21, following along Carter's Run, until they picked up Jerry's Run Road, thence to Leeds Manor Road and down to Templeman's Mill, on Thumb Run, a mile north of Orlean. They had traveled slowly, what with Sam's bad leg, and it was near suppertime when they came by the mill and up to the house. Yager and Grove had agreed to go that far with their friend and when they saw he was faring well enough they said their good-byes. But Sam asked them to wait while he wrote the letter to take back to Rebecca, so they had stayed the night.

By mid-July Chapman was ready to return to duty. But much to his chagrin, it would not be to Mosby's command. The army had acted upon the request of Major Dearing, made back in April, asking that the lieutenant fill a vacancy in Caskie's battery. In fact, orders had been issued once again for him to report to his new assignment. But Chapman was home on leave near Luray, replenishing his stolen clothing supply, when Mosby had made his excursion to Dumfries. When he returned, Sam was also back to accept command of the new mountain rifle, train the men, and set out with the command for Catlett's on May 29.

Special Order Number 119/16, was dated May 19, 1863, and read:

> Lieutenant S. F. Chapman, artillery, Provisional Army,
> Confederate States, will proceed without delay to
> Fredericksburg, Va. and report to General R. E. Lee,
> commanding, &c., for assignment to duty with Captain
> Caskie's battery. [370]

Where was Chapman on and after May 19 when the orders were issued? At home, or enroute to rejoin Mosby? In Salem? Apparently Sam and the orders never got together. Or did they? Whichever the case, he did not report to Fredericksburg for duty with Caskie. And after his subsequent wounding at Grapewood Farm, Dearing and Caskie would have to wait awhile for their new lieutenant.

The official records of the Confederate Adjutant and Inspector General (A&IG) have a lot of missing pieces, especially when it comes to Special Orders. Some of the missing pieces pertain to Sam Chapman. However, new orders caught up with him while he was recuperating from his wound. He was assigned to duty as first lieutenant with Company C, better known as the Hampden Light Artillery or Caskie's battery.[371]

When Chapman arrived at General Lee's headquarters at Culpeper Court House, with his parole in hand, Lee's adjutant, Colonel Walter Taylor, remarked: "You are at large again." Chapman had been exchanged for a Federal prisoner which permitted him to return to military duty. Maybe Sam was "at large" but only to the extent that he was back with the artillery. He reported to the 38th Battalion just as it was returning from Pennsylvania. The battalion had been part of the artillery barrage which preceded General Pickett's advance on the Union lines at Gettysburg on July 3. They arrived at Culpeper Court House on July 24 and went into camp about three miles from the town. By August 3, Sam was on the move again as the battalion left for a new camp, situated on the Stearn's farm near Orange Court House. [372]

Lee's army was now attempting to acquire some semblance of organization, and regain its confidence and morale, following Gettysburg. Among it's 20,451 casualties, were six general officers killed or mortally wounded, three captured, and eight wounded. This was one-third of the fifty-two officers above the rank of colonel who had entered Pennsylvania. Losses in the ranks of junior officers were much heavier. Thus, the need for rebuilding the command structure of the army. In Dearing's battalion, losses in the campaign were considerable, with seven killed, thirteen wounded, and thirteen captured. Thirty-seven horses were lost. Caskie's battery suffered three wounded, but none killed or captured. [373]

Chapman expressed his feelings about the life of an artilleryman, after having seen service with Mosby, while he was at Orange Court House: "It was a pleasant life, but a very inactive one." One thing he did get a chance to do—resume his religious activities. Sam had, of course, been much involved before the war, especially after being licensed to preach in 1858, but had not yet been ordained. Most of his time, however, between then and his enlistment in the army, had been spent in college.

A great revival was spreading throughout the army during this period and Sam was attending religious services regularly. "Mr. Duncan, an Episcopal clergyman was chaplain and called on me regularly for some assistance in his services, which I rendered." Sam always took part in the prayer meetings and "I enjoyed them very much." [374]

The relaxed atmosphere that pervaded the army at Orange this late summer was soon to be a memory; the order to strike camp came and, on September 8, Longstreet's Corps was on the march to Richmond. A day or so later the troops went the other twenty-five miles to Petersburg. The rumors heard in the ranks were apparently true. Longstreet's Corps was being sent to the West to team up with Braxton Bragg's Army of Tennessee. But the groans turned to smiles when it was announced that Pickett's division would not be making the trip. Instead, it was placed under the command of the Department of North Carolina and, on October 24, the 38th went into camp on the Birtchett farm outside Petersburg. Major Dearing would later marry Mr. Birchett's daughter. [375]

Chapman did not go into camp with the rest of the battalion. In fact, he would not even be sleeping on the ground, inside a tent, or in a hut with the other officers. He would have two rooms outside the city at a cost of thirty dollars a month, with heat, and twenty-five dollars for cordwood, all paid for by the army. On October 12, Sam had been assigned to duty as a member of the general courts-martial for the division. The Court was composed of Lieutenant Chapman, Captain Robert Stribling, formerly of the Fauquier Artillery, and Captain Caskie. [376]

Chapman would serve on the courts-martial board for the next three months, regularly holding forth in Petersburg, morning and evening. Although not a case for the general courts-martial, the most extreme case for the battalion was that of a private in the Fayette Artillery, charged with desertion and sentenced to a firing squad. The sentence was withdrawn before it could be carried out and the soldier was returned to duty, later being wounded at New Bern. Sam recalled a case at the other extreme: "Among a good many offenders we tried an officer charged with drunkenness. He was a preacher and pleaded guilty. A more humiliated man you could not imagine than he was during the time his trial went on. We all felt for him, and gave him a sentence not very severe, which I believe, made General Pickett, the reviewing officer, mad."[377]

On January 23, 1864 the men of the 38th Battalion were ushered onto cars of the Petersburg and Weldon Railroad. Pickett's division had been ordered into eastern North Carolina; a week later, the Hampden Artillery was firing on the Federal defenses in Fort Anderson, outside New Bern. But Sam Chapman wasn't with them.[378]

Major Mosby had written to the Confederate Secretary of War on January 5:

> I respectfully request the appointment of Lieut.
> Samuel F. Chapman as Adjutant of this battalion.
> Lieut. Chapman was originally a lieutenant in an
> artillery company which was afterward consolidated
> with another. He was relieved of duty in his company
> and appointed to the Conscript bureau, then was
> assigned to Caskie's battery, Dearing's battalion,
> Pickett's Division. He has rendered valuable services
> with my command & I would regard his appointment
> as a special favor. [379]

By January 25, Chapman's appointment as adjutant was confirmed, to be effective, retroactively, to January 11; he was notified and his acceptance was received in Richmond on February 6. By this time, based upon General Lee's glowing remarks to the Secretary of War, in a letter dated January 21, Mosby had been promoted to lieutenant colonel. On February 17, Sam Chapman was back in Mosby's Confederacy.[380]

PART V

FROM IRREGULAR COMMAND TO 43rd BATTALION

12. "Back with Joy"

Abraham Lincoln's Emancipation Proclamation took effect January 1,1863. Sam Chapman's emancipation was effective a year and a month later and the artillery lieutenant would always remember the day, in February of 1864: "The Division was ordered to North Carolina for active duty and at the time I received another order from the War Department to report there for a commission as adjutant to Lieutenant Colonel Mosby, who had requested the appointment. I went back with joy and reached Mosby's Confederacy about the middle of the month."[381]

Mosby's command had been quite busy since the affair near Grapewood Farm which had resulted in Sam's being wounded and absent from the command. Less than two weeks later, on June 10, 1863, sixty men had assembled near the Caleb Rector house at Rector's Cross Roads. These were hard-to-come-by Mosby men. The conscription law that forbade the enrolling of eligible men for the Partisan Corps had pretty much depleted Mosby's pool of possible Rangers. Additionally men like Sam Chapman, "Big Yankee" Ames, Sam Underwood and R. P. Montjoy, part of the core of his command, were absent because of wounds or capture. Nevertheless, the assemblage was witness to the formation of Company A, 43rd Battalion of Partisan Rangers.

They were now an official command in the Provisional Army of the Confederate States of America and as such, were subject to the same regulations governing the regular cavalry except where the dictates of the Partisan Ranger Act of April 1862 took precedent. The required election of officers was held, in the style of Mosby's "democratic process." One slate, picked by the leader, was presented to the command. The nominations were then closed and the vote taken. Needless to say it was a unanimous vote; not to vote for the candidate presented would result in transfer to the regular army.[382]

James William "Willie" Foster, Jr., the nineteen-year-old who had distinguished himself at Chantilly the previous March and in the Grapewood Farm fight following the Catlett's train ambush, was elected captain of the new company. He would not be in command for long. Two days later, while in a barbershop in Middleburg, Foster was captured by Major John Hammond's

5th New York Cavalry. He would remain in Union hands until almost the end of the war, never returning to the partisan command. [383]

Things had begun to get interesting in the ongoing relationship between Mosby and the U.S. cavalry. A communication from General Pleasonton, commanding the cavalry corps of the Army of the Potomac, to General Rufus Ingalls, chief of the Union supply command for all armies in the East, on June 12, asked: "How much of a bribe can (you) stand to get Mosby's services. There is a chance for him, and just now he could do valuable service in the way of information as well as humbugging the enemy." [384]

Just why Pleasonton thought "there is a chance for him," is unclear. And whether or not the dispatch was sent tongue-in-cheek, frustration was plainly showing in the Federal command and rightly so. On July 28, Mosby advised Stuart; "I send you...141 prisoners...I also sent off 45 several days ago; including in the number, 1 major, a captain, a surgeon, and 2 lieutenants. I also captured 123 horses and mules, 12 wagons, 50 sets of fine harness, arms, etc." Four days later, he sent another communiqué to Stuart: "I sent over...about 30 prisoners. Also captured about 30 wagons, brought off about 70 horses and mules, having only 10 men with me. A few nights ago I captured 29 loaded sutler's wagons, about 100 prisoners, and 140 horses. I had only 27 men."[385]

But the Yankees weren't the only ones feeling heat that summer. On August 18, General Lee, while endorsing a report of Mosby's, replied to Stuart: "I fear (Mosby) exercises but little control over his men. He has latterly carried but too few men on his expeditions, apparently, and his attention has been more directed toward the capture of wagons than military damage to the enemy. His attention has been called to this." [386]

On August 24, Mosby and about thirty men were in Fairfax County, scouting for unguarded railroad bridges that might make good targets to burn. Instead, they spotted a drove of horses with a cavalry escort of fifty troopers from the 2nd Massachusetts. Mosby divided his command in half, telling Lieutenant W.T. "Prince George's Tom" Turner to charge in their front while he, Mosby, attacked from the rear. In the meantime, thirteen more troopers had joined the escort. While the Yankees were watering their horses at Gooding's Tavern, near Annandale, Mosby and Turner attacked, scattering the Union cavalrymen. During the exchange of gunfire, Mosby was shot in the side and thigh. In great pain, the partisan leader was led from the fight, into some woods, where he was attended by Will Dunn, a doctor who had only recently joined the command. Two of the Rangers, Norman Smith and seventeen-year-old Charles Shriver, were killed, while three others from Mosby's band were wounded. Mosby was taken to the home of his father, in Amherst County, and in a month's time was back with his men.[387]

The guerillas continued to harass the Yankee wagon trains, much to the distress of General Lee. After his earlier admonition of Mosby for raiding wagon trains rather than inflicting "military damage to the enemy", Lee once again wrote to Stuart: "The capture and destruction of wagon trains is advantageous, but the supply of the Federal Army is carried on by the railroad. If that should be injured, it would cause him to detach largely for its security and thus weaken his main Army." But again on October 26, Mosby hit another wagon train on the road between Gainesville and Warrenton, carrying off "145 horses and mules and 30 negroes and Yankees, among them 1 captain." [388]

The command gathered on October 1 at Scuffleburg, a hamlet nestled at the foot of Brushy Mountain, on the headwaters of Deep Run, midway between Paris and Markham. Sixty men were selected to constitute a second company, Company B, and the officers were unanimously elected by the Mosby method. William Rowley "Billie" Smith was chosen to be captain. The former lieutenant in the Black Horse Cavalry was a brother of Norman Smith, who had been killed five weeks earlier at Gooding's Tavern.[389]

Two months later, December 7, the command was at Rectortown, where Company C was formed. Elected to the captaincy was William Chapman, who retained the rank he already held as an artillery officer.[390] But the success Mosby had been having, up to the time of the formation of this newest company, was coming to an end.

Frank Stringfellow had been a scout and aide to Jeb Stuart, but joined in with the partisans whenever the opportunity presented itself. Only five feet, one inch tall, the well-educated schoolteacher had earned the right to wear the insignia of a captain of cavalry. Stringfellow had been captured once and spent nearly two weeks in Old Capitol Prison before being exchanged. He had nearly been captured again in November following a fight at Bealeton Station. Now, in early January, 1864, Stringfellow was on a scout near Harper's Ferry. A winter storm left the snow above the knees of the bantam-size Stringfellow, but he brought back information for Mosby: a detachment of the Union 2nd Maryland Cavalry, under the command of Major Henry A. Cole, was encamped on Loudoun Heights and was in a vulnerable position for attack.

Stringfellow reported that Cole's camp was at the base of the east side of the Blue Ridge, between Hillsboro and Harper's Ferry, and only about one mile or less from the latter. Mosby left Uppervillle around the middle of the day on January 9 with about 100 men.[391] The harsh winter had set in with earnest in northwestern Virginia and William Chapman remembered: "The snow was quite deep and as the weather was intensely cold, the sufferings of the men were very great, many of the men having their hands and feet frostbitten during the night. The snow creaked under the horses' feet and the noise made had a ringing sound." [392] Around dusk the Rangers stopped at "Woodgrove," the home of Henry Heaton, a private in Company B, where they secured a hot meal to help them endure the intense cold of the night. After a short stay, the march was resumed and, several hours later, the partisans reached the Potomac River, a mile or two below Harper's Ferry. The column then traveled in a northwesterly direction, towards Harper's Ferry, until it was between the Ferry and the Federal encampment. The men dismounted, taking the horses' reins in their hands, and ascended, with great difficulty, a wooded, slippery hill in the rear of the sleeping Federals. [393]

"I rode a portion of the night with Capt. Wm. Smith," Chapman recalled, "and during the evening he showed me a beautiful gold watch which his wife had given to him, I think as a birthday present. We talked but little of the prospective fight, and indeed there was little conversation among the men. Some kept themselves from freezing by cutting a hole in the center of the blanket that was always carried strapped to the saddle, and inserting their heads through the hole and letting the blanket fall over them and on the horses."[394]

It would not be long before daylight and Mosby was anxious to put his plan of attack into action. Information at the time indicated that about 175 to 200 of the enemy occupied the camp. Stringfellow, with ten men, was to surround and take the house which Major Cole used for his headquarters; Captain Billie Smith, with another party, was to secure the horses standing outside the hospital building; Montjoy would go back to the bridge and, with six men, capture the picket they had avoided on their way in; Mosby, with the bulk of the command, was to attack the camp proper.

The Rangers, once shivering in the cold of the deep winter night, were now edgy with excitement and the cold was forgotten, except for the hands that grasped steel revolvers. Suddenly, there was a noise—a report from a pistol or carbine perhaps—and Stringfellow's men went charging into the camp, contrary to the plan laid out by Mosby. It was a scene to remember—and at the same time—one to try and forget. Mosby and his group, thinking the charging Rangers were Yankees, began shooting into their midst. Charlie Paxson was one of the first hit and he fell mortally wounded in the frozen snow.

With all the disorder in Mosby's command, the Federals were able to rally and pour their fire into the attackers. Some of the raiders took refuge in an old log house, while the others remained in the open, drawing the fire of the recovering Yankees. Lieutenant Turner, badly wounded, was taken away to a nearby residence; "Prince George's Tom" would die the following day. Suddently, in all the chaos, the signal gun from Harper's Ferry caught Mosby's ear, and he ordered a withdrawal, knowing that several thousand Federal troops were encamped there and would quickly be on the way. The shattered command made its way back on the road to Hillsboro, taking with them seven prisoners and thirty-five horses. The Federals did not follow. By sunrise the band was back at the Heaton home. [395]

William Chapman's remembrances of the chaotic scene that followed the attack were still vivid many years after the war: "...the men with Captain Stringfellow and those with Col. Mosby mistaking each other for the enemy (were) firing on each other. Some of the men did not hear (the order to withdraw) and hearing the cries of their own wounded comrades undertook to get them off the field." In all the confusion, Chapman, and some others still in the camp, believed that Mosby was among the wounded, being unaware that he had withdrawn. "I had the impression that Col. Mosby himself was wounded in the camp," Chapman recalled, and when he saw Captain Smith helping a wounded private—Henry Edmonds of Company B—he asked about Mosby's whereabouts. When Smith told him he was afraid their leader was wounded, Chapman "proposed that we go back and find him." [396]

As the two officers rode deeper into the encampment, they came upon the fallen Paxson, who begged them to remove him from the field. "He could not tell how he was wounded but was lying on his back," Chapman recalled, "and told us he could move neither hand nor foot." Chapman sent another Ranger after an extra horse and shortly afterward, "there was a shot fired at us from a group not twenty steps distant. Capt. Smith and I returned the fire and then a volley was fired at us. The volley for a moment blinded me and I had a feeling of thankfulness that I had escaped, and hoped that Capt. Smith had, when suddenly he leaped in the air and fell on the right side of his horse, his left foot drawing the stirrup over on the right side and both feet hung in the stirrups, with his head in the snow." [397]

With lighting instinct, Chapman jumped from his own horse, asking his friend how he was shot. Getting no reply, "I endeavored to lift him into the saddle but found it impossible. I then thought of the watch that was in his pocket and tried to unbutton his overcoat to take it from him, but my hands had become so cold after removing my gloves to go into the fight that I could not unbutton a single button." Realizing Smith was beyond help, Chapman knocked the dead captain's feet from the stirrups, mounted his own horse, and led Smith's mount from the encampment. But something always puzzled Chapman each time he thought of that cold night: " While this was going on the group of men who had fired the volley, whom I could distinctly see in the same position as when they fired, made no further demonstration towards me, neither by firing at nor by trying to capture me. Finding Lieutenant Robert Gray, Chapman asked for his help in recovering Smith's body and to look for Colonel Mosby. Only then did Chapman learn that he and Gray were apparently the only men in the camp: "This was the first I had heard of Col. Mosby's having withdrawn from the attack." [398]

Later that day, Captain Chapman, on Mosby's orders and accompanied by Private Montjoy, carried a flag of truce to Major Cole, "…with the proposition to exchange the prisoners we then had for our men who were killed or wounded." Cole refused to accept the communication. [399]

The ill-fated raid had cost the partisans dearly. Eight men were dead or would die from their wounds. Another three, including Fount Beattie, were wounded but would recover, and one man was taken prisoner. On the Federal side, Union reports put their losses at five killed, including one captain and two lieutenants, two mortally wounded, and one taken prisoner. (Mosby attested to taking six prisoners and 50-60 horses). [400]

Like Warrenton Junction, Loudoun Heights was, through costly error, a tragedy that the 43rd would remember for a long time to come.

Lee's criticism of Mosby's choices of targets to attack not withstanding, the effect of the command's harassing raids on Yankee wagon trains continued to take troops off the line and put them guarding the trains, both wagon and rail. Realizing this, Lee, on January 21, recommended Mosby's promotion to lieutenant colonel. General Stuart also recommended Mosby for promotion, alluding to the major's "…unswerving devotion to duty, self-abnegation, and unflinching courage, with a quick perception and appreciation of the opportunity…." Stuart's endorsement, ironically, was contained with Mosby's report of the debacle at Loudoun Heights. The promotion was approved, to take effect February 11, 1864. [401]

Just prior to Sam Chapman's return to the 43rd Battalion, the week after Mosby's promotion, he had the occasion to take part in a foxhunt. He could not help but make the comparison of the "running to the hounds" to his first cavalry charge, at Chantilly, nearly a year before: "The dogs behaved well, so the old hunters said—and so did the fox to my notion. I think he got away. The enjoyment of the old hunters, who had been in the army, seemed to know no bounds. To me it seemed tame enough. Having been in the cavalry, I only felt compensated for my participation in the hunt by the good dinner we all sat down to." [402]

Tomorrow Sam would be "back with joy" in the cavalry.

13. A Real Ranger at Last

Colonel John S. Mosby's first adjutant, Lieutenant Sam Chapman, was sleeping soundly. Next to him slept his brother, Captain William Chapman; also in the room was their cousin, Private Judah Forrer. Ranger Richard Montjoy and a Prussian army veteran by the name of Baron Von Massow, were sleeping elsewhere in the large home. The estate, "Highlands," owned by John Jeffries, was located several miles north of Salem in the area between Piedmont and Rectortown. Nearby was the home of Ranger Joseph Blackwell, used by Mosby as his headquarters when he was in this vicinity. These homes were considered to be safe-houses for the partisans. And a week from now, the Jeffries home would be the scene of the marriage of William Chapman and Jeffries niece, Josephine.

In anticipation of his marriage to "Josie" Jeffries, William had apparently asked Sam for a favor several weeks earlier. On February 5, William had taken a dozen or so men, crossed the Shenandoah, and rode on to Berryville. There he learned that a similar party of Federal cavalryman had just left the village heading for Charlestown. Attempting to cut them off, Chapman cut across country, but came upon their rear upon entered the pike. Later that day he penned the following note to Sam:

> *Dear Brother, I just returned from a scout near Charlestown.*
> *Met with a party of Yankees and attacked them killing three,*
> *wounding seven and capturing three Yankees and four horses.*

William then closed the note with: *"Do not get the ring I wrote to you about a day or two ago as I am going to send to Richmond today."* [403]

It was late the evening of February 17 when Sam arrived at Highlands and found his first cousin. Judah Forrer had been with Mosby only about three weeks. He had spent the last two years, following his discharge from the Dixie Artillery, working for the war effort in the Forrer ironworks. Sam also met the Baron Von Massow, who had served seven years in the Prussian army before coming to America; he was sent to Mosby through General Stuart, just as Sam's friend, the late Captain Hoskins, had been. The Barron was as colorful as Mosby when it came to dress; he rode into battle wearing a long, lined cape over a glittering uniform and from his hat waved a big ostrich plume. And he was not without the ever-present European sabre. [404]

The noise of horse's hoofs on the frozen ground, and the all-to-familiar rattle of cavalry tack and equipment, quickly brought the Rangers out of their slumber. The sounds emanated from a detachment of a larger force of Union cavalry, comprised of the 1st New Jersey, 1st and 3rd Pennsylvania, and the 1st Massachusetts, on a mission to try and locate Mosby and any of his men. The total force, numbering 350 men, had set out from Warrenton late the night before. John Cornwell, a deserter from the 43rd, accompanied the Federals. Cornwell had gotten into a disagreement with Walter Frankland, the battalion's acting quartermaster, over reimbursement for a bill and when he took his complaint to Mosby, the colonel had backed Frankland. It was then that Cornwell sought out the Yankees, twenty miles away, at Warrenton, where Brigadier General David M. Gregg's 2nd Cavalry division was encamped. The former Ranger told the Federals that he could guide them to Mosby and several of the others.

The information given by Cornwell was relayed to Union cavalry chief General Alfred Pleasonton. Pleasonton then instructed General Gregg to send a force as soon as possible "for the purpose of capturing Mosby and his party." Regarding the deserter, Pleasonton said that Cornwell was to accompany the party and "if he should lead you into a trap he will be shot." Gregg in turn gave orders to Lieutenant Colonel J. W. Kester, commanding the 1st New Jersey Cavalry, "...to proceed to-night at ten o'clock to Markham and Paris and vicinity where it is reported bands of guerrillas have their headquarters." (Kester's directive is incorrectly dated February 18, while the actual date was the 17th.)

When Kester reached Salem, he dispersed the 350 man detachment as follows: fifty men from the 1st Massachusetts to Upperville and on to Paris, meeting the rest of the command at Ashby's Gap; Kester to take the remainder to Piedmont where Captain Hart would take 150 men of the 1st New Jersey and continue on through the Piedmont Valley to Paris; Kester, with the remaining 150 troopers from the 1st and 3rd Pennsylvania, would start for Manassas Gap, where they would take a by-path north, meeting up with the rest of the command between Ashby's Gap and Paris. The different patrols were to search all houses along the way where a Ranger might be hiding. [405]

It was probably the fifty-man detachment of the 1st Massachusetts, under the command of Lieutenant Bradbury of the 3rd Pennsylvania, that awakened Sam and the others as the column passed on the way from Salem to Upperville. For reasons unknown, they did not stop to search either the Jefferies place or the Blackwell home. The night was very cold and the troopers were marching rapidly toward the rendezvous point at Paris, probably more interested in a warm fire than in locating sleeping Rebels in the middle of the night.

Mosby had been in Richmond for several days; it was on this trip that he secured Sam Chapman's appointment and transfer and where he accepted his own promotion to lieutenant colonel. He returned to Piedmont the evening of February 18, and was eating breakfast the next morning at the Blackwell home, when he learned of the Yankee search parties. With Cornwell guiding them, the cavalrymen had been successful in taking a total of twenty-eight prisoners; twenty-four of them Mosby's men, the other four simply innocent civilians.

Lieutenant Hunter and Captain Chapman had each gathered small bands to try to hit the Federal troopers and release the prisoners but they were too few to engage Kester's force. Mosby called for a meeting the afternoon of February 19 at Piedmont and sixty men, including Lieutenant Sam Chapman, set out to follow the Federals as they headed back to Warrenton, hoping for an opportunity to strike them. They were unable to catch up at a favorable spot and had to let the Yankees, with their prisoners, return unharmed. [406]

The next day, Mosby's adversary from the Loudoun Heights affair five weeks previous, Major Cole, brought about 250 men of his 2nd Maryland Battalion south from Harper's Ferry to Upperville, looking to flush Mosby out. From Upperville, the force proceeded to Piedmont Station on the Manassas Gap Railroad. Cole succeeded in surprising and capturing several Rangers along the way. Mosby was again at the Blackwell home near Piedmont when word came that Cole and his men were in Upperville. Sending some of his men to round up the others, Mosby started north, hoping to overtake Cole's column, which had turned around at Piedmont and taken a trail along the base of the Blue Ridge and back toward Upperville. The Rangers sniped at the column all along the road. About two miles beyond Upperville the Federals stopped to feed and rest their horses. This pause gave Mosby time to gather his men and, when the patrol started out again, he charged into the rear guard, just before it reached Blakeley's School House. This drove the rear of the column in on the others, causing confusion in the troopers' ranks. Reaching the schoolhouse, Cole's men dismounted and took a position behind a stone wall.

Sam Chapman remembered the ensuing fight: "They checked us by dismounting their carbineers and by posting them behind stone fences. These we could only dislodge—as we had no carbines—by flanking them." Mosby had gathered about sixty men by the time he engaged Cole. It took three assaults for the Rangers to dislodge the Federal cavalrymen and it was here that "Montjoy... won his captaincy." Montjoy, Chapman's companion when they were defending the little Howitzer at Grapewood Farm, had engaged in hand-to-hand fighting with Captain W. L. Morgan of the 1st New York Veteran Cavalry before killing him.[407]

The boys' school at Upperville was being recessed as the two adversaries passed by. Henry Cabell "Cab" Maddux was not yet sixteen years old. The chubby teenager jumped on his pony, with nothing but a McGuffy's Third Reader for a weapon, as Mosby's men went past, joining in the chase with a whoop and a holler. It would be his last day of school. Cab would spend the rest of the war riding with the 43rd.[408..]

Mosby's report to Stuart's headquarters on the fight: "They left 6 of their dead on the field, among them 1 captain, 1 lieutenant, and 7 men prisoners; also horses, army equipment, etc. The road over which they retreated was strewn with abandoned hats, haversacks, etc...It is a source of great pride to bring to your notice the names of some whose conspicuous gallantry renders their mention both a duty and a pleasure. They are Captain and Lieutenant Chapman,...Private Montjoy...My loss was 2 wounded."[409]

A spirited Sam Chapman later described the scene: "The three charges our men made were done with great dash. I remember the conspicuous figure of our leader, clad in a new black overcoat that had a cape lined with red flannel, and that (was) exposed to full view by the wind. He rode, as usual, in the forefront, looking into the very eyes of his foe, his pistol flashing at every step. I had not been in a fight for more than six months, and this affair, I thought, would do for a fresh introduction into partisan warfare."

Years later, Mosby would remember that it was Chapman who was always riding in the forefront: "His character as a soldier was more on the model of the Hebrew prophets than the Evangelist or the Baptist in whom he was so devout a believer. He was generally in front of everybody in a fight."[410]

Mosby told the Rangers to meet back at Piedmont the next day for the funeral of Private Joseph McCobb, who had been killed by Cole's men while trying to escape the house searches two days before. Not much was known about the Baltimore native; he had joined Mosby's command after serving in the 1st Maryland Artillery. While the men were at the Jeffries' home, assembled for the services, a report came in that a Yankee patrol was at Rector's Cross Roads, about eight miles distant. And riding with the patrol was an ex-Ranger.

Charlie Binns was a thirty-two-year-old former private in Mosby's first company. He was the stepfather of Ranger Dulany M. Richards. And he was a deserter. Binns had gone over to the Yankees the previous November to avoid arrest by Mosby on unspecified charges. Now he was guiding the Federal patrol, comprised of elements of the 2nd Massachusetts and the 16th New York Cavalries, under the command of Captain J. S. Read.[411]

Leaving their dead companion to be buried by others, the 160-man force set off for Middleburg, five miles east of Rector's. Upon reaching Middleburg, Mosby learned that the Federals had come from Vienna, in Fairfax County. While the rest of the command rode towards Dranesville, two of the Rangers were sent to follow the Yankees and report back to Mosby. He hoped to intercept them on their return route to Vienna. That night, Read's column camped on a farm, a short distance from Dranesville, where it was joined by another body of cavalry.

Sam Chapman picks up the story: "Mosby put the command in charge of my brother, the ranking captain, with orders to march to Guilford Station, in Lower Loudoun, in order that we might be in a position to intercept the raiders on their return to camp. The (Yankees) went through Leesburg, and bivouacked six miles beyond for the night."

The partisans camped for the night in the pines along the pike near Dranesville. "(Mosby) seemed confident of his success in meeting them just where he wished to meet them," Sam recalled. "I have been on the inside track in all this march," he remembered his leader saying. Chapman explained what Mosby meant: "... the enemy (in their movement) had described an irregular arc, but we had moved over the chord of the arc. Never had scouting been more successfully done, and never had its results been more satisfactory. The Federal troops were but a few miles off and we were on the road between them and their camp."[412]

Early the next morning, Mosby moved his command out on the pike to Anker's Shop, about two miles below Dranesville. Around the middle of the morning, the picket, Walter Whaley, reported the Federal column was on the move. Mosby divided the command into three parties in the piney woods, to await the enemy's arrival. Lieutenant Frank Williams' men were to charge in their front; Captain Chapman and his group were to charge the rear; Montjoy, with fifteen carbineers, was to fire into the center of the column. After each had been given his instructions, Mosby said, "Men, the Yankees are coming and it is very likely we will have a hard fight. When you are ordered to charge, I want you to go right through them." The signal to attack was to be a shrill whistle, which Mosby himself would sound. [413]

"On they came, rather leisurely, not expecting an attack." Sam remembered. "Everything…was still. Our nerves were wrought to a high tension as this deliberately moving host came near and were passing. We could not stir until the shrill whistle should be blown. An advance guard of the Federals came in sight of our picket down the road, fired a shot, and waved to their comrades to come on." [414]

The blast from Mosby's whistle reverberated through the stillness of the pinewoods. The crack of carbines from Montjoy's riflemen was followed by the charge of Captain Chapman into the column's rear and Lieutenant Williams into their front. "We met the enemy standing still and they attempted a fight, but with the invariable failure that attends cavalry that stands to receive a charge," recalled Sam. He was beside Mosby as they galloped at the head of Williams' detachmen, down the hill, each with both revolvers blazing, upon the front of Read's column. Remembering events such as these years later, Mosby spoke of Sam Chapman: "(He) was a Baptist minister who prayed through a six shooter, which he claimed was the most efficacious form of prayer, especially when dealing with Yankees." [415]

The road was quickly filling with the dead and wounded—men and horses— and riderless mounts galloping in terror everywhere. The attack was so devastating that many of the Union cavalrymen were driven into the Potomac River, a half-mile distant, and dead and drowned bodies were found days later. Included in the dead was Captain Read, leader of the Federal detachment. Read had supposedly surrendered to Baron Von Massow, when the Baron charged at him, sabre aloft, preparing to take off his head. Read had thrown up his pistol hand in a posture of surrender but as the Baron rode past him, toward another cavalryman, Read turned and shot Von Massow in the back, causing a severe, but not fatal, wound. William Chapman was a witness to the scene and placed a well-aimed shot into Read, killing him instantly. However, the Baron's fighting days with Mosby were over. [416]

Private John Munson would have an almost identical experience to that of the Baron. Toward the end of the fight, Munson, with one shot remaining in his revolver, pointed it at a Yankee trooper, who threw up his pistol hand, exclaiming "I surrender!" Munson rode past him, firing his last round at another trooper, when the first man turned and fired, wounding Munson in the back, one-half inch from his spine. Ranger Ludlow Lake saw the incident and shot and killed Munson's assailant. [417]

The extent of the loss to the Federal command speaks to the deadly ferociousness of the fight: fifteen killed, including Captain Read, and another twenty-five wounded; Captain Manning, three lieutenants, and several non-commissioned officers among the seventy-two prisoners taken, and ninety horses with equipment captured.

The loss to the Rangers was one killed and four wounded. The dead man was James Pendleton Chappelier. It was his first raid and he must have had a premonition of his death, from a conversation he had with Sam Chapman. "While we were waiting in the pines, he told (me) that he had hidden a considerable sum of money in one of his boots, and to look for it there if he should be killed. The money was taken to his father." [418]

Despite all the attempts to catch the deserter Binns, he escaped during the confusion at the beginning of the fight. Mosby's report to cavalry headquarters included the following: "My thanks are due to Captain Chapman and Lieutenants Williams and Hunter and Adjutant Chapman for their fidelity in executing every order." [419]

The Rangers called this fight "Second Dranesville" and it was as satisfying as the first Dranesville fight, the one better known as Miskel's Farm.

14. Winds of Change

The March winds blowing across the rolling hills of Mosby's Confederacy would bring significant changes in the conduct of the war in northern Virginia, both for the partisans and for the Yankee invaders.

On March 10, a short, unkempt, stogie chewing major general by the name of Ulysses Simpson Grant was brought east from the Western theatre of operations and made general-in-chief of the Union armies by President Lincoln. He was given unlimited resources to deal with the "rebellion" and would devise a policy of out-maneuvering rather than out-fighting Robert E. Lee. He would wage total war against Mosby, his men and their families; the citizenry in general would suffer, in the region inhabited by the Rangers, through destruction of their property and the harassment and detention of non-combatants.[420]

A second change also dealt with personnel, this time in the Union cavalry. Around the middle of the month, Grant replaced his cavalry chief, General Pleasonton, with a short, temperamental Irishman by the name of Phillip Henry Sheridan. And even though General Sheridan would not personally assume command of the Union Army of the Shenandoah until August, Grant's mandates to his Valley commanders, together with some of their own, would raise warfare on both sides of the Blue Ridge to a new and more devastating level.

March would also find the ongoing debate over the year-old Partisan Ranger Act heat up, cool down, and finally die in April, ironically, with both repeal and confirmation taking place. It began in January, with a request from Brigadier General Thomas L. Rosser, commanding officer of the Laurel Brigade, to General Lee, to take some action "in order that this partisan system...may be corrected." Rosser accused the partisan commands in general of being "without discipline, order, or organization. (roaming) over the countryside, a band of thieves, stealing, pillaging, plundering, and doing every manner of mischief and crime. They are a terror to the citizens and an injury to the cause. They never fight; can't be made to fight." He then singled Mosby out: "Major Mosby is of inestimable service to the Yankee army in keeping their men from straggling. He is a gallant officer, and is one that I have great respect for; yet the interest I feel...in the good of the service coerces me to bring this matter before you...." Rosser backed his play with two heavyweights: "Major General Early can give useful information concerning the evils of these organizations. If he cannot, Maj. Gen. Fitz. Lee certainly can...."

The communication met with a favorable endorsement from both Stuart and Lee and then from the Secretary of War. The days of the Partisan Ranger Act were numbered and March would see the last full month of its existence.[421]

The month began with a rather disappointing raid on a Federal patrol along the road from Bristoe Station to Greenwich. A previous attempt to capture the patrol, which numbered anywhere from fifty to one hundred men on any particular day, had been unsuccessfully tried by a party led by Lieutenant Richards; now Mosby himself would try.

Taking forty men, Mosby hid them in a pine thicket while he and Sam Chapman climbed a hill to watch for the approaching patrol. When it passed, the raiders charged into its rear. But by not putting a contingent of men further up the road, to attack the front of the column, and by not covering its flanks, the troopers were able to scatter when Mosby struck the rear, resulting in only nine prisoners, with horses, being taken. [422]

With miserable weather—there was a snow two feet deep on the Third—and the increasingly strong opposition to the partisan commands by the regular military establishment, and now by the politicos in Richmond, Mosby determined that a low profile would probably be the best course for awhile. Although the 43rd Battalion had been officially a part of the regular service since the organization of Company A in June of 1863, its detached status and freedom of operation placed it in the Partisan category as far as most of the regular army commanders were concerned. They made no distinction between Mosby and the rest of the guerilla bands. Even Mosby himself regarded his command as Partisan under the Act of April 1862.

With the exception of a raid by Richards and forty Rangers in the northern Shenandoah Valley on March 10, the rest of the month was spent in relative quietness. But the Richards' raid did have some positive results as far as showing the tenacity and courage of Mosby's partisans.

Richards and his band had been able to slip quietly into a Federal picket post, between Kabletown and Charlestown, and carry off twenty men and horses, with little resistance, although one Yankee was killed and four wounded before the raiders departed. The shots alerted the main camp at Charlestown and Major Jerry A. Sullivan with about thirty-five troopers from the 1st New York Veterans hurried to the post. Finding the Rangers gone, Sullivan started in pursuit. Six of the partisans, including Richard Montjoy, had lingered too long and were a good distance behind the rest of the group. As Sullivan caught up and started to overtake them, the Rangers initiated a patented Mosby maneuver—they turned and charged right into the oncoming Federals. Sullivan was the first to fall and the remainder of the bluecoats became panic stricken. The Rangers were able to capture six prisoners and horses and rejoin the main body before it crossed the Shenandoah. The 1st New York Veterans counted three dead. [423]

Relaxation and home cooking—and a chance to be with the girls—were things that the Rangers, as most soldiers, looked forward to with much anticipation; they could usually find all three at many of the numerous safehouses, scattered over the countryside, in Fauquier and Loudoun Counties. One such place was Belle Grove, two miles south of Paris in upper Fauquier. Owned by the Edmonds family, the large three-story house, with a two-story wing attached, could host several of the command at one time. In addition to the many bedrooms, there was a three-foot high cellar in which the men could be concealed when necessary. A trap door was located in the floor of a closet under the steps that went from the dining room to one of the servant's bedrooms above.

Amanda Virginia "Tee" Edmonds was a lively, good-natured and unmarried girl in her mid-twenties when war came to the area known as the "Debatable Land." Most of the fighting men in this area of the Piedmont Valley were members of Company A of the 6th Virginia Cavalry—or at least they were initially. Many of them migrated to Mosby's command, taking part in raids and scouts, although never officially becoming Rangers. On March 4-5, Belle Grove was host to seven of these soldiers and Tee was led to write in her diary: "I thought, were Yanks to pounce upon them, they would have a nice capture." And just the week before, "Our boys return and we give thirteen of them supper…Col. Mosby was here for breakfast." Following Lieutenant Richards' raid across the Shenandoah, Tee spoke of "All our boys (assembling) once more around the hearth to indulge in drinking "spirits" done up in apples and brown sugar. I made the toddy sweet and strong, for I am determined they should feel the effects and they did. They soon became a merry set…." [424]

An entry in Tee Edmonds's diary, from before the war, speaks of Eliza R. "Bec" Elgin and Tee calling on two of "our old schoolmates" in Salem. [425] "Bec" was Miss Beck, principal object of Sam Chapman's affections and the one who had "pained" him in Salem the previous summer.

If March, 1864, was a slow month for guerilla operations it was notable for being the month in which one of Mosby's most personally embarrassing moments of his wartime career occurred.

On March 25, while Mosby and six of his men were returning from a scout in the Valley, they learned there were four members of the 21st New York Cavalry at the home of a Union sympathizer, near Millwood, in Clarke County. The partisans were able to surprise the Yankees, as they were sitting down to supper, and make them their prisoners. Crossing the Blue Ridge through Ashby's Gap in a driving snowstorm, the small group stopped at the Triplett place, mid-way between Paris and Piedmont. Leaving Sergeant Wrenn in the barn to guard the prisoners, Mosby and the rest of the party went into the house.

While the Yankees were tying up their horses, a Corporal Simpson slipped the revolver out of one of Mosby's saddle holsters, and, in the darkness, dropped the reins from his own horse, while picking up those from Mosby's. He stepped into a stirrup, took a wild shot at Wrenn and bolted from the barn. Mosby, hearing the commotion, ran out of the house just in time to see Simpson, up on his favorite grey mare, ride by, followed closely by one of the other captives. Lost, along with his horse, were the Colonel's revolvers, overcoat, and other items, including his saddlebags, which contained several things personal. Among these were identification papers for some of his Rangers, his captain's commission, and Stuart's order, praising him for his raid on Fairfax Court House and the capture of General Stoughton. [426]

After arriving back at the command's unofficial headquarters, the Blackwell home near Piedmont, Mosby and Adjutant Chapman took care of some administrative matters. In a long communiqué to Stuart, a litany of things was discussed. Mosby had been able to develop considerable information, through reconnaissance and the use of informants, relative to the movements of the enemy. New picket lines were being established near Winchester and Charlestown where none existed before. New rails were being laid on the Winchester and Potomac. General Robert Milroy had been placed in command at Harper's Ferry. All these things could add up but to one conclusion: a movement up the Valley must be in the works.

The partisan commander also requested "$2,000 secret-service money, (which) I could use greatly to the public advantage...investing it in tobacco, and then converting it into greenbacks."

Another item in the communiqué was a request to halt the recruiting of men for Mosby's command by the enrolling officer in Richmond, men the partisan chief was having to send back; " ...for success in my operations (I must have) none but first rate men." [427]

March 28 would find the battalion gathered at Paris where its fourth company was organized. Richard P. Montjoy was elected captain of Company D, once more in Mosby's own version of the democratic election process. The company, made up primarily of Marylanders, would come to be called "Company Darling" by the girls of Fauquier because of the many beardless youths on its roster. They were the "beaux and fops" of the battalion, in the best uniforms and with the best equipment. Truly they were the "Darlin's" of the command. [428]

The same day the command were gathered in Paris, Colonel J. W. Fisher took 225 men of Major McCabe's 13th Pennsylvania Cavalry up the Little River Turnpike to Aldie, "...(searching) houses and other buildings where guerrillas might be concealed." Receiving information that the partisans, including Mosby, were at Middleburg, Fisher raced for that town, only to come up empty. Afraid to go into the mountain passes with his 225-man force, "having learned...that Mosby had nearly three times my number," Fisher returned to Aldie. He had a brief exchange with an unknown enemy "of considerable force" two miles beyond the village, causing him to withdraw his command and skedaddle back down the turnpike. There was no sizable group of Mosby's men in the area that day and it is unknown who or what "the considerable force" was. Suffice it to say, Fisher was glad to be safely back in camp, where he filed his report to his superiors, closing with: "From all I have learned I have come to the conclusion that we have not sufficient cavalry force attached to this division to drive Mosby out of the country...." To Colonel Fisher, the "gray ghost" had seemed awfully real. [429]

With the coming of spring to the gentle hills, lush meadows, and secluded valleys of northern Virginia, the "new" Union cavalry under Phil Sheridan would begin to step up its efforts to find and destroy Mosby or, at the least, to render him as ineffective as possible. The drain on Federal manpower, necessary to keep supply and communications lines protected, was hurting Grant's strategy for the conduct of the war in Virginia. It was taking entire brigades of blue-coated cavalry and infantry to keep the Orange and Alexandria tracks open, between the Potomac and the Rapidan, not to mention the long right-of-way of the Baltimore and Ohio through Maryland and Virginia. And the Manassas Gap Railroad, closed for two years, was now a light at the end of the proverbial tunnel for Grant and Sheridan. If the tracks could be rebuilt and the trains started running again—and kept running—it would open up the Shenandoah Valley to the huge supply bases around Washington. It would also provide a faster and easier means for moving troops from west of the Blue Ridge to the busy Eastern theatre around Fredericksburg and Richmond and vice versa. But, there was Mosby...always Mosby.

Tee Edmond's diary for February 23, 1864, contains this entry: " Mr. Flannery left yesterday and returns today with his long wished for banjo. We all drink of its sweet melodies as twilight darkens into night; an unusual instrument and sound at Bell (sic) Grove." Again, a month later, "Mr. Flannery tries to keep the blues from coming with a lively air on the banjo. He plays with spirit and the other boys join in the chorus. He is a lively soul...." [430]

Private M. W. "Pug Count" Flannery had enlisted with Mosby on August 20, 1863. He was one of the Mosby regulars at Belle Grove, using it as his safe-house, when not with the command. He was a perennial favorite around the area, with a personality that rivaled his lively banjo. No dance set could be complete without "Pug Count's" gleeful tunes.

On the evening of April 13, Flannery was at an outpost of the 13th Pennsylvania Cavalry, near Nokesville, in Prince William County. He had been known to enter Federal camps before, without being detected as a Confederate, presumably in company with a Doctor Edmunds, according to a Union report. On this occasion, a gust of wind blew open his overcoat, exposing his gray uniform. Private M. Locke, one of the pickets, fired once, the ball entering the young Rebel's chest. Before falling to the ground, Flannery was able to fire his revolver twice, wounding Locke in the left leg and arm. [431]

On April 20, Tee Edmonds lamented to her diary: " Oh! Oh! Oh! What bad, unlooked for, unwished for news the boys bring this morning. Poor Mr.

Flannery has been killed. Nearly two weeks ago he left Bell (sic) Grove expecting to return in a day or two, but alas Bell (sic) Grove will see him no more...Oh! how sad to think of it when we see his loved instrument sitting in the corner waiting; silent and mute as the soldier in his grave. Oh! will the anguish, trouble and sorrow of war never cease." [432]

A week after the death of Flannery, the Partisan Ranger Act was laid to rest. The Confederate Congress had repealed the law on February 17, but in so doing, authorized the Secretary of War to exempt those companies he felt were needed "... to (serve) within the lines of the enemy..." Two such commands fell into this favorable category—McNeill's Rangers, operating primarily in western Virginia and the Shenandoah Valley, and Mosby's 43rd Battalion. By Secretary Seddon's action on April 21, all other so-called partisan ranger organizations were to be disbanded or converted to regular cavalry companies. [433]

It appeared that April would end on an upbeat note for the Rangers with the good news about the Mosby and McNeill commands. The good news turned bad very quickly.

Colonel Charles R. Lowell, Jr., of the 2nd Massachusetts Cavalry, started from Vienna in Fairfax County on April 29 with a brigade of cavalry, supported by another brigade of infantry from Fairfax Court House. Dividing up as they proceeded west into Loudoun County, one body entered Leesburg. Several of the Rangers were in and around the hotel, unaware that the bluecoats were in the town. By the time Lowell's men were spotted it was too late. Several partisans were captured at the hotel; some were in the barroom and all these were made prisoners, except Private John DeButts. He was seriously wounded trying to get to his horse, which he had left at the blacksmith shop. DeButts had been a member of the Fairfax raiding party that captured General Stoughton the previous year. Private Tom Flack made it to the edge of town before he was shot and killed.

The Federals left Leesburg, traveling by way of Bloomfield, to Upperville. On the way they were able to pick up several more of Mosby's men, including Edwin Rowzee, George Ayre, and Champ Fitzhugh. All three would spend the rest of the war, plus two months, in Federal prisons. Another, Felix Ware, was shot and captured above Upperville. By May 1, Lowell was back in Vienna and filed his report. He listed "21 of Mosby's men...and from 20 to 25 horses" captured. His casualties, caused by some of the Rangers dogging the column and picking up stragglers, were three killed, two wounded, and four captured. [434]

March winds had blown change across northern Virginia. April breezes had brought a newer, more acrimonious war to Mosby's Confederacy.

15. Springtime in the Shenandoah

When General Grant assumed command of Mr. Lincoln's armies in March, 1864, he implemented a whole new way of running the war from the Northern side. His grand scheme called for a coordinated offensive on all fronts—General Sherman to move against Johnston's Army of Tennessee, into Atlanta, and then to the coast; Ben Butler to march up the James toward Petersburg and Richmond; Nathaniel Banks' Army of the Gulf to invest Mobile. In the Shenandoah Valley, German-born General Franz Sigel was to move up the Valley, neutralizing the Army of Northern Virginia's supply base. Grant would travel with General George Meade's Army of the Potomac, with the aim of crossing the Rapidan and getting between Robert E. Lee and the Virginia coast. These movements, if successful, would ensure a steady stream of supplies to the Union army while, at the same time, keeping Lee away from the Confederate capitol at Richmond.

When Grant arrived at the headquarters of the Army of the Potomac at Brandy Station, he found over 100,000 troops, encamped in the Virginia mud, over a ten-square mile area north of the Rapidan River. They had been there for six months now and were more than ready to move against "old Bobby Lee" and his Army of Northern Virginia, also in winter camps, south of the Rappahannock.

The first of the Union forces started across the Rapidan River at Germanna Ford, the morning of May 1, kicking off Grant's Overland Campaign. It would result in one of the bloodiest four weeks of the war, with major battles being fought at the Wilderness, Spotsylvania Court House, and Cold Harbor. Casualties for the three conflicts would total 48,800 killed and wounded on the Union side and 25,500 for the Confederates. At Cold Harbor, Grant would suffer 7,000 casualties in less than thirty minutes, in an ill-conceived frontal attack on the dug-in Southerners. But although Northern casualties were almost twice that of the Southerners, Lee could not afford to fight such battles of attrition.[435]

While the two great armies were going head-to-head, there was another happening that would devastate Southern morale almost as much as the death of Jackson exactly one year and a day before. On May 11, in a spirited engagement, Jeb Stuart's cavalry ran up against that of Phil Sheridan, at an old abandoned inn called Yellow Tavern, six miles north of Richmond. Before the day was out, Mosby's commander—and close friend—would be mortally wounded by a single shot from the gun of a dismounted private of the 5th Michigan Cavalry.[436]

Mosby, in the meantime, had decided to expand his area of operations. Things were starting to happen over in the Shenandoah Valley since Sheridan had taken command of the Yankee cavalry and Grant had begun his offensive. With the increased challenges his Rangers were now facing, Mosby had decided on a new strategy to help combat them. He now had four companies, a large enough force that he could break it up into smaller groups; they would have increased expansiveness and at the same time, be more difficult to defend against or to capture.

The Shenandoah Valley, from Lexington in the south to Harper's Ferry in the north had, for all practical purposes, been in the possession of the Confederates since the outbreak of the war, three years before. There had been battles, some fairly significant, during Jackson's Valley Campaign in 1862; and Harper's Ferry had belonged to the Federals for a good bit of the time. Winchester had changed hands almost more than one could count. But all in all, the better part of the war had seen the Valley owned and controlled by the Confederacy. Continued control was vital to the South. Its vast fields of corn and grain, its voluminous orchards and lush grazing lands, with cattle and sheep abounding—all this meant busy mills and filled barns and storehouses for the hungry soldiers of Lee's army. But there were other reasons Lee could not afford to give up the Valley. Like the protection it provided for the Virginia Central Railroad at Staunton; and Staunton itself, with its huge stockpiles of material. And both sides were acutely aware of the Valley's use as a pathway to the north and Washington. Yes, the Valley was vital to Lee. Grant was determined to have it or destroy it.

The last of April, and through the first part of May, Grant put his plan into operation. Franz Sigel started up the Valley from Martinsburg, moving timidly, and finally, after three days, reached Winchester on May 1; he had covered less than twenty-five miles. But he was on his way toward his objective—the railhead and supply depot at Staunton, ninety miles away. Around the same time, General's Crook and Averell were on the march from West Virginia into mountainous Southwest Virginia. Averell was to capture the major saltworks at Saltville, while Crook's aim was the Virginia and Tennessee Railroad at Dublin and the destruction of the bridge across the New River at Narrows.They would then march north and hook up with Sigel at Staunton.

Soon after Sigel arrived in Winchester, Mosby assembled his command at Rectortown and issued plans and orders for the coming days. One of these plans involved splitting up the command into smaller parties. Captain Dolly Richards was to take about twenty-five men, and Lieutenant Sam Chapman an equal number, and cross the river into the Shenandoah Valley. On May 8, the two took their commands and marched to Paris, in preparation for crossing the Shenandoah. Just before they were to leave Paris, Captain William Chapman, who had been on a scout with a few men from his company, returned and was invited to go along. [437]

The detachmnt crossed the Shenandoah and collected themselves in a wood near Berry's Ferry. Here Richards left on a scout to determine the strength of some Yankee cavalry reported in the area. Before he returned, the impatient Sam Chapman, along with his brother, had taken off with their men to Millwood. Sam and Richards had agreed to meet further east on the Valley Turnpike, so when Richards returned from his scout, and could not find Sam, he left for the other rendezvous.

The Chapman brothers had been lying in wait for a Yankee scouting party from the 1st New York Cavalry. The scouts were known to travel the Winchester Turnpike between that town and Berryville each day. This knowledge proved to be correct; the next day William Chapman took twelve men and attacked a Union patrol of the same number, as the Yankees were stopping to plunder a dairy on their way into Berryville. Chapman was able to kill two, capture five, and collect eight horses.

After gathering his prisoners, William hurried back to where Sam was waiting, telling his brother that fellow members of the 1st New York would be in pursuit of him in a few minutes and they had better retreat with what they had. The word "retreat" did not suit Sam, even when it came from his brother. When a regiment of bluecoats appeared a few minutes later, Sam, ever spoiling for a fight, charged into their advance guard, driving it back on the rest of the regiment. Then and only then did he retreat, falling back to Millwood with the prisoners and a portion of the command, while William left in another direction with the rest. [438]

Sam Chapman wasn't through with the 1st New York Cavalry. When he found there were only seven troopers in pursuit of him and his small party, he saw another chance for a fight. (Mosby once described Sam "as the only man I ever saw who really enjoyed fighting, and who generally went into the fray with his hat in one hand and banging away with his revolver with the other.")[439]

Chapman proceeded to send his prisoners off with a few of his men and, with the remaining six, turned about and ordered a charge into his pursuers. But some of his men did not want the fight as bad as Sam, for in a few minutes he found himself nearly alone against the Federal cavalrymen; only Private "Doctor" Sowers had stayed with him. Not hesitating, Chapman charged all the way through his pursuers, who, it turned out, were only the advance guard of the regiment. Stopping on the opposite side of the road, Sam awaited the shots of the startled Yankees as they passed him, heading back to their main body. Even with the odds he now faced, he was able to shoot and wound three of the cavalrymen; both he and Sowers had their horses shot from under them, however. Now dismounted, they took refuge in a brier thicket until the regiment had passed. [440]

The Loudoun Rangers were organized in 1862, with most of the roster comprised of Union men from upper Loudoun County. The command was organized specifically to counteract the various guerrilla bands operating in Loudoun and Fauquier Counties prior to the arrival of Mosby and his Rangers. Their success against these early guerillas had been remarkably good but was quickly eroded with the formation of Mosby's command. The Loudoun Rangers were held in very low esteem by Mosby and his men, particularly for their plundering of farms in the area. [441]

On May 16, Captain Richards learned that Captain D. M. Keyes and about forty-five of his Loudoun Rangers had crossed the Potomac from Maryland into Loudoun County. Richards, with thirty men, started from Bloomfield and by nightfall was on their trail. Catching up to the Union loyalists the next day at Waterford, he was able to draw six of them out of the town to where his party was waiting. In the ensuing skirmish, only one managed to get away—three were wounded and two captured. Charging at the rest and chasing them through the town, Richards, without a single casualty, proceeded to rout the Loudoun County bunch, killing two, wounding four and taking five prisoners and fifteen horses. Five days later, Mosby and his group rejoined Richards in the Valley near Cedarville, a few miles north of Front Royal, on the Winchester Road. The partisan command now totaled about one hundred men. [442]

Pine Hills is a low range extending from the Shenandoah River in Warren County, through Clarke and Frederick Counties, and into West Virginia where it terminates. About two miles from Cedarville, an elevated point of the range, called Guard Hill, rises above Crooked Run. The Federals maintained a picket post on this prominence.[443]

Mosby took his partisans to within one-half mile of the post the night of May 21. Wanting more information on the enemy position, Mosby sent Lieutenants Joe Nelson and Sam Chapman to reconnoiter. Chapman came back reporting that the encampment, which normally had about seventy-five men, had been greatly reinforced; there was now at least double the cavalrymen, and what looked to be a company of infantrymen, positioned on the road that ran along the backbone of the thickly wooded hill. Upon hearing this news, Mosby quipped, "So much the better. Now we'll get two good horses apiece instead of one."[444]

Mosby ordered Chapman to take fifteen men, armed with carbines, on foot to the camp; the rest of the command, on horseback, followed. Sam and his group struck the camp firing and yelling "like Modec Indians", according to Private John H. Alexander. "Our impetuous captain (sic) rather over-did our part...Instead of merely flushing the enemy out," as was Mosby's plan, "we drove so many of them out of reach into the darkness that only about sixteen of them were overhauled. I think, though, that we secured nearly every horse on that post, numbering about seventy."[445]

Following the fight, an incident occurred that would nearly cost a Union officer his job and career; he asked the wrong question of the wrong man. The total of the Union force at Guard Hill was about 250 cavalry and fifty to sixty infantry. All of the command was not up on the crest of the hill, where Mosby attacked; part of it was encamped at the base of the hill, near the river flat. Captain Michael Auer, commanding Company A of the 15th New York Cavalry, rode up on the hill to inquire of the "disturbance", supposing that it was the repetition of some "rioting" that had occurred the previous night. Riding up to Chapman he asked what all the fuss meant. "It means that Mosby has got you," Sam replied. The shocked captain, with the whites of his eyes expanding, remarked, "Well, this beats hell, don't it?" Two days later, Auer was dismissed from the service for "having grossly neglected his duty while in command of pickets." The dismissal was subsequently overturned.[446]

PART VI

CALICO AND RED ROSES

16. Missing the Trains

When Major General Franz Sigel marched his army, part of the Department of West Virginia, into Winchester on May 1, 1864, he had assembled a full division of infantry, nearly a full division of cavalry, and five field batteries of twenty-two guns. His command totaled 6,500-9,000 men, depending on just who was asked; Sigel opted for the smaller figure. It had taken the little German three days to cover the twenty-two miles from Martinsburg to Winchester. He would not march out of the city until May 9. [447]

Sigel was about as incompetent as he was slow. A well-placed political appointee, with an up and down career—mostly down—he had his greatest success at Pea Ridge, Missouri in March of 1862. Since then he had not tasted victory, having been defeated in the Valley by Jackson and sharing in the Union defeat at Second Manassas. The latter resulted in his going on extended sick leave to preserve his place in the military hierarchy. But politics had put him back on top and in command of the Department of West Virginia. As such, he commanded nearly 25,000 men and 118 pieces of artillery; the Department encompassed the entire state of West Virginia, all of Maryland west of the Monacacy, and the Shenandoah Valley, with Loudoun County thrown in.

Sigel's mission was an important part of Grant's plan: march up the Valley, clearing it of insurgents as he went, and carry the necessary supplies up to Staunton; there he would rendezvous with General's Crook and Averell These two should be marching from southwestern Virginia, after striking the Virginia and Tennessee Railroad at Dublin, destroying the saltworks at Saltville and the bridge over the New River. [448]

On the evening of May 13, Sigel's troops were spotted between Mount Jackson and New Market. Two days later, his army would be three miles north of New Market at a landmark named Rude's Hill. It had taken six days to go the fifty miles from Winchester. It was clear General Sigel was not General Jackson when it came to the moving of armies. [449]

Two days after arriving with his army at Rude's Hill, Sigel was on his way back down the Valley Pike, in a rout that didn't stop until the retreating Federals had crossed the Shenandoah at Meem's Bottom, more than three miles away, and burned the bridge behind them. Major General John C. Breckinridge's Confederate army, with the help of the cadets from the Virginia Military Institute, had stopped Sigel in his tracks, at the Bushong farm a mile north of the town of New Market. Symbotically, it was the first anniversary of the funeral of Stonewall Jackson.

Meanwhile, in far southwestern Virginia, Crook had fought a vicious hand-to-hand battle with 2400 Southern troops under Brigadier General Albert G. Jenkins at Cloyd's Mountain, before breaking through and burning the Virginia and Tennessee Railroad bridge over the New River. But Grant had not had success with Lee in a fiery hell called the Wilderness and, when Crook learned of the defeat there, he abandoned the rest of his raid and turned back into West Virginia. Staunton—and the Valley—remained under Confederate control.[450]

Sigel's defeat cost him his career. It would cost the Shenandoah Valley much more. Sigel's replacement was a scowling, baggy eyed, mustached sixty-two-year-old major general by the name of David "Black Dave" Hunter. His nickname was not derived from the firey ruination he was to bring to the Valley, but rather was a cognomen from his early army days, due to his swarthy, Indian-like complexion and gray eyes, that dilated into blackness and brillancy under excitement. Dyeing his long mustache and wearing a dark brown wig under a black slouch hat, only enhanced these features. [451] The name would prove to be discriptively appropriate. Hunter would leave a trail of flame, smoke, howling babies, crying women, and wanton distruction, the likes of which the Valley could never have imagined. By the latter part of May, Hunter had replaced Sigel as commander of all Federal forces in the Valley.

Major Harry Gilmor had good reason to dislike Yankees. The twenty-six-year-old self-assured—some said egotistical, but not to his face—Rebel was descended from a prosperous Baltimore shipping and mercantile family of Scottish origin. He had been put in prison for two weeks while Maryland was under martial law and Baltimore was a hot spot for those many Marylanders who favored secession and the Confederate cause. Following his release, Gilmor had come to Virginia, where he was commissioned a captain in the 12th Virginia Cavalry. But he was again imprisoned in August,1862, after being captured outside Baltimore while visiting a friend. This time he was charged with being a spy and, although not prosecuted, spent five months locked up at Fort McHenry. After being exchanged, Gilmor was granted permission to raise a partisan command. It was with this command, the 2nd Maryland Cavalry, that an incident would later occur which helped to initiate a new and harsher kind of warfare on the inhabitants of the Shenandoah Valley. [452]

Following Sigel's defeat at New Market, guerrilla activity in the Valley seemed to take on a new life. Mosby, with his scattered bands, had only recently begun regular operations on the western side of the Blue Ridge. McNeill, who normally raided on the other side of the Alleghenies, in West Virginia, was coming into the Valley with his independent cavalry company. Liege White's Comanches were already in the Valley, as was Gilmor's independent command.

The 43rd Battalion, some 150 strong, left Rectortown on May 28; they bivouacked near Front Royal that night, and the next morning Sam Chapman introduced Mosby to a twenty-one year-old former comrade in the Warren Rifles named Charlie Richardson. Sam felt that Charlie, now a private in the 7th Virginia Cavalry, would be a good guide for the current expedition. [453]

The next day, the command crossed the Shenandoah, picked up the tracks of the Manassas Gap Railroad, which paralleled the North Fork of the river, and followed this route into Strasburg. Here they spent the day watching for Union activity up and down the Valley Turnpike. Not seeing any wagon trains or patrols small enough to take on, they waited until the next morning and rode into Middletown, fifteen miles south of Winchester. Passing through the village they continued on to Newtown, where they discovered the still smoldering remains of a Federal wagon train that had been captured and burned by Harry Gilmor and his partisans. They also saw a barn ablaze beyond the town, the work of Hunter's men.

The 15th New York Cavalry had eighty-three troopers, under the command of Lieutenant Colonel Augustus I. Root, escorting a train of sixteen wagons. They were heading for New Market where Hunter was headquartered with his army. The train was carrying mostly medical stores, intended for a large field hospital, along with some forage.

Gilmor had been watching the train from a thick wood at Bartonsville, three miles north of Newtown. Following the column until it reached Newtown, he and his fifty-three partisans attacked it from the rear, after which they divided and flanked it on both sides. At this point, "seeing that there was great danger of loosing my whole command, I fell back," is how Colonel Root described his cavalry's abandonment of the train, as they turned about and raced down the pike in the direction from which they had just come. Gilmor's men proceeded to set the train ablaze, with the exception of four wagons, which they took with them. Several prisoners were taken, including six officers on the way to report to their commands; Captain R. H. Brett of the 1st New York Veteran Cavalry was among the mortally wounded. It was May 29.[454]

The order that came down on May 30 from Hunter to Major Quinn, commander of the 1st New York Cavalry, was unequivocal: "You will detail from your command 200 men to proceed to Newtown tomorrow morning at 3 o'clock, for the purpose of burning every house, store, and outbuilding in that place, except the churches, and houses and outbuildings of those who are known to be loyal citizens of the United States. You will also burn the houses of all rebels between Newtown and Middletown...."[455]

When Major Joseph A. Stearns arrived in Newtown the next day, with a regiment of cavalry to carry out Hunter's order, he was met by a contingent of the town's leading citizens. They knew Hunter by his reputation; they also knew him through first hand experience. One week before, someone had fired on a wagon train just outside the village. Hunter had ordered the house, from which the shots were believed to have come, burned. He then issued one of his soon-to-be notorious proclamations: "For every train fired or soldier assassinated, the house and other property of every secession sympathizer residing within a circuit of five miles shall be destroyed by fire...."[456]

The townspeople begged for their homes and their town. They had no control over what the Confederates had done or would do, they pleaded, and had even cared for Union wounded after Gilmor had left. Stearns determined that he would face Hunter rather than do harm to the innocent people of Newtown; in turn, the townspeople took the oath of allegiance to the United States. For his actions, Stearns would later take a merciless verbal assault from the furious Hunter. Only David Strother, Hunter's chief of staff, saved Stearns from dismissal from the army for disobedience of orders.[457]

Sam Chapman and Mosby's newest scout, Charlie Richardson, had spied a wagon train near Fisher's Hill, heading south. The train was one of Hunter's, enroute to New Market. Chapman and about twenty-five men were ordered to move around the cavalry escort and capture the wagons while Mosby and his men attacked the column from the front; Dolly Richards was to come in on the rear. When Mosby's men charged, the cavalry beat a hasty retreat, and when Richards attacked he found, to his surprise, that he was facing one hundred infantrymen lined up along a stone fence just off the road. In an attempt to turn the men around, Private William Embrey was shot and killed and another Ranger wounded. Meanwhile, as someone shouted "Mosby! Mosby!", the cavalry escort turned and raced pell-mell back down the pike, leaving Chapman in a good position to capture the wagons. Instead, seeing the fleeing escort heading toward him, Sam could not resist; he charged at them in return, turning them around and driving them back upon their infantry support. This allowed the wagons to speed away, part of them back down the pike toward Winchester and the rest in the opposite direction. Chapman's men managed to kill several of the Yankee cavalrymen and wound three, but much to Mosby's dismay, the wagon train he thought should have been captured had been allowed to escape. Sam Chapman, when it came to a decision between a capture and a fight, well....[458]

War can have its humorous side amid the inevitable death and devastation. On June 1, Dolly Richards and twenty-five men were hiding out along the double tracks of the Baltimore and Ohio Railroad between Kearnysville and Duffield Station; their orders were to capture the westbound express that ran out of Baltimore. With darkness approaching, the Rangers quietly slipped down to the tracks and observed that one set of rails was old and the other newer. Having information that the westbound train would be on the newer track, Richards instructed the men to tear up that set of rails. He divided his command into parties for boarding the train and waited. Soon the Baltimore express came hissing down the track and when it got to the place at which the Rangers had torn up the rails, the train roared right on by—on the undisturbed rails. Many a hearty laugh was heard at Richards' expense, not only that night, but on many an occasion afterwards. [459]

Despite the best efforts of the partisan groups, Hunter's army was picking up steam as it marched up the Valley toward Staunton. True, the attacks on his wagon trains had required him to draw men off from his columns to provide escorts and protection for the trains. Still, with his army of 8500 men, and an unlimited supply base, Hunter had reached Harrisonburg, twenty-seven miles north of Staunton, by June 3.[460]

On June 8, a Yankee scouting party from Colonel Lowell's Fairfax command, captured Privates George and James Gunnell at their home at Gum Spring in Loudoun County. Also picked up with the two brothers was another member of Mosby's command, Private Charles Fenton Beavers. The three prisoners were sent to Old Capitol Prison in Washington, D.C. On September 20, the Gunnells were transferred to the prison at Fort Warren, in Boston Harbor, where they would stay until paroled on June 12, 1865, a month after Lee's surrender. Beavers would not be so fortunate.

Fenton Beavers was a private in the 43rd Battalion when he surrendered to the Federals on Christmas Day of 1863. Two months later he took the oath of allegiance to the United States and was released. However, according to Colonel Lowell's report, "Beavers is the same man who feigned desertion from Mosby some two months ago, and, after taking the amnesty oath and spying around Alexandria and Vienna, returned to the enemy." Tried and convicted of violating the oath and of spying, Fenton Beavers was hanged on August 28, 1864. He was twenty-one years old.[461]

Francis Harrison Pierpont was as strong a loyalist as the Union could ever hope to find. A hard-line anti-slavery, anti-secessionist supporter of Abraham Lincoln, he was a lawyer with the Baltimore and Ohio Railroad and became governor of the "pretended" state government. The government was formed in the counties of western Virginia, which were in sympathy with the North, and was moved to Alexandria after that area was occupied by Federal troops.

The same day the Gunnell brothers were captured, thirty-five picked men, including Sam Chapman, gathered with Mosby at Rectortown. Mosby had a plan, similar to the one that had resulted in the capture of General Stoughton at Fairfax. This time the target was Pierpont. Mosby's well-laid plan was such: two men would wait on Telegraph Road, outside Alexandria, with a covered wagon. To take the picket off guard they would claim admittance as a market wagon. Securing the picket, the first group of men, with Mosby, would go after the Pierpont; Captain Richards would look for Brigadier General John Potts Slough, the military governor of Alexandria. Sam Chapman would lead the third group, whose task it was to "requisition" as many horses as possible from the government stables.

From the beginning things did not go as planned. The guide for the party got lost and failed to keep the scheduled rendezvous, which cost the raiders the nercessary darkness. So while the men whiled away the hours the next day, again awaiting darkness, Mosby was informed that the plot had been discovered and that a rude reception was being prepared for him that night. The raid, of course, was called off and the Rangers returned to the safety of the Debatable Land. [462] The best made plans of mice and men....

June 22, 1864, was a day for taking care of pressing administrative business within the command. It was also the day that the battalion would observe its first roll call, with 200 men answering to their names. Bothered by the capture of several of the Rangers while off duty and outside the confines of his "Confederacy," Mosby, in a General Order, reiterated the boundaries within which his men were to reside when not on duty. The bounds of this region were:

> From Snickersville, along the Blue Ridge Mountains to
> Linden, thence to Salem, to the Plains and then along the
> Bull Run Mountains to Aldie, and from there along the
> turnpike to the place of beginning, Snickersville. This
> area had approximately two hundred and twenty-five
> square miles and was contained in parts of two counties
> —Lower Loudoun and Upper Fauquier. Its geographical
> center was Rector's Cross Roads near the Fauquier
> and Loudoun County line. No member was to leave
> these bounds without permission. A roll was to be
> taken at each meeting and the missing of two successive
> meetings would result in transfer to the regular service. [463]

Following the roll call and other business, the command set out for Fairfax County, reaching White Plains and camping on the eastern side of Thoroughfare Gap for the night. The next morning, they were near Centreville, when one of the scouts brought information that a patrol of the 16th New York Cavalry was in the town. By the time the Rangers got there, the Yankees had gone; however, about one and a half miles beyond the village the partisans ran upon the column feeding their horses in a field. The New Yorkers, numbering about forty, were led by a Lieutenant Tuck. Since a portion of Mosby's command had previously been detached, he charged in on the unsuspecting cavalrymen with about sixty men. "Our party made no stand, and Lieutenant Tuck reports his men as appearing demoralized and panic stricken, scattering in all directions," according to a report of the affair filed by the brigade commander, Colonel Lowell. "Lieutenant Tuck is the only one of the party who has yet (6 p.m.) reached camp, the remainder being either wounded, prisoners, or straggling....I have considered it useless to start in direct pursuit of Mosby...." Mosby reported killing and wounding six and capturing thirty-one men and thirty-eight horses. [464]

The mountain howitzer was back. Well, not *the* howitzer, but another 12-pounder, recently arrived from Richmond, that would permit the old one to be there in spirit at least. On June 29, taking the howitzer and companies B, C, and D, Mosby rode to Duffield Station on the Baltimore and Ohio, with the intention of capturing a train. Sam Chapman, again in charge of the artillery, situated the gun on an eminence, a quarter of a mile away from the Federal garrison stationed there. Mosby then sent Captain Richards, with a flag of truce, to see the commanding officer, demanding his surrender. The lieutenant in charge asked Richards what would be the conditions of the surrender. He was told there were no conditions, but that he could see the attacking force if he so desired. After doing so, the capitulation was effected.

Around two o'clock, Chapman moved the howitzer to a new position where it could command the approaching train. The telegraph wires between Harper's Ferry and Martinsburg were cut and the attackers waited. After about an hour, Mosby assumed the train had already gone by, so he ordered the taking of the stores and the destruction of any that were not wanted. In his report of the incident, Mosby says: "We took Duffield's Depot...secured about 50 prisoners, including 2 lieutenants and a large amount of stores...." The raiders then set fire to the camp and the storehouses. What Mosby did not realize was the train had not passed—it was simply running late. [465]

The reports going back and forth through the Union command speak directly to the confusion that forces such as Mosby's were able to create. These began the evening of June 29, a few hours after Mosby captured the station:

> From the President of B&O RR to General Max Weber – Our
> mail train east passed Sir John's Run about 1 this p.m. and
> has not arrived at Harper's Ferry at 7...is it possible our
> trains may have been attacked. Can you inform us what are
> the facts? Is there a considerable force? I trust your arrange-
> ments are such that you will succeed in capturing the
> party. Our telegraphic communication west of Harper's
> Ferry was broken at 2 this p.m....

> G. J. Lawrence (rank unknown), Headquarters, Harper's
> Ferry, to Major T. Eckert Washington, D. C. – Gilmer (sic)

attacked our forces at Duffield's Station today...cut the wires; no communication west.

Colonel L. B. Pierce, Bolivar Heights to Captain Burleigh, Assistant Adjutant-General – Sergeant Rhodes returned to Duffield's and states that all the damage done there was the robbing of the store, and the burning of the shanties belonging to the infantry...who were all captured.

Lieutenant Colonel Gatch, Commanding at Kearneysville to Major Meysenburg, Assistant Adjutant-General – An escaped prisoner from Duffield's reports that from 500 to 800 rebel cavalry and infantry made their appearance there at about 1 this p.m. and captured the place. They have a battery of at least four guns. Mosby is in command.

General Weber to President of B&O Railroad – The enemy appeared in force...about 1 o'clock today...the wires were cut...the rebels appeared under a flag of truce...you express a hope that I may capture the party, but will not be surprised that I answer I fear not, when I tell you my whole force consists of 108 cavalrymen; the forces of the enemy are between 500 and 600.

General Weber to Major Meysenburg – information was received that the enemy had routed our men; had plundered and burned the camp, stores, and store-houses at Duffield's... the force of the enemy was not far from 400 men, with two pieces of artillery. [466]

The partisans returned home the last day of the month from what would come to be known as "The First Calico Raid." A lady of the area, after congratulating the guerrilla chieftain on his success, said that she understood that a large quanity of calico cloth had been captured. This being an item in short supply, she inquired as to his selling her some cheap, to which Mosby is reported to have responded, rather curtly, "Madam, you have mistaken my profession; I am a soldier." [467]

From Tee Edmonds' diary: "Mosby returned off a very successful raid yesterday having captured Duffield Depot, near Harper's Ferry, routing the

Yankees with several prisoners and as much goods as the soldiers could carry off. They were jubilant at their success...I am thankful they all returned safely home, unhurt, better than to capture the whole North and its trash." [468]

17. A Chance Lost

July came in with a heat that was stifling; before it would go out, some of the Rangers and many of the bluecoats would think it was more akin to Dante's inferno.

In the noonday sun of Sunday, July 3, between 200 and 250 men of the 43rd assembled at Upperville. They had with them their "new howitzer", the recently acquired 12-pound Napoleon. Marching at a leisurely pace because of the heat, the command camped that night at Wheatland, not far from the Potomac. By noon of July 4, they were opposite Berlin, Maryland; they proceeded a short distance down stream to a crossing, just about a mile from Point of Rocks, on the opposite shore. Mosby and a guide entered the water and went less than half way across before being fired on by some sharp-shooters hiding in the bushes on the other side. A force of cavalry was also lined up near the town.

After some short but brisk fire from both sides, Sam Chapman brought the Napoleon up to a position on a hill where it commanded the town on the opposite shore. Supported by some men of Company C, with carbines, Chapman sent a shell into the bushes from where the shots had been fired. This, and a second shot, quieted things down a bit, at least enough to permit the companies to cross, first to a small island, amid-stream, and then to the other bank. Some more fire from the Federals prompted Chapman to send another shell in their direction and the shooters could be seen running back up the towpath. [469]

The small village of Point of Rocks was important as a supply depot, situated as it was on the Potomac River and the Baltimore and Ohio Railroad, twelve miles east of Harper's Ferry; it served as the eastern terminus of a forty-four mile section of double track. Alongside the railroad, but separated by a fence, ran the Chesapeake and Ohio Canal with its towpath and barge traffic. Garrisoned in the town to protect these environs were two infantry companies, supplemented by two companies of the Loudoun Rangers commanded by the partisan's old nemesis' Captains D.M. Keyes and James Grubb.

Mosby and his column marched down the towpath until they reached a small bridge that crossed the canal into the town. After tearing out the floor of the bridge, the enemy situated themselves in a small rifle pit above the bridge.

While the partisans worked to repair the bridge, some of the men dismounted and went across on the timbers, driving the Federals from their entrenchment at the rifle pit. The rest of the command rode across when the floor was repaired, and the Loudoun Rangers were seen fleeing in the direction of Frederick while the infantrymen skedaddled to the nearby mountains.

After the Federals vacated the town, Mosby's men entered and went to work on the telegraph poles and wires, cutting both and breaking communications with Harper's Ferry. During this time a train passed by on the tracks adjacent to the canal. Lieutenant Chapman was still on the Virginia side of the river with the little howitzer and fired a shot, missing the train but causing it to back up the track. Meanwhile, the rest of the command was in the process of plundering the village and one of the items in demand was calico—keeping in mind that almost any dry-goods article of cloth was referred to as calico by the Rangers. Thus, this raid would become known as "The Second Calico Raid." [470]

After setting fire to the enemy camp, the Rangers crossed the river, back into Virginia, late on July 4; they spent most of the following day making demonstrations as if to re-cross into Maryland. The enemy was, at the same time, reinforcing the town and information was received that 200 cavalrymen and two companies of infantry were now in the village. Attired in confiscated bonnets, crinoline, and most every other imaginable article of apparel, it was a colorful, however strange, looking conglomerate of "calico rangers" that started back down the road toward Waterford.

Learning that a fairly large force of Union cavalry was at Leesburg, Mosby had taken a wide circuitous route to bring him near Waterford, where the command spent the night. The enemy force reportedly in Leesburg was commanded by the most-able Major William H. Forbes and consisted of portions of the 2nd Massachusetts and 13th New York, totaling about 250 men. Mosby on the other hand had only about 150 Rangers, due to a large number of the men returning to their homes following the raid at Point of Rocks. In addition to the size of Forbes' force, it was also reported by some scouts that Forbes knew of the recent raid and was spreading the word among the residents of Leesburg that he had Mosby in a box and would spring the trap on him the next day.

The morning of July 6, Mosby took his command and headed for Leesburg only to find that Forbes had already left, taking the road to Aldie. Mosby,

oping to cut him off and get between Forbes and his base at Fairfax, went
: a gallop toward the ford at Ball's Mill on Goose Creek, only to find the
ederal column had gotten there and crossed ahead of him. [471]

1ount Zion Church sits two miles east of Aldie on the Little River Turn-
ike. It was here that Mosby met with his first little band, the detachment
om the 1st Virginia Cavalry, fifteen months before, and set off on his ini-
al raids. Now it would be the scene of a major confrontation between his
attalion and the Federal cavalry under Major Forbes.

aking a short cut from Ball's Mill to Mount Zion Church, Mosby managed
o finally get in front of Forbes. Sam Chapman was ordered to set the cannon
t the road, while carbineers were deployed in the wood to Chapman's left.
he rest of the command was disposed so that they could charge the enemy
fter the first shots were fired. When Forbes column came in sight on the
urnpike, the little gun let loose with a shell that fell far short of the target.
he Federals formed in a field near a house belonging to a family named
kinner. The Rangers charged with a yell, to the front and on the flank of the
nemy, firing their six-shooters with effect. [472] The attack was described by
'harles Humphreys, a chaplain in Forbes' command: "Mosby and his rang-
rs were upon us, swooping down like Indians, yelling like fiends, dis-
harging their pistols with fearful rapidity, and threatening to completely en-
elop our little band." [473] The Yankees were unable to withstand this assault
nd broke and ran some distance to a fence, where they turned and formed
gain. It was of little use. The Rangers drove into them once more, this time
vith such unfettered fierceness that the bluecoats had no time to run. The
ght became one of hand-to-hand, sabre-to-sabre, revolver-to-revolver com-
at at point blank ranges. Chaplain Humphreys' first-hand account recalls
ie frightening fight from the Union side: "No words can picture the confu-
ion and horror of that scene—horses madly leaping in the pangs of death,
ders crushed beneath their ruthless feet; then the panic-stricken crowd gal-
oping over their fallen companions, and closely followed by the insolent
oe; here and there a rally, as some brave spirit, scorning defeat, inspired a
ttle courage in his companions and turned to face the enemy—but only to
ie." [474]

1ajor Forbes was astride his horse in the middle of the fray. He stood in the
tirrups, much as Sam Chapman had done at Miskel's, thrusting his sword at
nyone within range. Tom Richards, who had been wounded and captured in
ie fight at Warrenton Junction, felt the searing pain of cold steel as Forbes'

sabre drove into his shoulder. At the same time, Richards pulled the trigger of his revolver in the face of Forbes; the only sound was a click. Suddenly, a bullet ripped into Forbes' horse, sending both horse and rider to the ground with the major pinned underneath. One of his lieutenants fell wounded beside him and both men were forced to surrender. So vicious and close was the fighting that Willie Martin, like Richards, a former prisoner from the Warrenton Junction fight, was clubbed into insensibility by a Yankee cavalryman.

After Forbes and the lieutenant fell, the remainder of the command fled in a rout, with the Rangers at their heels. The chase lasted for some ten miles and well into the afternoon. When it was finally over, the dead and wounded littered the road and the field. The Skinner house was turned into a hospital and Doctor Will Dunn, Mosby's surgeon, treated men from both sides. [475]

The Rebels came out of the fight with seven men wounded, one mortally. For the Federals it was a far more tragic story: 17 killed, 40 wounded, 12 to 15 mortally, and 57 taken prisoner. Over 100 were captured and a dozen more were left dead on the field.

The severity of the fight at Mount Zion Church, and its pathetic aftermath, can be found in the recollections of John Henry Alexander, a seventeen-year-old partisan private in Company B: "I was placed on picket in the road below the (Skinner) house for the few hours we remained after the fight. I have never had as bad a two hours as I had that night. The groans of the wounded men and horses, the pitiful calls for relief, the prayers, the heart-rending laments for loved ones, were borne to me on the quiet summer night...To hear a poor fellow calling for water, or for someone to move his dead horse off his broken leg, or to raise his head and let him die in peace, was an awful trial...." [476] Less than four weeks later, Alexander would receive a head wound in a fight near Adamstown, Maryland.

The Rangers finally departed about midnight for Middleburg. Colonel Lowell, Forbes' commander, arrived the next day to bury the Federal dead and carry off the wounded. His report stated that only forty-five men of Forbes' command got back to camp alive. He added: "I think the chance was an excellent one to whip Mosby and take his gun. I have no doubt Major Forbes thought so too, as the wounded men say there was not enough difference in numbers to talk about. The chance was lost." [477]

'or Mosby, he had once again turned on a superior force and came away
ictorious. The frustration of the Union commanders could be seen in their
eports, which seemed to have a familiar ring following each fight with the
artisans.

A couple of days after the Mount Zion Church fight, the 43rd met at Upper-
ille. Once again Mosby took them in the direction of the Potomac, but fur-
her down stream, near Leesburg. They crossed the river at Conrad's Ferry
nd marched on into Poolesville, Maryland. There was thought to be a camp
f the 8th Illinois Cavalry a little further on, between Seneca Mills and
Muddy Branch. However, when the Rangers arrived there, they found the
amp had been hurriedly abandoned; tents were left standing with forage and
amp equipage scattered about. These were burned, along with a large
lockhouse and a frame building connected with the camp, by the raiders.
About thirty head of beef cattle, left behind by the Illinoisans, were rounded
p and taken back to Virginia. The Union detachment had apparently been
ummoned to the defenses around Washington in the wake of General Jubal
Early's threat to that city. [478]

A side-note to the capture of Major Forbes during the Mount Zion fight is
ound in a letter Mosby wrote to Sam Chapman's son, Willie, in San Fran-
isco years after the war: "Do you ever see or hear of the Forbes'? I enclose
ou my card of introduction to Cameron Forbes of the Philippines. He is a
on of Major Forbes of Boston, whom we captured. His family have been
ny warm friends ever since the War. I recently had a letter from his sister,
Edith." Then a post-script: "Just before I went to Hong Kong, your father
and I dined at the Arlington with Major Wm. H. Forbes (whom we captured,
he father of Cameron.) One of my men took Major Forbes' watch when he
vas a prisoner. Your father took it from the man and gave it back to Forbes.
After I returned from Hong Kong Forbes gave me a banquet in Boston. Then
met Mrs. Forbes, her daughter, Edith, & one of her sons at the Palace Hotel
San Francisco) in 1900 & dined twice with them.")[479]

18. Wedding Bells and Captain's Bars

Colonel Mosby had learned of General Early's plan to invade Maryland after returning from the raid on the Duffield depot. Mosby had run into one of Early's quartermasters who was passing through Rectortown on his way to join the general at Winchester. This accidental meeting was what precipitated the Point of Rocks raid—Mosby wanted to cut communications along that line to protect Early's movements into the region. Following the raid, Mosby sent Lieutenant Beattie and Private Henry Heaton with a message to Early. The two caught up with the general at Sharpsburg, Maryland and delivered Mosby's dispatch. In it, the partisan chief had given Early all the information he had about the number and distribution of Union troops east of the Blue Ridge.[480]

Early, in his memoir of the Valley campaign, alleged that he had sent a message back to Mosby from Sharpsburg, asking him to cut the railroad and telegraph on the northern side of the Potomac below Harper's Ferry and advise him of any information on the enemy east of the ridge. "He never crossed the river, and I received no information from him," Early wrote.[481]

Heaton and Beattie returned with a message from Early; this message could not have been requesting what Early was maintaining, because Early already had this information; this was the very reason the two envoys of Mosby's had gone to Early in the first place. The message Early sent back, according to Mosby, was that he, Early, was going to take his army on to Washington, after taking the enemy off Maryland Heights, overlooking Harper's Ferry. However, Early later abandoned the Maryland Heights idea, opting instead to take his army further north, through Boonesboro, and back toward Washington by way of Frederick. He neglected to advise Mosby of this change in plans.[482]

By July 14, Early had withdrawn from in front of the Washington defenses, recrossed the Potomac at White's Ford, and was resting near Leesburg. His grand march on Washington had gotten him to the very gates of the Capitol, but with reinforcements sent by Grant from Petersburg, any attempt to take the city was doomed to failure. Early's time schedule had been upset by a major skirmish at Frederick City on July 7, followed by an even larger fight at Monocacy on July 9. These delays had allowed time for the troops of the

XI and XIX Corps to come by steamship from Petersburg to the defenses around the city. [483]

General Hunter was returning to the war. The previous month, he had advanced his army up the Valley, taken Staunton, and moved on to the rail and supply center at Lynchburg. But here things had bogged down for Black Dave and he was unable to strike a match and make it all better. He not only failed to take Lynchburg, he had hardly fought at all. And then, under cover of darkness, amid the whistles and rattling of Early's phantom troop trains, Hunter withdrew his army. [484] Ten days later he wired Washington from Gauley, West Virginia, some 150 miles away. Perhaps Hunter had inhaled a little too much of the smoke from his senseless burnings, for he told his superiors that "...his campaign into Virginia had been extremely successful, inflicting great injury upon the enemy." Hunter would not stop running until he reached Charleston, only seventy-five miles from the Ohio border. Not only had he withdrawn from Lynchburg—he and his army of 20,000 had withdrawn from the war. Confederate general, John B. Gordon, in his memoirs, gives this assessment of Hunter's flight: "If I were asked for an opinion as to this utterly causeless fright and flight, I should be tempted to say that conscience, the inward monitor which 'makes cowards of us all,' was harrowing General Hunter, and causing him to see an avenger wrapped in every gray jacket before him." [485]

Hunter had taken his army and traversed the new State of West Virginia— twice. First, when he left Lynchburg and went to Charleston by way of Lewisburg and Gauley and then again from Charleston, back across to the northeast corner at Harper's Ferry. He had marched his men nearly 500 miles, over some of the most difficult mountain terrain in the East, since pulling his army from in front of Lynchburg in the darkness of June 18-19. After leaving Lynchburg, Hunter would fight only one time during the entire expedition—at Hanging Rock, on June 21. "Tiger John" McCausland's Confederate cavalry caught up with the rear of his wagon train as it started over Catawba Mountain, just west of Salem, in Roanoke County. Then he was gone. Until now.

On July 14, Grant was advised: "No news from Hunter, nor do we know where he is; at our last advices he was at Parkersburg." But Hunter showed up at Harper's Ferry later that day, the same day Early was resting his troops at Leesburg. The next day, Grant wired Major General Halleck, the army's chief of staff, in Washington, that "Hunter should make all the Valley south of the Baltimore and Ohio Railroad a desert as high up as possible. I do not mean that houses should be burned, but all provisions and stock should be removed and the people notified to move out." Then he added, "Your troops (are to) eat out Virginia clear and clean as far as they go, so that crows flying over...will have to carry their provender with them." [486]

On July 16, Early, despite Hunter's attempts to stop him, passed through the Blue Ridge at Snicker's Gap and entered the Shenandoah Valley east of Berryville. Here he met with Mosby, with the partisan chief offering Early complete cooperation, in anything that the general might need, within Mosby's ability to comply. Early failed to take advantage of the offer and Mosby operated for the next four months, while Early was in the Valley, without direction or assistance from Old Jubal. Ironically, during this meeting, Early presented Mosby with a small rifled cannon, while complimenting him on the energy and bravery of his command. [487]

The Rangers continued to harass the Yankees, who were now in the Valley trying to get to Early. Mosby broke his command up into several smaller parties, commanded by Captains Richards and Chapman, and Lieutenants Glascock, Nelson, and Hatcher and crossed into Maryland. Near Monocacy, Hatcher encountered a Federal cavalry detachment and attacked it, taking fifteen prisoners and killing and wounding an undetermined number. In all, the parties returned to Virginia with between twenty and thirty prisoners and about seventy-five horses. On July 18, near Snickersville, Richards and ten of his men struck a column of Federal cavalry, and in the ensuing skirmish, killed five, wounded two, and captured four; also taken were eleven horses with all their equipment. [488]

There is a corner of real estate, a little northwest of Paris, where the counties of Loudoun, Fauquier, and Clarke unite. Located in Ashby's Gap, it once was marked with a well-known landmark, the "Big Poplar" tree. The French general, Alfred N. Duffie, had replaced Stahel as Hunter's chief of cavalry six weeks before. He had posted a squadron of the 20th Pennsylvania, under Captain Montgomery here, to guard the Gap and the Federal night camp at Paris. Captain Chapman divided his company and, with Lieutenant Fox, was able to sneak upon the picket and capture two officers, fifty enlisted men and fifty-five horses; several of the enemy were killed and wounded. The raiders then raced through Paris, causing a great confusion, enabling them to take more prisoners and inflict additional casualties.

In Paris, General Duffie was aroused from his bed and attempted to gain control of the situation, shouting out orders, one of which was "all prisoners captured will be shot." Lieutenant Matthew Magner was the only Rebel captured and as he was being prepared for execution, one of the townspeople convinced the General that the soldier was not one of Mosby's men but belonged to another command; the Lieutenant had papers on his person from his former unit, the 6th Virginia Cavalry. He was sent to Harper's Ferry as a prisoner of war, but escaped on August 6. The Rangers lost one other man, not from enemy fire but from being thrown from his horse in the charge. He died several days later from his injuries. [489]

Tee Edmonds diary entry for July19 related: "Captain Chapman made a brilliant capture this evening at Ashby's Gap...capturing thirty-two, and forty horses...Mr. Magner was captured last night after leaving here." Magner was a frequent visitor and guest at Belle Grove and was thought to be one of Tee's more serious beaus. (He is mentioned at least thirty times in her wartime diary). He left the area after the war, returning to his native Mississippi, where he died of cholera in 1866. [490]

General Duffie, in his report, had this to say regarding the attack on the picket post: "I regret to report that through the shameful mismanagement and neglect of the officer in command...one squadron...was captured by Mosby's guerrillas, with all their horses, arms, and equipments. I have recommended the officer commanding this squadron for dismissal." [491]

While Duffie's cavalry was in the vicinity they were able to capture five of Mosby's men near Upperville. They also took about fifty horses, some of which formerly belonged to the 20th Pennsylvania. During this time, one Ranger was killed. Duffie's horses had been without forage since leaving Snicker's Gap two days before; the foraging parties that were sent out "were much annoyed by detachments of Mosby's guerrillas." The Yankee command, apparently upset over the disgraceful defeat Mosby had handed them, and the constant harassment they incurred, took their anger out on some unfortunate citizens along the road from Paris to Snickersville. The women of the area were to suffer the most. In addition to the personal attacks, the Yankee cavalrymen broke up furniture, killed stock, and stole provisions and wearing apparel. [492]

Hunter had wasted little time in carrying out Grant's orders of July 15. The only problem was he got it backwards. Grant had said, "I do not mean that houses should be burned..." Hunter burned houses. He had received the re-layed order from Halleck on July 17 and the same day he burned the home of his first cousin, Andrew Hunter of Charlestown. There was no reason for this, except that the prominent lawyer had prosecuted, on behalf of the United States, John Brown, for treason following his raid on Harper's Ferry in 1859. Soon after, Hunter set the torch to the home of Edmund Lee, a dis-tant cousin of Robert E. Lee; Edmund Lee had given refuge from the war to Hunter's own niece, Helen.[493] On July 18, John Garrett, president of the B&O Railroad, wired Secretary of War Stanton that one of Garrett's engi-neers at Harper's Ferry reported: "(Hunter) stated that he had burned An-drew Hunter's residence at Charlestown, and had given orders to burn Faulkner's house at Martinsburg, and that it is his intention if he finds guer-rillas at Charlestown to burn that town; and as Clarke County only polled two votes against the ordinance of secession, he will burn every house in the county."[494]

General Horatio Wright, commanding the Federal XI Corps, had been or-dered to take his 10,000-man army and pursue Early into Virginia and be-yond, as long as there was a chance of catching him. When Early slipped through Snicker's Gap and then fought off the pursuing Federals across the Shenandoah River, the XI Corps was ordered back to Washington; Grant wanted the army with him at Petersburg. As a result, the roads and the gaps were choked with the long blue lines. There seemed to be no end.

On the night of July 20, Mosby's men were in rear of what they thought was only a large wagon train, but could not understand the direction in which it was traveling. Sam Chapman crept out to the roadside and concealed himself in the bush to observe the train go by, attempting to make some sense of it. Flankers were riding on either side of the road and came close enough to Chapman for him to have reached out and touched them. The infantry was randomly firing into the roadside brush as it passed by and things got a little close for the hidden observer. The Rangers tried several times to cross the road, but the train seemed to just go on and on. Then, with the coming of daylight, they realized it was Wright's XI Corps on the way back to Wash-ington. The partisans decided to work on the rear of the column, harassing it and picking up stragglers.

Lieutenant Hatcher was sent off with fifteen men, while the rest of the com-mand rested the horses, and would soon follow. When they caught up with Hatcher along the turnpike, they found that he had picked up eighty-three prisoners—stragglers and men with broken down horses—from the rear of the long blue column. The battalion then moved along toward Purcellville, observing the evidence of Wright's large force having passed through the countryside—broken fences, trampled down cornfields, skins of hogs and calves, and feathers and heads of poultry, all scattered about. A few more stragglers were picked up and when Mosby arrived back in Fauquier he had 104 prisoners. [495]

The Yankees had invaded the Debatable Land with numbers never seen before. True, a lot of the bluecoats were actually withdrawing, instead of invading, but they had first come as the invaders. In order to be most effective against these hordes, Mosby again divided up his command into smaller groups. One party of twenty men, under Sam Chapman, was sent to Bunker Hill, near Winchester, to capture a picket post. At the same time Mosby took twenty men and proceeded toward Martinsburg, and Captain Richards, with ninety men rode toward Winchester. The three parties all returned safely, but with very little to show for their trouble. They started right away for home, with their few prisoners and few horses, to take a much-needed rest. [496]

Sam Chapman was glad to be back in Salem. Although he enjoyed the exciting life of the partisan and seemed to relish the inherent dangers that accompanied it, he had something else on his mind these days. In fact, it had been on his mind for quite awhile. "Something else" was Miss Rebecca Elgin.

After Sam left "Miss Beck" at Salem the previous summer and had written her his letter of good-bye from Yorkdale, he had tried to put her memory behind him. It was difficult to do, however, what with the war in a lull following Gettysburg and him back in the artillery at Orange. Things were pretty dull and routine then, a whole lifetime removed from the days with Mosby— Chantilly, Warrenton Junction, Miskel, and of course Grapewood Farm. So there was plenty of time to think, and thinking, at least about Salem and Rebecca, was something he could have done very well without. But then, when he went to Petersburg and was busy on the courts-martial detail, things got easier in this regard; there just wasn't that much time for such thoughts.

It may have been easier to avoid the thoughts—if Sam had wanted to avoid them. But he didn't. And on top of that, in November, he had again written to her; not the kind of letter he had written her from Yorkdale, but one that was, well, kind of self-assured and less intense; a comfortable letter. It was optimistic—like red roses just beginning to break their buds in the spring—and bright with promise. He wrote of the war and of his hope for the country in the coming months, of his duties, his comrades, the resurgence of his religious faith while at Orange; all these things were on his mind. He did not write of the things that were still on his heart.

When Rebecca had received Sam's "good-bye" letter that June, she knew she would probably never see him again. A great sadness seemed to overwhelm her then. No matter what she tried to do to escape her thoughts of him, they were always there. But then, when the letter came from Petersburg in November, the loneliness of those five months seemed to disappear. No longer did she run from her memories; she ran to them, trying to live every single one again in her mind. And after what seemed an eternity, the next letter came just after Christmas.

Rebecca had written to Sam after she received his November letter. She tried to keep it light and cheerful, as he had, and she thought she had done this very well. But it was difficult to hold back all she wanted to say to him. And his next letter to her was very much as the previous one—cheerful and non-committal—but no matter, she was glad just to hear from him and know that he was well.

The knock on the door that early February morning awoke everyone—Rebecca, her mother, Mr. Murray. They figured it must be the Yankees again, looking for deserters, and Mosby's men, whichever they could find. They had been there before and, just like before, they would not find anything. Mrs. Murray had opened the door and Rebecca heard her exclaim: "Sam!" and again "Sam!"

The months following Sam's return as Mosby's adjutant, he and Rebecca had been together as much as the war would allow. They had talked of many things and one of these was marriage. He had not asked her again. It just seemed to have come from a mutual understanding. They had settled on July for no particular reason—except perhaps because Rebecca liked red roses and Salem was usually bursting with red roses in July. So, Mosby and the war and the Yankees all permitting, July it would be.

(Authors note: Exactly what transpired between Sam Chapman and Rebecca Elgin, from the time of his letter in June 1863 and his return to Salem in February, 1864, is not known. Therefore, the events related in the last few paragraphs are to a degree supposition, although it is reasonable to assume that correspondence of some sort was exchanged, considering the resulting turnabout in their relationship.)

The morning of Thursday, July 28, gave every indication of being another hot mid-summer day in the town of Salem. There wasn't the slightest hint of a breeze and no clouds had yet formed to interfere with the hastily heating rays of the sun. Situated as it was, on the main line of the once busy Manassas Gap Railroad, which ran from Fairfax County into the Shenandoah Valley, the village of 300 residents was constantly astir, with its five stores and a learning academy along the half-mile Main Street. Additionally, several churches and some forty homes took up space in the village. One of these homes was occupied by William Murray, the fifty-seven-year-old gentleman stock-dealer, his wife, Catherine, and stepdaughter, Rebecca.[497]

The Murray home stood on Lot 36 on the south side of Main Street, near the center of the village. It was not owned by Murray, however, but rented to him by Decatur B. Hall, a local merchant. The house was an imposing one in the small town—a large, white, stone structure with numerous outbuildings, including a two-room slave quarters. It had been built by Daniel Flowerree, sometime after 1830, and the entire lot with all appurtenances was sold to Hall in 1849 for $1800.[498] The residence had been mentioned in a Yankee dispatch on Christmas Day of 1863; information was received by the Union cavalry that "Mosby has made great preparation to have a frolic, with his principal officers, at the house of...Mrs. Murray, in Salem, tonight...Mrs. Murray lives about the middle of the street, in a large white house." Colonel Taylor, commanding the 2nd Cavalry division, was directed to "send a party from the brigade which is at Warrenton, under the command of a smart-and-competent officer, to capture them." [499] Apparently the "frolic," if scheduled, was called off or curtailed, and the Federals came up empty-handed, save for two Rangers, Privates David Grafton Carlisle and John W. Davis, who were found in the town. Carlisle was later exchanged and returned to the command, only to be recaptured, and saw the end of the war from inside a Union prison. Davis died from disease less than two months after his capture. [500]

Now nearing twenty years of age, Rebecca Elgin was a pretty girl, with smooth, rounded features, deep-set eyes and a pleasant, sincere looking set to her lips that made it appear that she might, at anytime, break into a shy smile or soft laugh. Over a year had passed since her rejection of Sam's romantic overture, following his wounding near Greenwich. Now, today was to be her wedding day.[501]

The well-wishers crowded into the Murray home before ten o'clock on this increasingly warm July morning. Sam's brother, William, would stand up for him. The partisans had not been actively engaged for a week now, so several of the groom's fellow Rangers would most likely be in attendance. Orders had already been issued for the command to assemble that afternoon, some ten miles north, near Upperville.

Sam, in his recently acquired lieutenant's uniform, was as handsome as Rebecca thought she had ever seen him. But the man that Ranger Ludwell Lake called "the bravest man I ever knew" wasn't sure he would last long enough for the preacher to make them one. Yankees were a lot easier to handle then his nerves at the moment, Sam was probably thinking. And William, standing beside Sam, most surely was doing his best to keep from laughing out loud at his brother; a stern look from Reverend Herndon, however, made it much easier for him to control such inclinations.

Thaddeus Herndon was well known to the people of Fauquier County. His father had been a Baptist preacher, as were two of his brothers. He lived at Locust Grove, near Piedmont, but served two churches outside the county— one in Loudoun County and one in Prince William. His bother, John N. Herndon had baptized Sam at Luray (Main Street) Baptist Church before the war and was the pastor there when Sam was licensed to preach in 1858.[502]

Rebecca glanced up at Sam as she came to stand beside him. She, with the pleasant smile, looking as calm as a leaf on a windless day, and he, shifting restlessly to the other foot, managing a nervous, almost sheepish, grin. It was not a long ceremony and soon the crowd was dispersing. The Rangers' assembly that afternoon was rumored to be an important one, so the week-long respite for the partisans soon would be over. But for the next few hours, the newly joined couple could be together. The sun was nearly overhead as the people left the house; business was going on as usual up and down the street. The new Mrs. Chapman had a single red rose pinned to her simple wedding dress, made of recently acquired white calico.

Two hundred men gathered at Upperville in mid-afternoon. Ninety-six of them would constitute the 43rd Battalion's newest company. The usual election procedure was followed, and the just married, former lieutenant, Sam

Chapman, was now a captain, commanding Company E. Mosby had remembered his newest captain's venturing and courageous character, recalling the fight at Miskel's farm: "I made him a captain for it." Sam's junior officers were Fountain Beattie, first lieutenant; William Martin, second lieutenant; Ben Palmer, third lieutenant. At dusk the command would march toward the Potomac and into war once more.[503]

PART VII

SHERIDAN—SUFFER THE PEOPLE...

.

19. Bluecoats and Yellow Jackets

Because Sam Chapman had been in charge of the battalion's artillery, provision needed to be made for a change in this part of the command. Additionally, the appointment of a new adjutant was necessary. These items were on Mosby's agenda for the July 28 meeting, following Sam's promotion and the choosing of the other officers and men of the new company.

William H. "Willie" Mosby was the only brother of John Mosby. He had joined the command less than a year before, two months shy of his eighteenth birthday. He took Sam's place as company adjutant and would be the only adjutant besides Chapman the command would ever have.[504]

Since the battalion now had several cannons, the time had come for a regular company of artillery to be organized. Chosen captain was Peter A. Franklin, a veteran of Parker's battery, Virginia Light Artillery. Franklin had been with Mosby since the previous October, coming over from the battery after having been found guilty by courts-martial of an undefined offense. He had been serving as a captain and quartermaster of that company. The new Artillery Company would have a complement of twelve men—four officers, a sergeant, and seven privates.[505]

The two hundred men, with their three small cannons, started out that afternoon and reached Purcellville, in northern Loudoun County, late on the night of July 28. On July 30, three companies—A, B, and D—crossed the Potomac and moved on to Adamstown. The partisans had wanted to intercept a train on the B & O tracks, but arrived too late. Instead they cut the telegraph poles and wires. Company B then moved down towards Monocacy, but soon returned and stayed near the ford on the Maryland side of the river. Companies A and D marched toward Barnesville, and ran into a picket post of the 8th Illinois Cavalry. The Rangers divided and one party proceeded to get in the rear of the picket; the other party stayed in the front, drawing fire from the Yankees, who were using carbines atop a high bluff. Before long, however, the first party was in behind the carbineers and in a brief fight were able to capture between twenty and thirty men and about seventy-five horses.[506]

A Union report about the latest raid into Maryland sounded like many of the previous ones: "By the disgraceful conduct of Lieutenant Van Ness, of the Third New Jersey Infantry (several men and horses were captured and one man killed). Colonel Clendenin reports the conduct of the lieutenant as cowardly in a superlative degree." [507]

Before the Rangers met up with the 8th Illinois cavalrymen, they had stopped at a country store where the main commodity consisted of "wet goods". Some of the men tried to see just how quickly they could dispose of the confiscated stock; soon several of the members of Company A were disagreeing among themselves to the point of fisticuffs. Even Lieutenant Nelson got into it with a private named Moon and pistols were drawn. Friends interfered and settled things down. Private Bill Ellzey and another Ranger named Toller were so involved that, when the Yankees were sighted and the partisans had to move on, the two warriors were still in the road fighting. They would spend the rest of the war in a Federal prison. [508]

While the other companies were returning to Virginia soil, Sam Chapman and Company E were now on the Maryland side of the river, having crossed at a different place than the others. Probing further north toward Frederick, they ran into some of the 8th Illinois cavalrymen along the Monocacy, south of the town. Much to their surprise, they found that the fords were being closed and guarded, cutting off their retreat to the southern side. Unbeknown to Chapman, this was being done because the Federals wanted to trap the other Rangers; they had no knowledge of Company E being in the vicinity up to now.

With a much larger force of Yankees in their front, Chapman decided the better part of valor would be to get back on the other side of the river. He turned the command around and started for the ford. It was then that another force of the 8th Illinois was spotted, racing rapidly toward the same ford. The Southerners won the race and were in the water while the Yankee cavalrymen fired at them from the bank. One man fell from his horse and drowned. Many of Chapman's men jumped into the water and either swam across, mounting up on the other side, or let their horses pull them across. [509]

With such an innocuous beginning for the new company, Chapman must have thought about those other times when he had made a career move. Like his first time under fire, as a recruit with the Warren Rifles, when they had raced away from Alexandria without firing a shot; or his first ride with Mosby, when he and less than a dozen other partisans charged into what they thought was a rear guard, but turned out to be the whole command, and they had skedaddled for their lives. Now, his first time out as a company captain and....But there was no need for concern; Sam had, in the past, and would in the future, more than make up for a few harmless setbacks.

When the battalion was safely back in Virginia, Mosby and a couple of the men went to see General Early at his headquarters in Martinsburg, while the rest of the command returned home. [510] Sam of course made the ride all the way to Salem. He had been away from Rebecca for five long days.

The partisans next gathered at Upperville on August 6 and, with 250 men and four artillery pieces, set off once more for the Potomac. However, all the fords were heavily guarded and large patrols of cavalry were seen moving towards Harper's Ferry on the Maryland side. The next day, Mosby sent the artillery back to Fauquier while he took Company A on a raid into Fairfax. The remainder of the command was left to press corn along the river. [511]

What the Rangers were observing along the Potomac was part of Grant's plan for Hunter's offensive against Early. Major White, with 600 troopers from the 8th Illinois Cavalry, was guarding the river, from Point of Rocks east to Edward's Ferry at the mouth of Goose Creek. This was a shoreline distance of about seventeen miles. Meanwhile Grant was wiring Hunter to concentrate all his available force in the vicinity of Harper's Ferry: "The brigade of cavalry now en route from Washington may be taken into account....Three other brigades of the best cavalry, numbering at least 5,000 men and horses, are now on the way to join you." [512]

But Hunter would not be around to concentrate his force anywhere; General Orders No. 240 for August 7, 1864 would see to that:

> 1. The Middle Department and the Departments
> of Washington, of the Susquehanna, and of West
> Virginia will constitute the Middle Military Division.
>
> 2. Maj. Gen. P. H. Sheridan is assigned by the President
> to the temporary command of the Middle Military Division.

The same day, General Hunter directed a message to President Lincoln, from Harper's Ferry:

> With several thousand wealthy spies in our midst,
> constantly sending information and supplies to the
> enemy and pointing out Union men to their vengeance,

it is impossible to conduct the affairs of any department successfully. I most humbly beg that I may be relieved from command of the Department of West Virginia.

On August 8, 1864 Hunter became an unemployed general.[513]

Mosby returned with Company A from the Fairfax raid on August 9 and filed his report: "With a detachment of 37 men, I defeated a body of 100 cavalry at Fairfax Station, killing the captain commanding and 6 men, and capturing 21 prisoners and 34 horses. Two (other) detachments brought in 6 more prisoners and horses; another detachment of 5...brought in 10 prisoners with their horses." [514]

When Sheridan took command of what was soon to be redesignated the Army of the Shenandoah, Grant gave him an awfully lot of help in the way of manpower. His command totaled some 35,000 infantry and 8,000 cavalry. His artillery was composed of fifty-two pieces, divided among the VI, VIII, and XIX Corps'. The cavalry, reportedly made up of the best horsemen in the Union armies, was being issued more and more of the breech-loading, repeating Spencer and Sharp's carbines. [515]

What Sheridan did not know was the size of the force that was to contest him in the Valley. Early, who had been able to push Hunter back down and out of the Valley, had an army of approximately 13,000 men divided among 9,000 infantry and artillery and 4,000 cavalry. Sheridan believed he was facing an army of between 20,000 and 30,000. [516] The two armies would now square off, playing the chess game as armies are prone to do. Early was at Bunker Hill, midway between Martinsburg and Winchester. Sheridan's army was scattered about Harper's Ferry. In between was Opequon Creek, flowing clear and clean now, but soon to lap its banks with a crimson stain.

On August 12, after jockeying for position and moving west to east and north to south, Sheridan and Early faced each other across Cedar Creek at a prominence called Fisher's Hill, fifteen miles south of Winchester. On the same day, the 43rd Battalion, 330 strong, and boasting two howitzers, left Rectortown, bound for the Shenandoah Valley by way of Snicker's'Gap. Coincidently, on the same day, the 8th Illinois Cavalry was sent to Loudoun County to search for Mosby.

John Russell was a twenty-three-year-old scout in Company C and Mosby considered him his best scout. Like his commander, Russell had those deep-set blue eyes, always moving except when they settled on you; then they seemed to fairly pierce the person and just as quickly move away, but leaving their mark. At five feet, seven inches, Russell was just an inch shorter than Mosby, although more compactly built. A native of Clarke County, Russell knew the countryside well, and this knowledge of his home county, as well as that of the neighboring counties of Frederick and Warren, would be of immense value to Mosby in his operations against Sheridan in the Valley.[517]

Russell had been on a scout. Mosby wanted to find out the best approach to take against Sheridan, so as to disrupt his communications and cripple his army, as he moved up the Valley against Early. When the scout returned, he had news of a long wagon train, heading south on the Charlestown Turnpike, between Harper's Ferry and Berryville. The train, reported Russell, was big—really big—and it was accompanied by a large contingent of infantry and cavalry.[518]

Mosby was with his command, just out of Berryville, when the scouting report was delivered. After passing through Snicker's Gap, they had crossed the Shenandoah at Castleman's Ferry and stopped for the night. With the news of the wagon train, the Colonel awoke some of the Rangers: John Munson, sixteen-year-old John Beckham, and the command's eighteen-year-old color-bearer, Stockton Terry, who had enlisted only three weeks previously. Instructing William Chapman to gather the rest of the command and follow, the five men, with Russell in front, left camp. Staying about a mile ahead of Chapman and the main body, the riders arrived on a knoll where they could look down on the turnpike. The sun was just coming up over the Blue Ridge behind them and a low fog still lay on the Valley floor.[519]

The scene, spread out before the Rangers, was spectacular. As the fog slowly dissipated, the wagons, with their white covers, could be seen. For as far as the eye could behold, like a long white snake, moving slowly up the pike, the wagons came—555 in all. The train was so long that it required two and one-half hours to pass a given point. Inside the wagons were five day's rations for 2,250 soldiers and extra stores for the officers. Additionally, other wagons carried forage, officers' baggage, subsistence stores, forges, and various regimental and headquarters equipment and material. Several hundred beef cattle accompanied the train. The guard was made up of a brigade of infantry, about 2500 men, and a large force of cavalry. The rumbling of the wagons on the hard turnpike could be heard for a mile and it was like an incessant, monotonous roar. Now the train had come upon a small stream, Buck Marsh Run, flowing across the turnpike, and at this point the wagons began to turn off the road into a pasture, to rest, graze and water the horses and livestock. [520]

One of the two howitzers brought by the Rangers, in the hurry to get it through the woods and onto the hill, had received a broken wheel and was rendered useless. The other gun was wheeled into position where it could look down the pike at the train. Mosby gave the men their assignments— Captain Dolly Richards would lead the first squadron, consisting of Companies A and B, with Lieutenants Nelson, Hatcher and Albert Wrenn. They would charge toward the head of the train. The second squadron, made up of the commands of William Chapman and Alfred Glascock, would go down toward the rear of the train. Mosby and Captain Sam Chapman's men would be in reserve, keeping company with the single little howitzer, now placed no more than a hundred yards from the pike. Stockton Terry, the young color bearer would stay with Mosby. It was a bitter potion for Sam. Mosby, in his official report, says: "The gallant Capt. Sam Chapman, commanding Company E, although burning for the strife, was prudently held in reserve." [521] Prudently and Sam Chapman were not words normally used together.

Everything was in readiness. The Rangers sat nervously in their saddles, awaiting the signal to attack—a shot from the cannon, which would tell Richards and Chapman to charge. Only a minute or two remained and then the signal would be heard. But this was an eternity to the waiting attackers and gave Mosby time to think on what was about to take place. A successful blow against Sheridan's supplies and communications now would no doubt make a deep impression on the Union commander and have much influence on the results of the upcoming campaign; failure would, in all probability, mean the end of the command. Such were the stakes—and high ones they were. But before Mosby could ponder any further on the matter, something else was about to intrude on his musing.

Mosby was confident in the fact that he had made allowances, to the extent that he could, for all possibilities. The rest was in the hands of Providence. And Providence apparently wasn't ready just yet. The Rangers manning the little howitzer were about to ram a charge down the barrel when the sneak attack came. This unexpected enemy swarmed first about the gun crew and then spread out among the others. Horses whinnied and reared, men cursed and frailed wildly. "Yellow Jackets!" someone shouted, "Yellow Jackets!" The cannon had been placed squarely over their nest in the ground. Now they were out and on the attack and the skedaddle began. The swarming enemy settled down at last—on the battery horses. The drivers could not hold the excited animals and fight off the invaders at the same time. Gunners, drivers, and horses all ran off, taking the limber chest and caisson with them.

Mosby himself was not spared. Riding a spirited sorrel mare, captured the year before, he was suddenly jolted, nearly out of the saddle, as a swarm settled on her. The stinging made the horse so frantic that Mosby just about forgot there was anything else in the world but yellow jackets. Sergeant A. G. Babcock, one of the Artillery Company members, managed to get hold of the gun and wheel it off the hole; just as quickly as they had emerged, the attackers—or defenders, depending on one's point of view— disappeared back into the ground. Finally, order was restored and the horses and equipment recovered.

Remarkably, the sounds and commotion had aroused little curiosity from the bluecoats down on the pike. The early morning fog, coupled with the humdrum of activity all around the train, masked most of the disturbance; those who did chance to look upon the hill thought they were seeing some of their own cavalry standing watch over them. (Colonel Mosby recalled the incident in his memoirs years later: "My scheme was nearly ruined by a ludicrous incident, the fun of which is more apparent now than it was then.") [522]

Captain J. C. Mann was a quartermaster in Major General William H. Emory's XIX Corps of Sheridan's Army of the Shenandoah. When the wagon train was getting ready to leave its parking area, just north of Buck Marsh Run, the morning of August 13, Mann received an order—a prophetic one. Brigadier General John Reese Kenly, commanding a brigade of militia and home guards escorting the train, came up to Mann: "I consider this the most dangerous point in the route. I desire you to remain here, therefore, until every wagon has passed." Shortly after, the chief wagon-master for the corps advised Captain Mann that the cavalry trains were unhooked and feeding their stock. Mann immediately went to the trains, roused the officers in charge, and ordered them to hook up and start immediately, that the train might be in danger of an attack. About this time, Mann heard the explosion of a shell, then a second one. Mann would soon leave the rear train, pass around a hill, and catch up with the balance of the trains midway between Berryville and Winchester, advising them of the attack and urging them to move as quickly as possible toward Winchester.[523]

Lieutenants John J. Fray and Frank "Red Fox" Rham had control of the partisan's gun. As soon as Sergeant Babcock had it in position, the charge was rammed home, the primer fixed, and the correctness of the aiming double-checked. "Fire!" was the command and the lanyard was pulled. Twelve pounds of destruction went screaming toward the wagons, striking a mule and divorcing it from its head.[524] Everything and everyone, in and on the train, stopped. The gun crew moved the gun several yards away, rammed home another shell and sent it after the first. For those with the wagons, time seemed like minutes, torturously turning into hours, but in reality it was all happening nearly instantaneously. Shock was displaced by confusion. Then fear set in as yet a third shell exploded in the midst of the drivers. By this time, Richards and Chapman had started their squadrons charging off the hill. [525]

General Kenly's escort was responsible for the guarding of the train; the guard was made up of such inexperienced troops as two companies of the 3rd Maryland Potomac Home Guards and the 149th and the 144th Regiments, Ohio National Guards. The Ohio troops were known as "One Hundred Days" soldiers, this being the term of their enlistment. It is no wonder that, at the sound of the first exploding shell, the cavalry fled and the infantry retreated into some woods and behind stone fences that crisscrossed the fields. The Artillery Company was moving the piece with each firing, keeping the enemy confused as to how many cannon and how much force was being thrown at them. Dolly Richards, with his two companies, struck the turnpike south of Buck Marsh Run and headed toward Berryville and the head of the train. Not long after Richards had begun his charge down the turnpike, a company of hidden infantrymen rose up, firing a volley which severely wounded Sergeant Ned Rector. [526]

Richards' squadron continued down the pike, now only a few hundred yards from the town. With unbridled speed, the captain led his men through the chaos that had been the wagon train, creating additional alarm and confusion. When he reached Berryville, he cut across at an angle where the Charlestown Road intersects the Winchester Turnpike, both of which were clogged with wagons trying to escape the onslaught taking place north of the town. Several hundred yards up the Winchester road, Richards was able to cut off about twenty wagons. Not stopping here, some of the Rangers, led by their captain, charged for another mile up the road, trying to get in front of the lead wagon. But east of Opequon Creek they were stopped and turned by a volley from the train's advance guard, which had taken a position behind a stone fence. [527]

Meanwhile, Chapman and his squadron had hit the train on the north side of Buck Marsh Run, running into about 150 infantrymen. But these troops, like so many others of the guard, were in shock over the suddenness of the disaster that had befallen them. They took refuge in gullies and behind some of the many stone fences so abundant in this part of the Valley, keeping their heads down and not lifting a musket to fire a shot. However, a sizable portion of the infantry fled into an orchard and here, being reinforced, took a stand. Chapman charged, going over the fence; a bullet from behind the fence found its mark, killing Lewis Adie, a former student in the class of 1865 at the Virginia Military Institute, and a favorite of Mosby. The Colonel was directing the firing of the howitzer, when his sergeant major, Guy Broadwater rode up to him: "Colonel! Lewis Adie is killed!" Mosby, in the crisis of the fight, could only reply "I can't help it."[528]

Young Adie was one of two Rangers killed this day. When Richards and his command were turned back east of the Opequon, they were fired upon by some troops who had taken refuge in Buck Marsh Baptist Church, a brick building located in Berryville on the Winchester Turnpike, near its crossing with the Charlestown Pike. The shooters had already fired upon a group of Rangers, passing by with a large number of prisoners, killing Welby Rector, a private in Company A. They had also wounded Lieutenant Wrenn. Calling on Lieutenant Fray and the mountain howitzer, a shot was fired toward the church, forcing out its occupants. The Federals were then captured, after a solitary headlong charge by Lieutenant Willie Martin into their midst, while men from both sides looked on in amazement. [529]

Mosby had observed the fight from his place on the hill, directing the cannon and issuing orders regarding the prisoners as they were brought back from the turnpike. Now he called for the destruction of what was left of the train. The Rangers began to ransack and pillage the wagons, coming away with a grand assortment of spoils, among which were brilliantly lined Union officer's uniforms and a quantity of violins. All the teams that had not run away were unhitched from the wagons and the wagons set afire. The beeves were rounded up, as were the mules and some horses. One item overlooked was a strongbox containing $112,000, on its way to Winchaster with the paymaster. The tired but jubilant Rebels then started toward Castleman's Ferry and safety on the eastern side of Snicker's Gap. [530]

As for the Union army, a Board of Inquiry was convened at Harper's Ferry on September 8, 1864 to investigate the affair. It rendered its decision on November 13, finding "the guard was insufficient; (the officers in charge) failed to look after (their) train, and without orders permitted the train to go into park, the drivers to unhitch and unharness their animals, and lie down and go to sleep." However, no individual blame was accessed and no disciplinary action taken. [531]

The success of the raid can be viewed in a couple of ways. First, from the numbers themselves: 300 prisioners taken, 700 mules and horses and 230 head of cattle captured, over seventy-five loaded wagons confiscated and destroyed Also on the plus side were the casualties. Mosby only lost two men killed and three wounded and no one captured. The Federals had five dead and an undetermined number wounded, in addition to the 300 captured. Another way to view the success of the operation is the effect it had on Sheridan. He withdrew his army from Cedar Creek, although he may have been planing to do that before the news of the raid reached him. But Mosby's actions insured the withdrawal, which took Sheridan's troops all the way back to their original line near Harper's Ferry. And their rations were short for a week. [532]

Probably the biggest impact of the raid was what Mosby had tried to accomplish all along—cause the enemy to remove troops from the front in order to protect his lines of communications and supply in the rear. Every soldier not in the breastworks or the trenches, or not available to advance against the enemy, decreases an army's fighting strength. "My purpose was to weaken the armies invading Virginia by harassing their rear. To destroy supply trains, to break up the means of conveying intelligence, to confuse and isolate them from their base. The military value of a partisan's work is not measured by the amount of property destroyed or the number of men killed or captured, but by the number he keeps watching." [533]

A dispatch from General John D. Stevenson, commanding the Military District of Harper's Ferry, and who had been president of the Board of Inquiry, tends to confirm Mosby's analysis. Sent to Sheridan four days after the raid, it asks for increased numbers of troops, solely to guard against Mosby and other partisans: "Finding all trains threatened by guerrillas (in force) and largely increased by several organizations under Mosby...I am of the opinion that the only safety to our trains and couriers is a posting of a force at Charlestown, with General Duffie at Berryville, and 1,000 of Averell's force at Charlestown....As things now stand, no small party or train...is now safe." Stevenson went on to request a section of artillery with Averell's 1,000 men at Charlestown. All of the equipment, arms, and men requested would have to come from somewhere in the army, effectively excluding their possible use against Early in the Valley.[534] And of course, there were not "several organizations under Mosby." The tactic of dividing up his force into smaller parties probably led to this conclusion.

The exuberant Tee Edmonds was fairly beside herself back at Belle Grove. Her diary entry for August 13, 1864 reflects her mood: "Mosby's most successful and brilliant raid I must not fail to record. They left Fauquier yesterday morning and made a dash to Berryville early this morning, capturing two hundred and ten prisoners, four hundred mules, seventy-five wagons and one hundred and eighty cattle. Oh but didn't we clap our hands when we heard for joy!, joy!, joy! Hurrah for Mosby, my gallant Mosby, the guerrilla chief!" [535]

20. "No Quarter! No Quarter!"

On August 16, 1864, two dispatches came from General Grant, near Peters-burg, to General Sheridan's headquarters, 150 miles away at Winchester. These dispatches would bring a new kind of warfare to the lower Shenan-doah Valley and across northern Virginia. It could be rightly called "the in-temperate war," for "intemperate' is defined as "lacking in restraint; exces-sive; severe or violant." Any and all of these would describe it.

> 1:30 p.m. – The families of most of Mosby's men are
> known and can be collected. I think they
> should be taken and kept at Fort McHenry,
> or some secure place, as hostages for the
> good conduct of Mosby and his men.
> Where any of Mosby's men are caught, hang
> them without trial.[536]

> 3:30 p.m. – If you can possibly spare a division of cavalry,
> send them through Loudoun County, to destroy
> and carry off crops, animals, negroes, and all
> men under fifty years of age capable of bearing
> arms. In this way you will get many of Mosby's
> men. All male citizens under fifty can fairly be
> held as prisoners of war, and not as Citizen
> prisoners, if not already soldiers, they will be
> made so the moment the rebel army gets hold
> of them.[537]

Sheridan received Grant's first message early on the morning of August 17. However, he had already received the second one the night before, on August 16. That same day, Sheridan issued orders to General Alfred Torbert, his chief of cavalry. Torbert was told to "(destroy) wheat and hay south of a line from Millwood to Winchester and Petticoat Gap. You will seize all mules, horses, and cattle that may be useful to our army." The last sentence of the order was wholly unambiguous: "No houses will be burned, and offi-cers in charge of this delicate, but necessary, duty must inform the people that the object is to make this Valley untenable for the raiding parties of the rebel army." [538]

The area to be included in "south of a line" was all the Valley from roughly the Shenandoah River in the east, northwest to the Allegheny Mountain range in the west. It was to be open season on everything south of this imaginary east to west line. Grant had expressed his wishes to Sheridan and Sheridan had repeated them in his edict to Torbert, adding: "No houses will be burned..." These were the rules. The rules would soon be broken.

On August 16, Sheridan started moving his army back down the Valley from its deployment opposite Early along the north bank of Cedar Creek. He had three good reasons for doing so: First, he thought his defensive position was a poor one. Second, he had received information that the division of South Carolinian General Joseph Kershaw was enroute to reinforce Early. And third, because of Mosby's attack on his supply train, his men were left with only two days rations.

It must have seemed to the Union command that Mosby was everywhere at once. The spurt of dispatches emanating from and to the commands in the field and Washington underscore just how much the partisan chief was keeping the enemy off balance, with his various small detachments, operating over a wide area. On August 15, Major Waite of the 8th Illinois Cavalry, writing from the Maryland side of the Potomac, advised Washington: "A number of squads of rebel cavalry seen on the Virginia side today, all along my line, from Monocacy down as far as Great Falls." On August 16, Colonel Chipman wired Secretary of War Stanton from Harper's Ferry: "Guerrillas invest the country between here and Winchester. Trains require strong escorts...." [539]

The day before Chipman's message to Stanton, Dolly Richards had taken a small squad on a scout along the turnpike between Berryville and Charlestown when he ran into a party of Federal cavalrymen. A brief fight ensued and the Rangers managed to kill a first lieutenant, who was a carrier of dispatches, wound another lieutenant, and capture five men. Only one man managed to escape. When Richards reported to Mosby on the affair, the Colonel responded that he was glad one man had gotten away so that he could tell Sheridan what had happened to the rest of them. [540]

The same day that Richards had been near Charlestown, Lieutenant Glascock, with fourteen men from Company D, had ridden through Ashby's Gap, crossed the river at Berry's Ferry, and then taken a route that by-passed Millwood and brought them out near Kernstown, four miles south of Winchester. Here, without firing a shot, the Rangers overpowered a Yankee patrol, capturing all twenty-nine men, including several officers, with their arms, equipment and horses. [541]

On August 16, there was this dispatch from Colonel Edwards to Major Whittier: "...160 to 200 of the enemy, accompanied by Mosby himself...are now a short distance to the left and rear of Middletown. One of the party has been within the limits of our camp today." [542]

On August 17, General Averell wired General Stevenson at Harper's Ferry: "...200 of my command have been sent to...capture, kill or disperse the guerrillas at Charlestown. I have sent scouts in that direction. If they do not succeed in clearing out the place, I will send more." [543]

On August 18, Sheridan, in an attempt to "break up and exterminate any bands or parties of Mosby's," ordered Major Waite and the 8th Illinois Cavalry to scout through Loudoun County, by way of Upperville, Middleburg, and Snicker's Gap. "Mosby is reported to have within his reach and control from 400 to 500 men and two pieces of artillery." Sheridan then cautioned Waite "to move with the utmost caution." [544]

The sweep by the 8th Illinois involved 650 troopers. They managed to capture sixty-two "rebel sympathizers"—all, either too old to serve in the army, or convalescing wounded—before returning to camp. Sheridan "hoped the 8th Illinois has cleaned out Loudoun Valley." [545]

The following day, Jim Wiltshire returned from a scout into the Valley, reporting a brigade of Union cavalry in the vicinity of Berryville and eastward toward the river crossing. Upon receiving this news, Mosby decided to divide his force into three groups, each to operate along a portion of the turnpike from Berryville to Harper's Ferry, some seventeen miles to the north. The largest of the three, composed of Companies C, D, and E, he placed under command of William Chapman, directing them to cover the area between Berryville and Rippon. Company B was put under the direction of Captain Richards, responsible for that portion of the road from Rippon to Charlestown. Mosby took Company A, to operate along the remaining few miles from Charlestown to Harper's Ferry. The command crossed the Shenandoah River at Castleman's Ferry and then each group went its separate way. [546]

A rarely published photograph of John Mosby as a
lieutenant colonel in 1864. (Courtesy of Fauquier
Heritage Society)

Sam Chapman served as lieutenant and adjutant in Mosby's 43rd Battalion until promoted on July 28, 1864 to captain in command of Company E. This is the only known war-time photograph of him and was taken after his 1864 promotion. (Courtesy of Charles and Jeanne Lewis)

William H. Chapman, possibly in the uniform of the
University of Virginia's Southern Guard which was
disbanded May 8, 1861. He then enlisted in, and later
commanded, the Dixie Artillery before joining Mosby's
command in 1863. (Courtesy of Howard Hammond)

This is believed to be a previously unpublished photograph
of Captain Bradford Hoskins, a British soldier-of-fortune,
who joined Mosby about the same time as Sam Chapman
and was wounded, as was Chapman, at Grapewood Farm
on May 30, 1863. Hoskins would die from his wound
the following day. (Courtesy of John Daly)

THE FIGHT AT MISKEL'S (BROAD RUN).

Miskel Farm Fight, April 1, 1863. This 1895 painting by James E. Taylor depicts Sam Chapman, as described by Mosby, "standing in your stirrups whaling the Yankees with your sabre." Mosby is on horseback in center of painting. The rider at far left is probably Taylor's depiction of William Chapman. Sam Chapman owned the copy shown here. (Courtesy of Paul B. Lacy, Jr.)

"Yorkdale" was the home of the Templeman family who ran the mill on Thumb Run in southwestern Fauquier County during the war. The estate was located off of present day Route 688, near the village of Orlean. The date of this photograph is unknown, but the buildings are no longer standing. It was from here that Sam Chapman penned his "Miss Beck" letter on June 21, 1863. (Courtesy of Fauquier Heritage Society)

FEDERAL HOUSE-BURNERS ANNIHILATED BY MOSBY'S RANGERS,

On August 20, 1864, members of the 5th Michigan Cavalry, in the process of burning and looting the Morgan residence near Berryville, are set upon by a large contingent of Rangers led by William and Sam Chapman. (From a James E. Taylor drawing in *Mosby's Rangers*, by James J. Williamson)

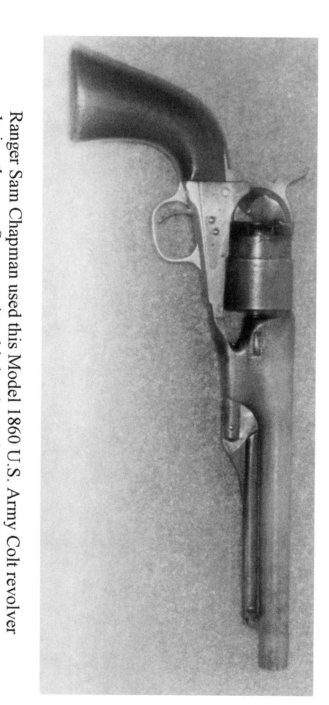

Ranger Sam Chapman used this Model 1860 U.S. Army Colt revolver during the war. Sam gave it to his brother John upon John's election as sheriff of Page County in 1888. It is one of two known revolvers still identifiable as belonging to and used by Sam Chapman in the conflict. (Courtesy of Horace Mewborn)

Rebecca Elgin Chapman, "Miss Beck," shown after her
marriage to Captain Sam Chapman on July 28, 1864.
(Courtesy of Mrs. Samuel Chapman Stephenson)

Rev. Sam Chapman, about 1882, when he was
beginning his ministry in and around Covington,
Va. (Courtesy of Mrs. Samuel Chapman Stephenson)

Rev. Thaddeus Herndon (left), the Baptist minister who presided over the marriage of Eliza Rebecca Elgin and Sam Chapman on July 28, 1864. (Courtesy Fauquier Heritage Society)

"Willie"Chapman (right) and his father's former commander, John Mosby, were very close when both lived in San Francisco during the decades after the war. "I feel towards him as if he were my son..." Mosby would say. (Courtesy Charles and Jeanne Lewis)

Covington Baptist Church soon after Rev. Sam Chapman arrived as pastor in 1882. The newly erected windmill (see page 297) can be seen at the rear of the church property. (Courtesy of Virginia Baptist Historical Society)

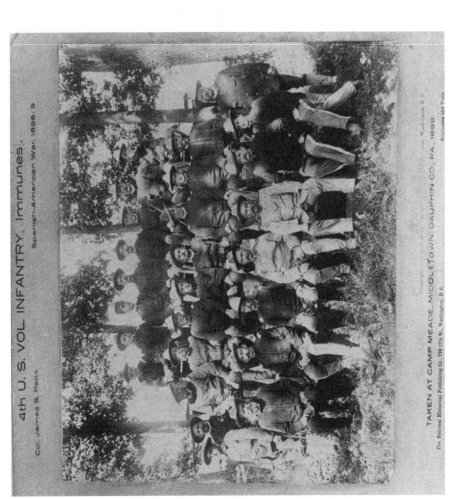

Officers of the 4th
U.S. Volunteer
Infantry Regiment
following their return
from Cuba in 1899.
Chaplain Sam
Chapman is seated
on left end of front row.
(Courtesy of Horace A.
Revercomb, III)

Sam Chapman's son, Willie, bought this house, now known as the Chapman House, and nearly 300 acres on Jackson River north of Covington, at auction in 1911. Rev. Chapman had a study on the second floor. This photograph is from a recent pen & ink drawing by the current owner and represents the house as it may have appeared when built, probably late in the 18th century. (Courtesy of Gertrude Lacy / Mrs. Paul B. Lacy, Jr.)

Former members of Mosby's Rangers attended the funeral of their war-time leader, June 1, 1916, in Warrenton, Va. Sam Chapman is second from right on the second row. (Courtesy of Fauquier Historical Society)

Grave site and monument for Sam and Rebecca Chapman and family in Cedar Hill Cemetery, Covington, Va. (Author's photos)

During the early part of the night of August 19, William Chapman and some of his men attempted to capture a picket post near the Ferry. In the ensuing fight, one of the pickets fired at Chapman and Chapman fired back, killing the Union soldier. Another of the pickets was wounded and the two remaining were captured. The Yankee soldiers were members of the 5th Michigan Cavalry, part of the Second Brigade, in Torbert's cavalry corps. This brigade was commanded by Brigadier General George Armstrong Custer. [547]

When Sheridan withdrew his army from its position along Cedar Creek on August 16 and started back down the Valley Pike, the residents of the lower Shenandoah Valley thought Black Dave Hunter had returned—with a vengeance. In compliance with Grant's orders—but also because of the constant annoyance and disruption of the guerrillas—Little Phil decided it was time to bring war to the Valley as it had never been done before. Mosby's raid on his supply train had been the icing on the cake; it was both a military and personal embarrassment. Well, these people needed to be taught a lesson in what war was all about.

Valley farmers were in the midst of harvesting their summer crops. Late summer gardens were reaching their peak. Yearlings were being fattened for their first full winter, while hogs were being fattened for the November and December butcherings. Mills were grinding along the clear rivers and streams. And Yankee soldiers were setting it all to the torch.

Barns, storehouses, smoke houses, mills, tanneries, fields—they all could go up in smoke if they happened to be along the route that a regiment or a squad or a company of horsemen happened to take. The smoke was beginning to lay like a giant gray blanket over the once green but now blackened landscape that was the lower Valley, as Sheridan's cavalry made its way back toward their previous lines near Halltown. The distance from Cedar Creek to Winchester is only about fifteen miles; the length of the Valley from Winchester to Lexington is 125. So there was a limit to the amount of destruction the soldiers could do during their short trek home.

Jacob R. Hildebrand was a Mennonite with farms in both Augusta and Rockingham Counties. He had two sons serving the Confederacy in the summer of 1864; a third would soon enlist. Hildebrand left his home in Augusta County on August 16 to visit his sons who were with Early's army at Cedar Creek. By the time he arrived in Strasburg, Early's forces had pulled out and were following Sheridan as he withdrew back down the Valley. On August 18, Hildebrand reached Winchester and spent some time with the boys, Benjamin, who was in the 52nd Virginia Infantry and Gideon, with the 1st Virginia Cavalry. On the way home the next day, he recorded in his journal: "Started home...the Yankees are burning Every (sic) barn they come across that has either hay or grain in it. I seen a good many that were smoking yet as I passed up the Valey (sic) Pike." [548]

For the most part, the rules were not broken as far as the burning of homes was concerned. That is, not broken by the main body of Sheridan's army. It was another matter when it came to Custer's brigade. When Custer learned of the attack on the picket post by Chapman's patrol, which had resulted in the killing of one of his lieutenants, he also heard that a person or persons in a nearby house had aided the Rangers. [549] For this, the yellow-haired avenger ordered five homes to be burned along the Leesburg-Berryville Pike, east of the town of Berryville. [550]

About thirty troopers from the 5th Michigan Cavalry were in the process of carrying out their general's order on the afternoon of August 20. They were under the direct command of Captain George Drake of Company H. The first house to be ignited was a large brick home belonging to Colonel Josiah Ware. All the inhabitants had been ordered out of the house and the blaze set. While the troopers still surrounded the house, they spotted William Chapman and two of his men. Chapman, along with John Hefflebower and George Lofland, was on his way to take three prisoners, captured near Hefflebower's father's house, back to the command; Chapman had left the rest of his men in a body of woods on the north side of the turnpike near Castlemen's Ferry.

The Federal troopers started after the Rangers but were unable to catch up to them before they reached the woods where the rest of the command was waiting. But this activity permitted the residents to put out the fire and save the house. Further down the road about two miles, Chapman observed smoke coming from the home of Province McCormick. By the time he arrived the house was past the point where it could be saved. Continuing west along the Turnpike, the Rangers next came upon the Sowers residence, likewise engulfed beyond the point of saving, the roof having already fallen in. Chapman directed Private James Flint to "gallop back to where I had left my men and tell Capt. Sam Chapman to bring the men on to Col. Morgan's, where the Yankees had gone to burn his house." The sight of the women and children standing outside weeping in their immense sorrow was too much for even the hardened partisans. The senseless arson would be avenged, vowed Chapman, and he passed the word to the rest of the men—there would be no prisoners taken. [551]

Captain Chapman—gathering the three companies under his command—his own Company C, Alfred Glascock with Company D, and Sam Chapman, commanding Company E, caught up with the house-burners at the home of Colonel Morgan, near the Sheppard's Mill Road, about one half mile from the McCormick place. Approaching the property, Glascock and the Chapmans could see the crops, fields and outbuildings already aflame. Spurring his horse and crying to his men "Take no prisoners! No quarter! No quarter today!" an enraged William Chapman—with his brother Sam only a horse's length behind—swept down upon the startled arsonists. By this time the entire command had taken up the cry, "No quarter! Wipe them from the face of the earth!" [552]

Captain Drake had gone with several of his force further up the road to another house, leaving the main part of his command under Lieutenant Allen. It was then that the Rangers struck. A war correspondent with the New York Times gave this account: "The men, overwhelmed by numbers, broke and fled in confusion.... The enemy were upon them, and no mercy shown, a majority of the men ran along a fence running at right angles with the road, hoping to find another passage, but finding none and reaching a corner, surrendered as a last resort."[553] But surrender was not a word that was to be used today.

A long stone fence, some three to four feet high, ran around the Morgan property. Trapped inside this enclosure, the burners tried desperately to find some way to escape the fierce onslaught. The Michiganders had earlier barricaded the road out of the estate and now, outnumbered by nearly ten to one, they found themselves enclosed within their self-made prison. Two of the mounted troopers jumped the fence and made their way across a field. Private William Patterson was on their heels but as he attempted to go over the fence his horse fell. A third trooper shot at him with his carbine, the bullet passing through his hat and tearing away half of a black plume. Patterson shot and killed the Yankee, who was carrying a bundle of silverware and jewelry, taken from some of the homes previously torched and sacked. Patterson would later record the incident, concluding, "It was a sharp, quick and clean little fight; no prisoners." [554]

"They hid behind the burning ruins, they crouched in the corners of the fences," a neighborhood woman who witnessed the affair recalled; " they begged for life, but their day of grace was past." [555] The once rich, black Clarke County dirt of Morgan's lane was now washed in the bright red blood of the Michigan troopers.

Colonel Mosby's report of the incident was brief. In reporting the enemy casualties, he had only this to say: "...no quarter was given, and about 25 of them were shot to death for their villainy. About 30 horses were brought off, but no prisoners." [556] It was not a day that Sam Chapman would soon forget.

21. The High Cost of Fame

The day before the Rangers annihilated the house-burners, Dolly Richards, with Company B, was at Myerstown, midway between Berryville and Charlestown. Learning from a citizen that Sheridan's army was encamped along the turnpike between Rippon and Charlestown, Richards gave serious thought to a daring plan. Why not get inside the camp, locate Sheridan and carry him off, much in the same manner as Mosby had taken Stoughton from his bed in Fairfax? A dauntless undertaking it would be, but one that, with some luck and the surprise factor, could work, Richards figured.

With eleven picked men, Richards was able to trick a sentinel and get his party inside the camp. Unable to obtain any information on the whereabouts of Sheridan's headquarters, the small band rode back to the turnpike, where they picked up a straggler from the 7th Michigan Cavalry. Forcing the Yankee to return with them, they used him to gain entrance back into the camp of the XIX Corps. But during a lull in the Ranger's watch over him, the prisoner was able to sound the alarm: "Wake up! Wake up! Rebels are in the camp!" Wheeling about and putting spurs to their horses, the twelve would-be abductors made it safely out of the camp. Richards' bold adventure had ended almost before it had begun.[557] What's more, serious misfortune awaited the small group just up the road.

On the way back to rendezvous with the rest of the battalion, Willie Martin was shot and killed by the accidental discharge from one of his comrade's revolvers. He had been Mosby's handpicked man for the position of first lieutenant to Sam Chapman in Company E when it was organized just three weeks previously. A saddened Mosby and Chapman attended the burial in Upperville the following day.[558]

Three hundred members of the 43rd Battalion rode east out of Rectortown at noon on August 23 accompanied by a 12-pound mountain rifle and a Napoleon gun. The large contingent rode on into the night, not stopping for bivouac, until they reached the Federal camp at Annandale. Located on the Little River Turnpike, halfway between Fairfax and Alexandria, the Rangers found that the garrison had sent off nearly all the horses and gone into stockade. After driving in the pickets, the two small cannon were brought into position and at dawn the next day Captain Montjoy was sent in to ask for the surrender of the post. He was refused. A few rounds were fired into the fort and this time Lieutenant Hatcher was sent in with a white flag. He was also refused. Moving the guns to another location, the partisans fired fifteen rounds at the camp; only one fell inside. The stockade was too well fortified to be taken without great loss, so the Rangers withdrew. But the mission had been successful in one important way: with the constant threat posed by Mosby and his partisans, the enemy would not dare release troops from this area to reinforce the Valley. [559]

On August 20, Major General C. C. Augur, commanding the Department of Washington, received a request from Sheridan: "I have 100 men who will take the contract to clean out Mosby's gang. I want 100 Spencer rifles for them. Send them to me if they can be found in Washington." [560]

Richard Blazer was a West Virginia native and a boat commander on the Ohio River when the war started. A loyal Union man, he joined an Ohio infantry regiment; he was soon elected captain and served in Crook's Army of West Virginia. An intelligent officer, with courage and good sense to go along, Crook tapped Blazer to command a new company of independent scouts. Better known as Blazer's Scouts, the company was organized with but one purpose—destroy Mosby. Equipping the untested company with the new Spencer rifles was an indication of the serious intent of Crook and Sheridan to "clean out Mosby's gang." [561]

Adopted by the army the year before, the Spencer should have seen more use than it did. For various reasons, such as the need to have preloaded cartridges with rimfire primers—unlike the commonly used percussion cap primers—and its heavy ten-pound weight when loaded, the new rifle never was widely used during the war; less than 15,000 were bought by the U. S. army. But it could be deadly. The gun was easy to load and would fire seven metallic cartridges without reloading. The primer in the jacket was sealed against moisture. The rifle had a long range, as opposed to that of the revolver favored by Mosby's men, and this may have been its biggest drawback. It was of limited use—except maybe as a club—in close cavalry combat. [562] (The Spencer rifle is not to be confused with the carbine of which some 46,000 were delivered to the army by war's end.) [563]

Toward the end of August, the Rangers gathered at Rectortown and Mosby again adopted the tactic of dividing his command. On this occasion, it was split into three detachments: Mosby took Companies A and B and started on a ride that would bring him in behind the Union forces at Charlestown; Montjoy, with Company D, was sent through Ashby's Gap, with the intention of crossing the river at Berry's Ferry; the third squadron—Companies C and E—under the command of Sam Chapman, passed through Ashby's Gap, then turned north to Sheppard's Mill, about three miles northeast of Berryville.

Chapman's squadron went into camp on the east side of the river crossing. That night John Russell was sent into Berryville on a scout. Near midnight, he returned with the information that a large body of Union cavalry, accompanied by wagons and ambulances, had passed through Berryville heading toward Front Royal, fifteen miles to the south. Early the next morning, Chapman marched his men to a place known locally as White's Burned Shop, just south of Berryville. Here, among the rolling hills of Clarke County, he saw what turned out to be skirmishers from the 6th New York Cavalry, which had been ordered from White Post to Berryville. They were silhouetted against the sky, on a small rise in a field on the Gold family farm. Because Chapman was unable to see beyond the hill, he decided caution was more desirable than recklessness.

Placing Company E under the command of Lieutenant Palmer, Sam told him to wait where he was, while he took Company C and went off to ascertain if the rest of the Federal cavalry was beyond the rise. Soon, orders came back to Palmer—charge the skirmish line, while Chapman did the same up the turnpike against the main body of the Federal command, on the other side of the hill. According to Private John H. Alexander, who was with the Rangers and later wrote of his experiences: "The Reverend Chapman considered that Mosby's men were organized for fighting purposes and that whenever Providence presented an opportunity for a fight, it was his simple duty to embrace it and trust the Lord for consequences."[564]

Advancing down a lane toward a closed gate, Palmer ordered Robert Jarman to get down and swing the gate open. The private obeyed, but just as he placed his hand on the gate, he toppled over, fatally shot by one of the Yankee skirmishers. Private Benjamin Iden was the next man to attempt to open the gate and he too fell dead from a well-placed rifle shot. Suddenly, Palmer, as if immune to the fate that had befallen his comrades, swung down from his horse, threw open the gate, and quickly remounted, leading the company through. Down the lane they charged, driving the skirmish line in against the remainder of the regiment on the other side of the rise. At the same time, Chapman came up with Company C. Having no time to re-form, the Federal cavalrymen, who were in columns of fours, fell back toward a wood. Without a defensive formation and with no one taking charge, the retreat turned into a rout. Unrelenting in their assault, Chapman's partisans pressed the bluecoats until they were against a fence, with a solitary gate as the only means of escape. The ones who could ran through the opening with the Rangers fast on their heels, while those who couldn't fell on the field, wounded—or dead.

The pursuit went on for a mile. And Sam Chapman was a relentless pursuer. When he was last seen approaching the woods, four Yankees were fleeing in front of him; when he eventually returned, he brought back four riderless horses. In the end, forty-two members of the 6th New York Cavalry were dead, wounded or prisoners. Thirty-eight horses were captured. On the Ranger's side, Jarman and Iden were dead on the field. Lieutenant Frank Fox was wounded and captured. Private Clay Adams, although not captured, was severely wounded. Both men would die agonizing deaths as a result of their wounds.

Fox was taken to a Union field hospital across the river from Harper's Ferry. His right arm was amputated, but pneumonia set in, along with secondary hemorrhaging, caused by the bullet entering his chest after exiting his arm. He died just over three weeks after the fight. Adams, who had joined the command after the regular services refused his enlistment due to his being deaf, was shot through the spine. Paralyzed in the lower part of his body, he lay on the field. That night, the scout John Russell and some other comrades went back across the river and carried him to Paris. Death was slow in coming; Adams finally died on January 7, 1865, four months after his wounding.

The final casualty count for Chapman's squadron was two killed, two mortally wounded, and several less seriously wounded. Sam had paid a high price for this victory. [565]

Mosby, on his expedition toward Charlestown, had gone as far as Myers Ford on the Shenandoah. Here, he took fifteen men from the squadron and crossed the river. Richards also took a small party and crossed, but hearing that a Federal scouting party was on the east side, he re-crossed the river and started in pursuit. After several miles, the trail turned and crossed back onto the west side of the Shenandoah. Believing that the Federals had gone on and were no longer a threat to his command, Richards sent Company B back to Lieutenant Nelson, while he took five or six men and started toward Rippon. This left Nelson with about seventy Rangers. The partisans went into a nearby wood, unbridled their horses and lay down in the warm September sun to rest, before rejoining Mosby and the rest of the command.

Richards had no way of knowing that he had been on the trail of Captain Blazer's independent scouts. After crossing the river, Blazer had ridden up stream toward Snicker's Gap, crossed once again to the east side, and marched back down stream until he came upon the lounging Rangers at Myers Ford.

The Scouts struck about two o'clock. Like a thunderbolt out of the cloudless September sky, it was sudden and totally unexpected. The sleepy Rangers took to their horses as the Federals came around the point of the woods and into the center of their makeshift camp. Nelson and Sergeant Horace Johnson of Company B tried to rally the men. The lieutenant got about twenty-five of them together and in typical Mosby fashion, charged into the Federals. But then a bullet from a Spencer seven-shooter found its mark in Nelson's leg, severely wounding him and causing him to fall back. The other Rangers interpreted this as an abandonment of the field. The skedaddle was on. Some of the men, unable to mount up, started down the hill toward a gap in a fence, with Blazer's men close on their heels. Blazer dismounted some of his men and sent them, with their Spencer repeating rifles, to fire at another bunch of Rangers trying to flee the onslaught by running across an open field. "After a spirited fight of several minutes I completely routed them," Blazer was to report; "(We) killed 13, wounded 6, took 5 prisoners and 17 horses. My loss was 1 killed and 6 wounded." [566] With the exception of the number reported killed (13), Blazer's report coincides with other reports. Mosby's seems to be the more accurate in the number killed (2) in this instance.

The surprise, the rout, the victory, were all Blazer's. It was one of the few times during the war, that any of Mosby's detached commands would allow themselves to be tricked, surprised, attacked and routed. When Mosby arrived at Myers Ford from his own raid near Harper's Ferry, he was told of the rout of Nelson's men. Following the trail of the retreat through Wormley's Gap, he found that his men had fled in disorder toward Fauquier. Colonel Mosby was not pleased. [567]

The months of August and September, 1864, had been busy ones for the 43rd Battalion. In a report submitted to General Lee on September 11, Mosby detailed the command's activities since March 1. He ended the report with this assessment:

> I have made no attempt, for it would be impossible, to embrace
> in this report a full recital of the innumerable affairs with the
> enemy in which the heroism of both men and officers of this
> command has been illustrated; yet the fame of their deeds will
> still live in the grateful remembrance of those whose homes
> and whose firesides their valor has defended.

Lee, in his endorsement of the report, summarized the activities:

> With the loss of little more than 20 men, he has killed,
> wounded, and captured...about 1,200 of the enemy and
> taken more than 1600 horses and mules, 230 beef cattle,
> and 85 wagons and ambulances, without counting smaller
> operations. [568]

On September 13, the command met at Piedmont and Company F, the sixth company of the battalion, was organized. Elected captain was Walter E. Frankland. It was Frankland who, with George Whitescarver, had walked thirty miles to Germantown in February of 1863 to "requisition" a Federal horse so that he could ride with Mosby. Two events—the first, ten days hence and the second, four weeks later—would be salient ones in Frankland's career as a Ranger. Elected second lieutenant was "Big Yankee" Ames, the deserter from the same Union camp at Germantown, who had supplied Frankland with information about the camp so that he could capture a horse.

Frank Fox's wounding and capture at the Gold's Farm fight yielded a vacancy among the officers of Company C. Third Lieutenant Frank Yager of Page County, enlisted by William Chapman a year ago, temporarily moved into the position but resigned his commission less than three months later. [569]

August and September had seen some of the costliest engagements that the 43rd Battalion was to endure. There had been victories but the price had been high. Now, with September nearly half over, two days yet to come in the month would serve to up the cost. One of these would be a day of ineffable sorrow for Captain Sam Chapman. The unsolicited, haunting, remembrance of it would summon forth the bitter taste that nothing, not even time, could enervate. It would become a part of him, just as his mind and his heart were a part of him, and it would only cease to be when the other two had gained their final rest.

22. An Uncivil War

Following the formation of his newest company, Mosby split up the command once more. Taking seven of the Rangers, he went on a raid to Fairfax County in the vicinity of Falls Church in an attempt to capture a quartermaster's establishment, belonging to the 16th New York Volunteer Cavalry Brigade. During the darkness of September 14, he entered the slaughter yard attached to the commissary but was detected before being able to do any harm. Abandoning this plan, Mosby sent five of the men back to Fauquier, while keeping his sergeant major, Guy Broadwater, and Private Thomas Love of Company D. The three stayed behind, intent on doing some scouting of Federal camps in the area. [570]

Colonel H. S. Gansevoort, commanding the 13th New York Cavalry, led a column of sixty-three mounted and 210 unmounted men on a scout into western Fairfax and eastern Loudoun Counties on September 8. On the night of September 12, the Yankee column ambuscaded the roads around Aldie and the next morning entered the village in search of Mosby or any of his command. Their efforts were in vain. However, they did receive information that Mosby had passed down the Aldie turnpike before the arrival of Gansevoort's troops. The Federals set out after him and by the morning of September 15 were between Chantilly and Fairfax.

Initial reports reaching Gansevoort were that Mosby had a large force of maybe 500 men in divided parties; later that day, Union scouts brought word to the Colonel that the guerrilla chieftain had been seen with two companions between the courthouse and Centreville. Five Yankee cavalrymen were dispatched to the Centreville Road to check out the report. [571]

Mosby, Broadwater and Love were on the turnpike, near Centreville, when they ran head-to-head into Gansevoort's five cavalrymen. Mosby, as was his want, was dressed in full uniform, and made an easy target for the Yankee shooters. Both parties began firing away at the same time; two of the Federal cavalrymen lost their horses and were killed. At nearly the same instance Mosby reeled in his saddle and then slumped onto the pommel, his face contorted from excruciating pain. A bullet from the gun of Private Henry Smith of Company H of the 13th New York had caromed off the handle of one of Mosby's belt pistols, striking him in the groin.

Love and Broadwater, who had started after the other Federal cavalrymen, heard their leader cry out. Turning around and racing back, they managed to catch Mosby before he fell from his horse. Propping him up in the saddle, the three partisans galloped away, stopping only after they were a safe distance from any pursuing Yankees. Broadwater procured a light wagon and the two men carried their leader to White Plains where he was cared for by James William Foster, a trusted friend. The wound proved to be painful but not life threatening and Mosby was soon taken to the home of his father in Lynchburg to recover. Gansevoort was unable to capitalize on his good fortune; he sent parties of both cavalry and infantry to the vicinity in search of the wounded guerrilla but all to no avail. [572]

The day after Mosby's wounding Union Brigadier General George H. Chapman, commanding the Second Brigade, Third Cavalry Division, sent a squadron of the 8th New York Cavalry into Snicker's Gap, while the main body of his expeditionary force of some 400 men rested near Snickersville. Chapman had been in the area trying to ascertain "what force of the enemy were rendezvoused " in the Ashby's and Snicker's Gap vicinity. Chapman was particularly interested in the narrow passage bounded by Snicker's Gap in the north and Ashby's Gap on the south, and protected by the Shenandoah River to the west and the Blue Ridge Mountains on the east. He had previously detached another party of fifty-five troopers and they were waiting at Snicker's Gap, having taken a ridge-top road north from Ashby's Gap. [573]

William Chapman had heard about the Federal force when it passed through Upperville. He was told that the troops had been killing sheep, poultry, etc. and had carried off a number of men and horses. Too late to catch the column at Upperville, Chapman took about forty men and climbed the east slope of the mountain. He took a cavalry trail along the crest and swooped down on the unsuspecting bluecoats in Snicker's Gap. A Union report of the incident stated that most of the men had unbridled their horses and had laid out in the warm September sun and fallen asleep. The partisans were able to retake all the prisoners and most of the horses held by the Yankees. In addition, they killed five of the Union troopers, wounded several more and came away with thirteen prisoners and forty additional horses. That was the good news. The bad news was the death of Private Joseph Johnson of Sam Chapman's Company E, plus three Rangers wounded and two taken prisoner. [574]

On September 21, William Chapman took seven men, including Lieutenant John J. Fray of the Artillery Company, and went on a scout into the Shenandoah Valley. On Dirt Road, between Harper's Ferry and Winchester, he spotted a supply train, accompanied by a heavy guard. The Rangers followed the wagons until they were about five miles north of Winchester. During this time they managed to capture the commissary officer of General Chapman's brigade, and two straggling cavalrymen. The partisans then decided that, due to the heavy escort, they would be unable to attack the train, so they let it go on its way.

Later that night, Captain Chapman came upon a house, around which were standing several horses and an army wagon. After gathering his men, he sent Lieutenant Fray and two others to search inside the building; Chapman took the rest and went to the stable yard. There they captured a commissary wagon, loaded with hard tack and drawn by six mules. The driver and a sergeant were also taken in. As for Fray, he found the alarm had been given and the house abandoned; evidently, the occupants had seen or heard the Rangers gathering outside and had quietly stolen away. Just as Chapman and the others were concluding their affair at the house, several cavalry officers, trying to catch up with a Federal escort between Winchester and Harper's Ferry, suddenly came upon them. One of the officers, a Lieutenant Gilliam, sensing something was amiss, made his escape in the darkness, but the others—Major Fry from the 16th Pennsylvania, and Captain Brown and Lieutenants Stone and Pressy with the 1st New Hampshire—were quickly captured.

The night's work was not over for Chapman's raiders. They started back on the road that would take them to the Shenandoah River and then across the Blue Ridge. The small band had only gone a mile or so when they happened upon a group of a dozen bluecoats accompanying two sutlers' wagons. Tricking the Yankees into thinking they were friendly troops, the partisans were able to gather in one enlisted man and eleven officers.

Chapman and his ever-increasing column passed through Ashby's Gap and down into Fauquier County on September 22. Without having fired a shot, eight Confederates had taken twenty-two prisoners, sixteen of them officers. The band looked so much like a Union detachment that, when they reached Piedmont, they were nearly attacked by some of their fellow partisans.[575]

On September 19 the waters of Opequon Creek east of Winchester had turned from clear to crimson, fed with the blood that spilled into its two tributaries—Red Bud Run and Abraham's Creek—out of the Berryville

Canyon. General Horatio Wright, commanding Sheridan's VI Corps, had pushed his entire supply train, together with artillery and 10,000 infantrymen, into the narrow confines of the ravine between Berryville and Winchester. The resulting logjam of men, mules, and wagons was unable to move because Rodes' and Gordon's divisions of Early's Valley army had, like a cork in a bottle, plugged up the other end. It was only a temporary Confederate success, however. Eventually, Sheridan would prevail and drive Early's army out of Winchester and back up the Valley Pike. At Fisher's Hill, south of Strasburg, the Southerners would make a stand, only to be driven in a rout from there. Nightfall of September 22 would find the remnants of Early's demoralized army another twenty-five miles further south at Woodstock. [576]

Sheridan had sent his chief of cavalry, General Torbert, into the Page Valley. He was to occupy New Market Gap, the only way from the Great Valley across the Massanutten range into Page Valley near Luray. The gap was a possible escape route for Early as he was being pushed up the Shenandoah Valley. But if Torbert could get up the Page Valley and through the Gap before Early could get past New Market, then he could cut off the Confederate retreat. This would put Early's army in a squeeze between Sheridan on his north and Torbert in the south. But it was not to happen; Torbert failed in his mission, largely because of Confederate General Williams Carter Wickham. With his two brigades, Wickham succeeded in stopping Torbert at Milford, midway between Front Royal and Luray. [577]

The same day Early was trying to hold his army together at Fisher's Hill, the Rangers met at Piedmont and Sam Chapman took about 150 men and started for the vicinity of Front Royal. Crossing from Fauquier County, through Manassas Gap, the partisans bivouacked midway between Front Royal and the Gap. [578]

Chapman had heard the guns from the engagement at Milford as he crossed the Blue Ridge. Leaving the command to sleep, he took a half-dozen men and went on a continual ride from house to house, along the road over which the Federal cavalry had marched the previous day, in an attempt to obtain any information he could. By daybreak of September 23, they were on a hill six miles south of Front Royal or about halfway to Milford. From here Chapman could see Torbert's cavalry camped on the north side of Overall's Run. Noting the size of the Federal cavalry and aware that the attack on the hastily prepared Confederate defenses the day before was not very vigorous, the partisan captain believed the fight would be renewed this day with more determination on the part of the Federals. [579]

As the small group of scouts watched, they saw what was estimated to be about 200 men move out of camp with some wagons and proceed north, down the Luray-Front Royal Turnpike, toward them. After the column had put about a mile between themselves and their main body, it did not appear that any more would follow. What Chapman was seeing was an ambulance train, escorted by about 175 troopers from the 2nd United States Cavalry, under the command of Lieutenant Charles McMaster. [580]

Figuring that they could successfully attack the Federal train, Sam Chapman hurried back down the turnpike toward his command. "I posted my Company at the angle of the Luray Pike, one-half a mile out of Front Royal, as you turn towards the river. I put Captain Franklin's (sic) Company about two hundred yards nearer town on the same road." Chapman saw that the column would have to pass through a narrow passage guarded by a high bluff on one side and the river on the other. He watched as Frankland led his men off, over Graveyard Hill, while he waited with his men near the turnpike toll-house. Concealed by the woods, the Federal column was allowed to pass so that Frankland's men could attack their front while Chapman's company struck their rear. "Down towards the river, a quarter of a mile off, I could see distinctly what was coming. Further back, up the river, my view was concealed by a field of tall corn, on the rise to the left," Sam recalled. [581]

As the head of the column passed him, Chapman suddenly caught his breath. He could still see men turning the angle of the road at the river! There was cavalry following the train—not just an escort, but long columns of smartly marching horsemen, colors waving in the September breeze! Instead of a mere escort for the ambulance train Sam was observing the Reserve Brigade of General Wesley Merritt's 1st Cavalry Division, Colonel Charles Lowell, Jr., commanding. It was the vanguard of Torbert's force, on a retreat toward Winchester. On they came and Sam's eyes could not discern the end of them. Then, as if awakened out of a dream, he thought of Frankland. He and his men would be striking the front of the train; there was no way the young captain could know what was at the other end. [582] Chapman turned to Lieu-tenant Beattie; "Take the men and get back to Chester Gap. I'll go after Frankland!" And with that, Sam put spurs hard into his horse's flanks and raced along side, and not fifty feet away from, the enemy cavalry in the direction of where Frankland should be. [583]

He was too late. Chapman found Frankland's squadron attacking the wagons in Gardner's Woods, just south of the town. They had pitched into the front of the escort, driving it back against the wagons and thus against the Reserve brigades. Sam was yelling as he rode up—"Call off your men! It's a division! You are attacking a division!" The excitement of the fight—or a penchant for not obeying disliked orders—brought a surprising response from Frankland: "Why Sam, we have whipped them!" Chapman repeated his order to call off the men and this time it struck Frankland square in the gut. The two captains raced in among the partisans, ordering them off the field and back up the Chester Gap Road. Sixteen-year-old Private Thomas Moss of Company D, recalled: "I remember distinctly the charge and driving back the Yankees, and whilst shooting...I felt a hand on my shoulder and heard these words: 'for God's sake, come out from here!' On looking around I found it was (Captain Frankland)" The two Rangers were alone among nothing but blue-coated soldiers.[584]

Alternately retreating and charging, the partisans tried to withdraw from the train. But the enemy was all over them—front, flanks, some had even gotten in behind them. They drove the larger part of the Rangers past Hockman's Mill and when they neared "Oak Hill," the home of Perry Criser, along side the Gap road, one of the men came back to Chapman in dismay, yelling "Captain, the Yankees have blocked the road in our front!" Sam told the soldier to go back and tell the rest "... to charge them, as that was our way of escape, and that the whole federal column was pressing our rear." When Chapman arrived, he discovered a line of Yankee cavalry assembled across the road, cutting off the retreat.[585]

Meanwhile, Beattie and the others were having a difficult time obeying their captain's order to get back to Chester Gap and safety. Henry Hatcher and Ab Minor, along with Beattie, attempted to form a line on a nearby hill. But a detachment of Federals got in between them and the rest of the command. Racing down the hill they charged into a group of about twenty Yankees guarding some Rangers who had been captured. "We routed the guards," according to Tom Moss, "and I was fortunate in saving Beattie's life by shooting a man who had his pistol within 12 inches of (him)." [586]

Lieutenant McMaster, commanding the ambulance train escort, had taken a portion of his cavalry and ridden hard up over the hill, raced up the Manor Grade, and brought his men onto the Chester Gap Road. It was he and his men who were lined up across the road over which Chapman's men must travel to gain Chester Gap and safety. When the retreating horsemen approached, McMaster, with sabre waving, led his men toward the partisans. But now Chapman's men were between McMaster and the main body of the Union soldiers. It was at this point that the keystone was laid for the wall of controversy that was to follow.[587]

After doing all he could to cover the rear of the retreat, Chapman caught up with his men on the Chester Gap Road. He remembered: "As I rode up I beheld a young officer wounded, and dismounted, standing by a large rock with his hand up. Some men new to the business, and in their panic, fired at him, which I promptly stopped." [588] The "young officer" was Lieutenant McMaster and the Rebels were bearing down on him and his small detachment. When McMaster was found, his body riddled by bullets, he was still alive—and still armed. According to Union sources, McMaster told his comrades that he had attempted to surrender but was instead shot. [589] (Despite reports to the contrary, McMaster, though mortally wounded, would not die that day, but some three weeks later.) [590]

The events surrounding McMaster's wounding, though still debatable, are clearer now than they were in 1864. As far as most of the partisans were concerned, no plausibility could be given to the report that the lieutenant was trying to surrender. In response to an 1896 speech by Dolly Richards, in which he held Custer responsible for the atrocities that followed the fight, Mosby set forth his views on just what happened to McMaster. "Merritt says Lieutenant McMasters (sic) was captured, robbed and shot; none of the other reports mention him. The truth is, McMasters (sic) was never a prisoner. He attempted to cut off the retreat of my men when attacked by a division of cavalry. He cut himself off and got killed. My men shot him and rode over him; they had no time to rob him if they had wished to do so; Merritt's whole division was behind and McMasters (sic) was in front of them...He may have intended to surrender, but it does not necessarily follow that my men knew it. They had no time to take prisoners or parley. They were surrounded by thousands and their only way of escape was to break through the ranks that enclosed them. McMasters (sic) got in the way; they shot him and rode on. It was not their business to ask him what he wanted to do." [591]

Still, much credence must be given to Sam Chapman's account, which would indicate McMaster was, in fact, trying to surrender, after being wounded ("As I rode up I beheld a young officer...with his hand up.") After all, it was Chapman who was in the better position to know and his account was based on what he saw, not on second-hand telling. With this said, however, Sam added: "The truth is he received his death wound in the midst of the melee, when men's blood was hot." [592]

Despite all the fighting, the Rangers came away with no one killed and only two wounded. The Federals lost about twenty killed and wounded. There were other casualties however; six of Chapman's men were captured. [593]

When McMaster told his comrades that he had been shot while trying to surrender, it was as if a short fuse had just ignited a powder keg among the Union troops. The six prisoners were taken into town amongst a fast growing mob scene. Not a citizen's mob but one comprised of well-trained and disciplined cavalry troops. These troopers were members of Merritt's division, which included Colonel Lowell's brigade. This was the same brigade that had suffered the most at the hands of Mosby in the wagon train attack at Berryville six weeks before. McMaster's own 2nd U. S. Cavalry was a part of Lowell's brigade. Custer's brigade of Michigan cavalrymen was also there. It included the 5th Michigan Regiment. The Berryville house-burners, annihilated by the Chapman brothers' squadron, had been members of this unit. So revenge—bloody, merciless, unforgiving revenge—hung heavily in the air. The eye-for-an-eye mind-set would come to rule this day. These avengers were not soldiers of an organized army, but rather ordinary men caught up in a different army—one of unrelenting hatred, fueled by the innate nature of man, which permitted such things.

When Hatcher, Beattie, Moss, and the others had ridden down the hill and charged into the bluecoats guarding a group of captured Confederates, Hatcher had given the reins of a riderless horse to one of the prisoners—Private William Thomas Overby of Company D. But before he could mount, Overby was again captured. Moss and Beattie made their way up into a pine woods. Beattie left in an attempt to round up some more men while Moss stayed hidden. He would remain there most of the day, until the enemy had left. And he would hear the disturbing sounds of what was to come, down in the village [594]

Besides Overby, four other Rangers were captured—Privates Thomas Anderson and Lucian Love—like Overby, members of Company D—and Private David Jones of A Company. The fourth one of Mosby's men taken was an unidentified private, believed to be named Carter. A sixth prisoner was young Henry Rhodes, a local lad, who found himself in the wrong place at the wrong time. The captives were marched into Front Royal where the word was spreading throughout the Federal commands about how McMaster had been wounded (or, as most accounts that day, killed.) Emotions were being aroused to an unbelievable pitch. The past defeats suffered by the Federals at the hand of Mosby and his band of partisans helped whip the inflamed passions of the blue-coated cavalrymen into a raging inferno that only the cold hand of Death would be able to extinguish. And Death was coming.

Tom Moss was still hiding in the pine woods when he heard the commotion down in the town. "I could see there was something going on in Front Royal and heard the shots," Moss recalled, "but did not learn until afterwards the fate of our comrades." [595] The shots he heard were the ones that killed Love and Jones and Anderson. Lucian Love and David Jones were taken to the graveyard behind the Methodist Church and gunned down. Anderson was marched a half-mile out of town, to Perry Criser's imposing home which overlooked the scene of the morning's fight. He was shot down while standing under the still green leaves of a spreading elm tree. The Yankee band mockingly played the tune "Love Not, the One You Love May Die" as the prisoners were led to their deaths. [596]

Henry Rhodes was a seventeen-year-old resident of Front Royal. He was not a member of Mosby's command—at least not in life. The sole support of his mother and sister, he had longed to ride with the famous guerrilla. Rhodes had borrowed an old horse and ridden out to the spot where the Rangers were gathered to await the wagon train; he believed he might be able to capture a horse that would enable him to become a member of the partisans. But the old horse had failed Rhodes during the retreat toward Chester Gap and he was captured. Taken back into the town, he was lashed with ropes between two horses and dragged, half-conscious, down Chester Street. . His mother ran to him and put her arms around his neck, pleading with his executioners. But they pushed her roughly away with the point of their sabres, jeering and admonishing her not to come near or she too would feel their deadly wrath. The youth was dragged to a field at the foot of "Rose Hill" and a single blue-coated trooper emptied his pistol into his body. The Richardson family, watching the terror unfold, was distressed almost beyond words that "poor Henry Rhodes should be shot in our field, nearly in front of our door." Doctor R. C. Brock was a young man living in Front Royal when the tragic events played out: "Rhodes was my friend and playmate and I saw him shot from a distance but did not know at the time who it was." [597]

The bloodletting of the Yankee troopers was not yet satisfied. Brock recalled seeing "Overby and Carter...carried to a large walnut tree upon the hill between Front Royal and Riverton and hung. They endured the taunts of their captors with proud and undaunted (bearing)." Overby stood hatless while the September breeze blew through his "black, wavy hair. (He had) a tall, well-knit frame—a splendid specimen of manhood—he looked like a knight of old." Both men were offered their freedom if they would tell where Mosby and his battalion could be found. The loyal partisans steadfastly refused and they were asked for any last wishes. Carter requested a Bible. Overby silently stared, unflinching, at his killers. Finally, as the rope was tightened around his neck, he bravely told his would-be executioners that he was proud to die as a Confederate soldier and as one of Mosby's men and that Mosby would swing in the wind ten Yankees for every man they murdered. The two prisonerss were made to stand on their horses' backs and then the horses were removed from under them. They hung there all night.[598]

Back at Belle Grove, Tee Edmonds heard a different version of the fateful day's events and recorded them in her journal the following day: "Some five or six of our dear soldiers were captured at Front Royal under Captain Sam Chapman and were brutally shot, two of them hung...Our men had captured a Colonel (sic)," she continued, "and were overtaken, surrounded by the enemy. Our men shot the Colonel (sic), giving him several shots after his begging and pleading with them not to kill him. He lived long enough to tell the Yankees what they did and these of our men who fell into their hands were treated so in retaliation. Oh! The innocent have to suffer for the cruelties inflicted by others," Tee lamented. "It would not have been so bad had they caught those whom committed the uncivilized act of shooting a defenseless prisoner."

Tee Edmonds' relating of the story meant she had talked with someone. That someone was most probably one or more of the Rangers who had returned to Fauquier. Anderson's body had been brought back, presumably by his comrades. "Poor Tom Anderson met his fate there. (His) body was brought down yesterday," Tee had written, meaning September 24. [599]

Blame for the executions—murders—varies, but the cover-up was complete. No mention was made of the happenings in any of the Union reports—not Torbert's, nor Merritt's, nor Lowell's; not Custer's, not Sheridan's. They were all there that day, except for Sheridan, and their silence inherently condoned what the troops had done. Young Brock had seen one of the Union commanders: "While I was looking at (Overby and Carter), General Custer, at the head of his division (sic), rode by. He was dressed in a splendid suit of silk velvet, his saddle bow bound in silver or gold. In his hand he had a large branch of damsons, which he picked and ate as he rode along, his yellow locks resting on his shoulders." [600] Though initially blamed for the atrocities, Custer was probably the least culpable. But he was an extremely visible figure in the town that day, as Brock so vividly relates. And certainly his silence can be taken as approval.

Responsibility for the killing of the Confederate prisoners probably falls most heavily upon General Torbert, commander of Sheridan's cavalry, if, for no other reason, because of his overall command of the troops involved. But Torbert would have more, much more, direct involvement. Culpability must also belong to General Merritt, commanding Torbert's 1st Cavalry division, and two of Merritt's brigade commanders, Colonel Lowell, commanding the Reserve Brigade, and of course General Custer of the 1st (Michigan) Brigade.

Of all the accounts of what took place that day, some stand out, primarily because of who authored them. First, there is the one by Captain Theodore W. Bean, provost marshal of Merritt's 1st Cavalry division, contained in a history of the 17th Regiment Pennsylvania Volunteer Cavalry. In his account, Bean relates the capture of the six partisans and how three of them were shot and the other three were brought back to the town. "One of these three, quite a youth, was surrounded by the Michigan Brigade on the outskirts of town and shot down. The other two were hung in a small grove between the town and the river. I witnessed the execution of these two men. Among the troops present was "... Lieutenant McMaster's troop of the Second United States Cavalry. (Their) non-commissioned officers and enlisted men requested the privilege of executing the order of General Torbert to hang them, which was granted." Bean's account specifically states that the Michigan Brigade (Custer's) shot the "youth", probably Henry Rhodes, and that the 2nd U.S. Cavalry (part of Lowell's Reserve Brigade) hung the other two on orders of General Torbert. [601]

A second account supports that of Captain Bean. Robert Craig Wallace was a member of Custer's 5th Michigan Cavalry and at the time of the incident, was detached for staff duty with General Torbert. Writing after the war, Wallace tells of the capture of "...some half a dozen of the enemy and they were shown no mercy. Some of them were told to run and as they ran were fired upon until they fell. I particularly remember the two who were brought to Gen. Torbert who told Capt. Bean of the staff to take them to the woods and hang them. Bean didn't like the job." Wallace further tells of a conversation which Bean had with the two prisoners, in which the division provost marshal told them he would spare their lives if they gave information that would be of use against Mosby and his command. They refused and were consequently hanged. [602]

Two other eyewitnesses authenticate these first two accounts. Samuel C. Willis was a sergeant in the 1st Rhode Island Cavalry. On March 27, 1902, in a letter to the postmaster of Front Royal, he wrote: "We were in the escort of Gen. Torbert and...captured some of Mosby's Men. Being questioned by Torbert, and being satisfied that they were from Mosby's command, he ordered them shot then and there. At the very time these men were being shot, two more were brought in, one a stout man, the other a small man." Willis goes on to relate how, after being questioned by Torbert and their subsequent denial to give up information about Mosby, Torbert ordered the provost marshal to take the men up to a tree and hang them. "As I was one of the non-commissioned staff of my regiment, my colonel said to me—'Go up and witness that and see that they do not recant.'" Willis says that after being again questioned by Captain Bean, with the same negative result, the two prisoners were hanged. [603]

The Reverend Frederic Denison was chaplain of the 1st Rhode Island Cavalry. He recorded his version of the events in a history of the regiment in 1876: "After a short chase, two of the guerrillas were captured, some were killed, and others made their escape. The two captured were given their choice, to lead a party to Mosby's haunts, or die. They preferred to be hung. Major Farrington, Provost Marshal (First Cavalry Corps), by order of General Torbert, notified the prominent citizens of the town that if like inhumanities (re: the "murder" of Lieutenant McMaster) were repeated the town would be laid in ashes. The criminals were led to a knoll a short distance away (and hanged.)" [604]

Although there are variations, such as the locales of the shootings and hangings, in these accounts, all—from those of the young lad Brock, and Ranger Tom Moss, to those of the numerous Union officers—reflect substantial agreement as to who was involved and where responsibility should lie.

The Union reports for September 23 are consistent in this respect—they make no mention of what took place with regard to the men of Chapman's command who were captured that day. In fact, they do not record that prisoners were taken at all. This omission is significant to the cover-up. Merritt's report on the affair states: "Near (Front Royal) the advance of the reserve Brigade encountered a body of guerrillas under a Captain Chapman, who was in the act of capturing an ambulance train of our wounded. The gang was quickly dispersed, with a loss of eighteen killed. Lieutenant McMaster of the Second U. S. Cavalry, was mortally wounded in this affair, being shot after he was taken prisoner and robbed." [605] The report of General Torbert is even less detailed, as he refers only to "...a skirmish with Mosby's guerrillas at Front Royal, killing two officers and nine men."[606] Lowell's report for September 23, states: "Moved to near Cedarville, dispersing enroute a detachment of Mosby's, under Captain Mountjoy (sic) killing thirteen." [607] This is, in all probability, Lowell's report of the Front Royal fight and he has confused Montjoy with Chapman. Cedarville is about three miles north of Front Royal and was the intended destination, on the way to Winchester. All the reports refer to casualties—killed and wounded—on the part of the Rangers, although there are no known records to support such losses, while not a single report refers to any prisoners being taken.

It is interesting that on October 5, almost two weeks after the affair, Lowell, in the midst of a letter to his wife, writes: "...I was sorry enough the other day that my Brigade should have had a part in the hanging and shooting of some of Mosby's men who were taken—I believe that some punishment was deserved—but I hardly think we were within the laws of war, and any violation of them opens the door for all sorts of barbarity—it was by order of the Division Commander, however." [608] The division commander was, of course, General Merritt.

On October 19, 1864, Colonel Lowell was mortally wounded at Cedar Creek and died the next day. He was promoted, posthumously, to brigadier general.

23. Following the Tracks

During the last week in September, Colonel Mosby had recovered sufficiently enough from his wound to travel from his father's home in Lynchburg to Petersburg to confer with General Lee. Mosby recalled the meeting: "When he saw me hobbling up to him on crutches, he came to meet me and said, as he extended his hand, 'Colonel, I have never had but one fault to find with you—you are always getting wounded.' " When his train stopped over at Gordonsville on its return trip to Lynchburg, Mosby ran into Dolly Richards and Alfred Glascock. The two officers were on their way to Richmond on a furlough. As he talked with the two men, it was apparent things were not going well within the 43rd during his absence. Although still requiring crutches to move about and not able to mount a horse without assistance, the commander resolved to return to his command. After arriving that evening in Lynchburg, Mosby gathered his belongings and the next morning was back on the train. This time, when he arrived in Gordonsville, he met another of his officers, Captain Montjoy—on furlough. "My command, I saw, was going to pieces from the jealousy of the officers. Montjoy volunteered to return, which showed his motive in leaving." [609]

The apparent discord focused on his two senior officers, Captains Adolphus "Dolly" Edward Richards and William Henry Chapman. The two men were much alike but, at the same time, different. Only twenty years old, Richards was the "dandy" of the battalion, with a demeanor that belied his youthfulness. Well built at five feet, ten inches, with dark hair and complexion, he sported a "frenchy" mustache, with blue eyes, that set off an already handsome face. The family home, "Green Garden," near Upperville, was often close by and afforded him the opportunity of maintaining the most immaculate and modish dress of anyone in the command. A most exquisite feather always topped off his hat. But beneath the trappings was a man of cool daring who knew what he wanted and how to go about obtaining it.

Chapman, the former commander of the Dixie Artillery, was a leader, through both a natural ability and experience. Though clearly not the "dandy" that Richards was, the twenty-four-year-old, former University student, had married the cultured and genteel Josephine Jeffries of Fauquier County in February 1864. Chapman had a dark complexion with deep, dark eyes, thick black hair, and a beard that seemed always in need of attention. He possessed an intense determination that, more often than not, let him achieve what he sought after. An oft-times rough exterior hid a keen intelligence and, like Richards, he had a competitive nature that made him a formidable adversary.

While Mosby was recovering from his wound, William Chapman commanded the battalion. "When I was wounded," Mosby later recalled, "Sheridan's line of communication was not over 10 miles in length and difficult to strike. Now it was 150 miles long and assailable in a hundred places (but) comparatively little (was) done. That was a chance for Dolly to win his spurs, but he thought Chapman would get the credit." [610]

The first person Mosby wanted to see when he got back to "Mosby's Confederacy" was Sam Chapman. Front Royal was much on the Colonel's mind and he wanted to hear first hand the tragic details. He was glad to see that no retaliatory action had been taken by his men against the Union prisoners they held. Much heated debate had ensued but cooler heads prevailed and it was agreed they would wait until their leader's return. The prisoners were sent on to Richmond. [611]

Something else had occurred during Mosby's absence that upset him. On September 26, Ranger Blackwell's home, "Heartland", near Piedmont, had been burned by a force of the 13th New York Cavalry, sent to escort an engineer examining the Manassas Gap Railroad. The home had served as Mosby's unofficial headquarters and as such, there was a large quantity of stores and material stored there. Among the items burned or destroyed, according to the Federal report of the incident, was "a large quantity of ammunition, artillery harness and equipments ... pistols and carbines, (and) articles of clothing." Tee Edmonds made note of Mosby's reaction in her journal: "Mosby returned last week and was very much enraged to find the Yankees had burned his headquarters—Joe Blackwell's. He calls for every man to meet as though he was going to do something rash." [612]

While Mosby was much disappointed that his officers had not taken advantage of Sheridan's situation in the Valley, during the time he was recuperating from his wound, he certainly intended to do something about it, now that he was back. He was keenly aware of the distance that existed between the bulk of Sheridan's army, located in the upper Valley near Harrisonburg, and his bases of supply and communications, over a hundred miles away at the railroad depots in Harper's Ferry and Martinsburg. Every weak link in that long chain would be susceptible to attack. [613]

Mosby's first order of business was to assemble the entire command, including artillery, at Piedmont on October 2. At the same time, Sam Chapman, with Company E, was dispatched to the Shenandoah Valley to strike Sheridan's lines of communication near Middletown. Things were quickly changing, however. When Chapman returned, bringing thirteen prisoners, he also brought the news that Sheridan was withdrawing his army back down the Valley.[614]

Sheridan had advised General Grant on September 29, that "I pressed Early so closely... that he gave up the Valley and took to the mountains...My impression is that most of the troops Early had left passed through the mountains to Charlottesville...Early's army was completely broken up and is dispirited." Believing the Valley cleared and secured, and with his supply lines getting longer each day, Sheridan decided to return closer to his base. By October 9, the Army of the Shenandoah had come as far north as Strasburg. And Jubal Early's supposedly "broken and dispirited" Army of the Valley was close on its heels.[615]

With Sam Chapman's news that Sheridan was proceeding back north, Mosby figured the Federal army would attempt to establish a base east of the Blue Ridge, using the Orange and Alexandria Railroad for this purpose. With this in mind, he took 300 men and two howitzers and headed for Thoroughfare Gap. That night his scouts reported a heavy concentration of Federal infantry near Gainesville, advancing west along the Manassas Gap Railroad. The next day, October 4, when Mosby neared the tracks at Gainesville, he received fire, which caused him to fall back across the Bull Run Mountains through Hopewell Gap, stopping near Piedmont. But what he saw and what had caused all the enemy activity was a construction train with infantry and cavalry guard. Now it was clear to the partisan leader—Sheridan's objective was not the Orange and Alexandria but rather the Manassas Gap Railroad. Plans had been made to reconstruct the tracks as far as Piedmont, then possibly through the Gap to Front Royal and into Strasburg.[616]

When Sheridan decided to retreat back down the Valley, due in part to the difficult task of supplying his army so far from its base, he also took the opportunity of denying the Confederate army a means of subsistence in the Valley. Sending his cavalry past him and south into Staunton, he had them destroy vast amounts of stores and material, so vital to Early's beleaguered army. "Torbert entered Staunton and destroyed a large quantity of rebel government property—harness, saddles, small-arms, hard bread, flour, repair shops, etc. He then proceeded to Waynesborough (sic), destroying the iron bridge over the South Branch of the Shenandoah, seven miles of tracks, the depot buildings, government tannery and a large amount of leather, flour, and stores, etc." [617]

Military stores were not the only objective. Continuing the kind of devastating warfare against the citizens of the Shenandoah Valley that had begun with Hunter, Sheridan now placed his name beside his predecessor's on the same infamous page in the history of the war. This part of his Shenandoah campaign would forever be known in the Valley as "The Burning". With Grant's approval, the Army of the Shenandoah spread out in a twenty-mile-wide swath across the Valley floor, from the Blue Ridge in the east to North Mountain and the Alleghenies in the west. Merritt's division held the center position, going down the Valley Pike and extending to the western base of Massanutten Mountain; Colonel William H. Powell, who had taken command of Averell's division, proceeded on the east side of the Massanutten through Page Valley. Custer was on the west flank, between the Valley Pike and North Mountain. By the time Sheridan reached Woodstock two days later, he was able to report to Grant: "I have destroyed over 2,000 barns filled with wheat, hay, and farming implements; over seventy mills filled with flour and wheat; have driven in front of the army over 4,000 head of stock, and have killed and issued to the troops not less than 3,000 sheep...Tomorrow I will continue the destruction of wheat, forage, & etc., down to Fisher's Hill. When this is completed the Valley, from Winchester to Staunton, ninety-two miles, will have but little for man or beast." [618] When the week was out, Sheridan could boast, according to one report, of having destroyed 800 barrels of flour, 50,000 tons of hay, and 600,000 bushels of grain, along with 50,000 head of livestock driven off; the dollar amount of the loss was put at 25 million. [619] Other reports varied in the numbers, but one thing they all were in agreement on—it was, for all practical purposes, complete physical ruination of the Valley. No price could be placed on the amount of human misery and suffering.

The torching of the Valley by the Union troops was part of the plan agreed to between Grant and Sheridan for the disposition of the Army of the Shenandoah. This followed the incorrect assertion that Early had been driven from the Valley. On October 3, General Grant, at City Point, near Petersburg, advised Sheridan: "You may take up such position in the Valley as you think you can and ought to be held, and send all the force not required for this immediately here. Leave nothing for the subsistence of an army on any ground you abandon to the enemy. I will direct the railroad to be pushed toward Front Royal, so that you may send your troops back that way."

The Union army's chief of staff, General Halleck, responded to Grant on October 4, relative to his plan for disposition of Sheridan's troops: "I perceive...that you propose to withdraw a large portion of the troops from the Valley, This will make it necessary to adopt a line of defense against rebel raids...I am of the opinion that the proper position...can be found at Manassas Gap, or its vicinity, so that the garrison can operate on either side of the Blue Ridge. The place should have several months' supplies and be capable of making a strong and long resistance to an attacking force." Halleck continued, setting forth the idea of rebuilding the Manassas Gap Railroad to Front Royal—and of his concern for Mosby: "It can be communicated with by the Manassas railroad....It will be necessary to send South all rebel inhabitants between that line and the Potomac, and also to completely clean out Mosby's gang of robbers who have so long infested that...country and Sheridan's cavalry should be required to accomplish this object before it is sent elsewhere. The two small regiments under General Augur have been so often cut up by Mosby's band that they are cowed and useless for that purpose." [620]

While Sheridan was reining terror in the Valley, Mosby was getting ready to rain cannon balls on the Manassas Gap Railroad. Following his discovery of the construction train and its escort near Gainesville, Mosby had taken his force toward Salem. He took a position on a rise known as Stephenson's Hill, just south of the town, setting up his two mountain guns to overlook the Federal camp one-half mile away. At three o'clock on the afternoon of October 5, the little guns opened fire. The Yankees, taken totally by surprise, quickly fled toward Rectortown where they formed a defensive line. One squadron of the Rangers, about eighty men, pursued the fleeing Federals, members of the 5th Pennsylvania Heavy Artillery and the 202nd Pennsylvania Infantry. Following was not hard to do—the way was well marked with discarded clothes and equipment. During the chase, the partisans managed to capture fifty of the enemy, while sustaining two wounded. One of the wounded soldiers, Private Charles R. Stinson of Company B, was captured and would die a week later in a Union hospital in Alexandria. [621]

The scene at General J. P. Slough's headquarters in Alexandria was one of self-admitted confusion on just what was taking place at Salem:

> 5:20 PM –"A telegram from Colonel Gallupe… announces an attack with over 400 men and two pieces of artillery, near Salem. The account is so confused it is hard to tell the result. His communication has been cut. He has 800 men with him. What shall I do? Shall I send a part of my artillery here and troops from Manassas Junction?"

> 6:40 PM – "The confusion of the dispatches… is such as to make it uncertain what troops have been engaged… Colonel Gallupe… should be strong enough to drive off the enemy if not over 400 strong."

By 7:40 p.m. Gallupe requested a section of artillery. Later that evening, General Augur advised he was going to the front himself. A short while afterwards an order was sent out "…to send all mounted men of First and Third Divisions, Cavalry Corps, and of Averill's division…to Colonel Gallupe at Rectortown….There will probably be 500 men and horses." [622]

While Mosby, with one squadron, was pursuing the Yankees to Rectortown William Chapman and the remainder of the battalion was tearing up the just completed track. That night, earthworks were built by the Federals at Rectortown, and they were joined by a force from near Piedmont that had been involved in rebuilding the bridge over Goose Creek. [623]

The next day, Mosby moved his guns to a new position at Salem and that afternoon the shelling resumed. The Union soldiers were forced from their earthworks and took refuge near Rectortown, in a deep gorge through which the tracks ran. A train, trying to make its way up from White Plains, was driven back; it made a later attempt and succeeded in getting through to the new Federal camp at Rectortown.

Mosby withdrew the evening of October 6, planing to assemble the next day at Blackwell's near Piedmont. The following day, the harassment and shelling of the Union troops and construction parties continued. The main body of the Federal force moved on to Salem, taking a position on Stephenson's Hill, which Mosby had vacated two days before. For all their efforts, the

Rangers were not able to halt the rebuilding of the tracks. On October 7, Tee Edmonds sat down in her journal: "The Yankees have run the cars as far as Piedmont. The old whistle and snort of the iron horse seems as natural as in days past." [624]

Although Mosby had been unsuccessful in halting the laying of the tracks, he continued to harass the trains that ran on them and the troops sent to guard them. On October 10, the same day that Augur advised Halleck he would commence building stockades along the entire length of the track, the partisans were busy with that same track. About a mile west of White Plains, Lieutenant Glascock and a few of the men displaced some rails and waited. That morning, a slow moving train was allowed to pass and then the Rangers open fire on the rear cars. Just as was planned, the engineer immediately put on steam and ran into the displaced rails, causing the locomotive to smash up and go off the track. The assistant superintendent of the railroad and several other people were killed; four Confederate prisoners on the train managed to escape. [625]

The day following the derailment, Mosby was with Montjoy's company at White Plains. Near a Federal camp, Mosby and thirteen of the Rangers ran into eighty Union troopers. The Yankees took up a position behind a stone fence, to fight with carbines at long range. Mosby called for Montjoy and then withdrew into some woods to draw the enemy out. When the Federals came out to follow the partisans, Mosby and the others suddenly turned and charged. A Yankee trooper shot Mosby's horse as he passed and the horse fell, pinning the guerrilla chief underneath. His men quickly extricated him, leaving Mosby with nothing more than a bruised ankle and leg, but it was sore enough for him to hobble for quite some time. The Federals lost six killed and wounded according to one unofficial report.[626]

While Mosby was operating against the Manassas Gap Railroad, Dolly Richards had taken thirty-two men and gone on a scout in the Shenandoah Valley. On October 11, he attacked an ambulance train on the Valley Pike, mid-way between Newtown and Middletown, on its way to join Sheridan at Cedar Creek. The train was carrying Lieutenant Colonel C. W. Tolles, Sheridan's chief quartermaster and Doctor Emil Ohienschlager, assistant surgeon and medical inspector on Sheridan's staff. They were escorted by twenty-five troopers of the 17th Pennsylvania Cavalry. Richards' men struck the rear of the train and the attack was so fierce that no one was able to escape. Three of the troopers were killed out-right, another five wounded, and nineteen prisoners were taken. Also wounded were Ohlenschlager and Tolles, both mortally so. Tolles, shot in the head, died three weeks later, while Ohlenschlager, wounded in the bowels, lasted but a few days. Twenty-three horses were captured and a quantity of papers, vouchers and documents taken, which were forwarded to Confederate authorities in Richmond. [627]

On October 12, Secretary of War Stanton decided to declare war on the civilian population "along the Manassas gap (sic) Railroad, ...in retaliation for the murderous acts of guerrilla bands, composed of and assisted by the inhabitants along the (railroad)." Every house within five miles of the line was to be destroyed, unless occupied by friendly persons. All males suspected to be or assisting the "guerrilla bands" were to be arrested and confined in Old Capitol Prison. Women and children would be displaced, going north or south, however they chose. Forage, animals and grain was to be confiscated. All timber and brush along the road was to be cut down and destroyed. Any citizens found within five miles of the railroad would be considered bushwhackers and treated accordingly. If further hostilities occurred "...an additional strip of ten miles will be laid waste and that section of the country depopulated." [628]

While concentrating on the Manassas Gap Railroad, Mosby had not forgotten the Baltimore and Ohio. On October 16, Lee sent the following report to Secretary Seddon: "On (October 14) Colonel Mosby struck the Baltimore and Ohio Railroad at Duffield's, destroying U. S. Military train consisting of locomotive and ten cars, securing twenty prisoners and fifteen horses. Among the prisoners are two paymasters with $168,000 in Government funds." [629]

On the night of October 13, Mosby, with about eighty-four members of the command, was lying in wait along the B&O tracks about two miles east of Kearneysville. The spot chosen was in a deep cut a little west of Brown's Crossing and just out from the Duffield depot. Lieutenant Hatcher had taken fifteen men and loosened one of the rails, using old ties and fence rails to elevate it above its companion rail. The Rangers then withdrew to a nearby wood to wait. Just after two o'clock the next morning, the slumbering raiders were awakened by the sound of a whistle, followed by the loud explosion of a locomotive's boiler. Within an hour's time, the cars had all been looted and the valuables taken from the passengers. The only casualties were the engineer, and his son who was the fireman, burned by the steam in the explosion of the boiler, and a Union officer, shot by Ranger John Hearn as he attempted to escape. The partisans took two prisoners—Majors Edwin Moore and David Ruggles, both paymasters headed for Winchester with $168,000 in payroll for Sheridan's troops. They then set the cars on fire. The raiders made their way back across the Shenandoah River to Bloomfield, in Loudoun County, and the next day divided up the spoils. Each participating man received about $2,000, from what was to be known as the "Greenback Raid". Colonel Mosby, as was his rule, would not accept any of the "rewards." [630] Unfortunately for the two paymasters, Treasury officials in Washington suspected there had been collusion between them and the raiders. Major Ruggles would die in a Southern prison and Major Moore was forced to petition the Congress for relief in clearing his name. Soon after the war, he visited Mosby in Warrenton and obtained a certificate attesting to the facts of his capture. [631]

While Mosby was making plans to strike the B&O at Duffield's, he told William Chapman to take a party and see if he could hit the railroad from some point in Maryland. The same day of the Greenback Raid, Chapman and eighty men crossed the Potomac River at White's Ford, about four miles below the Mouth of Monacacy and proceeded up the canal towpath toward Adamstown. Because of the raid on the railroad at Duffield's, no trains were moving out of Harper's Ferry. Along the way, Chapman burned several canal boats, with their freight, and captured some horses and mules; he then cut the telegraph wires between Licksville and Adamstown. By this time, the Federals were aware of the Rebels presence and were taking positions at all the crossing points back into Virginia. Various Union reports put Chapman's force at up to three hundred men. [632]

When the partisans turned away from Adamstown and started back, a company of Loudoun Rangers, numbering about 100 and led by Captain James W. Grubb, followed them. Sam Chapman, who was bringing up the rear of the column, proposed that the partisans turn and charge the Federals, but William told him: "Sam, I haven't got time to stop and go off on a fox hunt after Grubb," and started off at a trot. The Loudoun Rangers, thinking the partisans were about to skedaddle, speeded up after them. Then, when the enemy troopers were within striking distance, William Chapman turned the command around and, much to his brother's delight, ordered a charge. A short fight ensued before the Federals turned and ran. Grubb lost four men killed or wounded and seven taken prisoner, with their horses and equipment, before he finally retreated. Captain Burnette, commanding the post at Point of Rocks, showed his disgust with Grubb in a wire to General Stevenson, commanding at Harper's Ferry: "Captain Grubb returned here half an hour since, and said the enemy were retreating toward the river, but he thought it best not to follow. I ordered him immediately back....Grubb is reprehensible for this retiring....I have sent down the infantry."

When Chapman's contingent reached a bridge below Point of Rocks, they found an infantry detachment in the process of tearing up the bridge floor and throwing it into the water. They were able to scatter the infantrymen and replace the planking, and were soon safely across into Loudoun County.[633]

Once Mosby had diverted his attention away from the Manassas Gap Railroad and to the Baltimore and Ohio, he directed Captain Peter Franklin to take the artillery pieces to a safe place in the mountains and conceal them. The guns were taken a mile and a half up Little Cobbler Mountain, south of Piedmont, and hidden in a dense thicket, near Emory's. Sergeant A. G. Babcock and eight other members of the company then set up a camp at the base of the mountain. One of the men who had helped take the guns to their place of concealment was eighteen-year-old Private John H. Lunceford, of Company B. After coming off the mountain he was captured near Piedmont by troopers of Colonel H. S. Gansevoort's 13th New York Cavalry. Lunceford stated his desire not to be exchanged or otherwise go back to the command and agreed to lead Gansevoort to Babcock's camp. The New Yorkers were able to surprise the camp, making prisoners of Babcock and all his men. The search was then begun for the hiding place of the cannon. With some more help, apparently from another member of the Artillery Company, Gansevoort was able to locate the guns. "The location of the pieces was even a secret not imparted to many of Mosby's men. By intimidation, however, when almost relinquishing the task, a driver of the artillery was forced to discover the trail of the pieces," Gansevoort later reported. Along with the 13th New York, on the search mission were two companies of the 5th Pennsylvania Artillery and two squadrons of the 16th New York Cavalry.

The reward for the 13th New York Cavalry was a three-inch ordnance gun, a 12-pound howitzer and two small mountain howitzers, together with the limber, caisson, ammunition, and sets of harness. Colonel Gansevoort asked to retain one of the small mountain howitzers with his command.[634]

Mosby, in a report to General Lee in which he "...(desired) to make an explanation in reference to the capture of my artillery..." stated "one of my men deserted and guided the enemy to where it was. They captured no men or horses with it." It is uncertain just why Mosby would tell his commander that no men were captured. As a deterrent to Mosby's wrecking their trains, the Federals forced Babock and his fellow prisoners to ride in a box car next to the locomotive for a period of five weeks, as the trains were run between Rectortown and Alexandria. [635]

24. "Measure for Measure"

On October 13, while Mosby was waiting near Duffield's for the train that would soon be derailed in the Greenback Raid, the atrocities that had occurred at Front Royal only three weeks before would have a fateful reoccurence in the neighboring county a few miles to the south.

Brigadier General William H. Powell, in command of what had been Averill's Second Cavalry Division, Army of West Virginia, was in Rappahannock County with his troopers. What took place is best told in his official report: "Having learned of the willful and cold-blooded murder of a U.S. soldier by two men (Chancellor and Myers, members of Mosby's gang of cutthroats and robbers), some two miles from my camp a few days previous, I ordered the execution of one of Mosby's gang whom I had captured the day previous at Gaines' Cross Roads, and placing the placard on his breast with the following inscription: 'A. C. Willis, member of Company C, Mosby's command, hanged by the neck in retaliation for the murder of a U. S. soldier by Messrs. Chancellor and Myers.' I sent a detachment…with orders to destroy the residence, barn, and all outbuildings and forage, on the premises of Mr. Chancellor, and to drive off all stock of every description, which orders were promptly carried out." [636]

Albert Gallatin " Bert" Willis was a twenty-year-old ministerial student and Baptist colporteur, [637] who had joined up with Mosby ten months before and been assigned to Company C. On the day of his capture, he was at the blacksmith shop at Gaines' Cross Roads, a short distance from Flint Hill. (One account states he was in the process of taking some prisoners and stock back to the Confederate lines.) While sitting on the forge drying his feet, he heard the Union patrol approaching and tried to get up into a chimney to hide. But it was too late and he and another man at the shop were taken prisoner. Intent on executing one of the prisoners, straws were drawn and the fateful lot fell to the unidentified man with Willis. Breaking down, the weeping man begged for his life, expressing sorrowful concern for his wife and children. At this point young Willis, declaring that he had no such responsibilities and, as a Christian, was prepared for whatever fate might befall him, asked if he could take the place of the condemned. One of Powell's officers replied that it made no difference which it was but that one of the prisoners was to be hung in retaliation for the killing of the soldier of their command by who were thought to be Mosby's men. The execution was then carried out on a large poplar tree along the roadside. [638]

But Powell had been mistaken as to who he believed Chancellor and Myers were. Myers was a farmer—not a member of Mosby's or any other military command—who had befriended a man posing as a deserter from the Union army, but who in actuality was a spy. Chancellor was a Confederate solider, but not one of Mosby's men, on leave visiting his father, a neighbor of Myers. Chancellor had agreed to take the "deserter" out to the Confederate lines. Enroute, the man had tried to escape because he knew he would be found out if taken to the Confederate authorities; his attempts to flee only confirmed Chancellor's suspicions that the man was not a deserter but a spy. Knowing he would be hung when they reached Confederate headquarters at Gordonsville, the man tried once more to run; this is when Chancellor shot and killed him. None of the participants in the affair were associated with Mosby or his command.[639]

On October 16, Sam Chapman and his own Company E, together with Companies C and F, set out from Bloomfield to operate along the Manassas Gap Railroad. At the same time Mosby took the rest of the command towards Fairfax. Early in the morning of October 18, Captain Montjoy, with Company D, moved toward Falls Church, to attack a Federal camp. They succeeded in getting into the stable area and were moving the horses out, when the blowing of a horn was heard. Thinking it was only a signal to assemble some coon hunters, Montjoy were not alarmed and proceeded up the pike toward Vienna where he captured a four-man picket post of the 16th New York Cavalry. Also captured were the Reverend J. B. Reed and an unidentified Negro employee of Reed. It was then that Montjoy found out the horn he had heard was an alarm announcing the Rangers presence and that it had been sounded by no other than Reverend Reed. The partisans took the two men to a spot near Hunter's Mill and shot them both in the head, leaving them for dead. Reed was killed instantly, the back of his skull blown off by a pistol placed against his head; the Negro was lucky—the shot he received cost him an ear but was not fatal. After the Rangers left, he made his way back to a Federal post and told what had transpired. [640]

While the raiding was taking place in Fairfax, William and Sam Chapman had their men on the road between Piedmont and Paris in upper Fauquier County. Here they ran across a Federal foraging party, returning east toward their camp with a plunder of calves, pigs, sheep, turkeys, chickens, geese, apples, hay and whatever else they could manage to carry. Encumbered as they were with their booty, the Yankees were easy targets for the charging Sam Chapman and Company E on their flanks and William Chapman's men in their front. The Federal losses were great; up to forty men killed and wounded and twenty-nine taken prisoner along with fifteen to twenty horses, some of which were not corralled until the following day. The slaughter was so great that a complaint was lodged against the Rangers by the colonel of the Union regiment, accusing the partisans of shooting prisoners after they had surrendered. Colonel Mosby inquired into the matter and was assured by the Chapmans that no such thing had taken place. One Ranger, Private Joseph Kennerly, had, however, shot and killed two prisoners whom he was escorting after dark, after they managed to turn on him.[641]

One of Mosby's largest assemblies, some 400 men, gathered at Bloomfield on October 24. Planning on hitting at Sheridan's communications, they crossed the Shenandoah at Castleman's Ferry and by nightfall were encamped near Summit Point. The next morning the command proceeded to a point on the Martinsburg and Winchester Turnpike and Mosby, William Chapman, and a few other men went forth to reconnoitre the road. They soon spotted a light, two-horse ambulance wagon with an escort of ten cavalrymen. The wagon contained General A. N. Duffie, a former commander of the First Cavalry Division, Department of West Virginia, on his way to Hagerstown to establish a re-mount camp. This was the same General Duffie who, the previous July at Paris, had ordered that "all prisoners captured will be shot", after being aroused from his bed in an attack on his brigade by William Chapman and his company.

Duffie had started out from Winchester with an escort of fifty troopers. Believing the column was moving too slowly, Duffie took the medical conveyance and the small escort and pushed on ahead. They were about a mile and a half ahead of the main body when William Chapman, with twelve men, struck the rear of the escort while another detachment charged from the front. About this time, the attackers saw a large wagon train coming toward them from Martinsburg; Duffie saw the train also and attempted to reach it. The partisans were faster, however, and managed to stop the ambulance wagon and capture its occupants—Duffie, a captain, and a civilian, who was driving and carrying the mail. Three troopers from the escort were also captured. The rest retreated back to the main body, which then turned tail and raced back to Winchester.[642]

The wagon train that was coming along the pike from Martinsburg was a large one, comprised of an infantry brigade, a section of the 9th New York Artillery, the 5th Wisconsin Volunteers, and several detachments of cavalry.

The Rangers deployed for an assault on the column, with Captains Chapman and Montjoy taking one squadron and charging the front while Captain Richards took a squadron to strike the rear. They easily drove the calvery back on the infantrymen, but the artillery opened fire and the Rangers retreated. Mosby hoped the cavalry would attempt to follow and he could then isolate them from the rest of the column and hit them again. But they would not abandon the wagon train they were charged with escorting.[643]

As for General Duffie, he was quite an unwanted man. Mosby had him taken to the rear with the other prisoners and showed no further interest in the pompous Frenchman. Sheridan, in a report to Grant, stated: "Brigadier-General Duffie was captured between Winchester and Martinsburg. I respectfully request his dismissal from the service. I think him a trifling man and a poor soldier. He was captured by his own stupidity."[644]

Following the devastating reversal of fortune that turned a temporary victory by Early's Valley army into a retreat and then a rout, by Sheridan's forces at Cedar Creek on October 19, the struggle for control of the Shenandoah Valley was all but over. And with that there was no longer a need for the Union to have the Manassas Gap Railroad as a means of transporting troops and material into and from the Valley. On October 25, Union chief of staff Halleck issued orders to "take up the Manassas railroad back to Manassas Junction and all iron and material of the road, as well as the telegraph, will be brought in and disposed of…the troops will be drawn in as fast as the road is taken up." [645]

Early in the morning of October 28, a detachment of the 8th Illinois Cavalry, numbering 200-300 men, was sent to near Snicker's Gap to effect the arrest of one of "Mosby's boarding-house keepers." According to the Federal report, the detachment found the housekeeper and also fifteen of Mosby's men, seventeen horses and a number of revolvers and equipment. (This number may be the number captured the following day in a fight at the Dulany farm, instead of on the raid, as the Federal report implies.) The cavalrymen were on their way back when they were spotted between Middleburg and Upperville by Captain Walter Frankland, who had 207 men with him. When the Yankees reached Hatcher's Mill, Frankland, who was following, fell in with Mosby and a number of the other Rangers. Mosby ordered Frankland to get between the Union raiders and their camp at Rectortown, and he, Mosby, would do the scouting and keep Frankland informed of the column's movements. [646]

When the Federal force reached Upperville they turned south, toward Rectortown, crossing through a level pasture on the property of Henry Dulany, about a mile from Upperville; Frankland's position was now in front of the Illinois troopers. At this point, Mosby sent Captain Wright James, the battalion quartermaster, and Lieutenant Hatcher, back to Frankland to remind him of the previous order—to keep his position between the Yankees and their camp at Rectortown. But Frankland now deliberated on whether to make an attack in the open field against the enemy, who were now at the Dulaney house, or to fall back and form an ambuscade as Mosby had supposedly ordered. After conferring with Lieutenants Albert Wrenn and C. E. Grogan, Frankland decided to divide his force and make the attack. Mosby, commenting on the affair after the war, stated that Hatcher, "...who was the bravest man in the Southern Army, refused to go. He said it was murder in the first degree." Hatcher returned to Mosby, who was at Dolly Richards's home place, "Green Garden," near Upperville. James, however, like Frankland, was ever the fighter and supported the decision to attack.[647]

Frankland divided his men, with Grogan and about thirty men making a flank attack on the right, while the larger portion of his command with Lieutenant Wrenn, charged the front. When the Federal troopers saw the partisans forming for the charge, they divided up into three squadrons. Frankland's idea was for his two elements to coordinate their attacks so that they could unite after the initial charge. But the timing failed; when Wrenn topped a small rise that had hidden the Federal detachment from view, he found the Yankees drawn up in battle lines waiting for him. Wrenn was sucessful in breaking the ranks of the Federal's first squadron, but when Grogan attempted to hit their flank, he found he was hampered by a wide and deep ditch along side a ragged rail fence. The way was impassable and the group had to find another way to cross. This took them back up toward the Upperville road and broke the timing that Frankland had depended upon. Likewise, the Yankees were waiting for Grogan when he did enter the field. A rise hid Grogan from Wrenn's view during the initial phase of the fight, so that Wrenn had no knowledge of Grogan's dilemma. In addition, the Federals had taken a position behind a stone wall. Wrenn's men were held up by a barnyard gate, and Grogan by a gate to a high rail fence. The enemy squadron on the right of the gate sat their horses and, with their Spencer carbines, fired unrelenting into Grogan's flank. Fortunately, the Yankees did not decide to charge at this point, while the partisans were bunched at the gate. It was a scene eerily reminiscent of Miskel's Farm, only this time the shoe was on the other foot. [648]

The 43rd's losses were severe—two men were killed on the field and two more mortally wounded; four others were wounded but would survive, while somewhere between nine and seventeen were taken prisoner, depending upon which report was accurate. Federal losses were apparently light, although there is no mention of the number in their reports. [649]

One of the mortally wounded was an Irishman by the name of John Atkins, who, upon hearing of Mosby's exploits, had left his homeland and traveled to Virginia to join the partisan command. He was taken to the Dulany home and his dying words recorded by Mrs. Dulany: "I have come three thousand miles to fight for the Confederacy, but it is all over now. My poor mother— Jesus have mercy on my soul." He died within a few hours of his wounding. Mosby, as he stood over the dying soldier, remarked: "There lies a man I would not have given for a whole regiment of Yankees."[650]

There is controversy over just what Frankland did, and what Mosby ordered him to do, as it relates to the debacle at Dulanys. Mosby, in letters after the war, wrote that "Frankland, instead of halting and concealing his men so as to surprise the Yankees when they came up, (divided his men) and (had) Lieutenant Grogan to make a circuit of over a mile....Wren (sic) was defeated long before Grogan came in sight." He went on to make a damning accusation against the captain: "Frankland did not go with either party. He wanted to get the glory of beating them before I could get up. It was a perfect massacre. I can never forgive him. Some of my best men were killed." Sometime after the fight, Mosby supposedly relieved Frankland of his command, ordering him to send in his resignation. He also had him placed under arrest. But Mosby's later wounding and the removal of part of the battalion to the Northern Neck for the winter, delayed any further action. When Frankland returned from the Neck, he gave to Mosby a petition from his company, in which his men asked that he be allowed to remain as their captain. Mosby wrote that he refused to read the petition and that he told Frankland if the men wanted him they could have him, but he could never serve as an officer under him (Mosby) again.[651]

Was the fight at Dulany's another case of Frankland not wanting to obey a disagreeable order, such as in the affair at Front Royal in September when he questioned Sam Chapman's order to withdraw? Or was Mosby incorrect in what he recalled years later about the event? Did Mosby really make clear just what he expected of Frankland, or simply think he did, when he wrote of the event a long time afterwards?

While the Manassas Gap Railroad was being taken up, the Federals turned their attention to the short but vital track between Harper's Ferry and Winchester—the Winchester and Potomac Railroad. Construction crews that had been rebuilding the Manassas Gap line were sent to the latter road to hurry along its rebuilding. By the end of October, J. J. Moore, chief engineer for the military railroads, had been directed to put his whole construction force upon the Winchester railroad and to "push it forward to completion with the utmost vigor."[652]

The executions of his men by the Federals at Front Royal and more recently in Rappahannock County, were very much on Mosby's mind, as was the treatment being received by civilians along the right-of-way of the railroad and as passengers on the cars. On October 29, he sent a long message to General Lee, detailing the atrocities and his objective to "...hang an equal number of Custer's men whenever I capture them." It was not Mosby's intent to ask permission for the retaliatory measures he planned to take; however, the chain of command, from Lee to Secretary Seddon, endorsed Mosby's plan. From Lee: "I have directed Colonel Mosby...to hang an equal number of Custer's men in retaliation for those executed by him." And from Seddon: "General Lee's instructions are cordially approved. In addition, if our citizens are found exposed on any captured train, signal vengeance should be taken on all conductors and officers found on it, and every male passenger of the enemy's country should be treated as prisoners." [653] Mosby was of the belief that Custer was the force behind the executions and he would hold to this belief long after the war.

On November 6, the command assembled at Rectortown. Also there were twenty-seven Union prisoners. Mosby gave the order for the execution of seven of the prisoners and then he left the vicinity, unable to watch the painful scene that was soon to be presented. "This duty must be performed for the protection of my men from the ruthless Custer and Powell," he remarked before he left. The prisoners were made to draw lots—twenty-seven bits of paper but only seven of them with numbers, the rest being blank. The soldiers drawing the numbered pieces would be the ones to face the executioner. The others would be sent to Richmond as prisoners of war. The scene was emotionally painful for both captor and captive; one of the prisoners cried on the shoulder of a comrade while another prayed. When the lots had been drawn, the seven unfortunate men set out with a detail of Rangers, under the command of Lieutenant Ned Thomson of Company H, for the Valley. Thomson was to find a spot on the Valley Pike, as close to Winchester and to Custer's headquarters as he could safely go. While passing through Ashby's Gap, the detail met Captain Montjoy, returning from the Valley with additional prisoners from Custer's command. Recognizing two of the condemned men as being Freemasons, as he was, Montjoy, owing to his rank, was able to substitute two of his own prisoners for the two Masons. When Mosby later learned of the substitutions, he severely reprimanded Montjoy, reminding him that his command was not a Masonic lodge.

When the detail reached the vicinity of Berryville, one of the prisoners managed to release his bonds and make good his escape. Because the night was very dark and rainy, and fearful of other escapes, Thomson decided to halt and carry out the sentences here, at a place known as Beemer's Woods. The first three prisoners were hung; the next two, by their own request, were shot. The last man, waiting to be shot, managed to loosen his tied hands and strike Thomson, knocking him down, and run into the darkness, successfully escaping. Incredibly, the two men who were shot and left for dead would recover. Before the detail sat out from Rectortown, Mosby penned a note, which Thomson pinned to one of the men who was hanged: "These men have been hung in retaliation for an equal number of Colonel Mosby's men hung by order of General Custer at Front Royal. Measure for measure." [654]

On November 11, Mosby asked Grogan to take a letter, relative to the executions, to General Sheridan. But the lieutenant, thinking that his commander must be joking—the bearer of such a letter would most surly be hung himself—replied "Oh no, Colonel; I don't want to get a rope around my neck yet awhile." Mosby then entrusted John Russell with the letter: [655]

> General: Sometime in the month of September,
> during my absence from my command, six of my
> men who had been captured by your forces, were
> hung and shot in the streets of Front Royal, by the
> order and in the immediate presence of Brigadier-
> General Custer. Since then another (captured by
> a Colonel Powell, on a plundering expedition into
> Rappahannock) shared a similar fate. A label affixed
> to the coat of one of the murdered men declared that
> 'this would be the fate of Mosby and all his men.'

Since the murder of my men, not less that 700 prisoners, including many officers of high rank, captured from your army by this command, have been forwarded to Richmond, but the execution of my purpose of retaliation was deferred in order, as far as possible, to confine its operation to the men of Custer and Powell. Accordingly, on the 6th instant, seven of your men were by my order executed on the Valley pike, your highway of travel. Hereafter, any prisoners falling into my hands will be treated with the kindness due to their condition, unless some new act of barbarity shall compel me reluctantly to adopt a line of policy repugnant to humanity. [656]

Although the letter is dated November 11, it is apparent that Mosby had not been advised fully of the details surrounding the executions; he was of the impression that (1) the operation had taken place on the Valley Pike as planned, and (2) that seven of Custer's men had been executed. He was obviously unaware of the change in location and that two of the prisoners had managed to escape prior to being executed. Additionally, the two who were shot recovered and made it back to Union lines, although none of the Rangers would have been aware of this at the time.

The fact that Mosby had advised the Confederate high command of his intention "to hang an equal number of Custer's men," and they had given their endorsement, was not made known during the war. It was not until August 25, 1899, that Mosby sent an article to Joseph Bryan, a former Ranger and then owner of the Richmond Times newspaper, revealing the correspondence that had transpired between Mosby and Lee and the Confederate War Department. The day after he had mailed the article, Mosby wrote to Sam Chapman and detailed the same information, asking Chapman to "Take this letter with you & show it to the men & give them all my love." Sam was entrusted to take the letter to the dedication of the Front Royal monument the following month. In his letter to Sam, Mosby said "For the first time (the article) will give to the world a true account of the Front Royal affair. The world would never have known that I reported it to Gen'l. Lee and that both he & Secretary Seddon not only approved but ordered me to do it…You will see that my letter to Gen'l Lee does not ask for instructions—it tells him what I was going to do & I did it. I always kept it a secret that I had their order. I did not want to shrink responsibility for doing what I thought was right." The Colonel went on to say: " I never did anything that my conscience more thoroughly approved. That Torbert—Merritt—& Custer were ashamed of hanging my men is proved by their not alluding to it in their reports. My retaliation was a merciful act—It saved the lives of both our men & the Yankees—the war would have disintegrated in to a massacre." [657]

The world did not have to wait for Sam Chapman to reveal the letter at Front Royal on September 23, the 35th anniversary of the executions. Bryan's newspaper published Mosby's article on September 3. [658]

25. "A Terrible Retribution"

The Federal working parties that had been involved in the rebuilding of the Manassas Gap Railroad were now busy doing the same work on the Winchester and Potomac; as fast as the rails were taken up on one, tracks were being laid on the other. On November 6, Mosby advised Lee: "The enemy is engaged in removing the rails from the Manassas road for the purpose of reconstructing the Winchester and Potomac. The latter is already completed to Charlestown." On November 7, Sheridan told General Stevenson: "In case the railroad to Winchester is interfered with by guerillas I want you to arrest all male secessionists in Charlestown, Shepherdstown, Smithfield, and Berryville, and in the adjacent country, sending them to Fort McHenry, Md. You will also burn all grain, destroy all subsistence, and drive off all stock, belonging to such individuals, and turn it over to the Treasury agent. This order must be obeyed by you." The oppression of the civilian population along the Manassas Gap line had now become the plight of citizens along the Winchester and Potomac. [659]

Although Mosby tried to keep deserters and malingers out of his command, it was becoming ever difficult at this stage of the war. Desertions from the regular army were increasing day-by-day and many of these men were finding their way into Mosby's command for the sole purpose of plundering and robbing. To help alleviate this problem, he requested a formal inspection be made of the battalion.

Mosby called the 43rd together on November 20; some 500 Rangers assembled at Rectortown for the inspection, conducted by Lieutenant R. K. Meade. The inspecting officer's report gave generally high marks to the command: "From my observations and conversations with enrolling officers...Colonel Mosby has been very zealous in apprehending conscripts and deserters...Colonel Mosby has been very active in gleaning from his command such as were subject to conscription...." [660]

On Lieutenant Meade's recommendation, Mosby was directed to supply a detail of men to assist an officer from cavalry headquarters, Major B. S. White, "...to collect and bring out for the use of our cavalry such cavalry arms, particularly carbines, as he may find in the hands of citizens (which) have been captured from the enemy and deposited in the country by our soldiers or others." Many such weapons were in the hands of Mosby himself, as Meade stated in his inspection report: "Mosby has a considerable number of improved arms of all kinds which were not in use, that had been captured." [661]

During the month of November, following the execution of Custer's men by Mosby, the Rangers were busy on both sides of the Blue Ridge, primarily raiding in small groups at places throughout the countryside. One raid in particular was noteworthy. On November 16, Captain Montjoy was with Company D in the Valley. On the pike between Winchester and Newtown, he struck an unsuspecting Federal column of cavalry, scattering the bluecoats. A number of the enemy were killed and wounded and seventeen prisoners were taken, along with their horses and equipment. Montjoy proceeded to Berryville with his captives, where he allowed those of his company who resided in Loudoun County to cross the river at Castlemen's Ferry. He then took the rest of the command, numbering about thirty, and the captives towards Berry's Ferry.

When Montjoy was about two miles from the ferry, he was suddenly hit upon by an old nemesis, Captain Richard Blazer with his Scouts. So sudden was the attack that Montjoy was unable to rally his men. The partisans retreated to the home of John Esten Cooke, a former member of Stuart's staff, where they attempted to re-group and make a stand. But they were unable to turn the tide against their much stronger foe; the Rangers suffered one man killed and another mortally wounded and four or five less severely wounded. Blazer was able to re-capture all the prisoners and horses Montjoy had taken. [662]

When Mosby heard of Montjoy's defeat at the hand of Blazer, he determined that both he and "Old Blaze" could not occupy the same territory. Mosby summoned Dolly Richards and directed him to "Wipe Blazer out! Go through him." Taking 100 men from Companies A and B, Richards set out to find Blazer. On November 18, after being unable to locate his query, Richards encamped for the night in Castlemen's Woods on the west side of the Shenandoah River. Early the next morning, John Puryear and Charlie McDonough, two of the less disciplined Rangers, were scouting north toward Charlestown and near Kabletown, when they ran upon a small detachment of riders dressed in gray. McDonough, fearing a trap, turned and ran while Puryear approached the riders. McDonough's instincts were correct, but it was too late for Puryear. The riders were "Jessie Scouts"—Yankee soldiers dressed in gray. Puryear was captured and taken back to Blazer, who turned him over to Lieutenant Thomas Cole, Blazer's second in command. Meanwhile, McDonough had reached Richards and advised him of what had taken place.[663]

Richards caught up with Blazer near Myerstown—and Blazer, who was looking for Richards—saw his adversary at the same moment. Richards placed his men in a depression in the center of an open field, concealed from the road, which was about two hundred yards away. He hoped to surprise Blazer who was coming along the road. But when an intoxicated Ranger fired his gun, Blazer was alerted and took his column through a wood and toward a fence. He was now about seventy-five yards distant from Richards. Seeing the Federals dismount to take down the fence, Richards thought that they were dismounting in order to fight him with rifles from the wood. He directed Harry Hatcher to pull down a gap in a fence behind the Rangers so that he could trick Blazer into thinking the partisans were withdrawing; in this way, Blazer could be drawn out. The ruse worked and Blazer brought his men out into the field. At this point, Company B charged out of the recess, up a slope and into the Yankee cavalrymen. In the next moment, Hatcher turned and charged, hitting the Federals on their right flank.

When the forces collided, close hand-to-hand fighting ensued, with Richards' men having the advantage with their revolvers over the Federals with their carbines. The initial attack had taken several of Blazer's men out of the melee and as the fighting intensified, Blazer was unable to rally his fleeing soldiers. The majority of his command high-tailed it, through Myerstown and Rippon, toward Summit Point. They were not alone, for their commander soon followed, riding as fast as his horse would take him. Blazer was pursued by three or four of the Rangers but one, eighteen-year-old Syd Ferguson who, like Sam Chapman, would become a minister after the war, caught up to him just out of Rippon. Riding up beside Blazer, Ferguson dealt him a blow on the head with his revolver, knocking him from the saddle. [664]

Blazer had begun the fight with sixty-two troopers; when it ended, he had, depending upon which report is accurate, between sixteen and twenty-four dead, an unknown number wounded, and twenty-two captured along with some fifty horses. It marked the end of Blazer's Scouts. Richards had one man mortally wounded and a few others less seriously. [665]

While John Puryear was in the hands of Lieutenant Cole, attempts were made to extract information concerning Mosby's whereabouts from the oung Ranger. After less severe methods to persuade him to talk had failed, 'ole ordered a rope placed around the captive's neck, with the other end 1rown over the limb of a tree, in the normal manner for hanging a person. 'he rope was pulled tight and Puryear suspended until nearly unconscious; e was then lowered and questioned again. This scenario was repeated several times before Cole finally gave up. During the subsequent rout of 1lazer's command, Cole was captured by John Alexander. While Alexander /as disarming his prisoner, Puryear rode up. "His face was distorted with nger or excitement, and he was pointing a cocked pistol at the officer's ead," Alexander would later recall. Puryear had escaped during the fight, 1king his guard's gun in the process. Alexander shouted "Don't shoot this 1an; he has surrendered." Puryear, in a rage, replied that the prisoner had ·ied to hang him that morning. Alexander asked the lieutenant if this was so. There was a moment's hesitation, and no response; then the crack of a pis->l, and Lieutenant Cole fell against my side and rolled to the ground," Alxander remembered. When Puryear realized what he had done, all the emo.on of the events settled upon him as he burst into sobs, collapsing on the _round in uncontrollable shaking. [666]

\ loss greatly felt by all the battalion, and especially by Colonel Mosby, ocurred on November 27. Montjoy had crossed into the lower Valley a couple ·f days before with thirty-eight men. Not finding any targets, the band rossed back over the Blue Ridge into Loudoun Country. Word had been reeived that some of the Loudoun Rangers were harassing the civilian popu1tion and Montjoy set out to locate them. On the road from Waterford to .eesburg, the partisans ran into a detachment of the Federals, returning from . raid at Leesburg where they had captured two of Mosby's men. When the olumn reached Goresville, Montjoy struck them. The Loudoun Rangers ·roke into two groups, one group running for the Potomac while the other kedaddled back toward Leesburg. Montjoy and Lieutenant Grogan were in he pursuit, when a Yankee cavalryman turned his pistol over his shoulder, .ot aiming it at all. But when he fired, the bullet struck Montjoy in the fore.ead, killing him instantly.

'he twenty-two-year-old Mississippian, commander of the "darlins" of 'ompany D, was buried in the cemetery in Warrenton. On December 3, ./osby issued the following General Order:

> The Lieutenant-Colonel commanding announces to the
> Battalion, with emotions of deep sorrow, the death of

Captain R. P. Montjoy, who fell in action near Leesburg
on the 27th ultimo, a costly sacrifice to victory. He died too
early for liberty and his country's cause, but not too early
for his own fame. To his comrades in arms he has bequeathed
an immortal example of daring and valor, and to his country
a name that will brighten the page of her history.[667]

Sam Chapman was especially saddened by Montjoy's death. After all,
Montjoy had stood with him eighteen months before at Grapewood Farm,
defending the little howitzer to the last, before Sam was severely wounded
and they both were captured.

On November 2, the Confederate Secretary of War had directed that the
battalion's artillery company be disbanded. Inactive since the loss of its guns
and the capture of many of the members, there was no need to keep the
company organized. The day after the death of Montjoy, the command assembled to dissolve the Artillery Company and to form Company G. Elected
captain of the newest company was Thomas W. T. Richards, brother of
Dolly Richards. Thomas Richards had been sent to the Northern Neck of
Virginia the previous August by General Lee, upon the recommendation of
Mosby. His purpose was to organize the citizens into an armed civil defense
to protect their homes and property from the "outrages by the enemy." This
attempt was not very successful, however, and Richards soon returned. [668]

Now that Sheridan had disposed of major resistance from the Confederates
in the Valley, he would make the conquering of Mosby's Confederacy, and
with it the elimination of Mosby's command, his primary aim. On November 26, Sheridan sent a wire to Halleck: "I will soon commence work on
Mosby….Now there is going to be an intense hatred of him in the portion of
this Valley which is nearly a desert. I will soon commence in Loudoun
County, and let them know there is a God in Israel. Mosby has annoyed me
considerably, but the people are beginning to see that he does not injure me a
great deal, but causes a loss to them of all that they have spent their lives in
accumulating."[669]

The day after Sheridan's dispatch to Halleck, he had one sent to General
Merritt, commanding his First Cavalry division. Sheridan ordered Merritt to
take his brigades and operate on the east side of the Blue Ridge, in an area
bounded by the Shenandoah River on the west, the Bull Run Mountains on
the east, the Potomac on the north and the Manassas Gap Railroad on the

south; this would place Merritt in the heart of Mosby's Confederacy. His orders further stated that he was to "consume and destroy all forage and subsistence, burn all barns and mills and their contents, and drive off all stock in the region." Merritt's troopers were to take four days rations, a full supply of ammunition and fifteen pounds of grain on each horse. There would be no artillery or other wheels—save one wagon to serve as each brigade's headquarters—to slow the operation.

The Union cavalry's trail of flames had started with Hunter six months before and now it was to continue with Sheridan's latest order to fire the torch. The people in the Great Valley and in the Page Valley had been the earlier victims and now those in the beautiful rolling hills of the northern Piedmont, and in particular the Loudoun Valley, would become the latest.[670]

"They robbed the people of everything they could destroy or carry off—horses, cows, cattle, sheep, hogs, etc; killing poultry, insulting women, pillaging houses, and in many cases robbing even the poor negroes. They burned all the mills and factories, as well as hay, wheat, corn, straw and every description of forage. Barns and stables, whether empty or full, were burned." Thus Ranger James Williamson described the totality of the destruction. [671] The fires were visible in all directions at night, while the columns of dense, black smoke rose up and enveloped the landscape, watering the eyes and burning the throat.

Some evidence of the extent of the destruction can be found in the report of Lieutenant Colonel Casper Crowninshield, who was commanding the Reserve Brigade in Merritt's division. He reported destroying 200 barns, eight mills, 10,000 tons of hay, and 25,000 bushels of grain; additionally, he rounded up and carried off 474 beef cattle, 100 sheep, and 87 horses. Crowninshield estimated the monetary value of the property and animals at over $400,000. Add this to the sums from the other two brigades and some idea can be had of the extent of the operation. Sheridan, in his report to Halleck, reported 5,000 - 6,000 head of cattle, 3,000 - 4,000 head of sheep and nearly 1,000 fatted hogs had been driven off or destroyed by the combined efforts of his three brigades. Merritt also claimed capture of 500-700 horses. He finished his report by saying: "...the money value of damage done may be estimated by millions....The destruction in the valley and in the mountains bounding it is most complete."[672]

Charles A. Humphreys, a chaplain in Crowninshield's Massachusetts Brigade, remembered the devastation and human suffering: "This was the most unpleasant task we were ever compelled to undertake. It was heart piercing to hear the shrieks of women and children, and to even see men crying... begging that at least one cow—an only support—might be left. But no mercy was allowed...It was a terrible retribution on the country...." [673]

PART VIII

LAST HURRAH

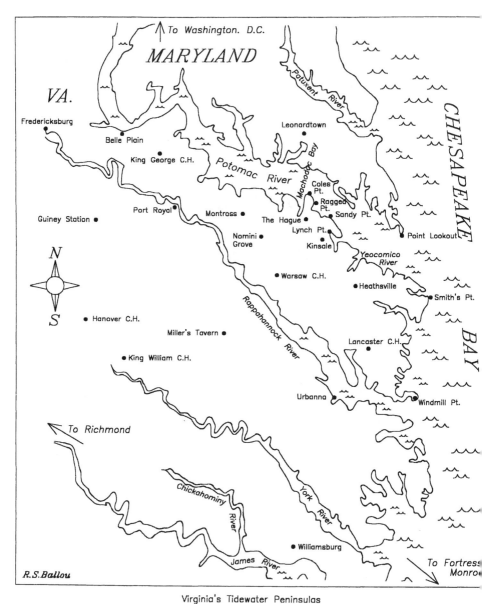

To Washington. D.C.

MARYLAND

VA.

Fredericksburg

Belle Plain

King George C.H.

Potomac River

Patuxent River

Leonardtown

Machodic Bay

CHESAPEAKE

Coles Pt.

Ragged Pt.

Sandy Pt.

Guiney Station

Port Royal

Montross

The Hague

Lynch Pt.

Point Lookout

Nomini Grove

Kinsale

Yeocomico River

N

S

Warsaw C.H.

Heathsville

Smith's Pt.

Hanover C.H.

Rappahannock River

Miller's Tavern

Lancaster C.H.

BAY

King William C.H.

Urbanna

Windmill Pt.

To Richmond

Chickahominy River

York River

Williamsburg

James River

To Fortress Monroe

R.S.Ballou

Virginia's Tidewater Peninsulas
Northern Neck lies between the Potomac and Rappahannock Rivers.
One—half of Mosby's command operated here from January to April 1865

26. A Command Divided

The 43rd Battalion offered no organized resistance, as a unit, while Merritt's brigades were burning the landscape and bringing the worst of the war to the people of Loudoun and Fauquier Counties. There were, however, small bands of the partisans operating on the fringes of the Federal cavalry, picking off stragglers and charging into their rear elements, inflicting what damage they could and retreating to safety before the Yankee raiders could react. Additionally, they managed to save some of the livestock by driving it from places yet to be burned back into those areas already torched. [674]

The first week in December, Mosby traveled to Petersburg to see General Lee. He found the commander in comfortable quarters at Edge Hill, home of the Turnbull family, about two miles west of the city. Lee had found it necessary to move his headquarters out of Petersburg, as Grant continued to extend the Union flank. The Confederate leader wanted to establish his quarters in a tent but had been persuaded by Mrs. Lee and his staff to accept the Turnbull's invitation to make use of their home.[675]

Mosby's purpose for seeing Lee was to gain approval for reorganizing his force into two battalions, each commanded by a major; William Chapman and Dolly Richards were recommended by Mosby for the command of the two units. Lee suggested that the request be put in writing to Secretary Seddon, which Mosby did on December 6: "I would recommend Capt. William H. Chapman...and Capt. Adolphus E. Richards...for the command of the two battalions proposed. They have both on many occasions been distinguished for valor and skill, to which my reports bear witness...."[676]

Mosby's request for reorganization of his command was denied, however its designation was changed to that of a regiment. Mosby was granted approval to promote William Chapman to lieutenant colonel, to be second in command, and Dolly Richards to major, thus allowing better and tighter control of the regiment, by delegation of authority at the field level through Chapman and Richards. At the same time, Mosby was recommended for promotion to full colonel. It was his thirty-first birthday. [677]

Both Chapman and Richards had been busy while Mosby was visiting Lee. The same day Mosby was composing his letter to Seddon the Rangers were striking a detachment of the 21st New York Cavalry south of Millwood in

Clarke County. Fifty-one of the Federal troopers had left Berryville that morning on a scout along the Shenandoah River. Returning on a warm December afternoon, a rare day for what was turning out to be a brutal winter they were suddenly attacked by about thirty-five yelling horsemen striking their rear and flanks. Unable to recover, the New Yorkers took to flight Twenty-seven Federals were captured, three killed; among the wounded was the commander of the patrol, Lieutenant Nelson B. Holcomb. The official Federal report stated: "There was apparently no fight at all, but a rapid and disgraceful flight." When the report reached Sheridan, he ordered Holcomb's dismissal from the army.[678]

The Union commanders were having a hard time when it came to knowing just where Mosby and his men were and what they were up to. On December 7, General Stevenson at Harper's Ferry cabled Captain Spencer at Point of Rocks, Maryland: "Have you any information to-day on Mosby? It is reported that he contemplates a raid into Maryland. Send more scouts...to remain out all night watching river." The same day, Sheridan informed Stevenson: " I had a report this morning that Mosby would collect at Rectortown today to raid toward Fairfax Court House.... Report also comes in this evening that he is on the Potomac with McCausland...." Stevenson then sent this response to Sheridan: "I have information to-day that Mosby was in the vicinity of Leesburg." Sheridan cabled back to Stevenson: "There is a report that a raid was intended on the Winchester road at Charlestown or Summit Point." Two days later, Sheridan inquired of Stevenson: "You telegraphed yesterday that Mosby was at or near Leesburg. Have you any information on the same subject this morning? "[679]

On December 10, Sam Chapman took about thirty men of his company through Ashby's Gap and into the Shenandoah Valley. They bivouacked in a terrible snowstorm on the riverbank and early the next morning attacked a Federal picket post near the Millwood tollgate. Five captives and eleven horses were gathered up without any losses to the command. [680]

A week after Chapman's raid, his brother, with 125 men, planned to attack a scouting party of the enemy that daily made the trek from Winchester to Berry's Ferry on the Shenandoah. To avoid any surprises, the Union detachment altered their route; some days they would come from the direction of White Post, returning through Millwood, while at other times they took a route through Millwood to the Ferry and returned by way of White Post Chapman divided his command so as to cover both routes—Lieutenant John

Russell took a position near Millwood and Chapman took up watch on the White Post road. [681]

The Federals—about a hundred of the 14th Pennsylvania Cavalry under the command of Captain William Miles—had been forewarned of the partisans plan to ambush the column and had put out flankers. Miles had mistaken the location, however, and the flankers were dispatched on the opposite side of the road where Chapman's group was waiting. Miles was with the advance guard of flankers, about twenty men in all, as they proceeded down the turn-pike from Millwood. With Chapman effectively cut off, Russell realized the Federals were between him and the river, blocking any escape by way of the river. Telling his men to charge, the forty or so Rangers struck Miles advance party. The onslaught was fierce and half of the Federal troopers turned and ran; the rest soon followed. Miles took a circuitous route through the pasture that bordered the south side of the turnpike in a vain effort to rally his troops. He was pursued by Lieutenant Jim Wiltshire and fatally wounded.[682]

The Pennsylvanians lost, in addition to Miles, ten killed, seventeen wounded, and twenty captured, according to the Federal report. There was no report of losses by the Rangers. [683]

The next major excursion by the Union cavalry into Mosby's Confederacy began on December 17 and would culminate with dire results for the partisans and for Mosby in particular. It would also prove to be of great embarrassment to the guerilla chieftain's adversaries.

On the morning of December 17 Lieutenant Colonel David Clendenin took a large raiding party, consisting of detachments of the 13th and 16th New York Cavalries and the 8th Illinois Cavalry, out of Fairfax and west, along the Little River Turnpike to Aldie. Here, the command separated into smaller groups and then united at Salem, where they dispatched a few of the Rangers.

On December 21, Mosby was alerted that the Federal column was moving toward Rectortown, looking for partisans or any other Confederates they could find. Mosby, who was attending a wedding just a few miles away, took his devoted follower, Private Tom Love of Company D, to reconnoiter the Federals, while sending a few other men to assemble the command. The troopers appeared to go into camp for the night, building fires and preparing their supper. Satisfied that the enemy would remain in camp until morning, Mosby and Love proceeded to the home of Ludwell Lake, a mile from Rector's Cross Roads. [684]

The Union cavalrymen were not content to stay in camp, however, and after finishing their meal, saddled up and struck out for Upperville. But their guide put them on the wrong road and by a fateful coincidence they took the road leading to Rector's Cross Roads. An advance guard of the 13th New York, under Captain Francis Brown of Company E, in passing the Lake home noticed saddled horses outside the house. These were the mounts of Mosby and Love. Mosby recalled the night: "As we were passing the house of a citizen, Ludwell Lake, who was famous for always setting a good table, the lights shining through the windows tempted me, as I was cold and hungry, to stop where I knew I would be welcome." [685]

The sound of the horses outside the house did not go unnoticed by the occupants inside. Mosby opened a door to the backyard and saw several cavalrymen. Shutting this door, he quickly turned to the other one, but at this time several of the Federals rushed into the room. Mosby hurried to hide the stars on his collar by covering them with his hand. He was dressed that night "...better than I ever was during the war." Having obtained new clothes on his recent trip to Richmond and Petersburg, he had "...a drab hat with an ostrich plume, with gold cord and star; a heavy, black beaver-cloth overcoat and cape lined with English scarlet cloth, and...over this a gray cloak, also lined with scarlet. My hat, overcoat, and cape were lying in the corner. I wore a gray sack coat with two stars on the collar to indicate my rank as lieutenant-colonel, gray trousers with a yellow cord down the seam, and long cavalry boots." (Mosby's promotion to full colonel had not been approved before he left Richmond.) [686]

It is not clear why the Federals outside the house began firing. Apparently several shots were fired before one passed through a windowpane, striking Mosby in the stomach. Major Douglas Frazar, in command of the 13th New York detachment, had arrived on the scene and was informed that a Rebel lieutenant had been wounded. Frazar entered the house, finding Mosby lying on the floor in apparent agony. When Frazar asked his name, Mosby replied he was "Lieutenant Johnson" of the 6th Virginia Cavalry. All signs of his rank had been removed and hidden; Mosby had on only a flannel shirt, and his trousers—no boots, hat or insignia. The Colonel was bleeding profusely and Frazar opened his shirt, looked at the wound, and assured himself that it was mortal. The bullet had entered the abdomen about two inches below and to the left of the navel; it had gone around the body and lodged in the right side. The troopers took Mosby's hat, boots, and trousers before leaving. They also took Tom Love. [687]

It seems incredulous that Frazar did not suspect this wounded "lieutenant" might be Mosby or at least one of his men. He was in the very vicinity in which his troopers were searching for the partisan. And they had captured Private Love, at the house, and seven other Rangers before leaving the area. Nevertheless, Frazar maintained in his report of the incident that it was not until he had arrived at Middleburg and gone into camp that Mosby's hat was brought to him. Still, he was not convinced that the wounded officer was, in fact, Mosby. The Union major questioned the prisoners and they all denied that it was Mosby and even denied that Mosby wore such a hat. "Nearly every officer in my command, if not all, saw this wounded man, and no one had the slightest idea that it was Mosby. Captain Brown and Major Birdsall were both with me when this occurred," Frazar related in his report.[688]

As soon as the troopers had left the house and the area, means were taken to remove Mosby to a place of safety and treatment. Mosby believed, like Frazar, that he was dying: "Shortly I became sick and faint. My own belief was that the wound was mortal; that the bullet was in me; that the intestines had been cut." Ludwell Lake procured an ox-cart and two oxen, with two Negro boys, to transport the wounded leader a short distance to the home of a neighbor, Aquilla Glascock. The trip, though not of a great distance, was excruciatingly painful for Mosby. He was rolled up in quilts and blankets and put in the cart. "It was an awful night—a howling storm of snow, rain, and sleet…over a frozen road cut into deep ruts. I was almost perfectly stiff with cold, and my hair was a clotted mass of ice." Two doctors—forty-seven year-old Talcott Eliason and twenty-five-year-old Will Dunn—both from Mosby's command, arrived soon after and successfully removed the bullet. Two weeks later Mosby was safely recovering at his parent's home in Amherst County. [689]

(Time has a way of soothing the remembrance of even the most intense physical pain and so it was in Mosby's case. Mosby was referring to a magazine article, written nearly thirty years later, when he wrote Sam Chapman: "I sent you a copy of the 'Call' with the account of my being wounded at old Lud Lake's. I had a particular object in publishing this to show that I was shot after having been taken prisoner. I did this not to reproach anyone but to show that acts of carelessness are often committed in both war and peace, for which those in authority cannot be held responsible. *Besides I have always felt very grateful to them for shooting me.* If some man of *our* command had done this, the whole command would have been denounced as cutthroats.") [690]

When the Federals determined—or strongly suspected—that the wounded man was indeed the infamous guerrilla leader, detachments were sent out in an effort to find him, all to no avail. But rumors were flying, as seen by the various Federal reports. From December 27 through the end of the year, reports placed Mosby as still being: (1) "...in the vicinity where he was shot," (2) "...lying in Middleburg...or five miles from Piedmont," (3)"...died from his wounds at Charlottesville." By the time these reports circulated, however, Mosby was well on his way to safety near Lynchburg.[691]

The fallout over Mosby's slipping through their fingers was still being felt within the Union command. On December 27, Colonel William Gamble, commanding the brigade that was involved in the affair reported on it to Lieutenant Colonel J. H. Taylor, chief of staff of the Washington Department: "Major Frazar did not search the house...the wounded rebel was not examined or brought in, which any good efficient officer should have done. I am also informed that Major Frazar was too much under the influence of liquor to perform his duty." On January 1, 1865, Gamble informed department headquarters: "I have given directions that all wounded officers and men of the enemy be hereafter brought in, although I thought any officer ought to have brains and common sense enough to do so without an order." That liquor may have been involved is also supported by Mosby's observations: "There was a good deal of whiskey in the crowd....My own belief is that I was indebted to whiskey for my escape, and I have always thought since that there is a deal of good in whiskey." [692]

The day following Mosby's wounding, William Chapman arrived to take command. He proceeded to harass the Union troops as much as possible in order to create diversions while Mosby was being moved. On December 19, General Torbert had taken 5,000 men, of Merritt's and Powell's divisions, and crossed the Blue Ridge with the intention of attacking the Virginia Central Railroad and capturing Gordonsville. They were driven off by Confederate cavalry under the command of General Lomax and, upon their return, learned of Mosby's wounding. They too commenced a search for him, and in the process took a number of horses and cattle from the citizenry. In return, they were constantly harassed by the partisans, who not only skirmished with them but at night disturbed their sleep by hanging around near the camps and sending rockets into the air. The Federal report of Torbert's expedition stated that "some thirteen enlisted men were captured and shot by guerrillas."[693]

On Tuesday, January 3, 1865, Virginia McLaurine Mosby recorded in her diary: "This evening... John arrived safely and doing well." [694] And the same day Mosby's mother was writing in her diary, William Chapman was writing to his father, at home near Luray: "Our part of the 43 Va. Battalion Mosby's Command left this evening for the Northern Neck, Sam in Command. They will probably reach their destination about Friday. They will have a cold and disagreeable night to start on." Referring to his wife of less than a year, William remarked: "Josie is sitting by me with a long face, thinking of my leaving in the morning, we have never been separated more than a week at a time." In a postscript he added: "I left Rebecca shedding a few tears at Sam's departure this evening." Sam and Rebecca Chapman had been married less than six months and this would become the farthermost distance and longest time they had been apart. [695]

The Northern Neck of Virginia is that area of the tidewater—a peninsula—lying between the Potomac and Rappahannock Rivers and extending from near the "fall line" at Fredericksburg, eastward to the Chesapeake Bay. It is roughly seventy miles in length, by twenty-five miles at its widest point, and comprises the counties of Northumberland, Westmoreland, Richmond, Lancaster and King George.[696]

There were two basic reasons why part of the battalion would be wintering on the Northern Neck. As far back as the middle of October, Mosby had contemplated sending part of his command there in response to the citizens' requests for protection from Federal raiding parties. Now, the destruction of food and forage by Merritt's cavalry, during the last week of November, ensured that the upper Piedmont would be unable to provide enough subsistence for the battalion through the harsh winter of 1864-65. [697]

"I received orders from Col. Mosby to proceed with Companies C, E, F, and G to the Northern Neck of Virginia," William Chapman recalled. "I was also directed to go to Richmond and to Petersburg and receive such instructions from Genl. Lee as he might have to give concerning operations in that section." Chapman assigned overall command of the four companies to his brother Sam and they left Salem on the long ride, southeast over frozen and rutted roads, to the Northern Neck. The following day, January 4, William departed the Jefferies' home in Fauquier County for Richmond. He was accompanied by Private James Phillip (Phil) Smith and Sergeant Ben Shipley, both of Company E, and Lieutenants Thompson and Talaiferro. [698]

Colonel Chapman and his group reached Richmond on January 7. "All were gay and happy at the prospect of spending a short furlough in Richmond," William wrote to his wife. On Sunday evening, they attended church with the elite of Richmond society. "The Mosby delegation…went to hear Rev. Mr. Minnigerode," William related to Josie. Reverend Charles Minnigerode was a German immigrant and the beloved rector of St. Paul's Episcopal Church, only a short walk from the seat of government; the church was frequented by President Jefferson Davis and his family. (It would be during Rev. Minnigerode's Sunday Communion service, less than three months later, that Davis would receive the dispatch from Lee, advising that Richmond was to be evacuated. And it was the same Rev. Minnegerode who would kneel to pray with Davis and his wife, Varina, in their suite in the Spotswood Hotel on May 10, 1867, the day the former president was released from Federal custody.) [699]

The next day, January 9, Chapman had a short interview with the Secretary of War. At one o'clock he visited "…the office of Mr. Chapman, Disbursing Office of the War Dept., who is a relative," to do some writing.[700] By three o'clock Chapman was on the train, enroute to Petersburg. In the letter to his father, the day before leaving for Richmond, the busy officer had written: "I was anxious to come by home but will not have the time owing to Col. Mosby's getting wounded. I will not have much leisure this winter."[701]

Colonel Chapman was shocked at the state of the Confederate army as he traversed the crowded road from Petersburg to Lee's headquarters outside the beleaguered city: "I left the cars…during a hard storm of rain and sleet. I passed through portions of regiments camped not in tents but in holes or burrows the soldiers had dug in the ground to find shelter from the cold weather. On that day I experienced my first depression and doubt of the success of our cause." He was equally surprised when he entered Lee's room at army headquarters. "There was scarcely any furniture in the room—some chairs and a table—and but little fire in the fireplace." Mosby's confidant was finding out first hand that the Rangers were engaged in a much different kind of war than was the regular army; defending a besieged city was far removed from the hit-and-run attacks of the partisans in the rural countryside of northern Virginia and the Valley. Sleeping in a bed and eating meals at a table, and in front of a fire inside a Fauquier safe-house, could in no way be compared to eating, sleeping and trying to keep warm in a hole outside Petersburg. Lee was apparently no more aware of Mosby's conduct of the war, and how it differed from that of the regular cavalry, than Chapman, observing the dug-in troops, was of Lee's mode of warfare. "He gave me instructions about taking care of my men, and cautioned me to move my camp frequently, lest we be surprised by the enemy. I saw plainly that Genl. Lee did not know how we had subsisted as soldiers in Fauquier and Loudoun Counties, and I did not enlighten him for fear he might interfere with the methods we had found most expedient for effective service, and for keeping the command together." While in Lee's presence, Chapman observed the commander giving his own coat to a courier who had arrived to pick up orders and mail and who had little to protect him from the terrible weather. "I left soon after with a despondent feeling"[702]

After leaving Lee's headquarters, Chapman again took the train; he was traveling north this time to Hamilton's Crossing on the Massaponax near its confluence with the Rappahannock River, four miles south of Fredericksburg. Here he was met by some of his men and, on January 14, took the ferry across the Rappahannock and proceeded on to King George Court House. They spent the night "...at the hardest hotel I ever saw, getting no forage for our horses," according to Sergeant Lemuel Corbin of Company C. By the next night they were within four miles of the Westmoreland Court House at Montross.[703] There Chapman found the command had taken up residence with the citizens of the region—Company C was in Westmoreland County, Company E in Richmond County, and Companies F and G in Northumberland and Lancaster Counties.[704]

The people of the Northern Neck had been asking for just such a force as Chapman's since at least the previous June. Bands of marauders, in the guise of Union soldiers, had been inflicting distress upon the people for some time. The previous June, a three-man committee, acting from a resolution of the citizens of Northumberland County, had written to President Davis of their "extreme peril:" "Recently a force of negro troops, with a squad of cavalry were landing above Westmoreland Court House. (They) broke into detachments...to pursue all the routes of travel down to the Neck. They were evidently in search of no armed force, and expected to encounter none. (They) were allowed unbounded license in pillage and waste....A large number of horses and mules, cattle and sheep, have been driven off; hogs were killed in mere wantonness; carts, wagons, and other vehicles taken off, agricultural implements broken into pieces...houses searched and ransacked, ladies and gentlemen, in many cases, stripped of all their clothing." The list of destruction and pillage went on for some length, involving "...300 negroes and fifty whites. The negroes were suffered to wander from house to house without control...ladies were insulted, cursed, reviled...four at least became unfortunate victims of brutal lust." [705]

On October 11, 1864, Major General Benjamin F. Butler, then commanding the Union Army of the James, ordered a gunboat to the waters off the Northern Neck, at Smith's Point in Northumberland County, there "...to seize some eight or ten of the most reputable citizens you can find and bring them to me." They were to be taken "as hostages for...the captain of the light-ship and six men who went on shore for water." It is not clear what had happened to the captain, J.R. McDonald, and his crew; nevertheless, Butler's actions were nothing out of the ordinary for him; he had earned the derisive sobriquet "Beast" for his treatment of the citizens of New Orleans—particularly the women—while he had been military governor two years earlier. [706]

Despite repeated requests for protection, the authorities in Richmond were not disposed to render much assistance, at least in the form of manpower, to the people of the Neck. President Davis: "...assure them of my deep sympathy and of the sorrow I feel at my inability to give them ample protection." Secretary of War Seddon: "The Department fully sympathizes and is doing all in its power to organize reserves and supply arms, etc., for home defense." General Lee was much less inclined to be sympathetic to their plight: "I have always heard that there were a great many men in that country who should have been in the army but who could not be got. I think the least they can do would be to turn out and defend their own homes;" and in reply to a later request: "It is impossible to detach troops from this army to defend the locality mentioned. if the people will do nothing to defend themselves....I can see no remedy for them. They could easily repel such marauding parties if they would exert themselves." Finally, at the urging of Seddon, Lee asked Mosby to recommend someone who could be dispatched to mobilize and train a local force for defense. In August, 1864, Tom Richards, later to become captain of Company G, was sent, but the exercise was a failure and he was soon back with the battalion. [707]

Mosby's choice of Tom Richards was not the partisan chief's alone—and there appears to have been an ulterior motive involved in the selection. Although, at thirty-five years, fifteen years older than his brother, Dolly, Tom had been passed over by Mosby for promotion. The jealousy for his younger brother showed; Tom had even been heard to remark about how "mortifying" it was to be in a command where a younger brother was his senior officer. For these reasons, Mosby—at Sam Chapman's suggestion—had sent Tom Richards to the Northern Neck.[708] But even when he was promoted to the captaincy of Company G some three months later, the older brother could not escape being his younger sibling's subordinate—Dolly Richards was promoted to major nine days afterwards. Tom Richards' bravery was never in question. It was he who led the initial charge against Blazer at Myerstown, the fight that resulted in the annihilation of the Federal unit. But here again, Tom felt he had not received the credit due him from his younger brother. Years later, when he and Mosby met in Los Angeles, he complained that "Dolly did him an injustice in the Blazer fight." Mosby, in writing to Sam Chapman about the meeting, remarked, "It rather gave me a contempt for him. You are in the same situation with your brother, William, but I would not have a very high opinion of you if I were to hear of you making such a speech. It was purely accidental that in yours and Tom's case that your (younger) brothers got ahead of you. I have no doubt that *you* were gratified at it."[709]

Colonel Chapman found, when he arrived on the Neck, that his presupposition to "not (having) leisure this winter" was not exactly valid. "Each company met regularly at a place designated for cavalry drill—there was little else for us to do. We could watch the gun-boats passing up and down the Potomac River, and on clear days look across to Point Lookout and grieve over the conditions of our soldiers imprisoned there, and try to invent some scheme by which to rescue them."[710] (Point Lookout could rightly be called the North's counterpart to the South's Andersonville. The largest prison in the North, it was situated on about forty sandy acres at the very tip of the Maryland peninsula, where the Potomac River flows into Chesapeake Bay. At times it held as many as 20,000 Confederate prisoners, who slept in tents, ate rats for food, and shivered and froze under their blankets from the fierce winter winds.) [711]

The severe winter weather did not spare the Rangers on the Neck. On January 28, William Chapman wrote to his wife: "Will you please knit or crochet me a pair of gloves. Somebody stole mine while in Richmond & so I have to borrow from some of my friends." (The same day, Tee Edmunds, in Fauquier, wrote in her diary: "This is without a doubt the coldest day since Creation. We can hardly keep the fire warm.") [712] Chapman later commented on the effect of the cold on Federal river traffic: "The Potomac is frozen nearly across. All of their vessels are blocked up. If it wasn't for the hardship our soldiers would have to undergo, it would be well if it would stay so until Grant's Army would starve out." And then, this personal note to Josie: "This is an intensely cold morning, though notwithstanding the cold & wind in my face, I should like to be on the road to see you." [713]

The Union army's attention to the Northern Neck intensified in early 1865. One reason, of course, was the fact that Chapman was there with about 400 Rangers. But the primary reason can be found in a communiqué, dated February 21, from Grant to Sheridan, requesting troopers be sent to the region: "Many supplies have been collected on the Northern Neck, and many more are smuggled in from Philadelphia and other places and taken to Richmond over this road" (meaning the Fredericksburg Road.) "70,000 pounds of bacon alone have gone to Richmond the last week....Cannot General Augur send a force to break that trade up?"[714] The entire region, between the Potomac and Mattaponi Rivers, which included the counties of Essex and King and Queen, as well as the Northern Neck counties, concerned the Federals, as seen in Sheridan's reply to Grant: "There is a large amount of provisions and forage. Last summer, when I was in this section, I found the finest crops of corn I ever saw, and every acre planted." [715]

About the time the Federals were contemplating a move against the Confederates on the Northern Neck, Captain Thomas Richards and several men from Company G were on a scout to Williamsburg. From their base in Westmoreland County it was a trip of 125 miles to the Colonial Capitol. It is difficult to understand just what the small group—seven to twenty-five men depending on what source is accurate—hoped to accomplish on a mission of such distance. In any regard, at three o'clock in the morning of February 11, the little band came upon a Union picket post on the Richmond Road. The partisans attacked the reserve force of the post, routing the garrison, and succeeding in capturing several horses, while killing one soldier and wounding four. The Union report states "a number of (Rangers) wounded, which they carried off with them," however there is no other record of just what Richards' casualties were, if any. The partisans made their retreat up the road toward New Kent Court House. [716]

Although Chapman's command had been received with apparent open arms, it was not long before rumblings of discontent were heard from some of the natives. On February 24, a citizen of Northumberland County, where Company F was quartered, wrote a letter to Elias Edmonds, a member of Virginia's House of Delegates from that area. The complaint was made that "a number of men, claiming to belong to Colonel Mosby's command," had forcibly taken personal property of some of the citizens, "even the boots off of some of their feet." While praising Mosby and "men who have distinguished themselves by bravery and patriotism," R. K. Ford, a justice of the peace, requested the representative's assistance in apprising Mosby of the conduct of some of his command, "for if this thing is not checked, life and property is in jeopardy." In forwarding the letter to the Secretary of War, Edmonds added "that this is but a single instance of the numberless outrages committed by some of these rogues...which are being brought to my attention by every letter I receive from home."[717]

On March 4, Grant sent explicit and detailed orders to Colonel Samuel H. Roberts, commanding the 139th New York Volunteer Infantry. Roberts was to take a brigade of infantry and a cavalry detachment and proceed from Fortress Monroe, up the Rappahannock as far as safely possible, and then disembark and travel overland to Fredericksburg. Two army and two navy gunboats would accompany the transports. "The object of your expedition is to break up...a very considerable contraband trade carried on across the Potomac by way of the Northern Neck and through Fredericksburg to Richmond." Roberts was further ordered by Grant to "seize or destroy all property...being used in barter for unauthorized articles of trade between the rebel armies and Northern cities...destroy the railroad depot and as much of the Richmond Road) as you can...You will arrest and bring with you all persons engaged in smuggling or trading between the North and South."[718]

Colonel Chapman was at Fredericksburg on March 6. Going down the river about five miles he spied the Union force under Roberts. "I saw ten transports and three gun-boats loaded with troops." After dark, Chapman took three men and tried to get as close to the anchored boats as possible, "...to learn the object of this raid or expedition." Unfortunately, the observers were spotted by a picket on the shore who fired at them, slightly wounding one of the men, named Pearson—a flesh wound to the calf of the leg—causing the small band to abandon their mission. The following morning Chapman had part of the answer to his question. "They burned the depot and stores at Hamilton's Crossing and captured some Confederate wagons, and then, about three o'clock, they went aboard their transports and started for For-tress Monroe." [719] (It is not certain just which Ranger was the one wounded; there were six Rangers named Pearson on the roster of the 43rd Battalion, all privates. Five of these men were in Company C, which was one of the com-panies under command of Colonel Chapman on the Northern Neck.) [720]

A full report of Roberts' expedition was sent to Grant on March 9, and the details reveal the huge success of the raid. The force consisted of five regi-ments of 1800 infantry and a detachment of 300 men from the 1st New York Mounted Rifles. Four gunboats accompanied the transports. Reaching the wharf at Fredericksburg at dusk on March 6, a squadron of cavalry took pos-session of the town without opposition, while another detachment of cavalry proceeded to the railroad bridge over the Massaponax River just south of the city. Here, twenty-seven freight cars, seventeen of which were loaded with tobacco, were captured, and near Hamilton's Crossing a train of fourteen army wagons, with forty mules, was taken. The 120-foot long railroad bridge was burned; the depot and telegraph office were also destroyed. In the city itself, a house-to-house search resulted in the capture of thirteen Con-federate soldiers. When the command returned to Fortress Monroe on March 7, they had "...45,000 pounds of tobacco, eighty bushels of grain, 46 mus-kets, 15 sabers, two horses and 12 mules..." which they turned over to the authorities. The remaining mules and wagons were retained for further use. Roberts ended his report by saying: "A careful estimate of the whole prop-erty captured shows its value to be about $700,000 in U. S. currency." [721]

Roberts must have been pleased with the success of his raid and he had every reason to be. However, there was no enemy to contend with and he had a force of "between 2,000 and 3,000 men" to accomplish his objec-tives. [722] So perhaps the brigade commander can be excused for being some-what delusional about what he could accomplish further down river. The same day he returned to Fortress Monroe, Roberts sent a dispatch to Grant: "The guide for the lower counties of the Northern Neck having reached me to-day, I propose, if the lieutenant-general permits, to take my command to some point on the Potomac River and march down. There are some 500 cav-alry in the country living upon the people and ready to collect conscripts and horses for the Confederates. I think the better part of the soldiers can be captured and a great many horses and cattle collected...It will take about five days to do the job well." [723]

At five o'clock on the morning of Sunday, March 12, Roberts landed his force for a second time in less than a week from a waterway of the Northern Neck. Intending to disembark at Machodoc Bay and advance inland to Montross, he found there was no place to rapidly land his troops. The flotilla then sailed southeast, around Coles Neck, passing Coles Point, Ragged Point, and Sandy Point and entered the mouth of the Yeocomico River near Lynch's Point; it then steamed into Kinsale, at the southern end of Westmoreland County. At eight o'clock the same morning, William Chapman was at the home of a Mr. Beale near The Hague, seven miles northwest of Kinsale. Receiving word "that the Yankees were landing infantry and cavalry at Kindsale (sic)....I at once sent couriers to the company commanders." [724]

Chapman collected about fifteen of his men who were in the vicinity and started in the direction of Kinsale. Not more than a half-mile along the way, he met Lieutenant Wat Bowie of Company F who, with two or three other men, was escorting a couple of prisoners. Advising Bowie that a regiment of cavalry was coming up behind him, Chapman directed the lieutenant and his group to continue on, in an attempt to draw the advance guard as far from the main body as possible; Chapman then concealed his men in the woods along side the road. When the advance guard of the Federal cavalry reached the point where Chapman had entered the wood, they observed tracks and came to a halt directly in front of the Rangers. "There was nothing for us to do but to charge them, which we did with such a yell that they must have imagined that we had a whole regiment," Chapman recalled, figuring that the same tactic used by Mosby in the Piedmont and in the Shenandoah Valley should be just as effective on the Northern Neck. The thirty or so troopers in the advance guard turned and ran back toward their column, with the Rangers in close pursuit. They soon caught up with the fleeing Federals, capturing some of them, while passing many others, before meeting the head of the column at the top of a small hill. [725]

The sudden flight of the advance guard back into the head of the main column threw the 1st New York Mounted Rifles into confusion and it was with some difficulty that their commander, Colonel E. V. Sumner, kept the remainder of his troopers from also being put to flight. Chapman "was riding a mare that was very fast and was hard to hold when excited, and I was carried into the head of the column and I distinctly heard this officer scolding his men, asking then if they were 'going to let a dozen men whip a regiment.' I had to pull my mare into the corner of a rail fence before I could turn, and I could see splinters flying from the rails from the bullets fired at me." [726]

Chapman, Wat Bowie, and one other Ranger found themselves trapped in the fence corner. The air was hot with lead and, when they wheeled around to go back, they found themselves facing the same enemy cavalrymen they had passed and not captured or disarmed on the charge into the head of the column. The three partisans took a road that ran off to the right from a blacksmith's shop. The Federals followed the main road to The Hague and found that "at every crossroad the enemy would separate, each squad taking a different path, until our cavalry found themselves pursuing only three men. These were captured and sent back toward the main column." Meanwhile, Chapman and his two companions "made a detour and reached a body of woods which we kept in until we came to the road over which we had passed in going into this charge." Here they were able to retake the three captured Rangers and make prisoners of the guard and two other Union troopers.

After the skirmish at The Hague, the Union force burned the blacksmith's shop and an extensive wheelwright's establishment along with a granary containing 500 bushels of wheat. Roberts then turned his men around and proceeded back in the direction of Kinsale. On the way they destroyed four small storehouses filled with grain, tobacco, and bacon and picked up twenty-six head of cattle and fifty sheep.[727]

Later, on that Sabbath day, Chapman collected his entire command and made repeated efforts to separate Sumner's cavalry from the main infantry body. Finally, stationing his men in a wooded area close by, Chapman and Sergeant William Biedler, of Company C, rode out into an open field in view of the Union cavalrymen. By exposing themselves in the open, Chapman and Biedler hoped to draw the troopers out to pursue them so that the rest of the command, concealed in the woods, could strike the New Yorkers. But the ruse did not work; in fact, it almost had disastrous results for Chapman. "I observed some sharpshooters passing into a body of pines on my left and called Mr. Biedler's attention to it and we started to move out of range. Just as I turned my mare, a shot from one of them struck her in the hind leg at the hock joint. A volley was fired at the same time and the mare, while in this excited state, ran for over 100 yards on three legs and carried me under a hill out of range of the bullets. She was the most valuable animal I owned during the war and I regretted her loss very much."[728]

Just about dark, Sam Chapman, with a portion of Company E, made an attack on the rear of the Federal column while his brother was just ahead scouting the flank. Reminiscent of Sam's wounding at Grapewood Farm nearly two years before, a Yankee bullet once more found its mark. While the freezing temperature slowed the stream of blood, oozing from the hole in his thigh, the captain was carried by some of his men to the nearby home of Reverend George H. Northam.[729]

The Reverend Northam was a thirty-four-year-old Baptist minister living with his wife and four young children in Nomini Grove, a few miles southeast of The Haque. He had pastored several churches on the Neck and was now serving Menokin Baptist Church in adjoining Richmond County. The church had a membership of 365, just over one-half of whom were black slaves and hired hands of the well-to-do families in the area. In the year immediately prior to the war, Reverend Northam himself recorded real estate valued at $8,000 and personal property of over $14,000.[730]

Word of Sam's wounding was carried to Rebecca and she immediately began the long and difficult journey from Salem. Her arrival and the kindly care of the minister's family hastened the recovery of her severely wounded husband.[731]

At 11:00 p.m. of March 12, Roberts began loading his force on the transports. "By 3 o'clock all were on board, and we dropped down to the mouth of the river, the army gun-boats throwing a few shells as a farewell present to the rebels, who were concealed in the background of woods." [732]

The opening sentence of Colonel Roberts' initial report from across the bay best sums up his latest incursion: "I regret to report that my expedition to the Northern Neck has not been very successful so far. I find the enemy in stronger force than I expected and superior in cavalry and perfect knowledge of the country." Federal casualties were confined to Sumner's 1st New York Mounted Rifles—five wounded, including one commissioned officer and five cavalrymen captured, including two of the wounded. The Rangers lost two men captured.[733]

Although unintentional, Roberts had probably best characterized the whole of Mosby's Rangers as well as anyone could: "...superior in cavalry and perfect knowledge of the country."

A few days after the fight with Roberts' force, Colonel Chapman met a former U. S. Congressman, the Honorable Willoughby Newton. Newton had witnessed, from his house, the charge that Chapman and the fifteen Rangers had made against the advance guard of the Federal column, driving it back into the main body, and acclaimed the incident: "A handful of men charging a regiment. It was equal to the charge of Balaklava!" [734] referring to the event in the Crimean War immortalized in Tennyson's *Charge of the Light Brigade:*

> When can their glory fade?
> Oh, the wild charge they made!
> All the world wondered.
> Honor the charge they made! [735]

27. "Collect Your Command"

John Willis McCue was a private in Company C, William Chapman's old company before his promotion to lieutenant colonel. McCue was an eighteen-year-old cadet at the Virginia Military Institute, class of 1867, when he enlisted with Mosby in August of 1864. On March 29, McCue and five comrades crossed the Potomac River from the Northern Neck to scout the enemy force at Leonardtown, Maryland. Afterwards, McCue and two of the partisans made an attempt to capture the post office in the small town of Croom. They were surprised by four government detectives and an armed postmaster who fired upon the three Confederates. While his two comrades fled, McCue engaged in a gunfight in the darkness; the postmaster, Jeremiah Coffron and one of the detectives were wounded. The detective, Richard N. Ryon, who would die from his wound, told McCue that he had fought bravely, had done his duty, and being in a Confederate uniform, he hoped he would be treated as a prisoner of war. Despite this, the young Ranger was taken to Baltimore where he was to stand trial before a military commission on a charge of murder. (On May 18, 1865, McCue was found guilty and taken to Clinton Prison, New York to serve a life sentence at hard labor. Through the efforts of various persons, including the president of the Commission that tried him, Colonel Samuel M. Bowman of the 84th Pennsylvania Volunteers—and at the personal request of General Grant—President Andrew Johnson eventually pardoned John McCue in November, 1865.) [736]

Prior to McCue's ill-fated excursion, the Federals continued to work on plans to eliminate Mosby's partisans on the Northern Neck. Commander Foxhall A. Parker, of the Potomac Flotilla, sent a message on March 16, three days after taking Colonel Roberts' invaders off the narrow peninsula, to General Augur, commanding the XXII Army Corps, in Washington: "With the home guards and Mosby's guerrillas the rebels on the Northern Neck now number about 800, most of whom are mounted. By landing a large cavalry force at Belle Plain these fellows could all be captured. I now have a sufficient force of gun-boats to encircle the whole Neck from Belle Plain, on the Potomac, to Port Royal, on the Rappahannock, at distances apart of fifteen miles, and can send a co-operating force ashore also." During the next three weeks, numerous dispatches traveled between the various army and navy commands and even between the Secretary of the Navy, Gideon Welles, and War Secretary Stanton, concerning just what to do about the Confederate force on the Neck. [737]

More than three weeks after his first dispatch to Augur, Parker sent another: "I learn that a force of 500 men, well mounted, are now on the neck collecting provisions, forage, horses, and cattle, and gradually moving up toward Falmouth, where they will cross the Rappahannock a few days hence... Cannot you send a force to intercept these fellows? Please answer." [738]

General Augur did answer Parker, immediately upon receiving the message: "A plan for sending a command to the Northern Neck is under consideration by the Secretary of War and General Halleck. I can do nothing until the matter is decided by those who have it under advisement." [739] The date was April 9.

John Mosby, looking pale and gaunt, had returned to the upper Piedmont by February 25.[740] During his absence, the three companies under Major Richards had seen infrequent, but mostly successful, action on both sides of the Blue Ridge. One such fight took place on February 19 near Mt. Carmel Church in Ashby's Gap. Richards, with a hastily collected group of forty-three Rangers, attacked a column of the 14th Pennsylvania Cavalry, hitting their rear guard while it was forced to march, by file, on a narrow path between the rocks on the Shepherd's Ford Road. The Federals offered almost no resistance and were soon routed. Of the 124 enlisted men and four officers, thirteen were killed and nearly an equal number wounded. Sixty-three of the Pennsylvanians were made prisoners and ninety horses rounded up. Nineteen Southerners, who the Federals had picked up along the road, were set free. Aside from a flesh wound received by one, Richards' men had no casualties. [741]

With Mosby's return to command, the Rangers continued to raid in small parties. However, they were also busily involved in the business of conscription and looking for forage in the scorched landscape of the upper Piedmont. Various Federal reports placed Mosby at Waterford, in northern Loudoun County the first week in March, "...conscripting all the inhabitants capable of bearing arms." Later that month he was reported to be "...scattered about the county of Loudoun, conscripting and impressing horses and provisions." [742]

As the winter waned and spring began to thrust its way out of the thawing ground, the luck of the Rangers seemed to wane also. More and more skirmishes, with seasoned Federal troops, were now resulting in the loss of more and more men—to death, wounds, and capture. In a fight at Harmony, just east of Purcellville on March 21, the command lost James Keith and Wirt Binford, both killed instantly, and at least five men wounded. One week later, three Rangers were captured, includung the battalion's quarter-master J. Wright James, while attempting to destroy a distillery; four more were capt-ed a few miles away. And on March 30, Charlie Wiltshire and George Gill were mortally wounded and two of their comrades slightly wounded, all by a single courageous Federal officer—Lieutenant Eugene Ferris of the 30th Massachusetts Infantry—whom they had seemingly trapped just inside a stable door in Berryville.[743] Tee Edmonds, writing in her diary, lamented the loss of another friend: "Oh! Who should be the fallen brave but dear Charlie Wiltshire. A braver man never fell...Oh! Why should the brave and loved ones fall?" [744]

On March 27, Lee, through his adjutant Colonel Taylor, sent orders to Mosby: "Collect your command and watch the country from front of Gor-donsville to Blue Ridge and also Valley. Your command is all now in that section, and the general will rely on you to watch and protect the country. If any of your command is in Northern Neck call it to you."[745] With the mass-ing of the Federal armies before the entrenched Confederates at Petersburg, all that Lee had, to "protect" the vast area west of Gordonsville, was ap-proximately 800 partisans. The handwriting was on the wall and Mosby knew it. What he didn't realize was how close the end really was.

Mosby assembled his men at North Fork Church in Loudoun County April 5, where the eighth—and last—of Mosby's companies, Company H, was or-ganized. George Baylor was elected captain in the style Mosby had used to select most all his officers—one name placed in nomination and one vote taken. The company set out the next day, some fifty-two strong, for the Valley, passing through Snicker's Gap and crossing the Shenandoah at Rock Ford. When the command reached Charlestown, Baylor learned that the Loudoun Rangers were encamped just a few miles away near Halltown. He immediately headed in that direction and when he was about fifty yards from the camp, ordered a charge. The surprise was complete and Baylor's men captured between forty and sixty-five men and over seventy horses, killing and wounding half-a-dozen of the Federals, while suffering the loss of only one man to wounds. [746] General Stevenson, sent a message to Middle Mili-tary Division headquarters: "Mosby surprised camp of Loudoun Rangers near Keyes' Ford and cleaned them out." When Union General Hancock heard the news, he is reported to have laughed heartily and exclaimed, "Well, that is the last of the Loudoun Rangers!" [747]

News of Lee's surrender on April 9 was slow in reaching Mosby and his command. Oh, there were unofficial stories circulating but nothing that Mosby could put his trust in. On the same Sunday morning that Lee was discussing surrender terms with Grant, Captain Baylor assembled Companies D and H and proceeded to White Plains, remaining there until afternoon; he then set out for Fairfax, intending to capture a train carrying wood to Alexandria. It had rained all night and the next day and as the force approached Fairfax, Baylor learned that the train would not be making the run after all. On the way back to Fauquier, the Rangers stopped at Arundel's Farm to rest, and most of the men dismounted. Suddenly, seemingly out of nowhere, they were set upon by a detachment of the 8th Illinois Cavalry under the command of Colonel Charles Albright. Confusion reigned. Some of the partisans were able to collect themselves enough to temporarily check the initial charge of the Federal cavalrymen. But it was of no use. Baylor's men had to skedaddle as best they could with Albright's troopers in fast pursuit. The chase ended at Wolf Run Shoals near where Bull Run meets the Occoquan River. The Rangers lost five men captured, one of whom, Private Richard McVeigh, was seriously wounded. Union casualties were two wounded.[748]

The Union officers minced no words in ballyhooing their victory over Mosby's men: "I just come... from a fight with a battalion of Mosby's men, under command of Captain Baylor. I whipped him like thunder..." reported Colonel Albright. And Colonel William Gamble, in his report, boasted: "The detachment of the Eighth Illinois Cavalry...met Mosby's battalion...and, as usual, whipped it like the devil." [749]

Ironically, the last company to be formed and the last captain elected in the 43rd had fought the regiment's last fight.

While Baylor was on his way to Fairfax, Mosby, with John Russell and several of the other Rangers had crossed the Shenandoah River where Mosby halted the group. He and Russell, with a small party, proceeded on a reconnaissance toward Berryville. Years later, The partisan chief recalled this last raid in vivid detail: " It was a dark, rainy night. We stopped at a house. Not far off we could see a picket fire on the Pike." Mosby sent Russell and some other men to capture the picket. "That was the last order I gave in the war to make an attack. I think I went to the house to get a cup of coffee made. Pretty soon we heard pistol shots & clatter on the Pike. I laughed & said 'John has got them.' Mosby was right—Russell soon returned with half a lozen Union cavalrymen as prisoners. Most of the waiting command was ent back across the river with the captives, while Mosby and the remainder ode on to Jordan Springs. On their return the following night, the group topped at a farmhouse near Berry's Ferry. "About midnight we heard the oar of artillery at Winchester. We knew instinctively what it meant. They vere celebrating Lee's surrender. It was the funeral knell of the Southern Confederacy," Mosby lamented. Nearly forty years after the occurrence Mosby revealed the reason for this final excursion: "The last raid that I went on was after I had heard of the fall of Richmond, but before we had heard of he surrender. I took the men on the raid to keep them from becoming demoralized, as it was my intention to hold out as long as Lee & Johnston." [750]

n response to Lee's order of March 27, Mosby had ordered William Chapman back to Fauquier County. The command left the Northern Neck on April 9 and reached Warrenton on April 12; that night they camped at the ome of James Blackwell, father of Joseph "Chief" Blackwell, of Company 3, near Bethel. Chapman would remember: "I reported that night or the next lay to Col. Mosby." [751] Their movement had not gone unnoticed. General Augur cabled (Brevet) Brigadier General Gamble, commanding at Fairfax Court House, on April 14: "I have information that 300 of Mosby's command passed through Falmouth on the 11th for Fauquier and Loudoun Counties." [752]

28. "Farewell"

Sam Chapman was still asleep when Rebecca arose on this unusually raw, windy morning a full month into spring. She was up earlier than usual and her husband was sleeping later than usual. She had tried not to awaken him when she got up; he had been restless most of the night and she knew he had not slept well. When Sam came into the kitchen a short time later he kissed her on the cheek and sat down at the table. Rebecca poured his coffee and he told her not to prepare him any breakfast—maybe just warm bread and butter—as he pulled on his best pair of long cavalry boots. He had shined them to a brilliant jet-black luster last evening and had asked her to lay out his best uniform and plumed hat. Sam was unusually quiet this morning, as he had been the night before. Rebecca had learned after nine months of marriage—lacking one week—not to ask things of her husband when he was reluctant to talk. Not that he minded; it was simply that when he did not feel like talking—a rare thing for her normally effusive mate—he did not.

Rebecca could only guess as to what was transpiring among Sam and the other Rangers. Sam's sister-in-law, Josie Chapman, had told Rebecca that her husband, William, had been across the mountain to Winchester and Millwood in the past several days and that some discussions were taking place with the Yankees.[753] It was now April 21, nearly two weeks since General Lee had surrendered his army. Four days before, after the battalion had gathered just outside of town, Sam had told Rebecca that a truce had been declared between Mosby and the Federals. But then there was some talk in the village about the truce being extended for ten more days, but that any agreement to an extension had not materialized and the truce had, in fact, ended at noon yesterday.[754]

Just what had taken place with regard to the truce was this: On April 17, Colonel William Chapman and Doctor Aristides Monteiro, one of the command's surgeons, had met with General Hancock at Union headquarters in Winchester. An agreement was reached whereas Mosby would refrain from any operations whatever and no offensive operations would be made against his command. This cessation of hostilities was to give Mosby an opportunity to meet the following day with General George H. Chapman to discuss a possible surrender. "I have no doubt but that Mosby will surrender his whole command.... " Hancock had wired chief of staff General Halleck in Washington.[755]

Mosby arrived at the meeting in Millwood the next day, about thirty minutes before the truce was set to expire. The ensuing discussions with General Chapman resulted in an agreement to have a "suspension of hostilities for forty-eight hours, expiring at noon on the 20th, and a conditional agreement for a further suspension for ten days."[756] The extension of the truce after the April 20 deadline was contingent upon approval from General Chapman's superiors. Hancock in turn reported these developments, requesting that he be notified if the truce was not to be extended. General Grant's acrimonious response was immediate: "If Mosby does not avail himself of the present truce, end it and hunt him and his men down. Guerillas, after beating the armies of the enemy, will not be entitled to quarter."[757]

Rebecca thought her husband had never looked as fine in his uniform, not since the day they were married anyway. But there was a sadness in his face that she had not seen before. He had not asked her to go, but said the battalion was assembling just out of town. Soon after Sam had left she took the buggy and, with a couple of the other wives, rode to the place, a large field to the north of the village.

The early morning rain had stopped, except for a slight drizzle, which, together with the cool wind, sent a damp chill through the air and "a thick fog hung like a pall over the face of the country." [758] The Rangers continued to ride in during what was left of the morning and by noon about 200 of them had gathered. They were all—like Sam—attired in their finest uniforms, almost every one with a black plume or feather in his hat, and each with a brace of pistols on his belt. They milled around, in small groups mostly, talking quietly. Many were not there, for various reasons—nearly 200 were in Northern prisons while others were wounded and could not ride—and of course there were those who had fallen, never to rise again in this world. Each man was mounted on a fine horse, most on an excellent cavalry mount, bridled and equipped, compliments of the United States government. [759]

Mosby had ridden in from "Glen Welby," the home of Major Richard Henry Carter, a few miles northeast of Salem. It was at Glen Welby that the Colonel had spent some time before stopping in at Ludwell Lake's home, where he was so seriously wounded, exactly four months ago to the day. And this morning Mosby had asked for pen and paper—he had something he needed to write. [760]

After Mosby's arrival, the order was given to each squadron commander, Lieutenant Colonel Chapman and Major Richards, to form his command; Chapman and Richards in turn ordered the company commanders to form their companies. They were soon drawn up in eight ranks, one for each of the companies which, for the most part, was represented by about a fourth of its complement. Mosby sat his horse between Chapman and Richards, a few paces behind the regiment's adjutant, his own brother, Lieutenant "Willie" Mosby.[761] There was a hush from the onlookers and not a sound was heard on the green; nothing save the occasional neighing of a horse. Mosby cantered his horse up to the far end and began a slow ride down the long mounted line, looking each man in the face, as if to somehow register forever the image in his mind's eye.[762] When he appeared in front of Sam Chapman, the gallant captain saw in his beloved commander's face not the sadness but a sparkle from the piercing blue eyes—a look that he quickly recalled from that cold January day over two years ago, when he had seen "that fellow Mosby" for the first time. Was this to be the last time he wondered?

After he had finished reviewing the line, Mosby returned to his place between Chapman and Richards. The two squadron leaders each withdrew a piece of paper from his pocket and read to his respective command: [763]

> *Soldiers – I have summoned you together for the last time.*
> *The vision we have cherished of a free and independent country*
> *has vanished and that country is now the spoil of a conqueror.*
> *I disband your organization in preference to surrendering it to*
> *our enemies. I am no longer your commander. After an*
> *association of more than two eventful years, I part from you*
> *with a just pride in the fame of your achievements and*
> *grateful recollections of your generous kindness to myself. And*
> *now, at this moment of bidding you a final adieu, accept the*
> *assurance of my unchanging confidence and regard. Farewell!*
>
> *John S. Mosby*
> *Colonel* [764]

The silence that followed the readings lasted but a few seconds. The order was given to break ranks. Men clasped each others hands; many rushed up to Mosby and before the first few men had gained his side, his eyes were red and he often turned away or choked back words.[765] A like scene was now presenting itself among the men. Handshakes turned to embraces and the manly efforts of strong men to hold back emotions simply gave way, as if a giant wave had swept across the gathering. Sam Chapman was quickly surrounded by the men he had so often led, by example, into the very heat and heart of battle, showing undaunted courage to those who would follow him.

The scene that was now playing itself out on the long level green was remembered by James Joseph Williamson, a veteran of Mosby's first company, Company A, and who had been with the partisan chief since April, 1863:

> Strong men, who had looked unmoved on scenes
> which would have appalled hearts unused to the
> painful sights presented on the field of battle, now
> wept like little children. Mosby stood beside a fence
> and took the hands of those who gathered around
> him. His eyes were red, and he would now and then
> dash aside the struggling tears which he was unable
> wholly to suppress. Men would silently gasp each
> other's hands and then turn their heads aside to hide
> their tears; but at last it became so general that no
> pains were taken to conceal them. It was the most
> trying ordeal through which we had ever passed. [766]

Twenty-five years later, in a letter to Doctor Monteiro, Mosby would refer to it as "the sad, sorrowful, pathetic scene at Salem when I disbanded and took leave of my men." [767]

The next day, William Chapman gathered at Paris any of the Rangers who wished to be paroled and, with about 200 men, including his brother and several other officers, rode toward Winchester. When the group arrived at Millwood they were detained for a short time by Federal pickets; some two miles from Winchester they were again stopped for nearly twenty minutes. Within a mile of the town, they came in sight of the Union camps. Colonel Chapman took fifteen or twenty men with him and rode into Winchester. Soon after, the Federal provost marshal came out to arrange the paroles. [768] The men were required to read, or have read to them, the oath, which they were then required to sign:

I *Capt. S. F. Chapman* of *Co. 'E', Mosby's Batt*. C. S. Army
do hereby give this my parole of Honor, that I will not take up
arms against the United States Government until I am regularly
exchanged. And that if I am permitted to remain at my home
I will conduct myself as a good and peaceable citizen, and will
respect the laws in force where I reside, and will do nothing to
the detriment of, or in opposition to, the United States Government.

The document contained a physical description, and listed the place of residence, of the person being paroled. It was signed "E. B. Parsons, Provost Marshal General."

A copy of Sam's parole in the National Archives reveals that he, as the parolee, never signed it. [769]

The war was over and Captain Samuel Forrer Chapman, late of Mosby's Rangers, although accepting his enemies' conditions for terminating the fighting, had not officially acknowledged them. Three months later he would be compelled to take a second oath to ensure his freedom. [770]

PART IX

"AN HONORABLE AND USEFUL LIFE"

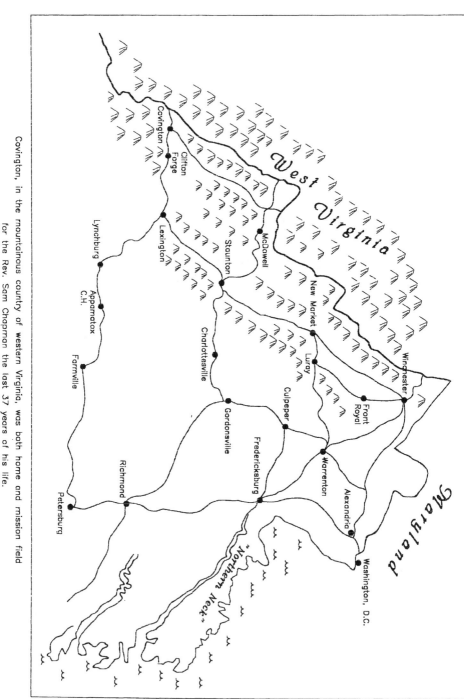

Covington, in the mountainous country of western Virginia, was both home and mission field for the Rev. Sam Chapman the last 37 years of his life.

29. A Qualified Citizen

After the emotional events that culminated with the disbanding of the Rangers at Salem on April 21, Sam and Rebecca Chapman traveled the same road that then-Lieutenant Chapman had traveled alone, in what seemed now to be a long two years before—from Salem, into Rappahannock County, through the Blue Ridge at Thornton's Gap and down to Luray. Then, Sam was heartbroken and trying to recover from wounds of both the flesh and the heart, following the fight at Grapewood Farm and the subsequent rejection by "Miss Beck" of his offerings of "Amo Te". Now, the heartbreak was of a different kind but felt just as keenly by them both. The "Great War for Southern Independence," that Sam had so completely enshrined, in mind, body, and spirit, was over and there was no "Independence". In its stead, there was military and political occupation, desolation of farms, homes and families, an unknown future. For Sam and Rebecca, there was each other, and together they would sort through the pieces, discarding the worthless and building on the promising.

The few weeks immediately following the end of the war would find them all at Luray—Sam with Rebecca, William with Josie, and Edmund, who had gone to the Purcell Artillery when the Dixie, commanded by his older brother, William, was disbanded in 1862. Also there were the younger brothers, John and George, and sisters, Kate, Annie, and Bettie. Bettie was soon to marry Joseph Milton Carter, once a member of William Chapman's company in Mosby's command. They reunited in the large house just north of town, with their parents—father, William and mother, Elizabeth—but too soon, they would again be apart.

Sam Chapman immersed himself in his first calling and, on July 1, was appointed a messenger from Main Street Baptist Church of Luray, to the Association meeting in Loudoun County.[771] However, a living had to be made, so he and Rebecca were soon back in Salem. But as a reminder that the war would not fast fade into memory, Sam found himself in the custody of the Federals—something they had accomplished but once in four years of fighting.

In Washington, D. C. for the purpose of buying livestock to take back to Fauquier County, Sam was arrested by the U. S. provost marshal on July 27, 1865.[772] General Grant, in a dispatch to General Augur, commanding the Department of Washington, explained that an agreement with General Lee had been made, following the surrender at Appomattox Court House, whereas, for any former Confederates, "...their paroles should be their pass for going through our lines where it was necessary for them to comply with their part of the agreement...All who come within your department in violation of this interpretation of the agreement between Lee and myself may be turned back or taken up and imprisoned for violation of their paroles unless they qualify themselves as citizens of the United States by obtaining the President's amnesty." [773] On August 2, Sam Chapman, traveling without a signed parole, took the amnesty oath to secure his release. [774]

Sam spent the next year working with Rebecca's stepfather, William Murray, raising and selling livestock. On July 12, 1866, the Chapman's first child, Ella Lee, was born in Fauquier County. On March 27 of the following year, their first son, Edmund Gaines, was born. [775] In 1868, Sam attended the Potomac Baptist Association meeting at Bethel Baptist Church in Clarke County. He was listed in the minutes as a licentiate minister, although not shown as serving any particular church. [776] June 6, of that year, was the day daughter Elizabeth would enter the world.

The influence of their parents, when it came to religious matters, did not end with Sam, but was felt in the lives of his siblings as well. On March 4, 1866, Kate, age 22, and Annie, age 21, "accepted conversion" and were baptized a month later into the fellowship of Main Street Baptist Church. A year later, eighteen-year-old brother John followed his sisters into the waters. [777]

As the calendar turned to a new decade, an interesting deed was recorded in the Circuit Court of Fauquier County, between William Murray, Rebecca's stepfather, and Sam Chapman. Entered on January 25, 1870, it had to do with "...monies belonging to his wife, Rebecca Chapman, which were collected and used by said Murray before the marriage of said Chapman with his said wife Rebecca." Murray had inherited an interest in the estate of a deceased uncle, and "...being anxious to pay off and discharge his indebtedness to the said Chapman," Murray conveyed to Sam "all of his right, title, and interest in the estate of (the deceased uncle), both real and personal." [778] The "monies" were, in all probability, the dower of $1,250 left to Rebecca by her father, when he died in 1845.

Sam was now teaching in the public schools of Fauquier County. In the summer of 1870, the family, including the Murrays, was living at Rectortown, north of Salem. The census for that year showed Sam with a personal estate valued at only $670, while Murray's real estate was valued at $7,000. In 1871, Sam was appointed by the State Board of Education to be the first superintendent of schools for Fauquier County, a position he would hold for only a year.[779] In August, at the Potomac Baptist Association meeting at Berryville, Reverend Chapman "pleaded" for assistance to aid Broad Run Baptist Church, at New Baltimore, near the Prince William County line in Fauquier County, in rebuilding their house of worship.[780] That same month, Rebecca gave birth to the couple's fourth child, William Allen, named for Sam's father.

Sam had relinquished his school superintendent's appointment by 1872. He was still being carried on the rolls as a licentiate minister in the Potomac Baptist Association when it held its annual meeting at Ebenezer Church in Loudoun County.[781] The year ended on a sad note for the Chapman clan when, just two weeks before Christmas, Sam's father died; he was one month short of his sixty-fifth year. The war that had so devastated the farms of the Shenandoah and Page Valleys had somehow ignored the Chapman place. The house, mill, and outbuildings were still standing and the 1870 census valued the real estate at an extraordinary $35,000. Mr. Chapman's personal estate was valued at $2,850 and he was recorded as having five black farm laborers and one black domestic on the premises.

The elder Chapman had served as clerk of Main Street Baptist Church since 1859. He was there to set down the minutes on April 5, 1863: "No preaching today, the pastor not being present, owing to the excitement from the invading Federal army having occupied the Valley of Va., about New Market and also threatening to overrun the Page Valley." And again, on a very personal note, on April 1, 1865, when several of the "Colored Members" were expelled and their names "stricken from the book for having left their homes and gone to the Yankees." Among these was "Evelina of Wm. Chapman," who had been baptized into the fellowship three years before the war. In addition to the baptism of his slave, Evelina, Chapman had witnessed the baptisms of six of his children, and watched with a father's pride, on that May day in 1858, as the church granted Sam his license to preach.[782] Some of the sadness Sam felt over his father's death was replaced by happiness when Rebecca gave birth to their third daughter, Kate, on March 31, 1873.

The next three years were ones of both great joy and overwhelming grief for the former Ranger and his wife. Following Kate's birth, Sam attended the annual Baptist Association meeting at Mt. Zion Church, near Aldie.[783] It must have been an emotional time for Sam, for it was in the field just across the road, ten years before, that he had unlimbered the little howitzer in anticipation of engaging the Union cavalry under Major Forbes. The ensuing fight in the Loudoun County countryside had resulting in a staggering defeat of the Federals at the hands of Mosby and his men.

By June of 1873, Sam had taken the family to Alexandria to live. There, along with his brother William, he was appointed Mail Agent at an annual salary of $1200, thanks to the friendship between Mosby and President U. S. Grant. Mosby's campaigning for his former foe in the presidential race—including a torrid, shoot-from-the-hip style of oratory—had helped Grant sweep Virginia in a successful bid for his second term. For his efforts, the president offered his old nemesis the post of U. S. Attorney for the Eastern District of Virginia. Mosby declined the offer, afraid that his motives for helping Grant might be misconstrued.

For any faults that John Mosby might have had, absence of loyalty was certainly not one of them. He was always ready to help the men who had served him so faithfully in any way he could. To this end, the former partisan used his friendship with Grant to secure several appointments to the patronage-heavy postal service, the Chapman brothers' being among them.[784] (Later speaking of these appointments, Mosby said: "My lieutenant colonel, William Chapman, a brave and good man, was appointed by General Grant in the postal service. At the beginning of President Hayes' administration, I was invited to call upon him (Hayes), and he stated that there was a great deal of trouble in the Internal Revenue Department of the South, and that he wanted a well-known Confederate soldier to take charge down there. He wanted me to accept the place. I, however, promised to name him a man who would suit him better for the place and upon my recommendation he appointed Colonel Chapman, who had proved a splendid official. Captain Sam Chapman, *the fighting parson*, was also appointed in the postal service by General Grant and served nine years.")[785]

The fulfillment of Sam Chapman's first calling was realized in 1875 when he was ordained into the Baptist ministry at Woodlawn Baptist Church, a few miles south of Alexandria. Sam had served the fledgling church as licentiate minister prior to his ordination. The church had its beginnings from a Sunday School class, started in May of 1859, at the Woodlawn Plantation mansion of Captain John Mason. The property once was part of nearly 2,000 acres owned by George Washington and given to his adopted daughter, Nellie Custis, upon her marriage to Washington's favorite nephew, Lawrence Lewis. It was subsequently subdivided and the portion on which the mansion stood bought by Captain Mason, a New England seaman. The church was organized in 1868 and services were held in the parlor of Woodlawn Mansion. In 1869, Woodlawn Baptist Church was constituted and received into the membership of the Potomac Baptist Association. The first building, a simple white frame structure, was completed in 1872, across the road from the mansion. The year following Sam's ordination, the enrollment of the church was recorded as "1 colored and 47 whites." Reverend Chapman would serve as the church's first minister until 1879.[786]

The year 1875 looked to be one full of hope and promise for Sam and Rebecca. On February 19 of that year, Samuel Forrer Chapman, Jr. was born. But then, on September 11, only three months after Sam's ordination, the seven-month-old baby died of cholera in a Washington, D. C. hospital. The devastation felt by the family was immense but their time of grief would not soon be over. On February 15, 1876, little Katie entered heaven at the age of only two years, ten months, and six days.[787] One month later, on March 16, Rebecca brought Gustavus Adolphus Elgin into the world. "Elgin" was named for his maternal grandfather, Gustavus Elgin, and for Aldophus "Dolly" Richards, Sam's friend and comrade in the 43rd Battalion.

Sam had apparently left the postal service upon his appointment as minister of Woodlawn Baptist Church. However, records show that on March 3, 1877, he was again appointed, this time as Railway Postal Clerk on the Washington, D. C. to Richmond run, at an annual salary of $1,150. In August, Sam and Rebecca sold their property near Rectortown in Fauquier County, consisting of slightly over twelve acres of land, to Patrick Murray for thirty dollars an acre, payable in two installments, with interest, over a period of twenty months. The contract of sale specifically provided that Murray was "...not to cut or remove any wood or trees from the said land except decaying wood already down and some for making or repairing fence on said land...." until the last payment was made. Apparently the payments were not made as called for; the deed transferring the land was not conveyed until December 22, 1879.

Son Paul was born in December 1878, bringing the number of children in the Chapman household to six. Also living with the family was Rebecca's mother, now widowed for a second time, and a fourteen-year-old house servant named Annie Coats.[788] On July 22, 1880, Sam received an appointment as Head Postal Clerk, paying $1300 a year, retroactive to July 1, on the Washington, D. C. to Charlotte, North Carolina route.[789] But nothing—not his preaching, nor his mail runs, nor the birth of two more sons —served to ease the aching heart of the veteran warrior, still grieving over the deaths of his precious Sam, Jr. and Katie. Only with time and distance, could Sam and Rebecca hope to gain some solace. Time was in God's hands; distance was in Sam's—or so he thought.

30. "A Land of Hills and Valleys"

Colonel Mosby once told the story of when he and Sam Chapman and some of the Rangers, with several Union prisoners, were being hotly pursued by Hunter's cavalry. They had come to a place on the Shenandoah River below Berry's Mill where they were faced with a seventy-five yard swim to escape capture, encumbered as they were with their prisoners. Mosby recalled asking: "Sam, do you remember that good old Baptist hymn 'When through the deep waters I cause thee to go, the river of woe shall not overflow?' Immediately he (Sam) took it up and the boys joined in and we swam for our lives."[790]

Perhaps the song—and the incident—were reverberating in Sam's thoughts as the decade of the 1880's, encumbering him with all its responsibilities and burdens, came charging into his life. Sam was still carrying the sorrow of having buried two children; he had six others to care for, in addition to Rebecca and her mother. Another child was on the way and with only $100 a month pay, to compensate for the days and nights away from home on the mail runs, it must have seemed to Sam that he was facing a long swim through deep waters indeed.

On March 3, 1882, Herbert was born in a Washington, D. C. hospital. Then, a few weeks later, the letter came. Would the Reverend Chapman answer a call to the mission field of western Virginia? Several small congregations were in need of a pastor, in the rugged country lying hard against the West Virginia border, nearly 200 miles west of Richmond. In addition to the outlying churches, the Baptist church located in the county seat of Covington would soon be without a pastor, the Reverend W. O. Harris having submitted his resignation on March 24, to become effective June 1.

Perhaps the distance Sam was seeking—like the time—was also in God's hands. Sam thought of God's promise to the children of Israel: "For the land, whither thou goest…is not as the land…from whence ye came out; but the land whither ye go…is a land of hills and valleys, and drinketh water of the rain of heaven. [791]

Sam had applied to the State Mission Board of the General Baptist Association of Virginia for a pastorate, available elsewhere in the state, somewhere away from northern Virginia. Covington—located in an upper valley of the Appalachian chain of mountains—and the surrounding Alleghany County region, was not unlike his native Luray and Page County—more rugged in nature and humankind perhaps, but just as picturesque.

Covington Baptist Church had its beginnings in 1841, being the first of the denomination to establish itself in the town. The Presbyterians and Methodists preceded the Baptists. On May 29, fourteen members organized themselves at the local Presbyterian Church and then met and began worship in the wooden structure that was the Alleghany County courthouse. The first convert was a black woman named Ann, who was baptized in the frigid waters of a local stream on February 13, 1842. The membership adopted the name of Covington Baptist Church of Jesus Christ. Growth was slow, inhibited by the war and its aftermath, and by 1871 only twenty-five souls, nine of whom were black, were on the rolls. A building fund was started in the 1870's and on the 17th day of September, 1874, for the sum of $250, the trustees bought a lot at the corner of Water Street and Second Street. Soon after, the congregation, then numbering thirty, moved into its own house of worship—a new wooden building on aptly named Water Street, only a few yards from the bank of the Jackson River. [792]

Sam arrived alone in Covington around the middle of May. Rebecca, with the new baby, and the rest of the family, were still in Alexandria, not knowing when—or even if—they might be moving. But her husband was anxious to present himself to the waiting churches and the members were just as anxious to hear—and see—just what sort of preacher this handsome forty-three year old ex-Ranger was. His coming was announced in *The Alleghany Tribune*: " Rev. Mr. Chapman, who has been with us for the past few days, was a captain in Colonel Mosby's command during the late war."[793] The new minister may have come at the request of the Baptists but immediately found himself before a different congregation, in nearby Clifton Forge, soon after his arrival: "The pulpit of the Methodist church here was filled last Sunday night by Rev. Mr. Chapman of Alexandria. Mr. Chapman is a Baptist minister and may be called to succeed Mr. Harris who leavs (sic) for Missouri next month." [794]

The following week Sam was back in Covington. "Rev. S. F. Chapman will preach in the Covington Baptist Church Sunday at 11 a. m. The ordinance of the Lord's Supper will be administered after the services." [795]

A month or so after Sam's arrival in the town, the following article appeared in the pages of the *Tribune:*

A windmill on the Baptist church lot, on the river bank, is a
novelty in Covington. It is to be used to raise water to supply
Mr. Parrish's residence on the avenue, a large reservoir on an
elvation (sic) above the house receiving the supply for
distribution. The cost of this water supply is something over
$700.[796]

Robert L. Parrish was a prominent lawyer, and Commonwealth's Attorney
for the town and county, as well as an entrepreneur. He had built a large
home on Maple Avenue, several blocks from the church lot; the house and
yard occupied half a block and with the water pumped from the river he
supplied an iron fountain on the front lawn. [797] Parrish's "novelty" was the
result of an agreement reached on March 1, 1882 with the trustees of the
church. At two dollars a year, for a period of thirty years, the church agreed
to lease a small parcel of the church lot to Parrish for "the erection and
maintenance of a wind engine and pump and other suitable machinery to be
used only for the purpose of pumping water from Jackson's River to such
points as (Parrish) may desire." The trustees had a reserve clause in the
agreement that allowed them to connect a pipe to the main water line, in the
event a baptistry was constructed, and to have free use of the water "…for
the purpose of immersing any candidate for baptism that their church may
have." Further, should the church erect a parsonage, "…the said parsonage
may be supplied with water in preference to any other building."[798]

Very soon after his arrival Sam found himself fully immersed in the Lord's
business. In addition to supplying the Covington Baptists, he was serving
the faithful at nearby Clifton Forge [799] and, on alternate Sundays, speaking at
the Union churches at Rich Patch and Low Moor. The larger congregation
at Sharon, a few miles east of Clifton Forge, was also on his field of service.
The new minister in the county was spending a lot of time on the train cars,
and on horseback and in the buggy, traveling between the churches. Again
the *Tribune* lends some hint to this—June 9,1882: "Rev. Mr. Chapman will
preach at Sharon church Sunday."—June 16, 1882: "Rev. S. F. Chapman
will preach in Covington next Sunday morning at 11 o'clock and at Low-
Moor in the evening at 8 o'clock."—July 21, 1882: "Rev. S. F. Chapman
will preach at Long-Dale furnace at 11 o'clock a.m. and at Clifton Forge at
8:15 p.m."—July 28, 1882: "The Rev. S. F. Chapman will preach next Sunday morning at Rich Patch."—August 4, 1882: "Rev. S. F. Chapman will

preach at Low-Moor next Sunday at 11:00 a.m. and at Covington at 8 p.m."[800]

The distance from Covington to Low Moor was eight miles and another couple of miles would take the preacher to the Rich Patch Church. Clifton Forge was almost thirteen miles from Covington and it was about six miles further to Sharon. Since travel in those days was sometimes difficult and slow, particularly to Rich Patch and Sharon which were not on the railroad line, Sam would often stay at the home of Mollie Murray in Clifton Forge when he was in that end of the county. "Mrs. Mollie" was known for boarding the various preachers who came to serve the Baptists of the area in the decades following the Civil War. Situated south of the river, the Murray home was also the site of Spout Spring to which the locals, including those on the north side of the river, came to get water.[801]

When Rebecca and her mother stepped off the train at the Covington station in the summer of 1882, carrying baby Herbert and with the other six children in tow, their eyes first spied McCurdy's Hotel just down the hill from the depot. Then they scanned the same dirt streets and hodgepodge of wooden, brick, and even log buildings—several housing the saloons that were in abundance near the station—that Sam had viewed upon his arrival. Once described as a "little, old, poor-looking town," [802] Rebecca must have wondered about the irony of it all as she recalled the Bible verses her husband had read to her of the "...land of hills and valleys (that) drinketh water of the rain of heaven."

The town of some 600 residents lay at the confluence of Dunlap's Creek and the Jackson River, although the former could be rightly called a river also. The area had been settled in 1746 and ten years later Fort Young was built, a little further south in a bend of the river, as protection during the French and Indian War. The early settlement was known as Merry's Store, and a short distance from the fort, in what was to become the town proper, was the actual store, named for Dr. James Merry, who, in partnership with Richard Smith, had opened the business on the site in 1817. In July of the following year, Dr. Merry had a plat for the proposed town drawn up. It consisted of 120 lots of approximately one-quarter acre each. A month later the lots were offered at public sale, with bids ranging from $65 - $150. The town became the seat of government when the new county of Alleghany was formed in 1822. The railroad arrived soon after the end of the War Between the States, but it would be another twenty years before Covington would begin to realize its full potential as a center of industry and trading in the western highlands.[803]

On August 16,1882, Sam and Rebecca were "received by letter" into membership of the Covington Baptist Church. The membership during Sam's first year in the pulpit was forty-eight.[804] That same month, he took part in the official organization of Clifton Forge Baptist Church.

Reverend Chapman had been integrally involved in the work of bringing the "Little Struggling Band" at Clifton Forge to fruition as a church. It had begun as a Sunday School in the small log school building, down in Slaughter Pen Hollow. Reverend John Pilcher, who was pastoring in Covington at the time, preached there first, on March 24, 1876, when the village that would become present-day Clifton Forge was called Williamson. Three years later, using funds from his own pocket and what he could collect by literally passing his hat among the crowd, Reverend Pilcher bought at auction the lot upon which the first church building, "a plain house for Church and Town Hall purposes," was to be erected. The price was forty dollars. On October 5, 1879, Reverend Pilcher led the inauguration service, an evangelistic meeting in which two persons made professions of faith.[805] The new building was a Union Meeting House, owned by the Baptists but to be used "by all denominations and any public meeting of a moral character that might be held in the town." There was nothing fancy about the meeting house: "...a frame structure roughly planked up and down with no inside finish, leaving cracks through which winter snows blew onto the benches." It cost $200 to build, plus lumber, and was in use within two months—whenever there was anyone to preach.[806]

About the time Sam arrived in Covington, the Augusta Baptist Association applied to the State Mission Board for help in having the new minister serve the Clifton Forge congregation as well. Reverend Pilcher had left in 1880 and his replacement, Reverend Harris, who served the Covington church in addition to the Baptists in Clifton Forge, was also gone. Sam accepted the call and on August 27, 1882, the Sunday marking his forty-fourth birthday, Sam led the organizational service of the Clifton Forge Baptist Church. Just as with the organization of the Covington church, forty-one years before, fourteen members constituted the membership of the Clifton Forge congregation. In the business meeting that followed, a Covenant of Principles, eight and one-half pages long, was adopted.[807]

Sam's first year on his new mission field was proving to be a busy one, what with the five churches scattered from the middle of the county eastward, almost to the Rockbridge County line. And the farthest congregation from Sam's home in Covington—the one at Sharon—was the largest of them all.[808]

Located adjacent to the old Lexington Turnpike, six miles east of Clifton Forge, Sharon Baptist Church was the mother church of the denomination in Alleghany County. In 1827, Colonel John Jordan and John Irvine, of adjoining Rockbridge County, had erected the Lucy Selina iron furnace, a short distance away on Simpson Creek, and named it for their wives. Colonel Jordan was a wealthy man of strong Christian beliefs, "...a Baptist layman advancing the cause of the Baptist faith in this section of Virginia." He had been a prime mover in the establishment of churches in adjoining Rockbridge County and Lexington. On June 16, 1832, one acre of land "...on the Bank of the Cowpasture River," was deeded to three men who, "...on behalf of themselves and sundry other persons,...by voluntary subscription have raised a certain sum of money and who have associated themselves together for the purpose of building a Meeting House for Public worship." When the structure was completed it was designated the Cowpasture Union Church. [809] Upon the death of Irvine in 1834, the original partnership was dissolved and Jordan brought two of his sons, Edwin and Ira, to the area to operate the furnace. The boys apparently inherited their father's strong Christian leanings. The Baptist church was organized with thirty-five members in August of 1839, for the benefit of the workers at the iron furnace—many of whom were slaves and other employees who had come to work for the company; Edwin Jordan was an active member. When Reverend Chapman arrived in the area, the Baptist congregation at what had become Sharon Union Church—later to be Sharon Baptist Church—boasted ninety-four members. Six of these would become charter members of the Clifton Forge church.[810]

Colonel Jordan wasn't the only one who saw a future in the iron rich mountain country of Alleghany County. In 1873, the Low Moor Iron Company, with investors from Kentucky, Ohio, and New York, as well as Virginia, was chartered by the Commonwealth. Located just west of Clifton Forge on the Jackson River and on the main line of the Chesapeake and Ohio Railroad, the company began mining operations on a portion of its 4,000 plus acres in 1875 and by 1880 had began smelting some of its own ore. The venture quickly grew and a large settlement around the furnaces grew with it. A letter by George W. Bagby, a visitor to Low Moor in 1880, gives some idea of the operation and of the surrounding landscape: "The cost of these works, first and last, will exceed $500,000—all this before a ton of iron has been smelted....A smoke stack 180 feet in height soars into the sky, piercing it just where the western mountain seems cut away in order to show its grandeur to most advantage. Beautiful at every point, so that it is almost impossible to keep the gaze from it." The house built for the general manager of the company sat atop a hill just south of the factory. Below it the village was laid out in caste-like fashion with middle management homes further down the hill and the employees' dwellings in the lowlands surrounding the factory. The home of the manager, a "big, square, honest, matter-of-fact gentlemen's house, with plenty of room and back porches (and) a wide hall extending through and through" was the site of numerous social gatherings.[811]

Soon after the iron works were establisheded, the company sat aside a parcel of land, near the company offices in the village, and had a Union church building erected on the site. The Baptists organized their Low Moor congregation in 1878 and it shared the Union building with the other three Protestant denominations of the area—Methodists, Episcopalian, and Presbyterians. [812] Then, on January 28, 1880, the trustees of Low Moor Baptist Church were deeded one acre of land near the Low Moor Iron Mines, by Charles M. McElwee and his wife for "the use and benefit of the congregation worshiping in the Baptist Church to be erected on the lot of land." It was "understood that the Trustees... will permit any other Protestant denomination of Christians to worship in the Church building at any time (it) was not in use by the Baptist denomination." [813] The building erected on this site, near Karnes Creek about three miles south of Low Moor, would be known to some as the "Rich Patch Mines Church" [814] and to others as just simply "Rich Patch Church". This small congregation of Baptists was made even smaller in the 1890's. A Union Church had been established on land owned by the Hook family, about three miles further south at Upper Rich Patch, apparently without the property changing hands. However, on January 17, 1896, the property was deeded to the trustees when Sallie Hook, a widow, and Samuel Hook, donated three quarters of an acre of land, including that on which the church building stood, "...for the joint use of the Presbyterian, Methodist, Baptist, and Dunkard Churches...(and to) permit other evangelical denominations of Christians to conduct worship in the church building...when it is not in use for the purpose of divine worship by any of the four denominations heretofore named." [815] (The church—Rich Patch Union Church—is still located on the lot near the intersection of the old Rich Patch Turnpike, now Roaring Run Road, and the Low Moor Road.) [816]

By the end of 1882, Sam Chapman's journey into "the land of hills and valleys" was well underway.

31. The Good of His Labor

"The doors were opened at a little before 7 p. m. and soon the house was filled to its utmost capacity and quite a number could not get in. The wax tapers on the trees were lighted and quite a handsome scene in the presents and decorations were presented." Thus one newspaper described Christmas evening, 1882, at the Low Moor Union Church. After a prayer and music, the presents were distributed: "Many were of considerable value, such as suits of clothes for the ministers present, a fine gold watch for a lady from her husband, a beautiful silver-headed cane to Rev. W. J. Cocke, superintendent of the Sunday school, from the Low Moor Iron Company and the Sunday school." [817]

Such gleeful scenes were no doubt repeated in the other area churches over this holiday season, the first for Sam and his family, among his newly adopted community of friends and parishioners. The same newspaper carried this letter to the editor on January 3, 1883: "I desire through your paper to make my grateful acknowledgement of the very kind remembrances I have received from my brethren and friends at Sharon, Clifton Forge, Low-Moor and Covington this Christmas and New Year. Their gifts were liberal and appropriate. I had hardly hoped that my acquaintance and ministry recently begun in their midst should have called forth such marks of esteem. Not only to Baptists but to members of other churches and to friends of no church connection am I deeply indebted." The letter closed with: "To those at the different places most active in raising these contributions, I return especial thanks. May the blessings and mercies of God come abundantly upon all throughout the year 1883. Very truly yours, S. F. Chapman." [818]

All the news this Christmas season was not of the cheerful variety, however. On Christmas morning a train derailment at nearby Millboro, in adjoining Bath County, claimed the lives of six men. The same day, six miles west of Covington, "A lad 13 years old…was induced to drink sufficient whiskey to cause his death in a few hours after." A local man was arrested and charged with the crime. [819]

The coming of a new year brought with it the announcement of a "Week of Prayer," beginning January 8, with special services in the Clifton Forge churches. The Tuesday night service was held in the Baptist church with Sam preaching on the topic "Confession of Sin." The Friday night preaching was also under Sam's charge, the subject being "Prayer for the Nations." On

Sunday, Sam would be holding regular services at Low Moor in the morning and Covington that evening. [820]

The Covington Baptist Church was the scene of an exceptionally joyous event on April 29 for Sam, as a father and a preacher. His first born, sixteen-year-old Ella Lee, presented herself for baptism, as did her fourteen-year-old sister, Elizabeth ("Lizzie"). The proud father performed both rituals. [821]

At the end of May, the Reverend Samuel Chapman ended his first year of missionary labor in Alleghany County. He had been on the field of service for forty-eight weeks, preaching a total of ninety-one sermons, at five "preaching stations" or churches. In addition, he had organized two new Sunday Schools, one new church, and performed six baptisms. And not the least of his labors was known officially as "Visits for Religious Conversions, etc." Sam recorded 416 for the year. [822] On May 16, the minutes of the Covington Baptist Church contained this entry: "On motion—Resolved that it is the desire of the members of the church to retain Bro. S. F. Chapman as pastor and request the same aid from State Missions that was received from it during the past year." The minutes of Sharon Baptist Church for May 27 had a similar entry, as did those for Clifton Forge Baptist two days later, but with an added note—a motion to call Sam for another year "…at $100 annual salary."

The second half of 1883, would be just as busy as the first for Sam as he continued to labor in the churches assigned to his care. The minutes of Sharon Baptist Church for September 23, 1885 reflect some of the success of his work. On that Sunday afternoon, following morning services, he baptized five converts. Three weeks later Sam would baptize five more in a stream close by the same church. [823]

The first month of the new year of 1884 found a new mouth to feed in the Chapman household when another daughter, Beatrice, was born. And the time Sam was spending ministering to his flock in the various congregations seemed to know no bounds. When the fiscal year ended in May, Sam had preached 133 sermons at five churches, baptizing sixteen converts and making 495 "Visits for Religious Conversions." [824]

The newly organized church at Clifton Forge, not yet two years old, was fast showing growing pains under Sam's pastorate. He was recalled in May for another year by the church and the same month a committee was formed to confer with the Masons about building a "...joint house of worship and Lodge." The idea was rejected by the Masons, but in October, "At a call meeting in Mr. Michael Ham's parlor..." presided over by Reverend Chapman as Moderator, "...it was resolved to ...sell the present building and part of the lots and denote the proceeds, after giving $50 to the Methodists, to the construction of a new church on the same lot." The following year, Sam dedicated a new building, complete with steeple, on Main Street. [825]

Reverend Chapman was quickly receiving candidates for membership in the Clifton Forge congregation. On a single day in September of 1885, he immersed twenty-one persons in the waters of either the nearby Jackson River or Smith Creek. [826] Two months later he had the honor and privilege of once again baptizing one of his own, when fourteen-year-old William, affectionately known as "Willie," was received into the fellowship of Covington Baptist Church. [827]

For the most part, the congregations being served by Sam were not wealthy by any stretch of the imagination. True, some assistance came from State Missions and helped to defray the "salaries" of the minister. But primarily, the financial state of these churches was such that local contributions – such as they were—were the main source of the pastor's subsistence. It is not known how much the various churches were paying Sam, but the minutes of a couple of them give some insight into the indeterminacy of their finances: Sharon Baptist Church, December 24, 1883: "A collection was taken up amounting to $1.10."—December 28, 1884: "Paid Rev. S. F. Chapman $23.00 on salary."—October 14, 1888: "The Church agreed to pay Bro. Tucker (Sam's successor) fifty dollars and as much as she (the church) might be able to raise." From Clifton Forge Baptist Church: January 11, 1886: " Motion approved to turn over a claim against the Freemasons of Covington for $49.60 to Bro. Chapman in part payment of his salary," and from the minutes of Covington Baptist Church for June 16, 1890: "The treasurer made an informal statement of the amount in hand to the credit of the church—$17.00. "

The local Personal Property Tax List for 1884 shows Sam Chapman was paying taxes on the most modest of possessions—a watch and a clock, valued at $15.00 and $2.00 respectively, a $10.00 sewing machine, and a cow valued at $25.00. Furniture and kitchen "equipment" carried a valuation of $200, but probably the family's most prized possession was an organ worth another $200.00. The amount of taxes paid was $2.28. (For some reason the organ was reduced in value to $50.00 the following year while all other property retained its value.) [828] With the uncertainties of his income from the churches, it is not surprising to find Sam relying on his experience as a teacher and school administrator to help defray the day-to-day expenses incurred in maintaining the large Chapman household. In 1885, in addition to his ministerial responsibilities, Sam served as principal of Covington Graded School. Whether or not he was a replacement during the school term is not known. However, this may well have been the case inasmuch as his name appears in the records as principal, following that of another gentleman in the same capacity.[829] But in the not too distant future Sam would take on a much larger role in the education of the children of the area.

The Staunton Female Seminary occupied three "elegant" buildings on the hillside of South Fayette Street, in the city that was once a major Confederate rail center and supply depot at the southern end of the Shenandoah Valley. Opened in 1870 by the Lutheran Church, its broad curriculum touched on nearly all subjects of interest and necessity to the young Christian ladies who matriculated there. Two such students were Ella and Lizzie Chapman, the eldest daughters of Sam and Rebecca. Candidates for graduation in the School of English, the girls were fully immersed in all the subjects available during the 1884 through 1886 school terms. History, Natural Science, Mathematics, Ancient and Modern Languages—these were but a portion of the courses pursued. Ella was also enrolled in Drawing, Oil Painting and Instrumental Music; Lizzie studied Vocal Music, Crayoning, Painting, and Mental and Moral Science. [830]

There are no records available to indicate whether Ella and Lizzie continued their studies at the seminary following the 1885-86 term. But a letter dated six years later—July 3, 1892—reveals both the burden and the obligation incurred by Sam to educate his children. Written by the principal of the school, Reverend James Willis, it acknowledges receipt "in full of all dues in settlement, Fifty Dollars. This is balance on Daughters' Tuition, Board, etc in Staunton Female Institute." The letter to the Reverend Sam goes on: "If you hear of any one at any time who will go away to school I shall be glad to hear from you & if I can in any way aid or favor you in the further education of your children let me hear from you as I will be glad to help you at any time." Unfortunately, the Staunton Female Seminary would close its doors four years later. [831]

As the decade passed its mid-point, some changes taking place within society—changes that normally occur within each new generation—were proving to have a somewhat profound effect on the ethos of the Church. In at least one of Sam's churches, some older members of the congregation were having difficulty accepting the secular practices of several of the younger members. The minutes of the Clifton Forge church reflect on one of these practices—public dancing. A resolution, adopted on January 22, 1886, stated: "...we regard dancing inconsistent in a professing Christian. Those that participate do themselves a great harm and the church a dishonor giving offence (sic) to the Brethren." Three weeks later, two members were "excluded for public dancing." On March 22, another member (female) appeared before the church "... to answer to a citation for public dancing." When she "promised to refrain from further violations of the Rules of the Church (she) was excused from the charges." But despite such distractions, the business of the church went on; on May 2, 1886, each male member was "...requested to pay 50 cents/m and each female 25 cents/m for and until the church debt is paid." [832]

In May of 1887, Mary Lewis Chapman was born, bringing to nine the number of Sam and Rebecca's children still living and to twelve the number of persons in the Chapman household, not counting a probable live-in person as a servant/cook. During this year, Reverend Chapman gave up the pastorate of Sharon Church but then took the pulpit of another, some fifteen miles to the north in Bath County.

Healing Springs Baptist Church sits along the main road between Covington and Warm Springs, the county seats respectively of Alleghany and Bath Counties. The church is the oldest one of the denomination in Bath, with services dating back as far as 1823. During the early years, when the debate was raging between the Missionary and Anti-Missionary Baptists, the congregation took the side of the latter. In 1842, a second church was established, this one accepting the stance of the pro-missionary faction. It was reorganized in 1845, calling itself "The Baptist Church of Jesus Christ of Healing Springs, Bath County, Virginia." From the beginning, its congregation was composed of both black and white members. In 1847 the total membership was fifty-five, of whom thirty-eight were white; ten years later there were fifty-two whites and thirty-five blacks. A new building was completed in 1856 and it was here that Sam accepted the call as pastor. In January of 1888, at a called meeting of the church, it was decided "...to raise $125.00 a year for the support of a pastor to preach twice a month." [833]

When the report was made to the General Baptist Association in May, 1888, for the previous twelve months, the Healing Springs church recorded ninety-nine members, almost evenly divided between male and female. For the same period, there was every indication that Reverend Sam was continuing with the heavy workload he had carried in previous years; he reported preaching 145 sermons during the fifty-two week period, while baptizing fifty-four persons. [834]

"With the best feelings of Christian love and fellowship toward all." With these words, Sam Chapman began his letter of resignation to the members of Clifton Forge Baptist Church. It was June 16, 1888. Sam had taken his place as Moderator at the previous meeting two weeks earlier, and the minutes of that meeting do not contain any hint of what was to come at the next regularly scheduled meeting. But Sam would not be present and his letter was read by the clerk:

> *My reason for this step is that it seems very evident to me that my work among you is done. Our relations for the past six years, ever since your organization, has been for the most part pleasant and I hope in a good degree profitable. If I might presume to offer some advice, I would say look carefully to the character and standing of the man whom you choose for my successor. More will depend upon this for real good than talents or ability.* [835]

The underlying reason or reasons are not given for Sam's leaving the leadership and pulpit of the "Little Struggling Band" that he had led, since before its organization, to the now substantial congregation, in a new building "with a steeple," on Main Street. His ministry here had, by all indications, been a successful one. There surely was something seriously wrong that caused him to take such terminal action on so short a notice and it is evident in the next two sentences:

> *It would be well and I hope what I desire that you will accept this without delay. My appointment to preach on the 4th Sunday, please consider as withdrawn. May the Lord bless you all.* [836]

It is known that just about the time of Sam's letter of resignation, the church "...felt that it could take care of a minister if he would give us all of his time." [837] Perhaps the people were appealing for Sam to give up his other churches and accept the full-time pastorate of the Clifton Forge church. If so, it must have been a very difficult time for him. He had his own church at home, in Covington, as well as the new one at Healing Springs, plus the Low Moor and Rich Patch congregations. Maybe there were factions within the church that wanted to call a new pastor altogether. All this is speculative, of course, but "It was moved and seconded that Bro. Chapman's resignation be accepted. A ballot was called for and the motion was rejected by a vote of nine in favor of the acceptance and twelve against it, some of the members not voting. After some remarks by the Brethren about the situation, the meeting was adjourned." Apparently, it was determined that Sam was not going to withdraw his letter and, on June 17, a committee was appointed to secure a pastor. A motion was approved for the clerk to prepare and forward, in the name of the church and its members, "...a farewell letter to Bro. Chapman on the occasion of his resignation as pastor." [838] There was no farewell sermon, no good-by party, only a "farewell letter," forwarded to the former pastor.

Within a month of Sam's resignation, the church called a new pastor, paying him thirty-five dollars a month. They would later share this minister with the Sharon congregation, which would pay him a minimum of fifty dollars a year—more if it could be raised. [839] A year later, the Clifton Forge church "...pledged itself to raise the sum of $325 for the pastor's salary for the ensuing year. Sharon agreed to raise $75...and the Virginia Mission Board was to be asked to give $200." [840]

Less than three years after Sam's departure, the prosperous Clifton Forge Baptist Church called a full-time minister for the sum of $700 a year "...to preach to us every Sunday morning and night..." and as the duties increased so would the salary." [841] If there had been any bitterness in his leaving, Sam Chapman could now look back and, like the writer of the scripture, find satisfaction "...that every man should eat and drink and enjoy the good of all his labour, it is the gift of God." [842]

32. For God, Family, Community

On August 28, 1888, the Augusta Baptist Association opened its annual meeting at Laurel Hill Baptist Church in the small Augusta County community of New Hope. The Reverend Sam Chapman had the honor of delivering the annual sermon in this historic church, the oldest Baptist church, not only in the county, but in the entire central Shenandoah Valley as well. [843]

Sam took the text for his message from Paul's Letter to the Church at Philippi:

> "...forgetting those things which are behind, and reaching forth unto those things which are before, I press toward the mark for the prize of the high calling of God in Christ Jesus." [844]

It had been just over two months since Sam resigned as pastor of Clifton Forge Baptist Church. Surely his thoughts must have been on that decision when he prepared his message for this occasion. But although he might not easily forget such happenings in his recent past, he had neither the time nor the energy to long dwell on them; his devotion to the business that lay ahead would be more than enough to occupy him.

It wasn't very long after Sam assumed his pastorate at Healing Springs that a matter, which had troubled the brethren of the Clifton Forge church, now caused concern within his new congregation. Sam was presiding at a called meeting, being held on the Saturday night before the second Sunday in February, 1889, to hear the report of a committee appointed by the Healing Springs church the previous month. The purpose of this committee was to "talk with several of the young brothers and sisters, that dancing had become common amongst them, this being in direct violation of a Rule of the church." [845]

The committee reported on the results of its discussions with five young men. These five had said that they did not think public dancing was "wrong" and further they were "not sorry." Four of the five requested their names "...be erased from the church Roll," and so it was done. The fifth boy likewise refused to admit any wrongdoing and offered no apology. However, he did not request to have his name removed, but it was "erased" along with the others. Oddly, the church minutes fail to make any further reference to the "young sisters." And there was something else that added to the unique-ness of this particular event.

Sam Chapman was presiding over the meeting this Saturday night because "Brother Hoover," who normally would have been in the chair, "advocated the cause of the offenders." It seems Brother Hoover had "...examined (the Rule against dancing) and (was) satisfied that the Rule was unwarranted." But he went a step further—if the church held to the Rule, then his name could "be Erased also." So, along with the five young men, the church also removed from its rolls a long time leader in the church. And before the night was over, another committee of three members was appointed to talk with three more young members about the same alleged violation and "report back." [846]

John Newton Chapman, one of Sam's younger brothers, was the sheriff of Page County. He had been appointed to the position to serve out the term of a local doctor who had resigned the position. Subsequently, he was elected in his own right to the four-year term 1888-1892. [847] Around this time, Sam was in Luray to conduct a revival. It seems that thirty-nine year old John had been persuaded to run for the office, not so much because he wanted the job, but due to pressure from the citizens of the county. While Sam was in town, his brother remarked that he really wasn't cut out to be sheriff—why, he didn't even own a gun. Sam replied that he had one, at his home in Covington, that he had no further use for and he would have it sent to John.[848] The gun was a Model 1860, .44 cal. Army Colt, one of the many such weapons captured from the enemy and used by Sam during his days with Mosby. Memories must have flooded over Sam when he once again took the pistol in hand. It had undoubtedly sent many Yankee "souls over the Stygian river without a prayer, " as Colonel Mosby once remarked when speaking of Sam in the fight at Miskel's farm twenty-five years before. [849]

Sam continued to carry an extraordinary workload as 1889 wound its way toward the half-year mark. He had been preaching an average of three ser-mons a week and performing, on average, one baptism for each week of the fifty-two week reporting period. [850] And not reflected in these figures were the numerous homes visited, and weddings and funerals he conducted.

Now, as the calendar page turned to the next decade, it found Sam taking on yet another major responsibility. His prominence in the community, as well as his education and experience, made him a prime candidate for the position of superintendent of schools for Alleghany County (this included the towns within the county also.) It was not unusual for a minister to be appointed to this post. The position could not be considered a full-time one; Sam would average about seventy-two days a year over his tenure, considerably more than any of his seven predecessors. What was unusual was the length of time he would hold the position—nine years—which was more than twice as long as any previous superintendent. And the job paid $200 a year. By 1891, Sam's third year in the position, this amount had increased to $270. Lizzie became a teacher in the Covington schools while her father served as superintendent. [851]

The appointment of the county superintendent of schools was made by the State Board of Education, from its offices in Richmond. But as a practical matter, and the exigencies of politics being what they were, the appointment more often than not was really a local matter. In addition to the appointment of the superintendent, the state board initially had the responsibility of choosing the trustees of the various district school boards. This arrangement was later changed and became the business of each locality, with the superintendent, Commonwealth's Attorney, and a qualified voter making the selections. One of Sam's primary responsibilities was to "set (the trustees) to work in taking the census of school population, determining the number and location of schools, and providing school accommodations. They (would) then began to examine and commission teachers." [852]

A tragedy, reminiscent of the ones that befell the family nearly fourteen years before, with the deaths of Sam, Jr. and Katie, touched the Chapmans again in 1889 when an infant daughter, born to Sam and Rebecca, lived only three months.[853] The illness and death of the baby, coupled with his new responsibilities as school superintendent, served to reduce the time Sam spent on his ministerial duties. For the annual report period ending May 31, 1889, he had served his churches a total of thirty-four weeks, preaching sixty-four sermons. The number of congregations he was now attending to had been pared to three—Covington, Low Moor, and Healing Springs. The following year, Reverend Chapman was no longer listed as being on the missionary field, all of his churches having become self-sustaining and not now under the wing of the State Mission Board. [854]

But life went on in the Chapman household. Like Sam as a young man, his offspring were becoming actively involved in the life of their church. On June 16, 1890, Lizzie was one of a committee of three women appointed to solicit contributions to be used in repairing and painting the doors of the building and the fences surrounding the property. Meanwhile, Willie was elected to serve as usher. And in addition to her other duties, Lizzie was also part of a committee " to consult and examine hymn books with a view of purchasing same for the church." The church minutes made note of another committee " to solicit contributions towards the pastor's salary." This one, of course, did not have any of the Chapman family as members. [855]

On July 28, 1891, Sam's mother, Elizabeth, died in Luray at the age of eighty. Death, which had been Ranger Sam Chapman's constant companion during the war years, had not been a stranger in the years following, either. And it would continue to be with him over the next ten years.

An economic boom—and its major by-product, land speculation—had swept through the Valley of Virginia in the late 1880's and eventually found its way into the mountainous country that was western Virginia. The town of Covington was already thriving as a center of trade and industry, due in large part to the rich iron ore deposits that served the numerous furnaces in the surrounding county, which in turn spawned more industries. The town was not, however, immune from the speculators and developers, the so called "improvement companies," that descended on the region. These people would buy up land at reasonably low prices, erect a grand hotel, and lay out lots—or, more often than not, entire towns—while promising the citizenry that industry and prosperity were certain to follow. Then the lots would be sold off, usually through auction at inflated prices, and the would-be developers would be gone. The panic of 1893 brought most of these ventures crashing down. But Covington, unlike the dozens of new "boom towns," was well established and would survive. Over 200 houses would be built—all occupied—and more than thirty stores, far more than the half-dozen or so existing in 1890, would occupy the town during this time. The town's population of about 700 would more than quadruple, to nearly 3,000, by the new century. [856]

Among the enterprises of the Covington Improvement Company was the Intermont Hotel, built on an entire city block overlooking the Chesapeake and Ohio Railroad tracks and depot. It was four stories high and boasted its own golf course. Billed as the finest hotel on the main line of the C&O between Cincinnati and Washington, D. C., it opened in May of 1891. The elaborately designed building would outlast the economic boom and the resulting panic, but by 1912, it too would be gone.[857] In addition to the hotel, the company bought several acres of adjoining land within the town, which were platted into residential lots and sold. Among the buyers were Sam and Rebecca Chapman.

On April 13, 1892, Sam paid "Seventy-five Dollars in Rent and Thirteen Dollars for Hay." On October 8, 1892, he made a payment of $45.00 for the rent of the family's home.[858] But on that same day, he and Rebecca purchased, for " two hundred and thirty-four dollars in cash and six hundred dollars in fifteen per-cent premium stock," two lots from the Covington Improvement Company. Not fully satisfied with the location of the lots, however, the couple soon after exchanged them for two others. On January 2, 1893, they used the property to obtain a mortgage, from the Eastern Building and Loan Association of Syracuse, New York, for the purchase price plus six per cent interest. The monthly payment on the loan was $19.01. A third lot, adjoining the other two was added soon afterwards. [859]

The new Chapman home was located on Wills Street, on the rear side of a hill that overlooked downtown Covington. It was a large ell-shaped house, of two stories with nine rooms, sitting in the middle of the block between Hawthorne and Locust Streets. A local builder, C. W. Rush, had built the house for "one thousand and eighty dollars in cash and a negotiable note for one hundred and thirty-seven dollars and fifty cents." [860] The family moved into their new residence on March 6, 1893. Sam built "a coal house, hen house, and a privy" on the back of the lot. He also put up "a shed for his cow and wagon, and a stable with hay loft." He completed his homestead by planting trees and encircling it with a fence. The cost of the improvements was about $2,200, not counting the labor of Sam and one of his sons. [861]

William S. Wills and his wife, Annie, lived opposite the Chapman home, on the hill overlooking the town. Wills ran the local drug store and his home was set on a large tract of land that was bordered on two sides by the lots of the Covington Improvement Company. By virtue of his and his wife's ownership in the property, the street running between the Wills and Chapman properties bore the family name. But a dispute arose between the Improvement Company and the Wills' which would eventually involve their friends, and soon-to-be neighbors, Sam and Rebecca Chapman.

A portion of the holdings of the Covington Improvement Company had formerly been part of the Wills property, owned by Annie Wills, who had inherited it from her father. A disagreement had arisen between Mrs. Wills and the Company, and in response to what Mrs. Wills believed was bad faith on the part of the latter, she had her husband dig postholes and string a wire fence down the center of Wills Street. The fence, which was erected about the time Sam began construction of his house, ran directly in front of his property. The result—what was once a forty-five-foot-wide street was now only half that wide, restricting access to the lots on the north side of the street. Mrs. Wills refused to take down the fence and the Covington Improvement Company, although requesting her to remove the fence, refused to take any other action. Rebecca, who held deed to the Chapman property, had no other remedy, other than a legal one, to try to have the fence removed. [862]

A lawsuit was filed by Rebecca in April of 1894 and, after a protracted civil trial, resulted in the removal of the fence and a declaration that Wills Street was a public right-of-way. The attorney representing Sam and Rebecca had a financial interest in the Covington Improvement Company, but was not acting on the Company's behalf in the matter. But it raised an interesting point when it was discovered that he was not even charging the Chapmans a fee. When questioned on this point by the attorney for the Wills', Sam and Rebecca's lawyer replied that "neither he nor any other attorney in Covington would ever charge a Minister of the Gospel" for legal work or representation. [863] Apparently there was no harboring animosity over the litigation; Sam Chapman and William Wills remained close friends and workers in the Covington Baptist Church. [864]

John Mosby had been an attorney for the Southern Pacific Railroad in San Francisco since 1885, following nearly seven years out of the country as the U. S. Consul in Hong Kong. After a short stint at the University of Virginia, Sam Chapman's son, Willie, had gone to San Francisco, where, with help from his father's former commander and long-time friend, he secured a position with a steamship company whose vessels plied their trade between San Francisco and the Orient. In letters to Sam and to Sam's brother, William, Mosby spoke of just how proud he was of his twenty-two-year-old *"protege* (and that Willie) *would make his mark and be successful."* [865] He also made mention, on more than one occasion, of Willie's being Sam's son, saying: *"He is an apt scholar; in fact, does not need a teacher—is the son of his father!"* [866] and again, *"That fighting boy of yours is evidently a son of his father!"* [867] He later told of his efforts to help Willie obtain a promotion: *"I went to see the superintendent about putting Willie a peg higher."* [868] He continued in his praise: *"He is a splendid boy—everybody takes a liking to him."* [869] The closeness of the two is reflected in a rare comment from the normally discerning Mosby, contained in an 1894 letter to Sam. *"The Belgic* (Willie's ship) *arrived a few days ago. Willie is here looking very well. I took him to see some ladies last night. I got sleepy and came home—left him with them!"* [870] The old soldier's affection for the young sailor is clearly shown in correspondence to Mosby's former captain some years later: *"Willie is due here on the 27th—he always comes straight to my room as soon as he lands. I feel towards him as if he were my son—everybody falls in love with him."* [871] Willie Chapman and Colonel Mosby would continue to see much of each other during the remainder of the decade, while both were in San Francisco, until Mosby left the West Coast permanently in early 1901.

Young Willie Chapman's decision to go to sea was met with some disfavor and anxiety by his mother, and Rebecca had apparently expressed her views in a letter to him. Writing to his "Dear Papa," Willie addressed his mother's concerns: "I do not see why Mama should not like the idea of my following the sea." He continued on, trying to alleviate Rebecca's fears for his safety: "The ship I am on is built of steel and has been running on this route for years & has gone right through typhoons, the fiercest tempest known, without sustaining any damage & has never lost a man." He summed up his feelings: "So all things considered, I am just about as safe at sea as on land; besides it is almost impossible to get anything at all to do on land that pays as well. These have been the hardest times out here that have ever been known."[872]

Some months followed, but it was apparent that Rebecca could not let go of the anxiety she felt for her son, sailing the seas to such far off ports. Such experiences were hard to imagine for a mother who had never traveled beyond the borders of her native state. Willie had just returned from "the longest voyage the Belgic had ever made across the Pacific." In addition to bad weather, the ship had been held in quarantine in Nagasaki, Japan due to the plague sweeping China. In a letter written to Sam the morning following his return, Willie told of his most recent trip: "Mama's advice came too late, even if it had been necessary, though the danger was slight. I haven't written before on account of the plague as I thought Mama would be uneasy." According to Willie, his mother may have had reason to be concerned. "I have been there (Hong Kong) twice since its visitation; between three & four thousand Chinamen died with it. In Canton it was very much worse, more than ten thousand died. This has been an eventful voyage in every way. Plague & war on one side & strikes & rioting on the other." [873]

Rebecca Chapman's mother, Catherine Murray, aged 74, passed away at her daughter's home on November 18, 1893. By now, Sam had given up the long ride to Healing Springs and was preaching only at Covington and Low Moor. The Covington congregation numbered only sixty-seven members, while at Low Moor, where quite a settlement had grown up around the huge iron works, the Baptist church could boast of a membership of 139. Sam was kept busy here, baptizing thirteen converts in 1893 and eighteen the following year. His duties as school superintendent required much of his time, also. On September 27, the Clifton Forge newspaper noted that "Rev. S. F. Chapman, county Superintendent of Schools, was in the city this week on official business."[874] Sam was also traveling to this end of the county for other reasons: "(Married) in the Rich Patch, by Rev. S. F. Chapman, at the residence of the bride's father...on December 27, 1893..." Two days later he was back in the area, performing another wedding. [875]

George Anderson Revercomb was "...a prominent attorney of the Alleghany bar, well known in Alleghany and the adjoining counties." [876] In later years he would serve in the Virginia Senate and become a leader in Republican Party politics in the state, unsuccessfully running for the United States Congress.[877] But on October 10, 1894, he was a thirty-four year old lawyer about to marry Lizzie Chapman. She was "...recognized as one of Covington's prettiest girls," said the reporter in one of the area newspapers. Reverend Sam Chapman performed the wedding of his twenty-six year-old schoolteacher daughter in front of a large audience "...that filled the (Covington Baptist) church to overflowing," that fall evening. "The bride wore a Canton white crepe" sent to her by her brother Willie from China.[878]

Just before Christmas, Sam received a circular from former Ranger John H. Alexander, of Leesburg, announcing a "Reunion of 'Mosby's Command' at Alexandria, Va., on Wednesday, January 16th, 1895." This would be the first of many annual gatherings of the old command and there was no way that Captain Chapman was going to miss it. Inclement weather kept many of the veterans away but Colonel Mosby was there, all the way from California. He sat in a place of honor at the head table in the Alexandria Odd Fellows Hall, flanked by Lieutenant Colonial William Chapman and Major Dolly Richards. In all, about 150 of the partisan band were in attendance. During a meeting, prior to the evening banquet, it was decided to form a permanent organization, to be known as the "John S. Mosby Camp, Confederate Veterans"; Sam Chapman was selected as Chaplain. [879]

Following the first toast of the evening, Colonel Mosby responded with sincere and heart-felt remarks, as he recalled a misty spring day nearly thirty years ago: "I have always felt that life cannot offer a more bitter cup than the one I drained when we parted at Salem, nor any higher reward to ambition than that I received as commander of the Forty-third Virginia Battalion of Cavalry." [880] But the old Colonel was not quite so conciliatory when it came to one veteran in particular who failed to attend the reunion.

Sydnor Ferguson had just turned seventeen when he joined the Rangers in November of 1863. He was the young private who captured Captain Richard Blazer following the fight at Myerstown on November 18, 1864. After the war, he attended college and seminary and was ordained a minister in the Methodist Church. [881] But Mosby could not excuse him for failing to make the fifty mile trip from Fredericksburg to Alexandria, and, eight months later, he was still thinking about it, when he wrote to Sam: "I think the Reverend Sid might have left the mourners *one* night to attend the reunion. I never could see the sense of people's *mourning* at the prospect of going to Heaven." This was in response to Ferguson having written that he couldn't come up "for fear several souls would be lost if he left (Fredericksburg)." And reminiscent of what Mosby would say about Sam Chapman, he concluded: "I suspect Sid could send (& has sent) more people to Heaven by shooting at them than by preaching." [882]

This initial reunion of the old battalion would be the only one Mosby ever attended. But he and Sam would see each other often and the Colonel would be a guest in the Chapman home many times over the years. Mosby could not attend Lizzie's wedding but less than a week later he was in Covington. "Colonel John Mosby, of Confederate fame, celebrated as a partisan leader during the war, passed through Clifton Forge on No. 4 Monday morning," a newspaper noted. "He had for the past few years lived in California, and was enroute to his old home in Warrenton. He stopped over at Covington Sunday and spent the night with Rev. Samul (sic) Chapman." The reporter ended with a familiar characterization of Sam: "The Rev. Chapman was, during the war, a member of Mosby's command and was celebrated as '*the fighting preacher.*'" [883] A couple of months later the former commander wrote to his "fighting preacher" and remarked on a book soon to be published by James J. Williamson, the former member of Company A, which contained wartime photographs of many of the Rangers. Mosby sarcastically observed that "(Sam's) picture in it did not suggest the idea of a minister of the Peace." [884]

Though sensitive to such remarks when directed toward him, Mosby often used belittling and derogatory language toward both friend and foe alike, sometimes in jest, but oft-times sincere. It was not the only occasion on which Sam was the subject of his old friend's caustic humor.

The Reverend Sam Chapman had occupied the pulpit of Covington Baptist Church now for over fourteen years, longer than any previous pastor. A rewarding ministry to be sure, though not an easy one, what with the other scattered congregations—at one time they had numbered six in all—under his care. Now, after nurturing and guiding the faithful over long hours, much traveling, and for little pay, he had grown weary. But at the Covington church, his own family—wife, mother-in-law, children—worked and worshiped. He had even baptized some of his children here, and for one, Lizzie, he had the exceptional honor of both baptizing and marrying her within its walls. So, it was with mixed feelings that, on October 30, 1896, at a regular meeting of the Covington Baptist Church, Sam submitted his resignation as pastor, to become effective on the first day of the new year. [885]

Over the next couple of years, the membership of the Covington church gradually increased, while that at Low Moor went in the opposite direction, due largely to the growth of the Baptist congregations at nearby Rich Patch Mines and further south at Upper Rich Patch. By 1897, the Covington church had a membership of nearly 100; Low Moor's had declined to about fifty and the little Baptist congregation at Rich Patch Mines numbered thirty-one. And Sam, while he was turning the pulpit of the Covington church over to someone else, had agreed, after a hiatus of some eight years, to again supply the Rich Patch churches. He would still keep the Low Moor church, thus giving him only three congregations to serve, in the same general area.[886] It would be a whole lot easier, from both a traveling and time standpoint, and the fifty-nine year old preacher needed the rest.

Sam had been principal of the first Covington Graded School during its 1885 term. The school was not exactly what the name might infer. It was divided into three parts, or grades, designed to separate the students by age. The first grade covered the primary years, the second grade the middle years, and the third grade the upper years.[887] On June 4, 1897, Sam, now in his final year as superintendent of schools, had the distinct pleasure of seeing the school graduate its first class—two girls and one boy—before a large audience in the town hall: "Exercises were opened with prayer by Rev. S. F. Chapman, County Superintendent of Schools," a newspaper account read.[888]

The U. S. battleship *Maine* floated easily in the tranquil, untroubled waters of Havana harbor the evening of February 15, 1898. But suddenly, shortly after nine o'clock, a deafening explosion, followed quickly by another, fractured the nocturnal stillness. The huge gray ship, ripped apart by the blasts, quickly went to the bottom, carrying with it 260 men.

Ever since native Cubans had declared open rebellion against their Spanish masters three years earlier, a large number of Americans' sympathies had been with the rebels. Reports of alleged atrocities, inflicted on the Cubans by Spanish controlled authorities on the island, only helped to fuel such feelings. The *Maine* had been sent to protect American lives and interests in Cuba, while Cuban rebel agents were permitted to operate freely in the U. S., gathering arms and money, and lobbying for American intervention. Spanish and American investigations of the cause of the explosions that sank the battleship were inconclusive, but tensions only heightened. Finally, with cries of "Remember the Maine" echoing from the nation's taverns and across the pages of its newspapers, Congress formally declared war with Spain on April 25, 1898.

When the United States went to war with Spain, it had been thirty-three years, almost to the day, since that April morning in Winchester, when Captain Sam Chapman laid down the arms he had taken up, against the same United States, four years before. But this cause seemed all too familiar to Reverend Sam Chapman—these Cuban rebels, fighting on their soil, for their homeland, against a foreign invader—and the stirring within him to be there, in the midst of the fray, was something the old warrior would not be able to still.

33. Donning the Blue

Events were moving rapidly in the spring of 1898. On April 19, President McKinley had requested—and received—from Congress a resolution authorizing his intervention in the Cuban affair. Although the Teller Amendment made clear that the U. S. had no thoughts toward annexation, in Spain's eyes the resolution spoke for itself and two days later the Spanish broke off relations. On April 25, Congress declared that a formal state of war existed between Spain and the United States. And the conflict was not to be confined to the Caribbean. Spain's interests in the Pacific, most notably the Philippine Islands, were included in America's plans of freeing Cuba and Puerto Rico of their Spanish yokes. But the objective in the Pacific was somewhat different—to secure an American territory in another ocean half a world away and establish a stepping stone to the Far East and its lucrative trade markets. Although such a thing was officially denied by Washington could it be that American imperialism, by whatever name, was about to replace European imperialism?

By June 1, the American navy had bottled up what was left of the Spanish fleet in Santiago harbor and a month later land forces stormed ashore. Meanwhile, Sam Chapman was working hard at getting himself involved. Age and lack of political influence forbade his obtaining a fighting commission. But with the help of a distinguished Confederate veteran who was now a United States senator, Sam was able to wangle a chaplain's commission in the volunteer infantry. [889]

Senator John Warwick Daniel had served his state and the Confederacy gallantly and at a terrific price. He was wounded early in the war while serving as a lieutenant with the 27th Virginia Infantry at First Manassas. Later promoted to major, he served on Jubal Early's staff until being permanently crippled by wounds suffered in the Wilderness in 1864. At the time of the conflict with Spain he was in his twelfth year in the United States Senate. [890]

Senator Daniel was a native and resident of nearby Lynchburg and Sam prevailed upon him for help in getting into the conflict. His old friend's efforts were successful and on June 13 Sam received his commission. He was sworn in on June 24 in Washington, D.C. and a week later reported as regimental chaplain of the 4th Regiment, U. S. Volunteer Infantry, at Camp Cobb near Fredericksburg. [891]

The U. S. Congress had passed, on May 11, an Act calling for the enlistment of up to 10,000 men, to be organized into ten "Immune Regiments." [892] The 4th Volunteer Regiment was one of these, comprised of soldiers from the District of Columbia, Virginia, Maryland, and West Virginia; it was mustered into service June 2-25, becoming part of the First Division in the Seventh Army Corps. The corps commander was none other than Colonel Mosby's old vexation from thirty-five years before, Major General Fitzhugh Lee. The law governing these Immune Regiments restricted the units to one commissioned chaplain each, to be appointed by the President, by and with the advice and consent of the Senate. Thus, it can be seen that the influence of Senator Daniel was critical in Sam's obtaining his commission, especially in view of the fact that applicants for the officers' commissions far outnumbered the vacancies available.[893]

The Immune Regiments had gotten their name from the belief that their members, from predominately Southern states, would have inherent immunity from Yellow Fever and other tropical diseases. The ten commands were hastily organized and put into service to relieve the National Guardsmen, and regular troops, who had been the first to occupy Cuba. The immunity theory was grossly misplaced and these troops—Sam included—would not be spared the afflictions contracted by so many of the other soldiers on the island. [894]

On August 17, the regiment broke camp at Fredericksburg and moved to Jacksonville, Florida, in preparation for eventual assignment in Cuba. But by this time, a cease-fire had been declared on the island and for all practical purposes the shooting war was over—less than four months after it had officially begun. Ten days prior to the regiment's departure from Camp Cobb, two privates, absent without leave and apparently not looking forward to the move, had been struck and killed by a train at Potomac Crossing north of the camp.[895]

In Florida, the next two months were spent taking light practice marches and holding inspections, along with occasional parades for visiting dignitaries. During this time, Sam was granted fifteen days leave, so "that I may visit my sick son at home in Covington, Virginia." [896] It is not known which son was so ill for him to request the leave. Three of Sam's sons were still at home—Elgin, then age 22, Paul, 19, and Herbert, 16. A likely possibility would be Elgin, who had been experiencing some problems and had recently returned from a stressful sojourn in San Francisco. But, of course, it could have been simply a physical illness of any of the three. [897]

On September 28, with Sam still on leave, the following order was received at regimental headquarters:

> By direction of the Secretary of War, the Fourth United States Volunteer Infantry is detached from the Seventh Army Corps and will be put in readiness for service in Cuba. The regiment will proceed to take station at Manzanillo....

Less than a week after his return to duty, Sam was at the port in Fernandine, Florida. On October 12 he set sail with the regiment, on board the U. S. army transport *Roumanian*. The soldiers arrived at their destination of Manzanillo, Cuba some 1079 miles and five days later—not as a fighting unit but as an occupation force. [898]

The port city of Manzanillo is located on the eastern side of the Gulf of Guacanayabo, some 100 miles west of Santiago. It is in Granma Province on the Caribbean Sea, or south side of the island, the side farthest away from the Unites States. After disembarking and marching to barracks, several of the companies of the regiment were dispersed, with orders to take possession of various towns and former Spanish garrisons in the rugged, albeit beautiful, countryside. [899] An example of the conditions experienced by the soldiers as they moved into the interior is reflected in a report filed by Company B: "Left Manzanillo 10 Nov., 1898, arrived in Bayamo Nov. 15, '98, distance marched 48 miles. At that season roads in bad condition, compelled to use carts (two wheels) drawn by oxen....The swamp 18 miles from Manzanillo is 3 miles across and very low." [900] At about the same time, Company H was enroute to Jiguani with 66 enlisted men and two commissioned officers: "Approximate distance marched sixty-five (65) miles; repaired roads and bridges whenever necessary to admit the passage of army wagons of six mules each, four escort wagons of four mules each, and one ambulance of four mules. Average load for team 3,300 lbs." [901] However bad the conditions might have been, there is no mention of any hostile resistance and all the towns were occupied without any apparent difficulty.

While the other men of the command were having their troubles traversing the roads and landscape of the interior, Chaplain Chapman was experiencing some difficulties of an entirely different nature back at regimental headquarters. Sam had been assigned duties and responsibilities in the care and distribution of the regimental mail, a job he neither had a taste for nor felt it required his time and attention. On November 23, he requested to be "relieved of the care of the mails of the regiment" in a letter to the commanding officer, Colonel James S. Pettil. "I have hitherto helped in the distribution but if I am no longer needed I can find plenty to do among the sick & the well in the regiment which I hope will conduce to their well-being and comfort." The same day, the Colonel responded by writing across the front of the request: "Leaving matter entirely in the hands of Mr. Chapman—was not appointed by R. O. & needs none to be relieved." [902]

Although American losses were less than 400 in battle, some 5,438 died of disease and exposure in the camps, in both the United States and the islands, and aboard the transports and other naval vessels. [903] The 4th Volunteer Infantry suffered the fatal loss of only nine enlisted men and one officer during its tour of active duty, aside from the two AWOL privates killed by the train while in station at Camp Cobb. The others all succumbed to disease. The officer—Captain John D. Tredwell, commanding Company K—died of typhoid in Florida, twelve days prior to the command's embarking for Cuba.[904] Nevertheless, once on the island, at least one officer had some trepidation concerning his future and sought out the regimental chaplain. On December 19, Doctor Samuel L. Hannon, the assistant post surgeon, put into Sam Chapman's hands a certified document, appointing Sam as Executor of the doctor's personal effects; he was to see that they all would be turned over to his wife in Washington, D. C., "in case anything should happen to me, death or otherwise." The effects were listed as "trunk & contents, 2 blankets, swords, machete, & clothing, monies in trunk, also money on person, watch, etc." [905]

Matters seemed to be going routinely along for Sam, and the regiment as a whole, at Manzanillo. He did write Rebecca of one incident that appeared to disturb him. In a hurried letter following services one Sunday in November—Sam wanted to post the letter with the steamer that would "go in an hour" for Santiago—he recounted that one of the command's soldiers, "full of mean Cuban rum, struck a Cuban who was already under arrest and fractured his skull. We are looking for the man to die and very much fear he will. It was a dastardly act....The Cubans will resent it and it would be worse if the fellow were to die....The Cubans will think it a miserable civilization that does such things." [906] The veteran partisan fighter seemed sensitive to such brutal acts and to the possible repercussions. Yet, the passing years have a way of fading such unpleasantness from one's memory. A long time ago, in a different world, Sam, and the men of Mosby's command, were intimately involved with events just as "dastardly"—and worse—taking place all around them.

On February 6, 1899, the U. S. Senate ratified a treaty with Spain in which Cuba would be an independent nation but under American protection. Less than two weeks later, Sam Chapman was in the Immune Regiment hospital, suffering with "remittent malarial fever"; it would be two weeks before he was back to duty. [907]

On May 11, with the "splendid little war" [908] now over, the 10th Regiment, U. S. Cavalry, relieved the 4th Immune Regiment. The same day, Sam's outfit began boarding the U. S. army transport *Dixie*; five days later they set foot on dry land, this time in New York harbor. The regiment boarded the trains for Middletown, Pennsylvania and encamped at Camp Meade on May 18. Three weeks later, Chaplain Sam Chapman was relieved of his commission and mustered out of service, along with the rest of his regiment—one year earlier than the original enlistment time of two years.[909]

Some years later, the old veteran of two distinctly different wars, would tell his fellow veterans of Mosby's command: "I was in a foreign country long enough to realize the full force of the American feeling. Comrades, get outside of the United States if you lack a feeling of esteem for our common country. The old flag that we shot at for four years will become a thing of beauty once more." Then, remembering the cause to which he had unselfishly devoted himself so many years before, but now proudly extolling renewed patriotism for his country, he said: " An American battleship was blown up in the harbor of Havana. There was a call to arms, and no section responded with more heartiness than the South. I, among great numbers, *not forgetting the grey, donned the blue* in our common country's service." [910]

34. "The Remnant of My Days"

While things were settling down in the Caribbean, such was not the case in the Philippines. Political wrangling over what to do with the newly liberated islands kept Washington in an uproar. The anti-imperialism sentiments in the U. S. bitterly opposed any thoughts of annexation. Holding an opposite view, expansionists felt the islanders incapable of self-rule and setting ducks for more European domination, particularly from Germany. President William A. McKinley finally caved in to those who did not want to surrender, so soon, such a valuable commodity, accepting the Philippines as an American territory. In this way, the smugly virtuous President said, we could "educate the Filipinos, and uplift and civilize and Christianize them." But these 'un-Christianized, uncivilized, and downcast' islanders did not wish to simply trade one foreign ruler for another. An organized group of insurgents started an uprising against their latest occupiers. America's troubles in the far-off islands were just beginning. [911]

Apparently, for Sam Chapman, the splendid little war in Cuba had ended much too soon to satisfy his desire to once again be where the action was taking place. And he must have expressed this to his friend, John Mosby, for six months after returning home he received a letter from his former commander: "John Daniel recently wrote me," Mosby said, "that he could have had you appointed Chaplain if the law had allowed them for the Philippines. I see there is a bill to allow them." Mosby urged Sam to "be in time and write to John. I shall do so, too." Ever looking out for the welfare of his old comrade, probably in light of Sam's bout with malaria, Mosby advised "An ocean voyage will help you. There will be very little exposure. If the climate doesn't suit, it will be easy enough to get a furlough and come home invalided (sic), drawing salary all the time. I have no doubt such a trip will be a benefit," he concluded.[912]

President McKinley, a captain and later major, in the 23rd Ohio Volunteer Regiment, had served with Sheridan in the 1864 Shenandoah Valley campaign. Mosby had supported his former foe in his successful bid for the presidency in 1896; he grew disenchanted with him soon after, however. In a newspaper interview just before the turn of the century, in which Mosby was discussing the officers who had served with him, he referred to the President (and in some way to Sam) in his ever increasing sardonic manner, "Captain

Sam Chapman—the same Chapman whom McKinley recently sent as a chaplain to preach humanity in Cuba—one of the ravages of time...."[913]

When Sam returned to Covington in June of 1899, following his stint in the U. S. army, he resumed his preaching in a limited fashion. He conducted services at Low Moor and at Healing Springs on an infrequent basis; however, Sam was not on the Association's Roll of Ministers for either 1899 or 1900.[914]

In the summer of 1896, Sam and Rebecca's son, Elgin, then 20 years old, had boarded the Number 1 train in Covington, en route to San Francisco. The trip would take several days, by way of Chicago, Council Bluffs, Cheyenne, and Ogden, Utah.[915] Elgin had a restlessness about him, not seeming to know just where his place was to be in life's scheme. A nervous sort, he would frustrate himself, and his father as well, with his aimless, undirected energies.[916] He looked upon his older brother, Willie, as someone to be admired and imitated, and in his quest for fulfilling his own destiny, persuaded his parents to let him join Willie in San Francisco. "(Elgin) left us in tears," Sam would write to Willie at the time. "Your Mama of course grieves after Elgin...but is not unreasonable. We are all glad there is some place for Elgin to go to. There seemed to be no place (remainder of sentence is missing)." In an aside for John Mosby, who was also living in San Francisco, Sam added: "Tell the Col. that his friends are still a trouble to him, but I know that his little colony out there will be a comfort and perhaps a joy to him. I'll speak for their fidelity to him. Give our love to the Col. & them all."[917]

Elgin arrived in San Francisco with dreams of a newer and far different life than the one he had known back in Virginia. He was able, through Mosby, now a lawyer with the Southern Pacific Railroad, to secure a job "on the cars." But his old frustrations still plagued him and soon he found himself disciplined and out of a job. In January of the following year, Willie, who was in the Orient, received a long letter from Miss Garber, a friend back in San Francisco. "Elgin had been late for several days so he was laid off....If Elgin will go every day he will be reinstated." Expressing hope for the young man's future, Miss Garber continued: "This seeming trouble may make a man of Elgin. I will frequently inquire for Elgin and you know he will not suffer for any thing, so do not worry about him. He may yet get a better place if he will learn to keep the hours when he begins again." [918]

Sam did not hear from Elgin for over six months after the boy had left home. Finally, in February he received a letter from his son, expressing remorse: "I feel ashamed for not having written to you all before now but I have intended to answer your alls (sic) letters but I have been putting off time and again to write to you all and now I think I can write you a short letter telling you I have kept well but have had a right hard time since I have been out here." Then Elgin revealed to his father that things were not going well for him at all: "My dreams about the West did not work as I thought it would...I was laid off from work a half a month but am back at it again."

Elgin diversed to tell about San Francisco's "nice buildings & fine residences & a very pretty bay & Oakland and Allameda (sic) just across the bay are very quiet places." He then rambled for several lines about the police who "seem to be going for the gamblers of Chinatown. I saw in the paper where they had a hundred or more Chinamen in the City prison." But then he returned to his own problems: " I thought when I first came out that I could bring all my friends out from Covington at first but find out I can hardly get along myself. I hope I can hold a job untill (sic) Willie comes but if I lose my place I will have to look homeward." Sam's concern must have been great for his son, so far away and in apparent despair: "I have passed through a pretty tough trial & they are pretty strict (the railroad men). I think of you all often. Your loving son, Elgin" [919]

The new century came in without fanfare in the Chapman household. There were still ten people in the large home on Wills Street. Ella, the oldest was teaching in the local school while the two teenagers, Mary and Beatrice, were attending school. Edmund, with Willie's financial assistance, was running the Chapman Bros. Cash Store, assisted by nineteen-year-old Herbert. Paul was a clerk down at the post office, while Elgin, back from his disappointing venture in California, helped his parents and the hired girl, Mary Johnson, with the chores around the house.[920] Now winter had given way to springtime and the once bare, stark, mountains were again lush and green with the promise that a new season brings.

The streams and creeks, overflowing with the late melting of snow, swept into the river, bringing the swift moving currents almost out of their banks as the river raced through the town. It was May 7, 1900. And Elgin was dead.

Suddenly, tragically, Sam and Rebecca's long-suffering dreamer had found his peace beneath the troubled waters.[921] But the peace that was Elgin's brought inconsolable grief to his mother—grief that only served to accelerate her increasingly worsening illness.

Rebecca was very, very sick. Sam had noticed the change in her soon after his return from Cuba. There had been a tiredness that was alien to his wife's normally endless vitality—a zest for living that until then seemed nearly inexhaustible. The doctor had told him then that her kidneys were affected in some way but no actual diagnosis had been determined at the time. Over the following months her illness progressed and now, with Elgin's death, her condition seemed to deteriorate at an even faster pace. [922]

On October 11, Ella took the train to Poolesville, Maryland, having taken a teaching position in the school there. [923] This was the same Poolesville where Mosby and Sam and the other Rangers had burned a camp of the 8th Illinois Cavalry in July of 1864. The burning followed by a couple of days the great victory at Mt. Zion Church, in which the Rangers, with Sam in command of the little howitzer, had defeated a large force of Union cavalry and captured their commander, Major William Forbes.

When Rebecca's condition grew worse, about three weeks later, Ella hurriedly returned to her mother's side. Two physicians were now in attendance and the prognosis was made that Rebecca had contracted Bright's disease, a then fatal affliction of the kidneys. Soon after, her weakened heart, unable to expel the veinous blood from the lungs, caused extreme shortness of breath. By the third week in November, doctors told Sam that his wife might live for a few months or could die at any time, as there was no cure and nothing that they could do.[924]

Paul was now working for the railroad in Pine Bluff, Arkansas and Willie was still sailing the Pacific. Sam wrote to both of them in late November, requesting they come home as soon as possible.[925] But they would not make it. Rebecca died at eight o'clock on Sunday morning, the second day of December, 1900. [926]

Sam's last days with his beloved "Miss Beck" were spent in trying to make her as comfortable as he could. She was never unconscious but was required to sit up much of the night and day because of the difficulty in breathing. "How she delighted to get out in the open air where she could breathe better," Sam wrote to Willie. "I took her out in the buggy when there was a good day. She loved to drink of the water at the running springs." He told

Willie of his mother's unrelenting faith of seeing all her children once more: "She talked about you and Paul a great deal and believed she would see you both. In fact, she would not think of dying, nor did we talk to her about it." Then the grief-sicken father wrote his son of the funeral, adding: " We buried her by the side of Elgin—the poor boy she talked and cried about every day that she survived him. His death greatly aggravated her trouble." [927]

The same day of Rebecca's death, Sam Chapman wrote what was probably his most poignant letter ever to someone other than a family member. The deep personal friendship between John Mosby, whom Sam always addressed as Colonel, and Sam Chapman—Captain Sam—his able and courageous subordinate, is reflected in the tone as well as the words. After describing his wife's illness and death—"We are in the deepest affliction,"—Sam wrote: "When you come in stop and see us. The presence of a friend is a great comfort to us all and no one would console more than yourself. She was a good woman and our only comfort is that she has gone to our Father's house, there to abide forever. I shall see her before many years." Sam continued to pour out his feelings to his friend: "The remnant of my days will drag wearily at first but they will pass away swiftly afterwards. I am not weary of life and intend to exert myself for the sake of my children....The children are inconsolable." Finally, he expressed his gratitude to both Mosby and Senator Daniel: "You have my grateful thanks for all your kindly interest and Maj. Daniel's kind offers are appreciated to an extent never to be forgotten." Aware that Willie was at sea, Sam did not write to his son until nearly a week later. He knew Mosby would be the one to inform the boy of his mother's death: "How distressed poor Willie will be. Good night my dear Colonel and may God bless you and yours is the prayer of your unworthy friend." [928]

The unremitting sorrow of the Chapman family continued when, five months later, on May 10, 1901, Sam's grandson, Elgin Revercomb, the nearly four-year-old son of Lizzie (Chapman) and George Revercomb, died from a probable complication of measles after an illness of several weeks.[929] The youngster's death came one year and three days after the untimely death of his uncle and namesake.

35. "God's Grace and Active Employment"

When Sam replied to a letter from Willie, some three weeks after Rebecca's death, he was keenly aware of his son's sorrow. "We have just read your letter of the 14th and all of us have cried over it. We know your distress was greater than ours and ours has been great enough." The father then offered this balm for healing in the days to come: "You must not think, however, that we are giving way to grief. We have too much to do for that. A living has to be made, as there is no one to give it to us. And it is better as it is. If I could afford idleness then most probably I would not work and the affliction would kill me. Next to God's grace there is nothing like employment to keep one from being consumed with grief when bereavement comes."[930] Sam had written earlier to Colonel Mosby in the same vein, that of keeping busy to overcome sorrow: "God's grace and active employment will do much for my comfort," he believed. [931]

Sam was now busy with the household responsibilities and helping Edmund out in the store. He was also preaching some but not on a regular basis. Healing Springs Baptist Church was still without a pastor and Sam was supplying there on occasion. However, misfortune was to strike the little congregation; the church minutes tell the sad news: "Our excellent church building which was built in 1855 & which was newly repaired & furnished with beautiful seats in 1900, was destroyed by fire on the 16th day of February, 1901."[932] Although the Reverend Chapman was "without a charge at the present time" he was back on the roll of Association ministers. Later that year, he was asked to deliver the prayer at the General Baptist Association's annual meeting being held at another of his former churches, Clifton Forge.[933]

Sam's daughter, Beatrice, had turned seventeen in January and, on August 28, her father wrote to Reverend Charles Fenton James, president of Roanoke Female College (RFC) in Danville, Virginia, about enrolling her there for the coming semester.[934] The school had its beginning, a few years prior to the outbreak of the War Between the States, as Union Female College. It was started by Baptists in the Roanoke Baptist Association, of which Danville was then a part. In 1864, after three years of embarrassment because of the word "Union" in the name, the college secured the approval of the state legislature for a change to its current name, based on the geographic and religious area in which the college was located. [935]

President James was a native of Loudoun County where Ranger Sam Chapman had spent a lot of time harassing Yankees. James was only sixteen years old when he enlisted in Company F of the 8th Virginia Infantry at Bloomfield in June of 1861. Two years later he was elected lieutenant and on August 19, 1864, became captain of the company. Converted to Christ and to the Baptist faith in a camp revival, at war's end James entered Sam's alma mater, Richmond College. He went on to graduate with a doctorate degree in divinity from Southern Baptist Theological Seminary. After pastoring churches for several years, the minister became president of RFC in 1892.[936]

On August 30, James replied to Sam's inquiry: "Am glad you have decided to send us your daughter. The rate I gave you is the same I give to ministers generally." Sam would not be asked to pay for tuition, only for Beatrice's boarding. James continued: "Am glad to have a daughter of one of Mosby's most gallant captains and glad to receive her on these terms. Hope she will be as good a student as her father was a soldier."[937] President James died suddenly on December 5, 1902, as a result of a heart attack suffered in his office three days earlier. The school would change its name again, in 1936, to Averett College, in honor of two brothers, both Civil War veterans, each of whom had served as head of the school.[938]

John Mosby was still working on Sam's behalf, trying to get him into a government position. Six months before Rebecca's death, the Colonel had written to him from California, reminding him of a previous letter in which he had encouraged Sam to apply for a place in the postal service. "Late disclosures show that integrity, as well as experience, is needed in it. I have written John Daniel & asked him to help you." The old commander, apparently thinking his former captain was not fully applying himself, offered a caustic rebuke: "I am sure you can get a place if you will only rouse yourself & try. (Take a few lessons in that art, tact & skill, from Colonel William & Josie!)" referring to Sam's brother and sister-in-law. "If you should get in now it will, in all probability, be a life appointment."[939] Seven months later Mosby himself was job hunting, having been dismissed by the Southern Pacific Railroad. To earn a living, he was forced to accept an appointment as a special agent in the Department of Interior's Land Office, working in the western states.[940]

The Reverend Sam Chapman returned to a regular, albeit limited, preaching schedule in 1902, holding services on the fourth Sunday of the month for the

Baptist congregation at the Rich Patch Union Church. The Association records reflect the unusual membership of one male member and seventeen females, and Sam's salary of $90 per year. The following year, services for the Baptists had been moved to the second Sunday of the month; membership was the same except for one less female member. Apparently Sam had agreed to either a reduction in salary, or he did not preach each month, as his salary was only $30.90 for the year. On the second Sunday in April, he made the journey to Bath County to examine—and approve—along with two fellow pastors, a candidate for ordination at the Healing Springs church.[941]

With the decline in his pastoring responsibilities, Sam resumed his lay activities in Covington Baptist Church. On September 27, he was called to be Moderator. Later, he would serve on a committee appointed to solicit contributions from delinquent members for the church debt.[942] That December, he presided over the marriage ceremony of his nineteen-year-old daughter, Beatrice, and Junious Winfred Young, of Charlotte, North Carolina. Much to Sam's regret, the couple would make their home in the husband's home state.[943]

As 1904 rolled around, John Mosby was in Alabama, still with the Land Office and still unhappy. But by spring of that year, he had managed to have himself transferred from the Interior Department to the Department of Justice in Washington, D. C.[944] And he was still working on Sam's behalf, trying to find his friend a place on the government payroll. Toward this end, in December he wrote Sam a note of introduction to President Theodore Roosevelt:

> Mr. President:
> This will introduce a friend, Captain Sam
> Chapman, whom I have known forty years
> as a noble, high-toned gentleman. He has been
> your earnest political friend & deserves the
> highest consideration from you.
> Respectfully,
> Jno. S. Mosby [945]

The note was extremely short on Sam's qualifications and experience, especially his service with the army in Cuba, where Roosevelt too had served, making a name for himself with his Rough Riders. Whether or not Sam ever used the introduction is not known, but by mid-January, 1905, he was no closer to employment than he had ever been. Apparently he was trying to obtain a position as special agent in the Land Office, the job Mosby had just left. The Colonel wrote to him in this regard on January 19, from his brother Willie Mosby's home in Bedford, where he was recovering from an illness. "From what I could gather whilst there (Washington), both through my brother and myself, I think your chances of securing the position in the Land Office are very poor. I am under the impression they have all been either given out to others or promised." [946]

Sam Chapman did not appear to be satisfied with the efforts of Mosby, Senator Daniel, and others on his behalf. One suggestion, with which Sam took offense, came from his former lieutenant and close friend in Company E, Fount Beattie. Beattie, like Sam's brother William, had many years of service with the Internal Revenue Service and thought Sam might land a storekeeper's job with the government. In a letter to Mosby, Sam had referred to Beattie as having his "mind in a state of eclipse" by suggesting such a thing. Six weeks after the letter from Bedford, Mosby again wrote Sam, this time from his office in the nation's Capitol, scolding him for his reaction to Beattie's suggestion: "I don't think so," Mosby replied to Sam. "He only suggested it as the best thing (available) as nearly all the other places are in the Classified Service. Some very good men have been (storekeepers.)... Col. Samuel Berkley was a storekeeper during Cleveland's first term. I recommended him to be retained under Harrison." [947]

Sam was still prevailing upon Mosby and Senator Daniel to try to get him into Mosby's former position with the Land Office. Charlie Pollard, a friend of Mosby and an old schoolmate and friend of Daniel, was also seeking such an appointment. Sam became upset with both Mosby and the Senator, believing they had recommended Pollard in lieu of him for the appointment and he had told the Colonel as much. Mosby responded: "I did go with you to see the Secretary (of Interior). Afterward, Charlie Pollard sent me a letter from (the U. S. District Attorney) of Birmingham addressed to the president recommending my friend Charlie Pollard of Alabama to be Special Agent." Mosby endorsed the letter and sent it on to the President. "There was no more inconsistency in this than my recommending at the same time yourself & Wm. Chapman to be postal clerks. You were both appointed. You & Pollard might have both been appointed. The Commissioner told you that you were too old....I can see no inconsistency in Daniel's recommending both you & Pollard to be Special Agents."

As Mosby continued on, his irritation with Sam became more noticeable with each sentence: "I do not think you ought to have been surprised at Daniel preferring his old schoolmate to anybody, especially as it did you no harm. Pollard was not appointed. Daniel <u>did give you</u> his endorsement. What more could he have done? What did he go with you to the Land Office for if not to recommend your appointment? " Before he ended his long discourse, Mosby expressed his disdain for the whole system, revealing why he may have been so upset with Sam for criticizing Fount Beattie in the first place: "I have no idea of mingling anymore in controversies over patronage. I wish I never had. In justice to Fount, *I ought to say that I first suggested to him to write to you and make the offer."* In closing, Mosby reproved Chapman somewhat, in case his old captain believed a storekeepers job too menial for him: "Pulling down fences is not as dignified as arguing cases in the Supreme Court, I have done both." [948]

John Mosby's position in the Justice Department finally paid off for Sam Chapman. In 1906, at the age of 68, Sam was situated as an office deputy in the U. S. Marshal's office, eighty miles from Covington, in Staunton. The position was strictly one of political patronage and it is very doubtful, in view of his age, if he would have been considered otherwise. In any regard, the job kept him busy. The Western District, headquartered in Staunton, covered sixteen counties, from Frederick on the north to Rockbridge on the south, a distance of nearly 150 miles, on both sides of the Allegheny and the Blue Ridge Mountains. The territory went east to take in Madison, Greene, Nelson, Rappahannock and Albemarle Counties. Sam's duties included the keeping of the funds book and the ledger, tracking the service of writs and processes, and in attending the courts within the district, when necessary, to perform the general work of the service. [949] Sam's youngest daughter, Mary, accompanied her father to Staunton, where they took up housekeeping in rented quarters at 208 East Beverley Street. [950]

Chapman's tenure as a deputy marshal gave him the opportunity to renew old friendships. On February 6, 1906, he joined the Stonewall Jackson Camp, United Confederate Veterans (UCV), in Staunton. Among the members was a local businessman and former comrade, Hugh McIlhany. McIlhany had served with Sam in the 17th Virginia Infantry at the beginning of the war although he was a member of Company K while Sam was in Company B. [951] Following the war, McIlhany prospered, becoming a partner in a real estate and fire insurance company. [952]

During the war, McIlhany had risen to the rank of captain by February of 1864, and held the position of assistant chief quartermaster for General James Longstreet's First Army Corps. But in August he resigned his commission; on September 10 he was enlisted into Mosby's command by Walter Frankland, also a one-time member of the 17th and then quartermaster of the 43rd. McIlhany would have a short life with the command. On December 21 he was captured, with several other partisans, in the sweep of the countryside by Federal cavalry; this was the same evening Mosby was severely wounded at the home of Ludwell Lake. The new Ranger would spend the duration of the war in Federal prisons.[953]

Mosby was not much impressed with a talk McIlhany made at the 1906 reunion of the battalion, in which he reminisced about the war and the hardships he had endured. Mosby wrote to Sam shortly thereafter: "I was amused at Hugh's speech. Now Hugh joined my command in Sept. 1864. He was captured Dec. 21, '64. Was with us three months. I don't suppose Hugh suffered much in the Commissary Dept., where he was until he joined us. Don't think he could have suffered much in the three months he was with us." Then, recalling the newspaper article on the speech, Mosby continued: "The report says the recital of his hardships drew tears (I would have laughed.) Then (quoting scripture) he says Mosby's men had neither scrip or purse. It was during the time Hugh was with us that we made the greenback raid. I think a majority of my men had purses with greenbacks and that they scattered them freely. I have no doubt that Hugh had a full stomach when he was captured—probably some greenbacks."[954]

In the same letter, the irascible Mosby took a swipe at another of his more unfavorable people—William Chapman's late mother-in-law—concerning a recent newspaper article: "If old Mrs. Jeffries were living I would ask you to explain to her that I am in no way responsible for your picture being in the Wash. Times & Josie's & Colonel William's not being there." [955]

Although there had been annual reunions of "Mosby's Men" each year since the inaugural meeting at Alexandria in 1895, Sam Chapman missed more than he made. In fact, he was not at the follow-up reunion that August in Marshall (formerly Salem), even though he had been elected Chaplain of the group. He did attend the 1896 and 1897 affairs in Richmond and Baltimore respectively. [956]

The July, 1896 Richmond reunion had been the grandest of all. Sam wrote extensively of it in a letter to his son Willie: "The best evidence of the complete success of the Richmond Re-union (sic) was the overwhelming enthusiasm among all classes and ages that made them forget the absurdity of bogus Col's and generals. The veteran was the man that day, and so, he had smelt (sic) gunpowder whether in the ranks or as a commissioned officer, it was all one." He then spoke of the banquet: "Over 125 sat down to such a supper as I have rarely seen. Mr. Jos. Brian (sic)[957] presided and did it well. The good feeling was abundant and super abundant. Four or five of us were preachers and we did our best to hold the boys down. We succeeded indifferently well. Brian (sic) put your Uncle Wm. on his right and me on his left." The march on the following day through the "thronged" streets of the State Capitol was attended by a crowd of "125,000 or 150,000" and went on for over a mile, though with "many halts" along the way. "All the spirit and vigor of 30 years ago seemed to come back to the old men," Sam told Willie. "A strange, indescribable feeling was the common experience of all. They will talk about it and tell it to their grandchildren by the fireside after they are done going to re-unions (sic)."[958]

And of course Sam was at the 1899 reunion in Front Royal, when the monument commemorating the six executed Rangers who had fought there under his command that day, was dedicated. Major Dolly Richards, the main speaker for the occasion, referred to the old Captain in his remarks: "Above all, it is most appropriate that we should today recall the fact that the gallant officer of Mosby's command who led the charge against the federal forces when these men fell in the streets of Front Royal, thirty-five years ago, was himself, during the Spanish war, a commissioned officer in the army of the United States, and there was no one who bore his commission with more honor, with more patriotism, with more devotion to his country's flag, than did our own comrade, Capt. Sam Chapman." [959]

Now, it was August 28, 1909, and many of the veterans, older in years but still able to make it to one of the larger of the reunions, were once more in Front Royal—forty-five years after the tragic events. One hundred and eight men, representing each of the eight companies that made up the command, were present; twenty former members of Captain Sam Chapman's Company E had come. It was fitting that the man who played such a primary role in the drama that had unfolded then would be the one chosen to address the gathering now.

Standing straight, Sam looked out upon the crowd, his voice still strong, but with a gentleness that bespoke his life's calling, rather than the calling he had answered for four years, nearly a half century before. His speech this day would be one of remembrance—and conciliation:

> Our thoughts at reunion are mainly reminiscent. We greet
> each other today with warmth and affection because of the
> stirring adventures of days long past; of associations and
> scenes pleasant for the most part, and at times painful, but
> whether pleasant or painful are full of thrilling interest.

He would go on "to recount the incidents of the distressing disaster...in which I was one of the principal actors. It was an event for which I may have been largely to blame, as some have thought it was the result of rashness. The only vindication of myself that I shall attempt today is a simple recital of the occurrences of the expedition."

After an amazingly detailed retelling of the long ago events, Sam brought the crowd back to the present—and to the future:

> I need say little more, the memory of our dead comrades is
> as dear to us as ever. No sensible man of any feeling in all
> this wide country thinks less of us for that; but the affectionate
> recollections of our comrades who have passed away do not
> need that our resentment should be kept alive....There is a
> great future before us....No 'Lost Cause' need damp the heart
> of a people who have the strength and opportunity to make a
> new cause, and even more to make it a better cause. [960]

Prior to Sam's leaving in August for the Front Royal reunion, he had delivered the opening prayer at a June 3rd Confederate reunion at the Masonic Theatre in Covington, held under the auspices of the Alleghany Chapter, United Daughters of the Confederacy. A "Confederate Battle Flag" was presented to the ladies by the Sons of Confederate Veterans, and the UDC chapter presented Southern Crosses of Honor to selected veterans. The Confederate Choir performed three numbers – *Dixie*, *The Bonnie Blue Flag*, and *Tenting Tonight*. [961]

Colonel John S. Mosby, founder and only commander of the group that would carry the name of "Mosby's Rangers" into the history books, never attended a single reunion of the group save the first, at Alexandria, in January of 1895. His view of such affairs was far removed from that of Sam Chapman and the other members of the command who did attend. Henry Cowles "Colie" Jordan was one such member, one who Mosby had once identified in a letter to the battalion's former surgeon, Doctor Monteiro, as "there not being a more gallant man in our command."[962]

Jordan wrote to Mosby on August 18, 1909, begging him to come to the reunion in Front Royal ten days hence. Mosby responded bluntly on August 23: "I shall not be there. I never attend these affairs because I am not in sympathy with their spirit. They are political conventions in the name of social gatherings. Nobody enjoys a talk over the old days more than I do, but I can't stand the speeches and the prayers that are made at these conventions. I prefer healing the wounds of the war; I do not enjoy making them bleed afresh. Let those who take pleasure in such things listen to them, but excuse me." [963] This was the same Mosby, however, who told Sam: "I say the Confederates who deny they are rebels are ashamed of it. I am proud of it."[964]

On March 25, 1910, the United States Marshal for the Western District in Staunton wrote to the Attorney General in Washington, D. C.:

> Samuel F. Chapman, one of the office deputies in the
> marshal's office has been appointed Postmaster at
> Covington, Virginia and will retire as deputy marshal
> April 1st, 1910. [965]

Thanks again to Mosby, Chapman was able to leave Staunton and return home to Covington.[966] The appointment, made by the President, with the advice and consent of the Senate, was effective April 5. He was now approaching seventy-two years of age and the postmastership, which paid in excess of $2300 a year, was for a term of four years, with reappointment in this patronage position always a possibility. Sam was replacing Charles Howard Revercomb, Covington's postmaster since 1897.[967] Howard was a brother to Sam's son-in-law, George A. Revercomb, who had married Lizzie Chapman.

Willie Mosby, who had taken Sam Chapman's place as adjutant of the battalion when Sam was promoted to captain, had been appointed postmaster of Bedford by President Grant. As soon as Willie heard of Sam's appointment, he wrote him a letter of congratulations and then offered some sage advise:

"Try to know every detail and every department of your work in the Office, for it is your only safeguard. If your Clerks find out you don't know the duties they will take advantage of it & get you in serious trouble before you know it....If at anytime you need advice or assistance you have only to call on me." And this: " I am delighted to know you will be provided for the next four years. I hope you will try to lay a little aside for Old Age." [968]

Chapman's duties as postmaster at Covington meant he had responsibility for mail deliveries in the city, as well as the large, mostly rural area served by that office. In many places, the rural routes were located in mountainous terrain that could only be reached over very bad roads, which was especially difficult during inclement weather. Wet weather meant muddy roads and really bad rains meant washed out bridges, putting the Postal Creed to a severe test. Sam wrote to his superiors in Washington of one such occasion, the flood of 1913:

> Owing to the storm, no mail was sent out
> over the Rural Route yesterday or today as
> one bridge was washed away, another injured,
> and the general condition of the road impass-
> able to vehicles and a part of it so to persons
> on horseback. [969]

The flood was continuing to cause Chapman problems nearly three months later as seen in a letter to his superiors in July:

> In reference to your letter of March 17th, 1913
> concerning change in rural route No. 1...I have
> this to say. I had not forgotten the matter nor had
> I neglected anything that might facilitate project.
>
> In the latter part of March, 1913, almost the
> whole road of No. 1 from Covington was torn
> up by a destructive freshet, making the extension
> impracticable and the whole service was much
> interrupted. The road of the extension project
> is now in the process of reconstruction. I shall
> make a visit to the scene of the extension in a
> day or two myself and report to you promptly. [970]

The same flood that was creating headaches for Sam Chapman in his mail deliveries had hit the eastern United States, causing between 5,000 and 6,000 deaths, and was probably the severest flood to ever occur in the local area. Among other damages, the C&O Railroad had hundreds of feet of track washed out on its main line, causing major delays in both freight and passenger service east and west. Several homes were washed away in Covington by the raging Jackson River. [971]

The hours Sam was scheduled to work at his office were not excessive if adhered to but they did not allow for much rest in between coming and going from home to work. In a report to the Post Office Inspector he listed "the hours I devote to the duties of the Post office:

> I go on duty at 6 A. M., off at 8 A.M.
> Return at 10 A. M., off at 12 N
> Return at 2 P. M., off at 6 P. M.
> Return at 8 P. M., off at 8:15 P. M." [972]

The fiftieth anniversary of the Battle of Gettysburg would occur in July 1913, and although Sam was not a participant in the battle, he planned on being at the commemoration. He requested time off from his duties by letter to the First Assistant Postmaster General:

> I would be glad to get leave of absence from 25th
> inst. to July 6th - twelve days. I wish to visit a
> friend who is in rather feeble health, and to take
> in Gettysburg on July 3rd and 4th. I am a Confederate
> Veteren. (sic) [973]

Sam's close friend, Willie Mosby, accompained him on the trip to Pennsylvania.[974] They rode, with two others, in Willie's automobile. Less than two months later, on August 27, Mosby died suddenly at age sixty-seven. Along with Sam, John Mosby grieved greatly for the loss: "I was eleven years the senior of my dear brother," the Colonel wrote to a family friend. "He was my Adjutant in the War and I was greatly attached to him. The older we grew the closer we grew together." [975]

Mosby's and Chapman's strong friend and political ally, John Daniel had died in office in 1910. The political landscape in Virginia was changing and a Democrat, Claude Swanson, was appointed to fill the seat in the U. S. Senate; in the subsequent election, he handily won the seat on his own. This placed two Democrats in the Senate from Virginia, and along with Governor Mann and Hal Flood running the state Democratic political machine, Sam Chapman feared for his continued appointment as postmaster.[976]

Mosby had lost his place in the Justice Department only two months after Sam gained his position in 1910—"kicked out" John Mosby would later write to Willie Chapman.[977] But the old warrior seemed to have gotten over some of the bitterness a few months later, after his return from an extended trip, for he wrote to Willie: "On my trip I made a complete circle. Much to my surprise, a bank sent me a check to pay my expenses on the excursion. It was a contribution from friends—all of which proves the truth of what I have often said—that the world is growing better every day." He added an aside for Willie's father: "Of course a lot of pretty girls showed their affection for me & I wish that the Reverend Sam had been there to enjoy the distribution of favors—not the kind, however, to send the Reverend Knott. Give my regards to Sam." [978]

After returning from his trip to Gettysburg, Sam expressed his concerns about his appointment in a letter to Mosby, who had been vacationing at Elkton Springs and Massanuttten in Rockingham County: "The P. O. Inspector Irving is with me now, checking me up. He told me that he had been ordered to check up this office and report in ten days. He is a right fair man and I believe he likes me. He will find nothing wrong here. I expect Flood or Martin has been at the P. O. Department arguing the appointment of their man here. I may be removed before the end of my term April 5th, 1914. Well, I shall not cry nor beg....I am thankful I am in good health. My kindest regards to the ladies. I would like to see them again."[979]

Chapman took the occasion, in the same letter, to voice his view of Henry Carter Stuart, nephew of General Jeb Stuart, Mosby's great friend and mentor. Henry Stuart was to be the next governor of Virginia but he was never a favorite of Mosby's, primarily because of his failure to take a stance against those who would criticize his famous uncle, for actions taken during the war, particularly at Gettysburg. Mosby had always been a zealous defender of Jeb Stuart and had clearly shown this in published articles and speeches over the years: "I was much pleased with your letter to Henry Stuart," Sam wrote. Then, in uncharacteristic fashion, he said: "He must be of different metal (sic) from his great kinsman. The older I get the less I like 'jelly fish' people.

I meet every day people of more ability & learning than I have and yet of so little moral courage that I do not care to stay about them." [980]

Since Mosby had been cut loose from the Justice Department, he was getting numerous requests to speak about his war experiences, even in the North. Referring to a request to lecture in New Haven, Connecticut, he wrote his old scout, John Russell: "I shall probably go this winter—not after glory—but money. I have been throughout the world & have to seek a living. If I can't get anything else to do I can join the Salvation Army. By the way, ask Major Hunter how he would like to join it with me. He is also in search of a job." [981]

Mosby did go to Connecticut and while there was given a tour of Colt's Arms Company factory. "I told them that I had a bullet in me & several bullet holes that Colt's revolvers had put in me," he wrote to Russell, "but I did not tell them that my men all carried two Colt's pistols & probably put some holes in people, too, especially you. They presented me with a fine pistol in consideration of the fact that my men had been their best customers." [982] Mosby's request of Russell regarding Major Hunter was repeated in a subsequent letter: "I asked sometime ago to suggest to Major Hunter that as he & I are both out of job, we might join the Salvation Army. We could beat their drum & the tambourine for them. Did you tell him?" Mosby inquired of Russell. [983] Later that year, on September 15, 1911, Major Hunter and Sam Chapman would help to dedicate the newly erected Confederate monument on the courthouse lawn in Covington. The orator of the day was Colonel Robert E. Lee, Jr. [984]

36. "But Little Fear of Death"

About four miles north of Covington, on the north side of the bridge cross-ing the Jackson River at a place called Deep Ford, sat an old two-story log house, the homeplace for the 290 acre farm that spread out in a mostly northwesterly direction from the house. Charles Dressler, who came from Rockingham County prior to 1795 and settled on the river, probably built the house. [985] His son, Peter Dressler, owned the farm and he and his wife Patsy had raised their family in the house and were living there at the time of Pe-ter's death in 1874. The story is told that the seventy-one-year-old Dressler had walked to nearby Mount Pleasant Church and planted two trees on the church and graveyard property. Returning home, he took a short cut through his hog pen and was bitten on the leg by one of the boar hogs. Infection set in and the leg was amputated, however Dressler died soon afterwards.

In the decade preceding Peter Dressler's death, the family, including Peter's son, Harrison, who lived with his wife and children several hundred yards up the river from the main house, was warned of the coming of Yankee sol-diers, then nearing Covington. Fearful of losing their property to the invad-ers, they took the precaution of carrying the cured meats to the river. Here, they were hidden back under the overhanging ground, in the roots of the numerous sycamore trees that lined the river's bank. The Yankees—if they eventually reached the farm—found no meats for their taking. Not long af-ter, however, the two families watched helplessly as several dogs floated the would-be booty down the stream. [986]

In September 1911, the heirs of Peter Dressler filed suit in the Alleghany County Circuit Court "for the purpose of having said lands sold in order to make partition thereof." The court appointed George A. Revercomb, Sam Chapman's son-in-law, Special Commissioner and the property was offered for sale at public auction in front of the courthouse on November 4, 1911. The highest bidder was William A. Chapman—Sam's son Willie—at $2,500. [987]

Sam spent the Christmas of 1913 with Colonel Mosby at his home in Washington, D. C. December 23 marked an anniversary Mosby could not forget and he recalled it in a letter to Sam on that day: "Just at this time 49 years ago I was lying at Aquilla Glascock's house suffering from the wound I got at Lud Lake's & the surgical operation afterward." He made no other mention of it but went quickly to another matter: "I had written Dolly Richards that you would probably be here to spend Xmas & asked him to come if he could." [988]

Soon after New Year's, Sam got the bad news that his sister, Mary Elizabeth ("Bettie"), had died on January 13 in Atlanta. She was the widow of former Ranger Joseph Carter, whom she had married after the war. Carter had died in 1906 while the couple was living in North Carolina. [989] On February 11, Sam saw his youngest daughter, Mary, wed George Stephenson, an employee of the Postal Service. [990] The couple would live in Covington, before going to Staunton and later to Richmond, where Stephenson served as a postal inspector. [991] Sam did not fare as well with the department. He failed to be reappointed and three months later, at age seventy-five, was replaced as the Covington postmaster. [992]

Sam's son, Herbert, had been in California. Much like Elgin, he admired Willie and thought that he might be able to emulate his older brother's success on the West Coast. Willie had been in San Francisco for over twenty years, having established himself very well in his work for a Japanese steamship company. He had also saved his money and made wise investments. On the other hand, Herbert, although now past thirty years of age, was just beginning and Willie sought to help his younger brother. He told Herbert of a friend in Nevada who was running a freight truck between a gold mining camp and the railroad station, and who possibly could find a place for Herbert in the future if his business expanded. In the meantime, Willie offered Herbert some advice: "I hope what you have now turns out well. Under no circumstances, if I were you, would I invest anything but my salary, & I would be mighty slow to do that," he wrote him. "Let me know how you like the work you are doing & what the prospects of that property are." The letter, written on May 5, 1913, was returned to Willie; Herbert had gone back home. [993]

While Herbert was in California, Edmund had been trying to do some farming on Willie's newly acquired place at Deep Ford, but he soon gave it up. During the summer of 1914 Willie returned home, at which time he made arrangements with Herbert to take care of the farm and to begin remodeling the old house. Before Willie returned to San Francisco, John Mosby paid the Chapman home a visit. The Colonel, along with former Ranger George Tuberville and some others, had attended the anniversary of the Battle of First Manassas on July 21. Prior to the trip, Mosby detailed some of his plans in a letter to Sam: "I shall not go to any resort this summer. I cannot afford the expense and want to keep at work." Mosby also mentioned the book he was working on: "I am really in no great hurry to publish my memoirs because if they appear a year hence they will probably be the last book written by a survivor of the war." [994] Unfortunately, he waited too long; *The Memoirs of Colonel John S. Mosby*, edited by his brother-in-law, Charles Russell, would be published posthumously. [995]

Willie's arrangement with Herbert, to fix up the house and to generally look after the farm, would not prove to be as satisfactory as Willie may have wished. Herbert lacked two essential ingredients to make the venture a success—an incentive for the work and his brother's business sense. In November Willie responded to a letter that Herbert had written him: "You don't write as though you enjoyed that painting job. I suppose it is rather tiresome & smelly. You also wrote that the people at Roanoke, who furnished it, were dunning you for the money. I suppose you mean creosote stain when you write of paint, as I have no recollection of ordering paint. I gave you a receipted bill for it before I left & as I paid for it by check, you can also get the cancelled check from the Covington Bank." [996]

Now that Sam was without gainful employment and had no income of his own, he decided to apply for the pension provided by the Commonwealth for veterans of Confederate military service. [997] On May 28, 1915, at the age of seventy-six, Sam completed the application and his friend, J. J. Hobbs, Clerk of the Circuit Court, witnessed and notarized his signature. The old Ranger, whose service with Mosby was well documented, did not list such service when he applied; neither did he show his service with the Dixie Artillery. He entered only his service with the "Warren Rifles, 17th Virginia Infantry", when he was asked for branch, regiment and company of service. "Infirmities of age" and "partially" were given by the applicant as the cause and extent of his disability. The physician's certificate stated "The applicant is deprived thereby of all ability to pursue his usual and ordinary occupation, or any other occupation for a livelihood on account of age." [998]

The application for the pension called for the giving of the "names and addresses of two comrades who served in the same command with you during the war." This time, Sam reflected back on his days in the 43rd Battalion and listed his good friends, Dr. Will Dunn, of Glade Spring, and Stockton Terry, living in Lynchburg. Dunn had enlisted as one of the command's surgeons, but became one of its most active combatants; Terry was a private in Sam's company and was the command's color bearer. Dunn and Terry should have been the ones to execute the "Affidavit of Comrades" that was a later part of the application. Apparently, Sam believed he was to enter the names of two additional comrades, so he gave two other former Rangers, Allen W. McKim, a private in Company B, and Charles E. Biedler, a private in Company C. Both men were from Page County and certified to having known Sam Chapman for "... 54 years." [999]

When Willie decided to remodel the house, he had in mind a place in the country where his father could go, away from some of the memories of years past that were forever present in the home on Wills Street. But in December of 1915, he suddenly had another reason. "My dear Papa," he wrote on December 15, "I was married Monday, almost immediately after my arrival here (Willie had been at sea since the first of the month and was now back in San Francisco), and have never been so happy before in my whole life. Am in hopes I shall be able to bring my wife to see you all next summer and am sure all of you will fall in love with her as I have done." Sam's captivated forty-four-year-old son continued exuberantly on: "My courtship and marriage had been very eventful & romantic & to look back on it seems more like one of Scott's novels rather than a twentieth century event. I find myself more in love with her every day as I find her character as beautiful as her physical charms." Leaving little unsaid, Willie confessed to his father: "I know you will think I am writing like a man in his early youth instead of one who has had much & varied experiences in life. I have always wished, but hardly dared hoped, that I should find just the right girl. I was married by one of my best friends, Judge Henshaw, who is a Justice of the Supreme Court." [1000]

Willie's credit and finances were on solid ground and he was in a position to try and expand his holdings as well as improve on what he already had. "I am trying to raise $500.00, to build the barn, before I sail," he had written to Herbert the month before his wedding, "& if I am successful I want you to start at once building it....I should like very much to see how the place looks now—get someone to take a photograph if you can." [1001] And in the same letter to Sam, in which he informed him of his marriage, he talked about an adjoining farm: "Get Revercomb to buy Saunders' place if he can buy it for 5000 or less. I shall not expect Herbert to oblige himself in any way." [1002] The Saunders property abutted Willie's farm on the southeast, not far from his house; it also fronted on the river. [1003]

As the year 1916 was ushered in, Willie was still trying to work out a deal on the Saunders farm. He wrote to Sam, telling him that Herbert had sent a list of farming implements that Willie felt were overpriced by Saunders. He then informed his father of probable financial arrangements in the event the property could be bought for no more than the $5,000 he had offered: "I suppose there will be no trouble about borrowing this amount from the bank as I could give a mortgage on the whole property. I should prefer however to get a private loan if possible, to run, say two years, with the option of renewal for the same length of time, if desired." The solvency of his financial condition was reflected as he told Sam: "I do not want a loan from the bank that falls due every three or four months, that would be an intolerable nuisance. I have investments out here I could easily get that amount out of, but I should have to dispose of them at a sacrifise (sic) at present as the war in Europe has depressed all business but arms and ammunition."[1004]

By February, Herbert Chapman had apparently gotten his fill of farming and remodeling. Willie wrote his father, enclosing a letter he had received from Herbert: "It seems that he has quit the farm entirely—well I don't blame him, as he can make nothing of it and sees no prospect of doing so," Willie related. But he was optimistic about the farm's success while being aware of his brother's shortcomings: "I am sure, however, that it could be made to pay if the right one could be employed to run it, someone who really understood the business. I wish you would get George Revercomb to see if he can get some one to run my place the same as his; that is to work it on shares. I would be perfectly willing to put all I get out of the farm back into the farm to improve it." Willie than told Sam "It would be just as well at present to call off that deal with Saunders." [1005]

After twenty-five years at sea, Willie had come ashore. "I have decided to quit the sea and I hope for good," he wrote Sam in March. His deep feelings for his wife, which he had never tried to disguise, dictated his decision. "The sea has no attraction at all for me now that I am married & never has had for Ruby." He told his father that he had no positive plans but he and his friends were constantly on the lookout "to find a suitable position ashore." Despite his unemployment, Willie was able to enclose "a draft for $100.00 to keep the farm going." [1006]

John Mosby was sick. About the time Willie was abandoning his long career aboard the ocean-going ships of the Pacific, his dear friend was boarding a boat outside Washington, D. C., for a trip south to Norfolk. He was hoping that the sea air of the Atlantic would invigorate him—restore some of the fire, physically and emotionally. The old warrior was saddened by what he perceived to be indifference and he longed for the affection of those closest to him. The impending death of his son, Johnnie, from cancer, hung like an opaque mantle over him. Three weeks later, he was back in the Capitol city, where he entered, first, Georgetown University Hospital, then Garfield Hospital.[1007] For a brief time some of the old feistiness seemed to return and he wrote Sam Chapman in April, taking his long-devoted friend to task for misunderstanding the status of a magazine article that had been accepted but not yet published. [1008]

On the morning of May 30, 1916, Colonel John Singleton Mosby died. He was buried two days later, in Warrenton. Sam was there, alone with his memories, amongst the 3,000 people who attended the funeral. One remembrance, tucked away in the recesses of his mind, came to the faithful minister of the Gospel as he watched the cool Virginia soil fall upon the mortal remains of his agnostic-leaning friend. It was something Mosby had expressed to him in a letter over twenty years before, when planning a visit to see Sam: "I would prefer to reach there in the daytime or early in the night," he had confided, "as I have a horror of being waked up at night." [1009]

Sam's oldest sister, Hannah Catherine ("Kate") and youngest, Margaret Ann ("Annie") had been living in Atlanta since 1890, along with brother Edmund. Kate died near there on July 14, 1916, after a lingering illness. In March Sam had received a letter from his brother, William, saying he had stopped to see Kate on his way to California from Greensboro. He had found her "looking better than I expected to see her & much more cheerful than most people would be, afflicted as she is." Kate died at the home of William's son, Doctor William A. Chapman, Jr., in Cedartown, Georgia. Sam made the trip from Covington to Luray for the funeral.[1010]

Following Kate's death, Edmund, now seventy-five, had gone to live at the Confederate Soldier's Home in Richmond. Sam received notice of his death there, less than a year later, on June 28, 1917. [1011]

The house on the farm was now in decent repair and Sam, Ella, and Edmund were spending considerable time there. Herbert was somewhere in Chicago, having left home under less than amicable circumstances apparently. A much saddened Sam wrote to him but the letter, addressed only "Mr. Herbert Chapman, Chicago, Ill.," was returned undelivered. "I hope this letter will find you," the dejected father had written. "I feel very badly whenever I think of how you left us. It was my fault as much as yours and I ask your forgiveness." [1012]

In late September 1918, Mosby's Men reunited once more at Front Royal, on the fifty-fourth anniversary of their fight there. Sam had told Ella early on that he wanted to go. He knew it was probably the last time that he would see most of the old partisans. When the time came, the two of them boarded the train in Covington, bound for Luray, where they would spend the night, visiting with loved ones in his old hometown. On a chilly fall morning, reminiscent of the many he had known when Mosby would assemble the men and reveal the plans for the day's ride and the coming night's raid, Sam and Ella left Luray for the short ride to Front Royal.

"The attendance of the old men was pathetically small," Ella recalled. "My father was greeted affectionately with tears by the men of his company who were there." Sam's close friend, Fount Beattie, who had stood by him defending the howitzer at Greenwich, stayed close by his side all day, as did Doctor Will Dunn. Tears were shed, unashamedly, as the veterans spied old friends and comrades, many for the first time since the war. Boyd Smith, Sam's First Sergeant in Company E, was one of the speakers, at the meeting inside the old courthouse. Though originally a member of the 4th Virginia Cavalry, Smith had ridden with Mosby and was formally enlisted by the Colonel on July 28, 1864, the same day Sam was made a captain and Company E was formed. "He frequently referred to my father as 'his gallant old captain' and my father's expression was as one who was seeing things a far way off," Ella noted. [1013]

That afternoon, they stood at the monument on the hill in the old cemetery, erected to those six who were with Sam's contingent of Rangers and were captured and executed by Union soldiers. There, the tears flowed anew and old men clasped each other's shoulders and hands and turned and walked away. It was Sam Chapman's last reunion.

Past his eightieth birthday now, Sam's health was not good. He had suffered several years from rheumatism; now he had a "nervous condition," in addition to having taken two hard falls, one while going down the stable steps. But he had heard from Herbert by January of 1919 and now had an address at which to write to him in Chicago. His health continuing to fail, he informed Herbert he was at the Revercomb home in Covington: "(I am) feeling very weak. Mr. Gathright brought me down in his auto. He carried me in his arms like a child." But he told Herbert not to try to make the long trip to see him, saying "It costs too much and I am better now. I might be some account yet."[1014]

By March, Sam did appear to have improved. Herbert wrote that he had gone to visit his brother Paul, now married and living in Michigan, and that the couple encouraged Herbert to live with or near them. Sam's reply to his son was longer and written in a much steadier hand than his earlier letters. "Their advice about buying 10 acres for yourself is good, I should think," Sam wrote back to Herbert. "Go over & see if the place suits you. You have had experience enough in farming to have a good opinion of a fit place." But then he expressed the longings of a father, approaching the sunset of his days, for his children: "I would be glad to have all my children near me as I can not expect to live long. But it won't do to think about that." He resigned himself to the separation: "I pray daily that I may meet all my loved ones in Heaven. I have but little fear of death."[1015]

Ten days later, Sam again wrote to Herbert. But things had taken a change for the worse in only that short span. "I am not in bed much," he wrote in a trembling hand, "but am much more feeble than ever I have been in my life before." He then talked again of his fall at the stable and recited those suffered by his friends. "Mr. W. S. Wills got one similar at home about the same time and died in a few days. I miss him so much. Mr. Hobbs, the Clerk, fell down about the same time and died. I am improving some but I shall never be right ever again." [1016]

Three weeks after Sam wrote to Herbert, Willie received a letter from Ella: "You will be grieved to know that Papa has taken worse again, ten days ago, and there has been very little change in his condition since. Someone has to be with him every minute, night and day." The sudden change did not bode well at all for Sam, and Ella knew it. His mind was now affected; he knew the family members well enough but was not aware of where he was. "(He) asks everyone who comes in to take him home," Ella wrote. "He has lost all sight of time and place and mixes up things that happened years back with the present, yet he is perfectly rational at times and talks of those away from home, saying he would like to see them." The prognosis for, and the extent of, any recovery for Sam, was uncertain, according to his doctor; possibly, he might get better but there was no way to know for sure. [1017] A few days after writing Willie, Ella wrote the "discouraging news" to Sam's brother,

William, in Greensboro, who in turn wrote to the widow of Ben Palmer in Richmond that Sam was "dangerously ill." [1018] (Palmer had been one of Sam's lieutenents when Sam was given the captaincy of Company E and Mrs. Palmer had stayed in close touch with many of the veterans of the command.)

Sam was more lethargic now. At times he would suddenly arouse, as if hearing an old command to "mount up" or to "charge." He would mutter a few words and then slip back into what appeared to be a peaceful half-sleep. What scenes were playing out in the mind's eye of the old Ranger—the wild fight at Miskel's farm and the sabre blow across his head? Perhaps he was once again swinging the ramrod at Grapewood Farm before feeling the burning in his leg from a Yankee bullet. Maybe the lump returned to his throat and the knot to his stomach as when he suddenly saw 200 Union cavalrymen turn into twenty times or more that number below Front Royal and the day would not end before six of his men were victims of enemy executioners. Or just perhaps he was once again standing beside Miss Beck, on that hot July day in old Salem, when the Reverend Herndon bonded them together, forever, before God....

The end came at 10:25 p.m., on May 21, 1919, at his home on Wills Street. The doctor officially wrote "arteriosclerosis" on the death certificate; he told the family that Sam had just worn out. It was lacking nine days of being exactly three years since John Mosby had died.

They buried him beside Rebecca and Elgin, on a slight hillside, looking across the nestled valley and facing the western sunset behind the Allegheny Mountains. His legacy—his life—is in the simple words chiseled into the gray granite:

A faithful minister of the Gospel
A brave Confederate Officer
An honorable and useful life

"I have fought the good fight
I have kept the faith" [1019]

NOTES

The following abbreviations are used for works cited in the endnotes:
CSR: Compiled Service Records of the Union and Confederacy; **GSPC**: Genealogical Society of Page County, Virginia; **MOC**: Museum of the Confederacy; **LOV**: Library of Virginia (formerlyVirginia State Library); **NA**: National Archives and Records Administration; **OR**: U.S.War Department, A Compilation of the Official Records of the Union and Confederate Armies (All **OR** citations are **Series I** unless indicated otherwise.); **PPL**: Page Public Library; **SHSP**: Southern Historical Society Papers; **USBC**: United States Bureau of the Census; **UVAL**: University ofVirginia, Alderman Library; **VBHS**: Virginia Baptist Historical Society; **VHS**: Virginia Historical Society; **WLUL**: Washington and Lee University, Leyburn Library; **WPA**: Works Progress Administration.

1. Courthouse Pleadings to Partisan Plans

[1] *The Religious Herald,* January 9, 1902

[2] Ibid.

[3] Mosby, *Memoirs,* p. 149/footnote

[4] Jones, *Ranger Mosby,* pp. 16, 18-20

[5] Ibid., pp.20-24; Wert, *Mosby's Rangers,* p. 26

[6] Mitchell, *Letters,* p. 301

[7] Keen & Mewborn, *43rd Battalion,* p. 2; Wert, *Mosby's Rangers,* p. 27

[8] Mosby, *Memoirs,* pp. 11-12; Jones, *Ranger Mosby,* p. 33

[9] Wallace, Jr., *Guide,* p. 40; Woodward, *The Confederacy's Forgotten Son,* pp. 33-35; Faust, *Encyclopedia,* pp. 727-728; Freemann, *Lee's Lieutenants, Volume I,* pp. xlix, 283

[10] Jones, *Ranger Mosby,* pp. 51-52; Mosby, *Memoirs,* pp. 49-53

[11] Jones, *Ranger Mosby,* pp. 52-53; Mitchell, *Letters,* pp. 13, 16; Driver, *1st Virginia Cavalry,* p. 24

[12] Jones, *Ranger Mosby,* p. 37; Mosby, *Memoirs,* pp. 22-23, 89

[13] Driver, *1st Virginia Cavalry,* p. 192; Blackford, *War Years,* p. 16

[14] Mitchell, *Letters,* p. 18 (The Mosby letter inadvertently gives the size of Colonel Lee's force as "8 men") Jones, *Ranger Mosby,* pp. 53-54

[15] Mitchell, *Letters,* p. 3 (The Mosby letter bears as incorrect year date of "1861"); Mosby, *Memoirs,* p.102; Jones, *Ranger Mosby,* p. 54

[16] Keen & Mewborn. *43rd Battalion*, p. 5; Jones, *Ranger Mosby*, p. 54

[17] Mosby, *Memoirs*, p. 60

[18] Ibid., Jones, *Ranger Mosby*, p. 56

[19] Jones, *Ranger Mosby*, p. 57

[20] Ibid., Coulter, *The Confederate States*, Volume VII, pp. 329-330

[21] Jones, *Ranger Mosby*, p. 57; Driver, *1st Virginia Cavalry*, p. 198; Faust, *Encyclopedia*, pp. 404, 728

[22] Faust, *Encyclopedia*, p. 420

[23] Mitchell, *Letters*, pp. 126-127; Mosby, *Memoirs*, p. 109

[24] Mitchell, *Letters*, p. 27

[25] Mosby, *Memoirs*, p. 101

[26] Wert, *Mosby's Rangers*, p. 29

[27] Sears, *To the gates of Richmond*, pp. (no nbr) Introoduction; Faust, *Encyclopedia*, p. 571

[28] Driver, *1st Virginia*, p. 35; Mosby, *Memoirs*, p. 110

[29] Faust, *Encyclopedia*, p. 667

[30] Freeman, *Lee's Lieutenants*, Volume I, p. 277; Sears, *To the Gates of Richmond*, pp. 158, 159

[31] Ibid.; Ibid., p. 152; Jones, *Ranger Mosby*, p. 58

[32] Mosby, *Reminiscences*, pp. 219-239; Mosby, *Memoirs*, pp. 110-111 Faust, *Encyclopedia*, p. 514

[33] Mosby, *Memoirs*, p. 112; Freeman, *Lee's Lieutenants*, Volume I, pp. 278, 282-299; Krick, *9th Virginia Cavalry*, p. 185

[34] Driver, *1st Virginia Cavalry*, p. 39

[35] Jones, *Ranger Mosby*, p. 61; Mosby, *Memoirs*, p. 119

[36] Sears, *To the Gates of Richmond*, pp. 343-345

[37] Mosby, *Memoirs*, pp. 121, 125

[38] Coulter, *The Confederate States*, Volume VII, p. 338; Keen & Mewborn, *43rd Battalion*, p. 13; Faust, *Encyclopedia*, 561

[39] Robertson, *Stonewall Jackson*, pp. 511-512

[40] OR 51, pt. 2, p. 594; Mosby, *Memoirs*, pp. 126-127

[41] OR 51, pt. 2, p. 594; Mosby, *Memoirs*, pp. 129-135; Robertson, *Stonewall Jackson*, pp. 510,539; Freeman, *Lee's Lieutenants*, Volume II, pp. 16-17

[42] Freeman, *Lee's Lieutenants, Volume II*, pp. 57-60, 71-72; Jones, *Ranger Mosby*, pp. 65-66; Mosby, *Memoirs*, pp. 135-137

[43] Mitchell, *Letters*, p. 36

[44] Mosby, *Memoirs*, pp.144-145

[45] Freeman, *R. E. Lee, Volume II*, pp. 415-417

[46] Ibid., p. 422

[47] Mosby, *Memoirs*, pp. 146-147

[48] Ibid., p. 147

[49] Freeman, *Lee's Lieutenants, Volume II*, pp. 399-406; Jones, *Ranger Mosby*, p. 68

[50] Freeman, *Lee's Lieutenants, Volume II*, p. 407

[51] Mosby, *Memoirs*, p. 216 (quote is from John Esten Cook's *Wearing of the Gray*)

[52] Scott, *Partisan Life*, p. 20; Keen & Mewborn, *43rd Battalion*, p. 7; Jones, *Ranger Mosby*, pp. 70-71

[53] Scott, *Partisan Life*, pp. 24-25

[54] Ibid., Alexander, *Mosby's Men*, p. 20

[55] Jones, *Ranger Mosby*, p. 15

2. Bloodlines

[56] The Page County valley, at various times, has been referred to as Massanutten Valley, Page Valley, and Luray Valley. For purposes here it will be called Page Valley.

[57] Strickler, *A Short History of Page County, Virginia*, pp 114, 116; Kerkhoff, *Old Homes of Page County*, pp. 105, 108; GSPC, WPA Historical Inventory of Page County, p. 522

[58] Bruen , *Christian Forrer, The Clockmaker*, pp 171, 193

[59] Ibid., pp 2, 7, 16. (The surname Forrer is derived from the name of the ancestral home, Fuhrer of Langnau, which means "furrow" or ploughed land)

[60] Ibid., pp. 15, 27

[61] Ibid., pp. 18-19, 21, 29.

[62] Ibid., pp. 27-28.

[63] Ibid.,p. 34; Strickler, *A Short History of Page County*, p 114

[54] Strickler, *A Short History of Page County*, p 114 (This part of the Page Valley was, at that time, situated in the county of Shenandoah; Page County would not come into being until 1831)

[55] Ibid., p. 23; Bruen, *Christian Forrer, The Clockmaker*, p 169.

[66] Bruen, *Christian Forrer, The Clockmaker*, pp 168, 171.

[67] Strickler, *A Short History of Page County*, pp 146, 150; GSPC, WPA Historical Inventory of Page County, p. 528

[68] Edmonds, *John Chapman of Spotsylvania County*, pp 3, 5, 12.

[69] Ibid.,p. 13; Yowell, *A History of Madison County, Virginia*, p 60.

[70] Dove, *Madison County Homes*, p 298

[71] Ibid. p. 13; Yowell, *A History of Madison County, Virginia*, p. 60; Bruen, *Christian Forrer, the Clockmaker*, p 193; The name of William Chapman's bride cannot be clearly substantiated. The Madison County "Marriage Bonds" show her to be "Caty Gaines, dau. of Edmund Gaines," while the contemporaneous "Index to the Marriage Bonds" shows "Hattie Gains" Some references, including genealogies, show William Chapman married Catherine Gaines, daughter of General Edmund Pendleton Gaines. No source was located to support this. On the contrary, sources cited here make this relationship impossible; Edmund Pendleton Gaines was born in 1777; "Catherine Gaines" was born in 1778, so he could not be her father. There is no record of General Gaines having a sister by the name of Catherine or Hattie. There is no evidence that any relationship existed between General Gaines and William Chapman's wife.

[72] Dove, *Madison County Homes*, p. 14

[73] Bruen, *Christian Forrer, The Clockmaker*, p 197; PPL, WPA Historical Inventory of Page County, pp. 428; 430

[74] GSPC, WPA Historical Inventory of Page County, pp. 428-430

3. Preparation for a Calling

[75] Strickler, *A Short History of Page County*, pp. 287-288; Bruen, *Christian Forrer, The Clockmaker*, p.182; Reader' Digest, *Family Encyclopedia of American Industry*, p. 563

[76] Strickler, *A Short History of Page County*, pp 154-155;

[77] Ibid., p 98n, p 225

[78] PPL, *An Interim Report on Catherine Furnace*, p. 31.

[79] Bruen, *Christian Forrer, The Clockmaker*, p 174

[80] Miller, *Mapping for Stonewall*, pp 12, 14-15

[81] Ibid., p 15

[82] Bruen, *Christian Forrer, The Clockmaker*, p 171;

[83] USBC, Augusta County, Virginia, 1850

[84] Lewis Collection, Report of Samuel F. Chapman in the School at Mossy Creek

[85] Ibid.

[86] Miller, *Mapping for Stonewall*, p 16

[87] UVAL, Hotchkiss Papers, (From a broadside for Mossy Creek Academy)

[88] WLUL, Hotchkiss Papers, *Fourth Annual Catalogue of Mossy Creek Academy*, Reel 60

[89] WLUL, Hotchkiss Papers, Miscellanious, Reel 60

[90] George Washington University Archives, *The George Washington University Through the Years*, pp. 1-3, (Columbian College became George Washington University when it was reorganized in 1904)

[91] Alley, *History of the University of Richmond*, p. 6

[92] Strickler, *A Short History of Page County*, pp. 254-255; Luray BaptistChurch, *A Historical Sketch*

[93] Strickler, *A Short History of Page County*, pp. 251; LOV, *Minutes* of Main Street Baptist Church, Luray Miscellaneous Reel No. 303 (Although the *Minutes* show William A. Chapman, who would be Sam's father, it is believed that William H., Sam's brother, was the other person baptized)

[94] .LOV, *Minutes* of Main Street Baptist Church

[95] Ibid.

[96] VBHS, *Catalog of Session of 1858-59, Richmond College*

[97] Alley, *History of the University of Richmond*, pp 18-22. (The school is now the University of Richmond and remains a Virginia Baptist school. The site of the old school is now in the Fan District of downtown Richmond.)

[98] Whittet & Sheperson, *The First Hundred Years*, p 27

[99] Alley, *History of the University of,Richmond*, p 43

[100] Ibid.

[101] VBHS, *Catalog of Session 1858-59, Richmond College*

[102] Alley, *History of the University of Richmond*, p 42

[103] Ministerials referred to those students who were studying for the ministry and, as such, were given special consideration in the cost of tuition and other fees.

[104] Alley, *History of the University of Richmond*, pp 43-44; VBHS, *Catalog of Session of 1859-60*

[105] *Richmond Enquirer*, December 2, 1859

[106] Ibid.

[107] Wallace, Jr., *Guide,* pp 9-10

[108] Lewis Collection, Clipping from an unnamed and undated newspaper

[109] Miller, *Mapping for Stonewall*, pp 23-24

4. A Call to Arms

[110] Coulter, *The Confederate States of America*, pp 40-41

[111] Ibid., pp 309-310

[112] NA, CSR: *17th Virginia Infantry*

[113] Wallace, Jr., *17th Virginia Infantry*, p.8; Wallace, *Jr.*, *Guide*, p.100

[114] Wise, *History of the Seventeenth Virginia Infantry, C. S. A.*, pp.11-14

[115] Wallace, Jr., *17TH Virginia Infantry*, p.11

[116] Ibid., p.12

[117] Ibid., p.13

[118] Ibid., pp.14, 17

[119] Stephenson Collection, From a memoir by William H. Chapman relating to the service of his brother Sam Chapman, May, 1925

[120] Wise, *History of the Seventeenth Virginia Infantry, C. S. A.*, pp.19-20

[121] Sanger, *James Longstreet, Soldier*; p. 29; Wallace, Jr., *17th Virginia Infantry*, p. 18

[122] Wise, *History of the Seventeenth Virginia Infantry, C. S. A.*, pp. 20-22, 287

[123] Wallace, Jr., *17th Virginia Infantry*, p.19

[124] Mitchell, *Decisive Battles of the Civil War*, p. 38

[125] Wallace, Jr., *17th Virginia Infantry*, p.19

[126] Ibid.

[127] *Religious Herald*, January 9, 1902

[128] Wallace, *17th Virginia Infantry*, p.19; Wise, *History of the Seventeenth Virginia Infantry, C..S.A.*, p. 35

[129] Ibid., p.132

[130] MOC, *J. Thomas Petty Diary*

[131] NA, CSR: *17th Virginia Infantry*

[132] MOC, *J. Thomas Petty Diary*

[133] Ibid.

[134] Ibid.; Franklin's name is spelled Frankland in CSR when he later enlists in 43rd Bn., Va. Cavalry;. Also, William Chapman's recollections of his brother's duties during this period place Sam assigned to the Signal

Corps 2-3 months prior or just after his stint with Beauregard's adjutant general (Re: e/n 119) . However, Petty's account of the time frame is more plausible, having been recorded at the time while Chapman's was written from memory over sixty years later.

[135] Ibid., Murphy, *10th Virginia Infantry*, p.11

[136] Wallace, Jr., *17th Virginia Infantry, p. 132*

[137] Wise, *History of the Seventeenth Virginia Infantry, C.S.A.*, pp. 37-38

[138] Sanger, *James Longstreet*, p.35

[139] NA, CSR:*17th Virginia Infantry; Chapman's Battery;* Moore, *The Danville, Eighth Star New Market and Dixie Artillery,* p.87

[140] UVAL, Daniel Papers; Wallace, Jr., *Guide,* p. 16

[141] Ibid; Ibid.

[142] Moore, *The Dixie Artillery.*, pp.87-88; NA, CSR *17th Virginia Infantry*

[143] Moore, *The Dixie Artillery,* pp.88-89; Wallace, Jr., *Guide,* p. 16

[144] NA, CSR *17th Virginia Infantry;* Bruen, *Christian Forrer the Clockmaker,* pp.171; USBC, Augusta County, Virginia, 1850

[145] LOV, CSR, *52nd Virginia Infantry*, Reel 936

[146] UVAL, Hotchkiss Papers, *A Description of the Elizabeth Furnace Iron Property, Augusta County, Virginia*

[147] Ibid; NA, CSR: *Chapman's Battery*

[148] Bruen, *Christian Forrer the Clockmaker*, p.180

5. Musketeer to Cannoneer

[149] OR, 5, pp.1095-1096, 1098

[150] Miller, *Mapping for Stonewall*, pp. 35-36, 43, 46

[151] Freeman, *Lee's Lieutenants*, Volume I, p.306; Robertson, *Stonewall Jackson*, pp. 332-333; Faust, *Encyclopedia*, p.415

[152] OR, 12:1,pp. 380, 385; Miller, *Mapping for Stonewall, p.* 47

[153] WLUL, Hotchkiss Papers, *Journal*, Reel 1 (Mr. Pendleton was First Lieutenant Alexander Swift "Sandie" Pendleton, Jackson's ordnance officer)

[154] OR, 5,pp. 1093, 2091; OR, 11:3, p. 405; Moore, *Dixie Artillery*, p. 90

[155] OR,. 11:1, pp. 273-276, 489-490, 615-617, 627-628, 630-632; Sanger, *James Longstreet*, p. 46

[156] Murphy, *10th Virginia Infantry*, pp. 4, 9-12

[157] Faust, *Encyclopedia*, p. 460; Strickler, *A Short History of Page County*, p. 177 (excerpts from the diary of Lt. John W. Mauck, Co. K, 10th Va. Inf)

[158] Faust, *Encyclopedia*, p. 391

[159] Strickler, *A Short History of Page County*, p.179 (Mauck diary)

[160] Murphy, *10th Virginia Infantry*, pp.25-26

[161] NA, CSR: *17th Virginia Infantry; Chapman's Battery*

[162] OR, 11:3, p. 615; *NA, CSR: 17th Virginia Infantry; Chapman's Battery; GSPC, The Hite Letters*, June 2, 1862

[163] OR,. 11: 2 , pp. 564, 625-626, 757-758; Sears, *To the Gates of Richmond*, p. 249

[164] OR, 11: 1, p.160; OR, 11: 2,p. 617;OR,.11:3,p. 256;

[165] OR, 11:2, pp. 494, 662; Moore, *Dixie Artillery*, p. 90

[166] OR 11:2, pp. 24-37

[167] OR (Supplement), Vol. 2, pp. 441-442

[168] Ibid., p. 443

[169] UVAL Daniel Papers, William H. Chapman to Samuel F. Chapman, November 18, 1904

[170] OR, .11:2, pp. 255-256, 293-296, 403, 405, 410, 566, 759, 763-764, 777-778, 793; GSPC, *The Hite Letters*, July 8, 1862

[171] Freeman, *R. E. Lee*, Volume II, p. 210

[172] Phrase coined by Colonel Jennings C. Wise, C.S.A.

[173] Sanger, *James Longstreet*, pp.74-75; Freeman, *R. E. Lee*, Volume II, pp. 208-209, 213-214, 218

[174] Sears, *To the Gates of Richmond*, p. 335

[175] OR, 11:2,p. 629

[176] OR, 11:3,p. 634

[177] OR, 11:2, p. 537

[178] Sears, *To the Gates of Richmond*, pp. 339, 344-345, 348; Faust, *Encyclopedia*, pp.332 ,571

[179] Ibid., 347

[180] Faust, *Encyclopedia*, p. 570; Freeman, *Lee's Lieutenants*, Volume *I*, pp. 614-615

[181] Carmichael, *Lee's Young Artillerist*, pp. 2-6

[182] OR, 11:3, pp. 646-648; OR, 12:2, p.547

[183] OR, 12:2, p. 569

[184] OR, 12:2, pp. 569-570; OR, 12:2, pp. 573-575

[185] OR, 12:2, pp. 563-564

[186] Freeman, *Lee's Lieutenants*, Volume II, p. 121; Sanger, *James Longstreet*, p. 88 and map facing page.

[187] Sanger, *James Longstreet*, p.88; Faust, *Encyclopedia*, p. 93

[188] Freeman, *Lee's Lieutenants*, Volume II, pp. 123-124

[189] OR, 12:2, pp. 565, 603

[190] OR, 12:2, p.511

[191] VHS, Letter from William Chapman to General James Longstreet, August 27, 1887

[192] Ibid.

[193] Ibid.

[194] UVAL, Daniel Papers, Letter from Samuel F. Chapman to Major John W. Daniel, Undated, c.1904

[195] Ibid.; Russell Collection, Letter from William Chapman to Mr. A. L. Henry, President of Bull Run Battlefield, March 26, 1923

[196] OR, 12:2, p. 578; Freeman, *Lee's Lieutenants*, Volume II, p.124 and map facing p.124

[197] Or, 12:2, pp.577-578

[198] Ibid., pp. 607, 640

[199] VHS, William Chapman to James Longstreet, August 27, 1887

[200] Ibid., OR, 12:2, pp. 598-599, 577-578, 564, 603-604

[201] Ibid.; Freeman, *R. E. Lee*, Volume II, pp. 329-332; Robertson, *Stonewall Jackson, pp.* 572-574

[202] OR, 12:2, p.565

[203] Ibid., pp.598-599

[204] Freeman in *R. E. Lee*, (Vol. II, p. 332), following Jackson's request to Longstreet for help, says "Samuel (sic) Chapman's company, the first to arrive, went quickly into action." Freeman goes on to say that Captain Robert Boyce and Captain James Reilly followed and that "Stephen D. Lee's eighteen guns were ready." Thus, Freeman appears to be saying that Chapman's Battery was the first to open on the assault.

[205] OR 12:2, p.511; Faust, *Encyclopedia*, pp.594-595

[206] Miller, *Mapping for Stonewall*, pp. 81-82

[207] Fox, *Regimental Losses*

[208] VSL, CSR: *33rd Virginia Infantry*, Reel 792

[209] Faust, *Encyclopedia*, pp.129-130; Robertson, *Stonewall Jackson, pp.* 580-581

[210] OR, 19:1, p.809

[211] Freeman, *R. E. Lee*, Volume II, p. 359; Robertson, *Stonewall Jackson*, p. 595

[212] Bailey, *The Bloodiest Day,* pp.11-12

[213] Freeman, *R. E. Lee*, Volume II, pp. 363-364

[214] UVAL, Daniel Papers, letter from William H. Chapman to Samuel F. Chapman, November 18, 1904

[215] Bailey, *The Bloodiest Day*, p. 44

[216] OR, 19:2, pp.605-606; OR,19:1, pp. 140,146, 1019

[217] Freeman, *R. E. Lee*, Volume II, pp.369-372; OR, 19:1, p. 140

[218] Freeman, *R. E. Lee*, Volume II, pp. 369-372; Bailey, *The Bloodiest Day*, pp. 44-52, with map, p. 48.

[219] Freeman, *R. E. Lee*, Volume II, p.374

[220] OR, 51:2,pp. 618-619

[221] OR, 19:1, pp.140, 147, 826, 854

[222] OR, 19:1,p. 140

[223] Robertson, *Stonewall Jackson,* p.,603

[224] UVAL, Daniel Papers, William H. Chapman to Samuel F. Chapman, November 18, 1904; OR 19.1-852-856, 863-864; (It is doubtful if Chapman's Battery ever caught up with Kershaw's Brigade on Maryland Heights. There is no mention of it in either Kershaw or McLaws' official reports although distinct references are made to other batteries that ascended the Heights. Also, Kershaw's men did not actually enter Harper's Ferry but went on to Brownsville and Crampton's Gap to meet the enemy there.. Chapman probably entered Harper's Ferry with Mclaws' troops which had been at Sandy Hook or defending Weverton Pass.)

[225] Ibid.

[226] Ibid., 19:1, pp.140, 147, 951;OR, 19:2, p. 608; Freeman, *R. E. Lee*, Volume II, pp.379-380

[227] Ibid., 19:1,pp. 148-150

[228] Ibid.

[229] Ibid., pp. 150, 988; Freeman, *Lee's Lieutenants*, Volume II, pp. 220, 222-224; Freeman, *R. E. Lee*, Volume II, pp. 401-402

[230] Freeman, *R. E. Lee*, Volume II, pp. 402-403; Freeman, *Lee's Lieutenants*, Volume II, p. 225.

[231] OR, 19:1, p. 150

[232] UVAL, Daniel Papers, William H. Chapman to Samuel F. Chapman, November 18, 1904

[233] Ibid., Samuel F. Chapman to John Warwick Daniel, undated, c. 1904

[234] OR 19.1, pp. 143, 151-152, 832-834; Moore, *The Dixie Artillery*, p. 95

[235] OR, 19:2, pp. 647

[236] Ibid., pp. 646-647, 649

[237] Ibid., p. 653

[238] UVAL, Daniel Papers, William H. Chapman to Samuel F. Chapman, November 18, 1904

6. Sojourner Behind the Lines

[239] NA, *CSR: Chapman's Battery*

[240] Freeman, *R. E. Lee*, Volume II, p. 411; SHSP, Volume 13, p. 13

[241] OR, 19:1, p.143

[242] Ibid., 19:2, p.590

[243] NA, *CSR:Chapman's Battery*

[244] OR, (Series IV:1), p.1152; Wallace, *Jr., The Richmond Howitzers, pp.* 4-5, 132

[245] OR, (Series IV:1), p.1095; Coulter, *The Confederate States of America,* , Volume VII, pp. 314-315

[246] OR, (Series IV:1) pp.1097; OR, (Series IV:2) p. 172

[247] Ibid., 19:2, p. 590;

[248] Ibid., p.657

[249] OR, (Series IV:2), pp.171, 217

[250] Ibid., pp..172; 217

[251] NA, *CSR: Chapman's Battery, Religious Herald,* January 9, 1902

7. Joining That Fellow Mosby

[252] Strickler, *A Short History of Page County*, pp. 170, 186-187; NA, CSR: *Chapman's Battery*

[253] OR, 12:2, p. 94-95, 97-98

[254] OR, (Series IV:2), pp 5, 7, .217; Keen & Mewborn, *43rd Batallion*, p. 305

[255] Scott, *Partisan Life*, p. 27

[256] *Religious Herald*, January 9, 1902

[257] Jones, *Ranger Mosby*, pp. 73-74; Mosby, *Memoirs*, p. 150

[258] Ibid., p. 151

[259] OR, 25: 1, pp. 38-39

[260] Mosby, *Memoirs*, p. 157

[261] Williamson, *Mosby's Rangers*, p.32f/n, Reports of Lieut.-Col. Robert Johnstone ; Jones, *Ranger Mosby*, p. 87; Scott, *Partisan Life*, p. 40; OR, 25:1, p. 667

[262] Ibid.; Scott, *Partisan Life*, pp. 40-42; Mosby, *Memoirs*, p. 160; *Religious Herald*,, January 2, 1902. (The recollection of Chapman differs somewhat from other accounts. His account more closely follows Scott than the others. Mosby, in his report of the affair (OR 25:1, p. 667), refers to the Vermonters as "(Gilmer's) rear squadron.", and goes on to say that he captured 19 of them. This coincides with the Union report of just who Mosby was actually attacking , although it was probably the Vermont detachment and part of Gilmer's men that he was charging.)

[263] Jones, *Ranger Mosby*, p. 314f/n; Williamson, *Mosby's Rangers*, p. 33f/n con't.

[264] OR, 51:2, p. 688; 25:2, p. 857-858

8. Of Recruits and Generals and Such

[265] Williamson, *Mosby's Rangers*, pp. 28-29, as related by Frankland. (White Plains is now The Plains and Salem is now Marshall).

[266] Ibid., p.29; Keen & Mewborn, *43rd Battalion*, p. 27

[267] Mosby, *Memoirs*, pp. 168-169

[268] Williamson, *Mosby's Rangers*, p 31-32

[269] Jones, *Ranger Mosby*, p. 64; Mosby, *Memoirs*, p. 162

[270] Ibid., p. 172; Williamson, *Mosby's Rangers*, p. 33

[271] Mosby, *Memoirs*, p. 172-173; Scott, *Partisan Life*, p. 44

[272] Faust, *Encyclopedia*, p. 724

[273] Mosby, *Memoirs*, p. 175

[274] Ibid., 174, 176; OR, 25:1, p. 1122

[275] Ibid., 25:1, p. 1121-1122; Mosby, *Memoirs*, pp. 178-180

[276] Mosby, *Memoirs*, p. 122

[277] Ibid., pp. 184-185

[278] OR, 25:1, p. 1122

[279] OR, 25:2, p. 856

[280] Faust, *Encyclopedia*, p. 724

[281] Williamson, *Mosby's Rangers*, pp.45-46

[282] Siepel, *Rebel*, p. 75 (as quoted in L. C. Baker, *History of the United States Secret Service*, p. 170)

[283] Scott,*Partisan Life*, pp. 64-65; Jones, *Ranger Mosby*, p. 102; OR, 25:1, p. 66

[284] OR, 25:2, pp. 856-858 `

[285] Scott, *Partisan Life*, p. 76; Siepel, *Rebel*, p. 84

[286] Scott, *Partisan Life*, p. 77

[287] Keen & Mewborn, *43rd Battalion*, p. 65

[288] OR, (Series IV:2), p. 26

[289] Keen & Mewborn, *43rd Battalion*, pp. 17-18, 330, 360; Scott, *Partisan Life*, p.34

[290] Scott, *Partisan Life*, p. 59; *Religious Herald*, January 9, 1902; p. 106; Armstrong, *7th Virginia Cavalry*; p. 147(roster)

[291] *Baltimore American*, Diary of Captain Bradford Smith Hoskins, reprinted, with commentary, from correspondent of the *Philadelphia Inquirer*, June 12, 1863

[292] *Religious Herald*, January 9, 1902;

[293] Ibid., OR, 25:1, p. 72; (The number of the Union reserve force varies depending on whose account is read. Scott puts the figure at 200, Chapman at 70, Mosby at 200 in his report of April 7, 1863, Johnstone (Union) at 70 in his report of March 23, 1863; Also. Mosby's report of the 3-17-63 action at Herndon is dated March 18, 1863 and is found in OR 25:1, p.66. His report of the Chantilly fight of 3-23-63 is contained in his report dated April 7, 1863 and is found in OR 25:1, p. 72. However, the date used by Mosby for the fight is "Monday, March 16", while he describes the Chantilly fight of March 23.).

[294] OR, 25:1, p. 72; *Religious Herald*, January 9, 1902

[295] *Religious Herald*, January 9, 1902

9. The String Breaks

[296] Williamson, *Mosby's Rangers*, p. 51

[297] *Religious Herald*, January 9, 1902

[298] Jones, *Ranger Mosby*, p. 101

[299] Ibid., p. 110; *Religious Herald*, January 9, 1902

[300] OR, 25:1, p. 61

[301] *Religious Herald*, January 9, 1902

[302] Russell Collection, Letter from W. F. Chapman to Mrs. A. M. Crane, June 25, 1910; Mosby, *Reminiscences*, p 104; Williamson, *Mosby's Rangers*, p. 52

[303] Scott, *Partisan Life*, pp. 63-64; Keen & Mewborn, *43rd Battalion*, p. 43(map)

[304] Keen & Mewborn, *43rd Battalion*, p. 43 (map); OR (Supplement), Vol. 4, pp. 533-534; U. S. War Department, *Atlas of the Civil War*, Plate VII-1

[305] Mosby, *Reminiscences*, p. 103-104; Russell Collection, Chapman to Crane, June 25, 1910

[306] *Religious Herald*, January 16, 1902.

[307] Scott, *Partisan Life*, p. 64-65; OR, 25:1, p. 77, 78; *Religious Herald*, January 16, 1902; OR (Supplement), Vol. 4, 531

[308] Keen and Mewborn, *43rd Battalion*, p. 43 (map); Scott, *Partisan Life*, p. 65

[309] Alexander, *Mosby's Men*, p. 17

[310] *Religious Herald*, January 16, 1902; Russell Collection, Chapman to Crane, June 25, 1910

[311] Ibid.; Ibid.; OR (Supplement), Vol. 4, p. 534

[312] Ibid.; Ibid ; Ibid., p. 531; Mosby, *Reminiscences*, p. 106

[313] Russell Collection, Chapman to Crane, June 25, 1910; Mosby, *Reminiscences*, p. 106

[314] Russell Collection, Chapman to Crane, June 25, 1910; Scott, *Partisan Life*, p. 67.

[315] Mosby, *Reminiscences*, p. 108

[316] Mewborn Collection, Letter from John Mosby to Sam Chapman, June 4, 1900

[317] *Religious Herald*, January 16, 1902; (The Union report of the Broad Run or Miskel Farm fight (OR 25:1, p. 78) states, "...Mosby, during his pursuit, is supposed to have received a saber wound across the face, which unhorsed him." There is no evidence of this having occurred; however, Sam Chapman who was near Mosby at times received a saber strike across the head which nearly unhorsed him; this could be the event described. Mosby, in his *Reminiscences*, also states that "(Sam) received a cut with a sabre.").

[318] Russell Collection, Chapman to Crane, June 25, 1910

[319] Ibid.

[320] OR 25:1, p. 77-78

[321] Russell Collection, Chapman to Crane, June 25, 1910 (Actually Flint had about 148 men to Mosby's 70 or slightly over 2-1. The reference to a sabre charge by Flint's men nearing the barn gate was probably confused with the sabre charge by Captain Bean's second squadron coming in relief of Flint. General Stahel's report was based on hearsay information he received from three officers who were not on the scene.)

[322] OR, 25:1, p. 72-73

[323] OR, 25:1, p. 78; Keen & Mewborn, *43rd Battalion*, p. 48

[324] *Religious Herald*, January 9, 1902

[325] OR, 25:1, p. 80

[326] OR, 18, p. 335; Wallace Jr., *Guide*, p. 9

[327] OR, 25:2, p. 860

[328] Faust, *Encyclopedia*, p. 720

[329] OR,25:1, p. 1057-1058

[330] Scott, *Partisan Life, pp. 78-83;* Keen & Mewborn, *43rd Battalion*, pp. 51-52

[331] *Religious Herald*, January 23, 1902

[332] Furgurson, *Chancellorsville, 1863*; pp. 216, 221

[333] Mosby, *War Reminiscences*, pp. 131-132; *Religious Herald*, January 23, 1902

[334] *Religious Herald*, January 23, 1902; OR, 25:1, p. 1104

[335] Jones, *Ranger Mosby*, pp. 119-120; Mosby, *War Reminiscences*, pp.133; Keen & Mewborn, *43rd Battalion*, pp. 54-56; *Religious Herald*, January 23, 1902

[336] Ibid.; Scott, *Partisan Life*, p. 86

[337] *Religious Herald*, January 23, 1902

[338] Keen & Mewborn, *43rd Battalion*, pp. 56, (roster:pp. 301, 315,330, 336, 345, 350, 361, 377)

[339] OR, 25:1, p. 1105

[340] Mosby, *Reminiscences*, pp.134-135

[341] *Religious Herald*, January 23, 1902

10. Paroled on the Field

[342] *Religious Herald*, February 6, 1902

[343] Mosby, *Reminiscences*, pp. 137-138; Scott, *Partisan Life*, pp. 89-90; OR 25:2, p. 861

[344] *Religious Herald*, February 6, 1902; Mosby, *Reminiscences*, p. 139

[345] OR 25:2, P. 862

[346] Munson, *Mosby Guerrilla*, p. 68; *Religious Herald*, February 6, 1902

[347] Evans and Moyer, *Mosby's Confederacy*, P. 38; *Religious Herald*, February 6, 1902

[348] Mosby, *Reminiscences*, p. 143

[349] *Religious Herald*, February 6, 1902; Williamson, *Mosby's Rangers*, p.65; Keen & Mewborn, *43rd Battalion*, p. 60

[350] Scott, *Partisan Life*, p. 92; *Religious Herald*, February 6, 1902 (Accounts differ on just how the train was halted. Some have the Rangers tying a telegraph wire to a loosened rail and pulling the rail away as the locomotive neared, while others have Chapman putting a shot through the boiler to stop the engine. Chapman's account disputes both, especially regarding the timing of the shot through the boiler, since Montjoy was away with the lanyard).

[351] Williamson, *Mosby's Rangers*, p. 65; Munson. *Mosby Guerrilla*, p. 69; *Religious Herald*, February 6, 1902

[352] *Religious Herald*, February 6, 1902

[353] Mosby, *Reminiscences*, pp. 146-148; Scott, *Partisan Life*, pp. 94-95; Evans and Moyer, *Mosby's Confederacy*, p. 38

[354] Mosby, *Reminiscences*, p. 147

[355] Mosby, *Reminiscences*, pp. 149-150; Williamson, *Mosby's Rangers*, p. 65

[356] *Religious Herald*, February 6, 1902

[357] Munson, *Mosby Guerrilla*, p. 73

[358] *Religious Herald*, February 6, 1902

[359] Ibid.

[360] *Baltimore American* newspaper (from a correspondent of the *Philadelphia Enquirer*), June 12, 1863

[361] *Religious Herald*, February 6, 1902

[362] Mosby, *Reminiscences*, p. 151; Wert, *Mosby's Rangers*, p. 184

[363] OR 25:1, pp. 1117-1119

11. "Miss Beck"

[364] *Religious Herald*, February 6, 1902

[365] USBC, Fairfax County, Virginia, 1850, Fauquier County, Virginia, 1860; VBHS, *Index of Obituaries*; Stuntz and Stuntz, *This Was Tysons Corner, Virginia*, p. 129; Fauquier Heritage Society Collection

[366] Crawford Collection, *Chapman Letter dated June 21, 1863*

[367] NA, CSR, *43rd Bn., Va. Cav.*

[368] Crawford Collection, Chapman Letter, dated June *21, 1863*; Bank of Fauquier Map

[369] Crawford Collection, Chapman Letter of June 21, 1863

[370] LOV, Special Orders of the Adjutant and Inspector-General's Office, p. 237

[371] NA, CSR, *38th Battalion*; LOV, Special Orders of the Adjutant and Inspector-General's Office (While the CSR refers to S.O. Nos 119/16,186/14 and 186/16, only 119/16 is a correct S.O. number for the matter referenced. S.O. Nos. 186/14 and 186/16 do not pertain to either Chapman or to the dates of July 18, 20, or

30. 1863 as the CSR and other sources cite. No other S.O. was located in the original records of the A&IGO at The Library of Virginia, which pertains to this matter)

[372] *Religious Herald*, February 27, 1902; Moore, *The Hampden Artillery*, p. 81-82

[373] Freeman, *Lee's Lieutenants*, Volume III, p. 190; Moore, *The Hampden Artillery*, p. 81

[374] *Religious Herald*, February 27, 1902; (The "Mr. Duncan" Sam mentions may have been Rev. J. A. Duncan, a minister of the Methodist Episcopal Church, South, not simply Episcopal, as Sam relates. This is the name the southern Methodist Churches adopted in 1845 when the national Methodist Episcopal Church split over the question of slavery. Reverend Duncan is listed as a chaplain in the A.N.V. (SHSP).

[375] Moore, The *Hampden Artillery*, p. 84

[376] *Religious Herald*, February 27, 1902

[377] Moore, *The Hampden Artillery*, pp. 84, 86, 165; *Religious Herald*, February 27, 1902

[378] Moore, *The Hampden Artillery*, p. 86-90

[379] NA, CSR, *43rd Bn., Va. Cav.*

[380] NA, CSR, 43rd Bn., Va. Cav.; OR 33, p. 1113

12. "Back With Joy"

[381] *Religious Herald*, February 27, 1902

[382] Mosby, *Reminiscences*, pp. 157-158; Jones, *Ranger Mosby*, p. 132

[383] Keen and Mewborn, *43rd Battalion*, p. 64, 67

[384] OR 27:3, p. 72

[385] OR 27:2, p. 992

[386] Ibid.

[387] OR 29:1, p. 80; Scott, *Partisan Life*, pp. 120-121; Keen and Mewborn, *43rd Battalion*, p. 366, 369-370

[388] OR 29:1, p. 495; OR 29:2, p. 652

[389] Scott, *Partisan Life*, p. 141; Keen and Mewborn, *43rd Battalion*, pp. 369-370

[390] Scott, *Partisan* Life, p. 159

[391] Keen and Mewborn, *43rd Battalion*, p. 372; OR 33, pp. 15-16;

[392] Russell Collection, W. H. Chapman's account of *Raid on Major Cole's Command Near Harper's Ferry*

[393] Ibid; Scott, *Partisan Life*, p. 179

[394] Russell Collection, *Raid on Major Cole's Command*

[395] Scott, *Partisan Life*, pp. 180182; Williamson, *Mosby's Rangers*, pp. 124-128; Mosby, *Memoirs*, pp. 168-269

[396] Russell Collection, *Raid on Major Cole's Command*

[397] Ibid.

[398] Ibid.

[399] Ibid.

[400] OR 33, pp. 15, 16; Mosby, *Memoirs*, p. 269

[401] OR 33, pp. 1113; Keen and Mewborn, *43rd Battalion*, p.351

[402] *Religious Herald,* January 9, 1902

13. A Real Ranger at Last

[403] Russell Collection; Scott, *Partisan Life*, p. 184, Williamson, *Mosby's Rangers*, p. 133

[404] *Religious Herald,* February 27, 1902; Munson, *Mosby Guerrilla*, p. 87

[405] *Religious Herald,* February 27, 1902; *Williamson*, pp. 136-137; OR 33, pp.156-157

[406] Williamson, *Mosby's Rangers*, pp. 136-137; Keen and Mewborn, *43rd Battalion*, pp. 108-110; OR 33; p. 571

[407] *Religious Herald,* February 27, 1902; Keen and Mewborn, *43rd Battalion*, p. 111; Bonnell, *Sabres*, .pp. 24-25

[408] Munson, *Mosby Guerilla*, p. 83

[409] OR 33, p.. 157

[410] Mosby, *Reminiscences*, p. 108

[411] *Religious Herald*, March 20, 1902; Williamson *Mosby's Rangers*, p. 142

[412] Ibid.; Ibid.

[413] Ibid; Ibid

[414] *Religious Herald,* March 20, 1902

[415] Ibid.; UVAL, *Scrapbooks of John S. Mosby;* Scott, *Partisan Life*, p. 202;

[416] Williamson, *Mosby's Rangers*, p. 145; Munson, *Mosby Guerrilla*, p. 86; *Religious Herald*, March 20, 1902

[417] Munson, *Mosby Guerrilla*, pp. 86, 88-89; Scott, *Partisan Life*, pp 202-203

[418] *Religious Herald,* March 20, 1902

[419] Williamson, *Mosby's Rangers*, p.144; OR 33, p. 159

14. Winds of Change

[420] OR 43:1, p. 811

[421] OR 33, pp. 1081-1083

[422] Scott, *Partisan Life*, pp.204-205

[423] Williamson, *Mosby's Rangers*, pp. 150-151

[424] Baird, *Journals*, pp.ix, 185-186

[425] Ibid., p. 15, 250fn

[426] Bonnell, *Sabres*, pp. 26-27; Williamson, *Mosby's Rangers*, p.153

[427] OR 33, p. 124

[428] Scott, *Partisan Life*, p. 209; Baird, *Journals*, p. 264/15fn, 190

[429] OR 33, pp. 259-260

[430] Baird, *Journals*, pp. 184, 189

[431] OR 33, p. 269; Williamson, *Mosby's Rangers*, pp.155-156

[432] Baird, *Journals*, pp. 191-192

[433] OR 33, pp. 1252-1253

[434] Ibid., pp. 315-316; Williamson, *Mosby's Rangers*, pp. 160-161

15. Springtime in the Shenandoah

[435] Fox, *Regimental Losses*, pp. 540, 552

[436] Driver, *1st Virginia*, p. 82-84; Freeman, *Lee's Lieutenants*, Vol. III, p. 424

[437] Williamson, *Mosby's Rangers*, pp. 162; Scott, *Partisan Life*, pp. 222-223 (Scott's account has this and the succeeding operations in he Valley involving Sam Chapman and Dolly Richards as taking place after the Guard Hill fight; however, Scott has the Guard Hill fight as being on May 8 when it was actually on May 21.Williamson's account has it taking place before the Guard Hill fight and he has the Guard Hill fight taking place on the correct date of May 21. For the dates, Williamson's account will be used.. Scott's account will be used, along with Williamson's, for the events that took place).

[438] Scott, *Partisan Life*, pp. 223-224

[439] Mosby, *Memories*, p. 356

[440] Scott, *Partisan Life*, pp. 224-225; Williamson, *Mosby's Rangers*, pp. 167

[441] Scott, *Partisan Life*, pp. 213-214

[442] Williamson, *Mosby's Rangers*, p. 168-169

[443] Scott, Partisan Life, pp. 216-217

[444] Alexander, *Mosby's Men*, pp. 59-60; Williamson, *Mosby's Rangers*, p.169

[445] Ibid., p. 61; Ibid., pp. 169-170

[446] OR 37: p. 572; Alexander, Mosby's *Men*, pp. 61-62 (Mosby, in an interview with the *Baltimore Star*, speaks of this occasion when talking about Sam Chapman. He remembered that Chapman fired and badly wounded Captain Auer when he rode up. (See *Scrapbooks of John S. Mosby*) No other accounts record this. The interview took place several years after the war and Mosby may of had this incident confused with the fight at Blakeley Grove School House, in which Auer had his horse shot from under him. (See Scott, *Partisan Life*, pp. 218-219)

16. Missing the Trains

[447] Judge, *Season of Fire*, pp. 6, 8, 12-13

[448] Ibid., pp. 10, 22

[449] Ibid., p. 33

[450] Ibid., pp. 51, 56-57

[451] Miller, Jr., *Lincoln's Abolitionist General*, pp. 5, 52

[452] Frye, *12th Virginia Cavalry*, p. 130; Jones, *Gray Ghosts*, p. 47, 114

[453] Scott, *Partisan Life*, p. 226; Williamson, *Mosby's Rangers*, p.171

[454] Judge, *Season of Fire*, pp. 65-66; OR 37:1, p. 161

[455] Williamson, *Mosby's Rangers*, pp. 172-173

[456] Osborne, *Jubal*, p. 250, Judge, *Season of Fire*, pp. 65-66

[457] Patchan, *The Forgotten Fury*, p. 54, 61

[458] OR 37:1, p. 2; Scott, *Partisan*, pp. 226-227; Williamson, *Mosby's Rangers*, pp. 174-175; Keen and Mewborn, *43rd Battalion*, pp. 129-130 (This account is based on both Williamson and Scott, as well as the Official Records; however, the accounts differ, not only in the date and place of the fight, but in which of the Chapmans was involved and to what extent. Mosby's report of 9-11-64 has the incident occurring "about May 20", however it is believed to have occurred nearer to the end of the month)

[459] Scott, *Partisan Life*, p. 230

[460] Judge, *Season of Fire*, p. 67

[461] OR 37:1, p.593; Keen and Mewborn, *43rd Battalion*, pp. 131, 295-296

[462] Jones, *Ranger Mosby*, p. 154; Scott, *Partisan Life*, pp. 230-232

[463] Williamson, *Mosby's Rangers*, p. 175

[464] Ibid., p. 177; OR 37:1, p. 2, 167

[465] Williamson, *Mosby's Rangers*, p.182; Scott, *Partisan Life*, pp.236; OR 37:1, p. 2, 358

[466] OR 37:1, pp. 692-695, 358

[467] Scott, *Partisan Life*, p. 238

[468] Baird, *Journals*, p. 200

17. A Chance Lost

[469] OR 37:1, p. 4; Williamson, *Mosby's Rangers*, pp. 184-185; Scott, *Partisan Life*, pp. 239

[470] Ibid., p. 4; Ibid., pp. 185-186; Ibid., pp.241-243

[471] Ibid., p. 4; Ibid., pp. 187; Ibid., pp. 244-245; Munson, *Mosby Guerrilla*, p. 94

[472] Williamson, *Mosby's Rangers*, pp. 187-188; Scott, *Partisan Life*, pp. 247-248, Munson, *A Mosby Guerrilla*, pp. 96-98

[473] Humphreys, *Field, Camp, Hospital, and Prison*, p. 96

[474] Ibid., pp. 97-98

[475] Williamson, *Mosby's Rangers*, pp. 188; Scott, *Partisan Life*, pp. 248; Munson, *A Mosby Guerrilla*, pp. 97-98

[476] Alexander. *Mosby's Men*, p. 95

[477] OR 37:1. pp. 358-360

[478] OR 37:1, p. 4; Williamson, *Mosby's Rangers*, pp. 189-191; Keen and Mewborn, *43rd Battalion*. p. 146

[479] Mewborn Collection, Letter from John Mosby to William (Willie) A. Chapman, January 22, 1911

18. Wedding Bells and Captain's Bars

[480] Keen and Mewborn, *43rd Battalion*, p. 137; Scott, *Partisan Life*, pp. 491-492

[481] Scott, *Partisan Life*, p. 491-492

[482] Ibid.; Judge, *Season of Fire, p. 151

[483] Williamson, *Mosby's Rangers*, p. 192; Judge, *Season of Fire*, pp. 237-238

[484] Osborne, *Jubal*, p. 258. On the night of June 17, Early had an empty train run up and down the tracks, in and out of the Lynchburg depot, punctuating the sounds of locomotives and cars clanging and thundering over the switches with cheers, band music, and sounds of rejoicing. Hunter believed that Early was being reinforced, with the troops arriving by train throughout the night..

[485] Gordon, *Reminiscences*, p. 301

[486] OR 37:2, p 329

[487] Wert, *Mosby's Rangers*, p. 181; Williamson, *Mosby's Rangers*, p. 192

[488] OR 37:1, p. 4; Williamson, *Mosby's Rangers*, p. 192

[489] Williamson, *Mosby's Rangers*, pp. 193-194; Bonnell, Jr., *Sabres*, pp.118-119

[490] Baird, *Journals*, pp.202, 272-273

[491] OR 37:1, p.322

[492] OR 37:1, p. 322; Williamson, *Mosby's Rangers*, p. 194

[493] Osborne, *Jubal*, p. 300

[494] OR 37:2, p. 374-375

[495] Williamson, *Mosby's Rangers*, pp. 194-196; Scott, *Partisan Life*, p. 255; Judge, *Season of Fire*, pp. 208, 261

[496] Scott, *Partisan Life*, p.256 - 258

[497] Wert, *Mosby's Rangers*, p. 119; USBC, Fauquier County, Virginia, 1860

[498] *Old Homes and Families of Fauquier County*, p. 33; Gott, *High in Old Virginia's Piedmont*, pp. 18, 44-45, 166, 189

[499] OR, 29:2, , p. 585.(Some sources refer to Mrs. Murray as being Jane Welch O'Bannon Murray, wife of James E. Murray, then residing in the Hall house on Lot 36. However, Jane O'Bannnon had purchased a house on Lot 37, across the side street from Lot 36, in 1839, prior to her marriage to James Murray. After the death of her husband, Presley O'Bannon, she married Murray and they sold the property to her brother, Sylvester Welch, in 1846. During the war, the Lot 37 property – as well as the Lot 36 property – was owned by Decatur Hall. The Lot 37 property was known as "Liberty Green." (See Gott, p. 190) It is not known if Jane Murray lived in the Lot 37 house following her sale of it to her brother in 1846. Further evidence that William and Catherine Murray lived in the Lot 36 house is found in *Old Virginia Homes* (p. 33) which states "Mrs. Murray lived in the house opposite the present (1937) Marshall National Bank. Her daughter, Miss Beck, married Captain Sam Chapman, one of Mosby's bravest soldiers." (p. 33) The Marshall National Bank occupies Lot 17, directly across Main Street from Lot 36.

[500] Keen and Mewborn, *43rd Battalion*, pp. 303, 304, 312 (roster)

[501] Author's description of Rebecca Elgin derived from photographs in Alleghany Highlands Genealogical Society and in the Stephenson Collection.

[502] Luray Baptish Church, *Minutes*

[503] Mosby, *Reminiscences*, p. 108; Williamson, *Mosby's Rangers*, p. 197; NA, CSR, *43rd* Bn.

19. Bluecoats and Yellow Jackets

[504] Keen and Mewborn, *43rd Battalion*, pp 149, 351

[505] Ibid., pp.149, 320; Musselman, *The Caroline Light, Parker and Stafford Light Virginia Artillery*, p. 80;

Williamson, *Mosby's Rangers*, p. 486

[506] OR 37:1, p.5

[507] Williamson, *Mosby's Rangers*, p 200 f/t.

[508] Alexander, *Mosby's Men*, pp. 100-101

[509] Williamson, *Mosby's Rangers*, pp. 197-202

[510] Ibid., p. 202

[511] Ibid., p. 204

[512] Ibid., p. 204 f/n

[513] OR 43:1, p. 719, 723

[514] Ibid., p. 633

[515] Osborne, *Jubal*, pp. 316-318

[516] Ibid., pp.319-320

[517] Mosby, *Memoirs*, p. 290; Keen and Mewborn, *43rd Battalion*, p. 364 (Russell took Mosby's middle name, Singleton, as his own after the war)

[518] Munson, *Mosby Guerrilla*, p. 102; Williamson, *Mosby's Rangers*, pp. 207-208; Mosby, *Memoirs*, p. 290

[519] Mosby, *Memoirs*, p. 290; Munson, *Mosby Guerrilla*, pp. 102-103; *New York World*, Mosby interview, March 31, 1895

[520] OR 43:1, pp.484, 621, 629; Mosby, *Memoirs*, pp. 290-291

[521] OR 43:1, p. 634; *New York World*, Mosby interview, March 31, 1895; Scott, *Partisan Life*, p. 276 (It is not clear which company Mosby kept in reserve with the Artillery Company – Glascock's or Sam Chapman's. Scott and Williamson, for example, indicate Captain Glascock's, while Mosby, in his Memoirs and at least one post-war interview says Sam Chapman's company was kept in reserve. In another interview, he says Glascock. In his report dated 9-11-64, less than 30 days after the raid, he says Sam Chapman's company was kept in reserve. Therefore, this is the version used here)

[522] *New York World*, Mosby interview, March 31, 1895; Mosby, *Memoirs*, pp. 291, 367

[523] OR 43:1, p. 629

[524] Mosby, *Memoirs*, p. 367; Williamson, *Mosby's Rangers*, p. 209

[525] Ibid., p. 356

[526] OR 43:1, p.628; *New York World*, Mosby interview, March 31, 1895; Scott, *Partisan Life*, p. 277

[527] Scott, *Partisan Life*, p. 277

[528] Ibid., p. 278; Mosby, *Memoirs*, p. 366; *New York World*, Mosby interview, March 31, 1895

[529] Scott. *Partisan Life*, p. 277

[530] Ibid., p. 278, OR 43:1, p. 485.

[531] OR 43:1, p. 612, 619

[532] Ibid., p. 279; OR 43:1, p. 484

[533] UVAL, *Scrapbooks of John S. Mosby*

[534] OR 43:1, p. 826

[535] Baird, *Journals*, pp. 204-205

20. "No Quarter! No Quarter!"

[536] OR 43:1, p. 811

[537] Ibid.

[538] Ibid., p. 43

[539] Williamson, *Mosby's Rangers*, pp. 211 f/n, 212 f/n

[540] Munson, *Mosby Guerrilla*, pp. 113-114

[541] OR 43:1, p. 634; Keen and Mewborn, *43rd Battalion*, p. 160

[542] Williamson, *Mosby's Rangers*, p. 212 f/n

[543] Ibid.

[544] OR 43:1, p. 831

[545] Ibid., p. 898

[546] Scott, *Partisan Life*, pp. 279, 280;

[547] *Clarke County Historical Association, p. 46*

[548] Hildebrand, *A Mennonite Journal, 1862-1865*, pp. ix, x, 51

[549] The house referred to was very possibly the Sowers residence; Chapman, in an account written after the war and appearing in the *Proceedings of the Clarke County Historical Association*, said "The picket was killed near Mrs. Sowers' house in the early part of the night of August 19, 1864."

[550] Jones, *Gray Ghosts*, p. 280-281

[551] Scott, *Partisan Life*, pp. 281; Williamson, *Mosby's Rangers*, p. 215; *Clarke County Historical Association*, p. 59

[552] Jones, *Gray Ghosts*, p. 281; Scott, *Partisan Life*, p. 280

[553] Williamson, *Mosby's Rangers*, p. 215f/n (as related in the *New York Times*, August 25, 1864)

[554] Williamson, *Mosby's Rangers*, pp. 214-215; Jones, *Gray Ghosts*, p. 281; *Confederate Veteran*, Vol. XII, p. 472

[555] Jones, *Gray Ghosts*, p. 281

[556] OR 43:1, p. 634

21. The High Cost of Fame

[557] Scott, *Partisan Life*, pp. 282-284

[558] Ibid., p. 286; Munson, *Mosby Guerrilla*, pp.201-202

[559] Williamson, *Mosby's Rangers*, pp.218-219

[560] OR 43:1, p. 898

[561] Scott, *Partisan life*, p. 364; Munson, *Mosby Guerrilla*, pp. 115-116

[562] Time-Life Books, *Echoes of Glory-Arms and Equipment of the Union*, pp. 27, 49

[563] Bilby, Joseph G., *Civil War Firearms*, p. 198

[564] Alexander, *Mosby's Men*, p. 170

[565] OR 43:1, p. 634; Williamson, *Mosby's Rangers*, 223-225; Scott, *Partisan Life*, pp. 286-288; Crawford, *Mosby and His Men*, pp. 255-257; Alexander, *Mosby's Men*, p. 170

[566] OR 43:1, p. 616; Williamson, *Mosby's Rangers*, pp. 226-228

[567] Scott, *Partisan Life*, pp. 291-292

[568] OR 43:1, p. 634-635

[569] Scott, *Partisan Life*, p.305; Williamson, *Ranger Mosby*, p. 239; Keen and Mewborn, *43rd Battalion*, p.386

22. An Uncivil War

[570] OR 43:1, p. 90; Williamson, *Mosby's Rangers*, pp. 232-233

[571] OR 43: 1, pp. 90, 617

[572] OR 43: 1, pp. 112, 617; Williamson, *Mosby's Rangers*, p. 233; Scott, *Partisan Life*, p.304, 320; Mosby, *Memoirs*, p.298

[573] OR 43:1, p. 543; Ibid., p. 234

[574] OR 43:1, pp.. 542-543; Williamson, *Mosby's Rangers*, pp. 235-236

[575] OR 43:1, p. 177-178; Ibid., pp. 237-238; Scott, *Partisan Life*, pp. 315-317

[576] OR 43:1, p. 47; Osborne, *Jubal*, pp. 341-344

[577] OR 43:1, p. 442

[578] Lewis Collection, From an account by Sam Chapman, August 29, 1909. Other accounts put the number of Chapman's men at anywhere from 80 to 120. Chapman also says he was in command of two companies, "my own, Company E and that of Captain Walker Franklin (sic), Company F." However, it is known that several of the Rangers making up the command were not members of either E or F Companies, but of other companies in Mosby's Battalion. This dispersing of men was not unusual when the battalion was broken up into smaller groups for operations.

[579] Ibid.

[580] Ibid., OR 43:1, p. 442

[581] Lewis Collection, From an account by Sam Chapman; Hale, *Four Valiant Years*, p. 429

[582] Lewis Collection, From an account by Sam Chapman; Scott, *Partisan Life*, pp. 317-318; SHSP, *A Horror of the War*, Vol. 25, pp. 239-240; *Confederate Veteran, Mosby and his Men – The Seven Martyrs* , Vol. VII, p. 510

[583] Williamson's and Scott's accounts say that Chapman told Lt. Harry Hatcher to take the men out, but Chapman's personal account states he ordered Fount Beattie to do it. It is reasonable to assume that Beattie would be the one since he was Chapman's lieutenant, while Hatcher was in another company.

[584] Lewis Collection, From an account by Sam Chapman; Williamson, *Mosby's Rangers*, pp. 240-241; 241 f/n (from a letter to Captain Frankland from Tom Moss)

[585] Lewis Collection, From an account by Sam Chapman; Hale, *Four Valiant Years*, p. 431

[586] Williamson, *Mosby's Rangers*, pp. 241-242 f/n (from a letter to Captain Frankland from Tom Moss); Scott, *Partisan Life*, pp. 318-319

[587] SHSP, *Hanging of Mosby's Men*, Vol. 24, p. 109 (from article by R. C. Brock in the Warrenton *Virginian* newspaper, February, 1896); Williamson, *Mosby's Rangers*, p. 240

[588] Lewis Collection, From an account by Sam Chapman. Sam Chapman's version of the events is the only known one by a Confederate participant that asserts that Lt. McMaster may very well have been trying to surrender and this version has heretofore either been ignored or is largely unknown. It was contained in a memorial address Chapman made at Front Royal in 1909. The address, as far as can be determined, was not reprinted in any of the newspapers of the day, which may account for its anonymity.

[589] Williamson, *Mosby's Rangers*, p. 240; Scott, *Partisan Life*, p. 319

[590] Fagan, *Custer and His Times, Book Three*, p. 26

[591] SHSP., *The Monument to Mosby's Men*, Vol. 27, pp. 273-274

[592] Lewis Collection, from an account by Sam Chapman

[593] SHSP. *The Monument to Mosby's Men*, pp. 319-320; UVAL, *Scrapbooks of John S. Mosby; Confederate Veteran, Mosby and His Men*, Vol. VII, p. 510

[594] Williamson, *Mosby's Rangers*, p. 242 f/n (from a letter to Captain Frankland from Tom Moss)

[595] Ibid.

[596] Ashby, *The Valley Campaigns*, p. 293; Hale, *Four Valiant Years*, p. 429, 431

[597] Ibid.; Ibid., 431, 433; SHSP, *Hanging of Mosby's Men.* Vol. 25, p. 240

[598] Ibid., 293-294; Ibid., 433; Ibid.

[599] Baird, *Journals,* p. 206

[600] SHSP, *A Horror of the War,* Vol. 25, p. 240

[601] Fagan, *Custer and His Times, Book Three,* p. 42-43

[602] Wallace, *A Few Memories of a Long Life,* p. 50

[603] Fagan, *Custer and His Times, Book Three,* pp. 40-41

[604] Ibid., p. 40

[605] OR 43:1, p. 442

[606] Ibid., p. 428

[607] Ibid., p. 491

[608] Emerson, *Life and Letters of Charles Russell Lowell,* p. 353

23. Following the Tracks

[609] Mitchell, *Letters,* p. 98

[610] Ibid.

[611] Williamson, *Mosby's Rangers,* p. 241

[612] OR 43:1. p. 618; Baird, *Journals,* p. 207

[613] Mitchell, *Letters,* p. 98-99

[614] Ibid., Scott, *Partisan Life,* p. 321

[615] OR 43:1, p. 29-30; Freeman, *Lee's Lieutenants,* Vol. 3, p. 596

[616] OR 43:2, p. 618; Williamson, *Mosby's Rangers,* p. 247, 250

[617] OR 43:1, p. 29

[618] OR 43:1, pp. 30-31

[619] Hale, *Four Valiant Years,* p. 434

[620] OR 43:2 pp. 266, 272-273

[621] Williamson, *Mosby" Rangers,* p. 251; Keen and Mewborn, *43rd Battalion,* p.371

[622] OR 43:2, pp.298-300

[623] Scott, *Partisan Life*, p. 324

[624] Ibid., p. 326; Williamson, *Mosby's Rangers*, pp. 253-254; Baird, *Journals*, p. 207

[625] OR 43:2, pp .334-335; Williamson, *Mosby's Rangers*, p. 257

[626] Alexander, *Mosby's Men*, pp. 104-105; Williamson, *Mosby's Rangers*, p. 258

[627] OR 43:1, p. 32; Williamson, *Mosby's Rangers*, p. 259

[628] OR 43:2, p. 348

[629] OR 43:1, p. 633

[630] OR 43:2, pp. 368-369; Scott, *Partisan Life*, pp. 335, 338,339; Williamson. *Mosby's Rangers*, pp. 261-263

[631] UVAL, *Scrapbooks of John S. Mosby* (From an account by Mosby in *The Illustrated American*, June 27, 1896

[632] OR 43:2, pp. 369, 370, 371; Williamson, *Mosby's Rangers*, pp. 264-265; Scott, *Partisan Life*, pp. 340-341

[633] OR 43:2, pp. 371, 372; Scott, *Partisan Life*, pp. 341-342

[634] OR 43:1, p. 618; Williamson, *Mosby's Rangers*, p. 266-267; Keen and Mewborn, *43rd Battalion*, p. 200

[635] OR 43:1, p. 635; Williamson, *Mosby's Rangers*, p. 267

24. "Measure for Measure"

[636] OR 43:1, p. 509

[637] A colporteur was a traveling distributor of religious tracts, Bibles, etc., and was a familiar sight within the armies during the war.

[638] *Reunion Journal*, Volume 1, Number 4, August 9, 1970 There are several accounts of the events surrounding Willis' execution. The account related here has been taken from two supposedly eyewitness' recollections.

[639] Williamson, *Mosby's Rangers*, pp. 289-290; SHSP, *Retaliation*, Vol. 27, p.320-321

[640] OR 43:2, pp. 414- 415; Williamson, *Mosby's Rangers*, p 271

[641] Scott, *Partisan Life*, pp. 348-349

[642] OR 43:1, p.186; 43:2, p. 350, 374; Scott, *Partisan Life*, pp. 350-351; Williamson, *Mosby's Rangers*, pp. 280-282

[643] OR 43:2, p. 461; Williamson, *Mosby's Rangers*, p. 283

[644] OR 43:1, p. 35; Scott, *Partisan Life*, p. 350

[645] OR 43:1. p. 465,466

[646] OR 43:2, p. 487; Scott, *Partisan Life*, p. 352; Williamson, *Mosby's Rangers*, p. 284

[647] Scott, *Partisan Life*, pp. 353-354; VHS, Frederick F. Bowen Papers

[648] Williamson, *Mosby's Rangers*. p. 285; Munson, *Mosby Guerrilla*, p. 169; Alexander, *Mosby's Men*, pp. 132-136

[649] Williamson, *Mosby's Rangers*, p. 285; Scott, *Partisan Life*, p. 354; Keen and Mewborn, *43rd Battalion*, p. 207

[650] Wiliamson, *Mosby's Rangers*, p. 286; Crawford, *Mosby and His Men*, p. 284

[651] VHS, Frederick F. Bowen Papers

[652] OR 43:2, p. 495

[653] OR 43:2, p. 910, 918

[654] Williamson, *Mosby's Rangers*, pp. 288-293; Scott, *Partisan Life*, pp. 356-360

[655] Williamson, *Mosby's Rangers*, p. 294

[656] OR 43:2, p. 921

[657] Kincheloe Collection, Letter from John Mosby to Sam Chapman, August 26, 1899

[658] *Richmond Times*, September 3, 1899; SHSP, *Retaliation*, Vol. 27

25. "A Terrible Retribution"

[659] OR 43:2, pp. 565, 918

[660] NA, Adjutant and Inspector General's Office, C. S. A., (Microfilm M-935, Roll 9)

[661] Ibid.; OR 43:2, p 926

[662] Williamson, *Mosby's Rangers*, p 300; Scott, *Partisan Life*, p. 363

[663] Mosby, *Memoirs*, p. 319; Munson, *Mosby Guerrilla*, pp. 118, 121-122; Scott, *Partisan Life*, p. 367

[664] Ibid., p. 120-121; Ibid., pp. 367-371; Williamson, *Mosby's Rangers*, pp. 304-305

[665] OR 43:2, p. 654; Williamson, *Mosby's Rangers*, pp. 305-306

[666] Alexander, *Mosby's Men*, pp. 125-126; Munson, *Mosby Guerrilla*, pp. 123

[667] Williamson, *Mosby's Rangers*, pp. 311-312; Scott, *Partisan Life*, pp. 374-375

[668] OR 43:1, pp.991-992; Williamson, *Mosby's Rangers*, pp. 313=314

[669] OR 43:2, p. 671-672

[670] OR 43:2, p. 679

[671] Williamson, *Mosby's Rangers*, pp. 317-321; Scott, *Partisan Life*, p.376

[672] OR 43:1, pp. 672, 730

[673] Humphreys, *Field, Camp, Hospital and Prison in the Civil War, 1863-1865,* p. 192

26. A Command Divided

[674] Williamson, *Mosby's Rangers,* pp. 322-323

[675] Freeman, *R.E. Lee,* Vol. lll, p. 525

[676] OR 43:2, p. 937

[677] Mitchell, *Letters,* pp.125, 235; Wallace, Jr., *Guide,* p. 71

[678] OR 43:2, p. 752

[679] Ibid., pp. 754, 755, 771

[680] Crawford, *Mosby and His Men,* p. 315

[681] Scott, *Partisan Life,* p. 381; Williamson, *Mosby's Rangers,* p 325 (Scott has Captain Richards taking the second group of Rangers, not Lieutenant Russell, but has Russell making the initial assault with Richards following up. Williamson does not mention Richards at all)

[682] Ibid, p. 382; Ibid., pp. 325-326

[683] OR 43:2, p. 798 (Williamson places the Union losses at thirty killed and wounded and sixty-eight taken prisoner)

[684] Scott, *Partisan Life,* pp. 386-387; Mosby, *Memoirs,* pp. 335-336

[685] Ibid, p. 387; Ibid., p. 336; OR 43:2, p. 843

[686] Mosby, *Memoirs,* pp. 337-338

[687] Ibid; OR 43:2, p. 843

[688] Ibid.

[689] Mosby, *Memoirs,* pp. 342, 344, 345; Scott, *Partisan Life,* p. 389; Keen and Mewborn, *43rd Battalion,* pp. 315, 316, 317

[690] Brown Collection, Letter from John Mosby to Sam Chapman, September 6, 1894

[691] OR 43:2, pp. 832, 838, 845; Scott, *Partisan Life,* p. 389

[692] OR 43:2, pp. 831, 845; Mosby, *Memoirs,* pp. 342, 343, 344

[693] Scott, *Partisan Life,* pp. 389, 390; Williamson, *Mosby's Rangers,* pp. 336-337; f/n p. 337

[694] Mosby, *Memoirs*, p. 354

[695] Russell Collection, Letter from William H. Chapman to William A. Chapman, January 3, 1865

[696] Dowdy, *The Virginia Dynasties*, pp. 7, 128, Survey Map (inside covers)

[697] Russell Collection, William Chapman's *Account of Operations of a Portion of Mosby's Command in Northern Neck of Virginia in 1865*; Scott, *Partisan Life*, p. 390

[698] Russell Collection, *Account of Operations in Northern Neck*; Letter from Wiliam H. Chapman to his wife, January 9, 1865; Letter from Josie Chapman to her husband, W. H. Chapman, January 12, 1865 (There is no certainty as to the identity of Thompson and Talaiferro. There was a Lt. Edward "Ned" Thomson (note difference in spellling) in Company H, but he was not promoted to that rank until 4-5-65. There was no Lt. Talaiferro known to be in the 43rd; there was a Pvt. John K. Taliaferro in Company D. (note difference in spelling of last name). The Lt. Talaiferro is mentioned in both William's and Josie's letters, with all indications that he was returning to Fauquier County soon after the Richmond trip; he could very possibly have belonged to another command)

[699] Andrews, *Scraps of Paper*, p. 92; Davis, *The Long Surrender*, pp. 21, 223

[700] Russell Collection, William H. Chapman to his wife, January 9, 1865 (The Chapman "relative" may have been Alfred Chapman who was a Disbursing Clerk in the War Department as late as 10-8-1864 (See OR, Series IV:3, p. 771)

[701] Ibid; Russell Collection, William H. Chapman to William A. Chapman, January 3, 1865

[702] Russell Collection, *Account of Operations in Northern Neck*

[703] Evans and Moyer, *Mosby Vignettes*, Vol. III, Chapter 2, p. 17

[704] Russell Collection, *Account of Operations in Northern Neck*, Freeman, *Lee's Lieutenants*, Vol. III, p. 415 (map); U. S. Government, *Atlas*, Plate XXXIII –1

[705] OR 40:2, p. 704,705

[706] OR 42:3, p. 175; Faust, *Encyclopedia*, p. 98

[707] OR 40.2, p. 684, 689, 706: OR 40:3, p. 744; OR 43:1, p. 991

[708] Brown Collection, Mosby to Sam Chapman, September 6, 1894

[709] Ibid.

[710] Russell Collection, *Account of Operations in Northern Neck.*

[711] Faust, *Encyclopedia*, p. 588

[712] Baird, *Journals*, p. 213

[713] Russell Collection, Letter from William H. Chapman to his wife, January 28, 1865

[714] OR 46:2, pp. 649, 662

[715] Ibid;, p. 665

[716] OR 46:1. pp. 458, 459; Scott, *Partisan Life*, p.466-468; Russell Collection, *Account of Operations in the Northern Neck*

[717] OR 46:2, pp. 1282, 1283

[718] Ibid., p.832

[719] Russell Collection, *Account of Operations in the Northern Neck*

[720] Keen and Mewborn, *43rd Battalion*, p. 356 (roster)

[721] OR 46:1, pp. 542, 543, 544

[722] OR 46:2., p. 892

[723] Ibid., p. 891

[724] OR 46:1, p. 549; U. S. Government, *Atlas*, Plate CXXXVII; Russell Collection, *Account of Operations in Northern Neck*

[725] Russell Collection, *Account of Operations in Northern Neck*

[726] Ibid.; OR 46:1, p. 342

[727] OR 46:1. p. 549; Russell Collection, *Account of Operations in Northern Neck*

[728] Russell Collection, *Account of Operations in the Northern Neck*

[729] Ibid.

[730] USBC, Middlesex County, Virginia, 1860; VBHS, *Minutes* of Rappahannock Baptist Association

[731] Russell Collection, *Account of Operations in the Northern Neck*

[732] OR 46:1, p. 549

[733] Ibid.; p. 550; OR 46:2, p. 954

[734] Russell Collection, *Account of Operations in the Northern Neck*

[735] Cook, *One Hundred and One Famous Poems*, p. 7.

27. "Collect Your Command"

[736] OR 46:3, p. 108; Scott, *Partisan Life*, pp. 469, 480, 482; Keen and Mewborn, *43rd Battalion*, p. 346 (roster)

[737] OR 46:3, p. 16, 17, 25, 618, 681

[738] Ibid., p. 682

[739] Ibid.

[740] OR 46:2, p. 666; Mosby, *Memoirs*, p. 354 (extract from diary of Mosby's mother)

[741] OR: 46:1, pp. 463-467; Scott, *Partisan Life*, pp. 449, 451; Williamson, *Mosby's Rangers*, p. 349

[742] OR 46:2, pp. 898, 911; 46:1, p. 552

[743] Scott, *Partisan Life*, pp. 457, 460-461; Williamson, *Mosby's Rangers*, pp. 355-358, 360, 361-362

[744] Baird, *Journals*, p. 218

[745] OR 46:3, p. 1359

[746] OR 46:1, p. 1309; 46:3, p. 617; Williamson, *Mosby's Rangers*, pp. 363-364; Scott, *Partisan Life*, pp. 463-464 (Scott places the Federal losses at two killed, four wounded, sixty-five taken prisoner, and eighty-one horses captured; Williamson gives five or six killed and wounded, forty-three taken prisoner and over seventy horses captured. One Federal report states that forty men were taken prisoner while another report says twenty-five)

[747] OR 46:3, p. 617; Scott, *Partisan Life*, p. 464

[748] OR 46:1, p. 309; Williamson, *Mosby's Rangers*, pp. 367-369; Munson, *Mosby Guerrilla*, pp. 256-258, 263; U. S. Government, *Atlas*, Plate LXXIV-1

[749] OR: 46:3, p. 700, 701

[750] Duke University, John S. Russell Papers, Mosby to Russell letter, August 21, 1904

[751] Russell Collection, *Account of Operations in Northern Neck*   .

[752] OR 46:3, p. 753

28. "Farewell"

[753] Munson, *Mosby Guerrilla*, p. 266; Williamson, *Mosby's Rangers*, pp. 377, 384

[754] OR 46:3, pp. 830, 841

[755] Ibid., pp. 799-800

[756] Ibid., p. 839; Williamson, *Mosby's Rangers*, p. 385

[757] OR 46:3, p. 839.

[758] Williamson, *Mosby's Rangers*, p. 393

[759] Ibid.; Scott, *Partisan Life*, p. 476; Jones, *Ranger Mosby*, p. 269; Keen and Mewborn, *43rd Battalion*, p. 271

[760] Munson, *Mosby Guerrilla*, p. 269

[761] Jones, *Ranger Mosby*, p. 270

[762] Williamson, *Mosby's Rangers*, p. 393; Munson, *Partisan Guerrilla*, p. 270

[763] Scott, *Partisan Life*, p. 476; Williamson, *Mosby's Rangers*, p. 393

[764] Russell Collection; This copy of Mosby's address bears the notation "Copied from the original, October 21, 1935 S. F. Chapman" (This S. F. Chapman was the son of William and namesake of his uncle)

[765] Williamson, *Mosby's Rangers*, p. 395; Scott, *Partisan Life*, p. 477; Munson, *Mosby Guerrilla*, p. 271

[766] Williamson, *Mosby's Rangers*, p. 395

[767] Mitchell, *Letters*, p. 63

[768] Williamson, *Mosby's Rangers*, pp. 395-396; OR 46:3, p. 897

[769] NA, CSR, 43rd Bn.

[770] Ibid.

29. A Qualified Citizen

[771] LOV, *Minutes* of Main Street Baptist Church, Luray

[772] NA, CSR, 43rd Bn.

[773] OR 46:3, pp. 868, 869

[774] NA, CSR, 43rd Bn.

[775] LOV, Fauquier County Records of Births (Cemetery records and tombstone inscription, Cedar Hill Cemetery, Covington, have Ella Chapman's date of birth as 7-28-1866. The official birth record in Fauquier County is the accepted one here)

[776] Gott Collection, *Minutes* of Potomac Baptist Association

[777] LOV, *Minutes* of Main Street Baptist Church, Luray

[778] Fauquier County Circuit Court Deed Book, No. 62, Page 191-192

[779] Weaver, *The History of Public Education in Fauquier County*

[780] Gott Collection, *Minutes* of Potomac Baptist Association

[781] Ibid.

[782] LOV, *Minutes* of Main Street Baptist Church. Luray

[783] Gott Collection, *Minutes* of Potomac Baptist Association

[784] *Alexandria Gazette*, June 9, 1873; Siepel, *Rebel*, pp. 182-183

[785] *Washington Times*, April 23, 1894

[786] Woodlawn Baptist Church, *A Century of Growth*, 1869-1969; VBHS, Minister's Biographical Sheet; *Minutes of* Baptist General Association of Virginia, 1875 (In Chapman's Biographical Sheet he gives the date of his ordination as June 1875, while the *Minutes* of the Association show October 1875)

[787] *Religious Herald*, September 30, 1875, March 23, 1876

[788] USBC, Alexandria City, 1880

[789] NA, Official Register of the United States for 1877, 1881; Division of Railway Mail Services Rosters, 1855-1897

30. "A Land of Hills and Valleys"

[790] UVAL, *Scrapbooks of John S. Mosby*, from an article in the *Baltimore Star*, date unknown (The "Berry's Mill" referred to by Mosby may actually have been Berry's Ferry)

[791] *Holy Bible*, King James Version, Deuteronomy, Chp. 11, Vs. 11, 12

[792] Covington Baptist Church *Minutes*; VBHS, Report of the General Baptist Association of Virginia for the period May 31, 1882 to May 31, 1883; Alleghany County Circuit Court Deed Book 7, pp. 303, 304

[793] *The Alleghany Tribune*, May 19, 1882

[794] Ibid.

[795] Ibid.

[796] Ibid., June 16, 1882

[797] *Virginian Review*, May 2, 1996

[798] Alleghany County Circuit Court Deed Book 9, pp. 100, 101

[799] Clifton Forge Baptist Church, *The Road We Came*

[800] *The Alleghany Tribune*

[801] Clifton Forge Baptist Church, undated letter (c. 1905) in Church's records from Mrs. Robert F. Murray, Excelsior, WV; "Mollie" was Mrs. Robert Palmer Murray who lived in South Clifton.

[802] Morton, *A Centennial History of Alleghany County*, p. 75

[803] Ibid., p. 74, 75; *Virginian Review*, May 2, 1996

[804] Covington Baptist Church, *Minutes*

[805] Clifton Forge Baptist Church, *Minutes*; *The Road We Came*, pp. 10-11

[806] Ibid.; Ibid., pp. 14-15

[807] Clifton Forge Baptist Church, *Minutes*

[808] VBHS, Report of the General Baptist Association of Virginia, 1882-83

[809] Alleghany County Circuit Court Deed Book 3, p. 315; *Virginian Review*, May 2, 1996; Corron, *Clifton Forge, Virginia*, p. 16

[810] VBHS, Report of the General Baptist Association for 1882-1883; Everhart, *Of Saints and Sweet Potatoes;* Corron, *Clifton Forge, Virginia*, p. 16

[811] *Virginian Review*, May 2, 1996; Low Moor Presbyterian Church, *Low Moor Presbyterian Church*

[812] Low Moor Presbyterian Church, *Low Moor Presbyterian Church*; Everhart, *Of Saints and Sweet Potatoes*

[813] Alleghany County Circuit Court Deed Book 8, p. 89

[814] Grose, *Alleghany County Heritage*

[815] Alleghany County Circuit Court Deed Book 20, pp. 43, 44

[816] Morton, *Centennial History of Alleghany County*, pp. 94, 95 (Morton says that Rich patch derived its name from a small level field at Upper Rich Patch, located near the crest of the hill and behind a store, where the Rich Patch Turnpike intersected the Low Moor Road. "When the white settlers came it was an Indian old-field and the rankness of the vegetation, caused by the wash from the neighboring heights, gave it the name of the 'rich patch' ")

31. The Good of His Labor

[817] *The Alleghany Tribune*, January 3, 1883

[818] Ibid.

[819] Ibid.

[820] Ibid.

[821] Covington Baptist Church, *Minutes*

[822] VBHS, Report of the General Baptist Association for Virginia, May 31, 1882 to May 31, 1883

[823] Sharon Baptist Church, *Minutes*

[824] VBHS, Report of the General Baptist Association, 1883-84

[825] Clifton Forge Baptist Church, *Minutes*

[826] Ibid.

[827] Covington Baptist Church, *Minutes*

[828] LOV, Personal Property Tax Lists for Alleghany County

[829] Linkenhoker, *A History of Schooling in Alleghany County, Clifton Forge, and Covington, Virginia*, p. 105

[830] Lutheran Theological Seminary Archives

[831] Ibid.; Hudnall Collection

[832] Clifton Forge Baptist Church, *Minutes*

[833] Healing Springs Baptist Church, *Minutes*; Everhart, *Of Saints and Sweet Potatoes*

[834] Ibid.; VBHS, *Minutes* of General Baptist Association of Virginia, 1887-88

[835] Clifton Forge Baptist Church, *Minutes*

[836] Ibid.

[837] *Clifton Forge Baptist, The*, Vol. 1, No. 3, September, 1905

[838] Clifton Forge Baptist Church, *Minutes*, June 17, 1888

[839] Ibid., July, 1888; Clifton Forge Baptist Church, *The Road We Came*, p. 17; Sharon Baptist Church, *Minutes*, October 14, 1888

[840] Clifton Forge Baptist Church, *Minutes*, August 1889; Clifton Forge Baptist Church, *The Road We Came*, p. 19

[841] Ibid., December 1890; Ibid..

[842] *Holy Bible*, King James Version, Ecclesiastes, Chp. 3, V. 13

32. For God, Family, Community

[843] VBHS, Augusta Baptist Association, *Minutes*, 1876-1900; Everhart, *Of Saints and Sweet Potatoes*

[844] *Holy Bible*, King James Version, Philippians, Chp. 3, V.13,14

[845] Healing Springs Baptist Church, *Minutes*

[846] Ibid.

[847] Strickler, *A Short History of Page County; Page News & Courier*, January 16, 1934

[848] John K. Gott conversation, April 29, 1997. Gott later owned the pistol, given to him by John Chapman's daughters.

[849] Mosby, *Reminiscences*, p. 108 (The exact quote by Mosby, when speaking of Sam was; "I doubt whether he prayed that day for the souls of those he sent over the Stygian river.")

[850] VBHS, General Baptist Association of Virginia, *Minutes*

[851] Linkenhoker, *A History of Schooling*, pp. 65, 317, 318

[852] Ibid., pp. 63, 64, 71

[853] City of Covington, Virginia, Records of Cedar Hill Cemetery (Extensive research was unable to uncover any additional information concerning this child. The tombstone, like the records, has no name, only the words "Infant Dau." and the date "May 1889 – August 1889." The monument for the family plot contains the inscription "Infant daughter of Rebecca Chapman.")

[854] VBHS, General Baptist Association of Virginia, *Minutes*

[855] Covington Baptist Church, *Minutes*

856 *Virginian Review*, May 2, 1996; Morton, *A Centennial History of Alleghany County*, p. 75; The *Covington Virginian*, September 23, 1964

857 *Virginian Review*, May 2, 1996

858 Hudnall Collection, Receipts from A. A. McAllister to Rev. S. F. Chapman

859 Alleghany County Circuit Court Deed Book 15, p. 51; No.17, pp. 438, 535; Alleghany County Chancery Court records, *Rebecca E. Chapman vs. Annie S. Wills*, 1894

860 Lewis Collection, Receipt from C. W. Rush & Co. to Mrs. Rebecca E. Chapman and S. F. Chapman, March 21, 1893

861 Alleghany County Circuit Court , *Rebecca E. Chapman vs. Annie S. Wills*, 1894

862 Ibid.

863 Ibid.

864 *Virginian Review*, May 2, 1996

865 Duke University, Mosby Collection, Letter from John Mosby to William Chapman, February 12, 1894

866 Kincheloe Collection, Letter from John Mosby to Sam Chapman, April 14, 1895

867 Ibid., August 18, 1895

868 Brown Collection, Mosby to Sam Chapman, September 6, 1894

869 Duke University, Mosby Collection, John Mosby to William, Chapman., January 19, 1894

870 Brown Collection, Mosby to Sam F. Chapman, November 12, 1894

871 Mewborn Collection, c. 1899

872 Hudnall Collection, Letter from Willie Chapman to Sam Chapman, April 8, 1894

873 Ibid., September 5, 1894

874 *Clifton Forge Review*

875 Ibid., January 5, 1894

876 *Clifton Forge Review*, October 12, 1894

877 *Virginian Review*, May 2, 1996

878 *Clifton Forge Review*, October 12, 1894

879 Ibid., *Washington Times*, January 16, 1895

880 Williamson, *Mosby's Rangers*, p. 496, 497

881 Keen and Mewborn, *43rd Battalion*

[882] Kincheloe Collection, Letter from John Mosby to Sam Chapman, August 18, 1895

[883] *Clifton Forge Review*, October 18, 1895

[884] Keen Collection, Letter from John Mosby to Sam Chapman, December 18, 1895

[885] Covington Baptist Church, *Minutes*

[886] VBHS, Baptist General Association of Virginia, *Minutes*, 1896-97

[887] Linkenhoker, *A History of Schooling*, p. 94

[888] *The Covington Virginian*, June 16, 1959 (reprinted from an 1897 newspaper)

33. Donning the Blue

[889] Stephenson Collection, misc papers of William Chapamn, c. 1919

[890] *National Cyclopedia of American Biography*, p. 218

[891] NA, Record Group 094, *Regimental Returns, 4th U. S. Volunteers, Spanish War*

[892] Miles, Nelson A., *The War with Spain, Part 1, North American Review*, May, 1899, p.516

[893] Alger, *The Spanish-American War*, pp. 17-18

[894] Millis, Walter, *The Martial Spirit*, The Literary Guild of America, 1931; NA, Adjutant-General's Office, U. S., A *Statistical Exhibit of Strength of Volunteer Forces*, 1899; Record Group 094, *Record of Events Cards*

[895] NA, Record Group 094; *Company M, Muster Roll*

[896] NA, Record Group 94, *Record of Events Cards.*

[897] Lewis Collection, S. F. Chapman papers; Hudnall Collection, S. F. Chapman papers

[898] NA, Record Group 094, *Regimental Returns*

[899] Ibid.

[900] NA, Record Group 094, *Company B Muster Roll*

[901] NA, Record Group 094, *Company H Muster Roll*

[902] NA, Record Group 094, *Misc. correspondence*, Adjutant General's Office

[903] Alger, *The Spanish-American War*, p. 452; Reader's Digest, *Family Encyclopedia of American History*, p. 1053

[904] NA, Adjutant-General's Office, U.S., *Statistical Exhibit, Strength of Volunteer Forces*

[905] Hudnall Collection, S.F. Chapman papers

[906] Lewis Collection, Letter from Sam Chapman to 'My Dear Wife," November 20, 1898

[907] NA, Record Group 094, *Regimental Register of Patients*, Adjutant General's office

[908] Attributed to former U. S. diplomat and Secretary of State (1898-1905), John Milton Hay

[909] NA, Record Group 094, *Regimental Returns*

[910] Lewis Collection, Memorial Address, 1909 Reunion of Mosby's Men, Front Royal

34. "The Remnant of My Days"

[911] Alger, *The Spanish-American War*, pp. 344-374; Reader's Digest, *Family Encyclopedia of American History*, p. 865

[912] Daly Collection, Letter from John S. Mosby to Captain Sam Chapman, December 22, 1899

[913] UVAL, *Scrapbooks of John S. Mosby*, unknown newspaper article, c. September, 1899

[914] VBHS, Reports of the Augusta Baptist Association, 1899 and 1900

[915] Lewis Collection, Letter from Sam Chapman to Willie Chapman, July 28, 1896

[916] Paul B. Lacy, Jr., Conversation

[917] Lewis Collection, Sam Chapman to Willie Chapman, July 28, 1896

[918] Ibid., Letter from Elvina (?) B. Garber to Willie Chapman, January 21, 1897

[919] Ibid., Letter from Elgin Chapman to Sam Chapman, February 16, 1897

[920] USBC, Alleghany County, Virginia, 1900

[921] Although not doumented, information from several family members and one unrelated acquaintence of the family indicates Elgin Chapman drowned in Jackson River near downtown Covington, probably a suicide.

[922] Lewis Collection, Letter from Sam Chapman to Willie Chapman, December 6, 1900

[923] Ibid., Letter from Sam Chapman to Willie Chapman, November 20, 1900

[924] Ibid., Sam Chapman to Willie Chapman, December 6, 1900

[925] Ibid.

[926] Ibid., Letter from Sam Chapman to John S. Mosby, December 2, 1900

[927] Ibid., Sam Chapman to Willie Chapman, December 6, 1900

[928] Ibid., Letter from Sam Chapman to John Mosby, December 2, 1900

[929] Howard R. Hammond conversation, December 14, 1998 (from a Covington, Virginia newspaper obit, c. May 11, 1901)

35. "God's Grace and Active Employment"

[930] Lewis Collection, Sam Chapman to Willie Chapman, December 19, 1900

[931] Ibid., Sam Chapman to John Mosby, December 2, 1900

[932] Healing Springs Baptist Church, *Minutes*, February 16, 1901

[933] VBHS, Repor*t* of the Augusta Baptist Association, 1901; Repor*t* of the General Baptist Association of Virginia, 1901-1902

[934] Lewis Collection, Letter from Rev. C. F. James to Rev. S. F. Chapman, August 30, 1901

[935] Hayes, *A History of Averett College*, pp. 24-25

[936] Devine, *8th Virginia Infantry*, p. 69; Hayes, *A History of Averett College*, pp. 49-50

[937] Lewis Collection, Rev. C. F. James to Rev. S. F. Chapman, August 30, 1901

[938] Hayes, *A History of Averett College*, pp. 24-25, 32, 49, 56

[939] Mewborn Collection, Letter from John Mosby to Sam Chapman, June 4, 1900

[940] Siepel, *Rebel*, pp. 256, 262

[941] Healing Springs Baptist Church, *Minutes*

[942] Covington Baptist Church, *Minutes*, September 27, 1903, October 9, 1904, September 27, 1905

[943] Alleghany County Circuit Court, Marriage Records

[944] Siepel, *Rebel*, pp. 273-174

[945] Stephenson Collection

[946] Lewis Collection, Letter from John Mosby to Sam Chapman, January 19, 1905

[947] Cockrell Collection, Letter from John Mosby to Sam Chapman, March 1, 1905

[948] Ibid.

[949] NA, General Records of the Department of Justice, Record Group 60

[950] LOV, Personal Property Tax Lists, City of Staunton, 1901-1910

[951] Wallace, Jr., *17th Virginia Infantry*

[952] Duke University, Mosby Collection, Letter from Hugh McIlhany to John Mosby, January 29, 1910

[953] Wallace, Jr., *17th Virginia Infantry*; Keen & Mewborn, *43rd Battalion*

[954] Mewborn Collection, Letter from John Mosby to Sam Chapman, October 13, 1906

[955] Ibid.

[956] MOC, *Ledger of Reunions – Mosby's Command*

[957] Joseph Bryan, veteran of Company D, was one of Mosby's closest post-war friends and publisher of *The Richmond Times*

[958] Lewis Collection, Letter from Sam Chapman to Willie Chapman, July 28, 1896

[959] *Confederate Veteran*, Volume VII, 1899

[960] Lewis Collection, Memorial Address at Reunion of Mosby's Men, August 28, 1909

[961] Hammond Collection, *Program* of the Reunion, June 3, 1909

[962] Mitchell, *Letters*, p. 67

[963] Duke University, Letter from John Mosby to H. C. Jordan, August 23, 1909, Copy in John S. Russell Papers

[964] Fauquier Historical Society Collection, Letter from John Mosby to Sam Chapman, August 24, 1907

[965] NA, Correspondence Related to Deputy Marshals, 1910-1914, Record Group 60

[966] Mewborn Collection, Letter from John Mosby to Sam Chapman, April 1, 1910

[967] NA, Postal Records, Roll 130, Page 27; Mays' Collection, *Request to Qualify as Presidential Postmaster*, April 7, 1910, (Sam Chapman's copy) ; Canceled check for $95.83, payable to "*S. F. Chapman, Postmaster, for ½ mos. salary*"

[968] Lewis Collection, Letter from W. H. Mosby to Sam Chapman, March 30, 1910

[969] Mays' Collection, Letter from S. F. Chapman to Fourth Asst. Postmaster General, March 28, 1913

[970] Ibid., Letter from S. F. Chapman to Fourth Asst. Postmaster General, July 19, 1913

[971] *Virginian Review*, May 2, 1996

[972] Mays' Collection, Report from S. F. Chapman to J. H. Irving, Post office Inspector, July 21, 1913

[973] Ibid., Letter dated June 19, 1913

[974] Mitchell, *Letters*, (Mosby to Spottswood Campbell, a grandson), pp. 188-189

[975] Ibid.

[976] Heinemann, *Harry Byrd of Virginia*, pp. 11-14

[977] Mewborn Collection, Letter from John Mosby to Willie Chapman, January 22, 1911

[978] Mewborn Collection, Letter from John Mosby to Willie Chapman, August 26, 1911, ("Reverend Knott" may have been Richard Knott, a former Ranger in Company F)

[979] Duke University, Mosby Papers, Letter from Sam Chapman to John Mosby, July 23, 1913

[980] Ibid.

[981] Duke University, Russell Papers, Letter from John Mosby to John Russell, October 5, 1910, (Major Hunter was probably Major Robert W. Hunter, a Virginian and former Chief of Staff for General John B. Gordon)

[982] Ibid., December 10, 1910

[983] Ibid., January 27, 1911

[984] *Confederate Veteran*, Vol. XX, August, 1912, p. 374-375; *Covington Dispatch*, September 14, 1911

36. "But Little Fear of Death"

[985] Brown Collection, King's Land Grant, by virtue of Military Warrant Number 1141, to Charles Dressler from Governor of Virginia, Robert Brooke, August 5, 1795

[986] Jackson Interview. Peter Dressler was the great-great-grandfather of the author and these stories were related by the author's grandmother, "Maggie" Dressler Jackson, daughter of Harrison Dressler. The exact time of this particular coming of Union forces is not known. Most likely it was when General William W. Averell's cavalry came through the area on its way to and from West Virginia and a raid at Salem in December of 1863; or it could have been the following June as General George Crook's Army of West Virginia pushed through the area against General John McCausland's vastly outnumbered Confederate cavalry.

[987] Alleghany County Circuit Court Deed Book 44, Page 445-447, Plat Book 15, Page 6

[988] Daly Collection, Letter from John Mosby to Sam Chapman, December 23, 1913

[989] Bruen, *Christian Forrer the Clockmaker*, p. 206

[990] Alleghany County Circuit Court, Marriage Records

[991] Mrs. Samuel Chapman Stephenson conversation, March, 1998

[992] NA, Postal Records, Roll 130, page 27

[993] Lewis Collection, Letter from Willie Chapman to Herbert Chapman, May 5, 1913

[994] Keen and Mewborn, *43rd Battalion*, p. 376 (roster)

[995] Mosby, *Memoirs*

[996] Lewis Collection, Letter from Willie Chapman to Herbert Chapman, November 24, 1914

[997] LOV, *Act of the General Assembly of Virginia*, approved April 2, 1902

[998] LOV, *Applications of Disabled Soldiers, Sailors, or Marines of the Confederacy*, Form No. 2

[999] Ibid.; Keen and Mewborn, *43rd Battalion*, pp. 315, 373, 296-297, 347 (roster)

[1000] Lewis Collection, Letter from Willie Chapman to Sam Chapman, December 10, 1915

[1001] Ibid., Willie Chapman to Herbert Chapman, November 24, 1914

[1002] Ibid., Willie Chapman to Sam Chapman, December 10, 1915

[1003] Alleghany County Circuit Court, Deed Book 44, Page 445, Plat Book 15, page 6

[1004] Lewis Collection, Letter from Willie Chapman to Sam Chapman, January 10, 1916

[1005] Ibid., February 23, 1916

[1006] Ibid., Letter from Willie Chapman to Sam Chapman, March 10, 1916

[1007] Siepel, *Rebel,* pp. 290-291

[1008] Wood Collection, Letter from John Mosby to Sam Chapman, April 10, 1916

[1009] Brown Collection, Letter from John Mosby to Sam Chapman, November 28, 1894

[1010] *Page News & Courier*, Luray, July 21, 1916; Lewis Collection, Letter from William Chapman to Sam Chapman, March 5, 1916

[1011] *Page New & Currier*, July 21, 1916; Moore, *Dixie Artillery*, p. 99 (roster)

[1012] Lewis Collection, Letter from Sam Chapman to Herbert Chapman, June 29, 1918

[1013] Lewis Collection, From informal writings of Ella Chapman, date unknown, (subsequent to the 1918 reunion); United Daughters of the Confederacy, Alleghany Chapter, 1926

[1014] Lewis Collection, Letter from Sam Chapman to Herbert Chapman, January 22, 1919

[1015] Ibid., March 21, 1919

[1016] Ibid., March 31, 1919

[1017] Ibid., Letter from Ella Chapman to Willie Chapman, April 22, 1919

[1018] MOC, Letter from William H. Chapman to Mrs. Ben Palmer, May 2, 1919

[1019] The Chapman family plot is in Cedar Hill Cemetery, Covington. As for the house on Wills Street, it has long since been leveled and, fittingly, the site and adjoining property is now home to a Baptist church.

BIBLIOGRAPHY

Published Sources

Books and Periodicals

Alexander, John H., *Mosby's Men*, The Neale Publishing Company, New York and Washington, 1907

Alger, R. A., *The Spanish-American War*, Harper & Brothers Publishers, New York and and London, 1901

Alley, Reuben E., *History of the University of Richmond*, University Press of Virginia, Charlottesville, 1977

Andrews, Marietta Minnigerode, *Scraps of Paper*, E. P. Dutton & Co., Inc., New York, 1929

Armstrong, Richard L., *7th Virginia Cavalry*, H. E. Howard, Inc., Lynchburg, Virginia, 1992

Ashby, Thomas A., *The Valley Campaigns*, The Neale Publishing Company, New York, 1914

Bailey, Ronald H., *The Bloodiest Day / The Battle of Antietam*, Time-Life Books, Inc., Alexandria, Virginia, 1984

Baird, Nancy Chappelear (Editor), *Journals of Amanda Virginia Edmonds, Lass of the Mosby Confederacy, 1857-1867*, Commercial Press, Stephens City, Virginia, 1984

Bilby, Joseph G., *Civil War Firearms*, Combined Books, Inc., Conshottocker, Pennsylvania, 1996

Blackford, Lieut-Col. W. W., C.S.A., *War Years With Jeb Stuart*, Charles Scribner's Sons, New York, 1946

Bonnell, Jr., John C., *Sabres in the Shenandoah / The 21st New York Cavalry, 1863-1866* Burd Street Press, Division of White Mane Publishing Company, Inc., Shippensburg, PA 17257

Bruen, Frank (Compiled by), *Christian Forrer the Clockmaker and his Descendants*, The Tuttle Publishing Company, Inc., Rutland, Vermont, 1939.

Carmichael, Peter S., *Lee's Young Artillerist / William R. J. Pegram*, The University Press Of Virginia, Charlottesville, 1995

Clifton Forge Baptist, The, Clifton Forge, Virginia (Privately printed), Volume 1, September, 1905

Confederate Veteran (40 Volumes), Volumes VII, XII, XX, XXXI, Nashville, Tennessee, 1893-1932

Cook, Roy J. (compiled by), *One Hundred and One Famous Poems*, Reilly & Lee Publishers, Chicago, 1958

Corron, Elizabeth Hicks, *Clifton Forge, Virginia, Scenic/Busy/Friendly*, Revised Edition, Stone Printing and Manufacturing Co., Roanoke, Virginia August 1, 1971

Coulter, E. Milton, *A History of the South* (10 Volumes), Volume VII, *The Confederate States of America*, Louisiana State University Press, 1950

Crawford, Marshall, *Mosby and His Men*, G. W. Carleton & Co., New York, 1917

Davis, Burke, *The Long Surrender*, Random House, Inc., New York, 1985

Delauter, Jr., Roger U., *McNeill's Rangers*, H. E. Howard, Inc., Lynchburg, Va., 1986

Devine, John E., *8th Virginia Infantry*, H. E. Howard, Inc., Lynchburg, Virginia, 1983

Dove, Dee, *Madison County Homes*, Kingsport Press, Kingsport, TN, 1975

Dowdy, Clifford, *The Virginia Dynasties*, Little, Brown and Company, Boston, 1969

Driver, Jr., Robert J., *1st Virginia Cavalry*, H. E. Howard, Inc., Lynchburg, Virginia, 1991

Edmonds, Elsie Chapman, *John Chapman of Spotsylvania County, Virginia and Related Families*, (Privately Printed), 1971

Emerson, Edward W., *Life and Letters of Charles Russell Lowell*, Houghton Mifflin Company, Boston and New York, 1907

Evans, Thomas J. and Moyer, James M., *Mosby's Confederacy: a Guide to the Roads and Sites of Colonel John Singleton Mosby*, The White Mane Publishing Company, Inc., Shippensburg, PA, 1991

Mosby Vignettes, Volume III, (Privately Published), Vienna, Virginia, 1994

Everhart, Joan, *Of Saints and Sweet Potatoes*, (Privately Printed), n.d.

Fagan, Roberta E., *Custer and His Times, Book Three*, Little Big Horn Associates, Inc., n. d.

Faust, Patricia L. (Editor*)*, *Historical Times Illustrated Encyclopedia of the Civil War*, Harper & Row Publishers, New York, 1986

Fox, William F., Lt. Col., U.S.V., *Regimental Losses in the American Civil War, 1861-1865*, Albany Publishing Company, Albany, N. Y. 1889

Fry, Dennis E., *12th Virginia Cavalry*, H. E. Howard Inc., Lynchburg, Virginia, 1988

Freeman, Douglas Southall, *Lee's Lieutenants, A Study in Command* (3 Volumes), Charles Scribner's Sons, New York, 1942

-------- *R. E. Lee, A Biography* (4 Volumes), Charles Scribner's Sons, New York, 1934

Furgurson, Ernest B., *Chancellorsville 1863 / The Souls of the Brave*, Alfred A. Knopf, Inc., New York, 1992

Garnett, Marion Gordon (Compiled by), *Reunion Journal*, Volume 1, Number 4, August 1968 to August 1970 (Privately Printed), Hampton, Virginia, 1970

Gordon, General John B., *Reminiscences of the Civil War*, Charles Scribner's Sons, New York, 1904

Gott, John K., *High in Old Virginia's Piedmont*, Published by the Marshall National Bank and Trust Company, Marshall, Virginia, 1987

Grose, Shirley and Associates, *Alleghany County Heritage, 1746-1997*, Volume 1, Summersville, WV, n. d.

Hale, Laura V., *Four Valiant Years In the Lower Shenandoah Valley, 1861-1865*, Shenandoah Publishing House, Inc., Strasburg, VA, 1968

Hayes, J. L., *A History of Averett College*, Averett College Press, 1984

Heinemann, Ronald L., *Harry Byrd of Virginia*, University Press of Virginia, Charlottesville and London, 1996

Hildebrand, John R., (Editor), *A Mennonite Journal, 1862-1865*, Burd Street Press, Shippensburg, PA, 1996

Holy Bible, The, Authorized or King James Version, The John A. Hertel Company, Chicago, 1937

Hotchkiss, Jed., *A Description of Elizabeth Furnace Iron Property, Augusta County, Virginia, Belonging to Forrer & Forrer*, McGill & Witherow, Printers, Washington, D. C., 1869

Humphreys, Charles A., *Field, Camp, Hospital, and Prison in the Civil War, 1863-1865*, Press of Geo. H. Ellis Co., Boston, 1918

Jones, Virgil Carrington, *Ranger Mosby*, University of North Carolina Press, Chapel Hill, 1944

Judge, Joseph, *Season of Fire: the Confederate Strike on Washington*, Rockbridge Publishing Company, Berryville, VA, 1994

Keen, Hugh C. & Mewborn, Horace, *43rd Battalion/Virginia Cavalry/Mosby's Command*, H. E. Howard, Inc., Lynchburg, Virginia, 1993

Kerkhoff, Jennie Ann, *Old Homes of Page County, Virginia*, Lauck and Company, Incorporated, Luray, Virginia, 1962

Krick, Robert K., *9th Virginia Cavalry*, H. E. Howard, Inc., Lynchburg, Virginia, 1982

Linkenhoker, Paul Douglas, *A History of Schooling in Alleghany County, Clifton Forge, and Covington, Virginia*, UMI Dissertation Services, Ann Arbor, Michigan, 1993

Miller, William J., *Mapping for Stonewall, The Civil War Service of Jed Hotchkiss*, Elliott & Clark Publishing, Washington, D. C., 1993

Miles, Nelson A., *The War with Spain, Part 1, North American Review*, May 1899

Miller, Jr., Edward A., *Lincoln's Abolitionist General/ The Biography of David Hunter*, University of South Carolina Press, Columbia, S. C., 1997

Millis, Walter, *The Martial Spirit*, The Literary Guild of America, 1931

Mitchell, Adele H. (Editor), *The Letters of John S. Mosby* (Second Edition), The Stuart-Mosby Historical Society, 1986

Mitchell, Lt. Col. Joseph B., *Decisive Battles of the Civil War*, G. P. Putnam's Sons, New York, 1955

Moore, Robert H., *The Danville, Eighth Star New Market, and Dixie Artillery*, H. E. Howard, Inc., Lynchburg, Virginia, 1989

---------*The Richmond Fayette, Hampden, Thomas, and Blount's Lynchburg Artillery*, H. E. Howard, Inc., Lynchburg, VA, 1991

Morton, Oren F., *A Centennial History of Alleghany County, Virginia*, J. K. Ruebush Company, Dayton, Virginia, 1923

---------*Annals of Bath County, Virginia*, The McClure Co., Inc., Staunton, Virginia, 1917

Mosby, John S., *The Memoirs of Colonel John S. Mosby*, Edited by Charles Wells Russell, Little, Brown & Co., Boston, 1917

---------*Mosby's War Reminiscences*, Dodd, Mead and Company, New York, 1898

Munson, John W., *Reminiscences of a Mosby Guerrilla*, Moffat, Yard and Company, New York, 1906

Murphy, Terrence V., *10th Virginia Infantry*, H. E. Howard, Inc., Lynchburg, Virginia, 1989

Musselman, Homer D., *The Caroline Light, Parker and Stafford Light Virginia Artillery*, H. E. Howard, Inc., Lynchburg, Virginia, 1992

National Cyclopedia of American Biography, The, James T. White & Company, New York, 1931

Old Homes and Families of Fauquier County, Virginia (The W. P. A. Records), Virginia Book Company, Berryville, Virginia, 1978

Osborne, Charles C., *Jubal / The Life and Times of General Jubal A. Early, CSA, Defender of the Lost Cause,* Algonquin Books of Chapel Hill, Chapel Hill, North Carolina, 1992

Patchan, Scott C., *The Forgotten Fury, The Battle of Piedmont, Virginia,* Sergeant Kirkland's Museum and Historical Society, Inc., Fredericksburg, Virginia, 1996

Reader's Digest Association, Inc, The, *Family Encyclopedia of American History,* Pleasantville, New York, 1975

Religious Herald, (The Memories of "Mosby's Men"), by Former Captain Samuel F. Chapman, Richmond, Virginia, January, February, March, 1902

Robertson, Jr., James I., *Stonewall Jackson, The Man, The Soldier, The Legend,* Macmillan Publishing, USA, New York, 1997

Sanger, Donald Bridgman, *James Longstreet, The Soldier,* Louisiana State University Press, Baton Rouge, 1952

Scott, Major John, *Partisan Life with Col. John S. Mosby,* Harpe & Brothers, Publishers, New York, 1867(Reprint edition Olde Soldiers Books, Inc., Gaithersburg, Md., n.d.

Sears, Stephen W., *To the Gates of Richmond,* Ticknor & Fields, New York, 1992

Siepel, Kevin H., *Rebel, The Life and Times of John Singleton Mosby,* St. Martin's Press, New York, 1983

Southern Historical Society Papers, (52 Volumes), Volumes XXIV, XXV, XXVII, Richmond, Virginia, 1876-1953

Strickler, Harry M. *A Short History of Page County, Virginia,* The Dietz Press, Incorporated, Richmond, Virginia, 1952.

Stuntz, Connie Pendleton and Stuntz, Mayo Sturdevant, *This Was Tysons Corner, Virginia,* (Privately Printed), Vienna, Virginia, 1990

Taylor, George Braxton, *Virginia Baptist Ministers,* Sixth Series, 1914-1934, J. P. Bell Company, Inc., Lynchburg, Va., 1935

Time - Life Books, *Echoes of Glory/Arms and Equipment of the Union,* Alexandria, Virginia, 1991

U. S. War Department, *War of the Rebellion: A Compilation of the Official Records of the Union and Confederate Armies (*128 Volumes), U. S. Government Printing Office, Washington, D. C., 1881-1901

-------- *Atlas to Accompany the Official Records of the Union and Confederate Armies,* 1891-1895, (Reprint Edition), Arno Press and Crown Publishers, Inc., New York, 1978

Wallace, Robert C., *A Few Memories of a Long Life,* Ye Galleon Press, Fairfield, Washington, n. d.

Wallace, Jr., Lee A., *A Guide to Virginia Military Organizations, 1861-1865* (Revised Second Edition), H. E. Howard, Inc., Lynchburg, Virginia, 1986

------- *17th Virginia Infantry,* H. E. Howard, Inc., Lynchburg, Virginia, 1990

------- *The Richmond Howitzers,* H. E. Howard, Inc., Lynchburg, Virginia 1993

Weaver, Hazel F., *The History of Public Education in Fauquier County, Virginia, 1871-1954,* The American University, Washington, D. C., 1955

Wert, Jeffry D., *Mosby's Rangers* (paperback edition), Touchstone, New York, NY, 1991 (Original edition published by Simon & Schuster, New York, N. Y., 1990)

Whittet & Sheperson, Printers, *The First Hundred Years, Brief Sketches of History of the University of Richmond*, May, 1932

Williamson, James J., *Mosby's Rangers*, Ralph B. Kenyon, Publisher, New York, 1896

Wise, George, *History of the Seventeenth Virginia Infantry, C.S.A.*, Kelly, Piet, & Company, Baltimore, 1879 (Reprint edition, R. W. Beatty, LTD, Arlington, Virginia, 1969)

Woodward, Harold R., *The Confederacy's Forgotten Son, Major General James Lawton Kemper, C.S.A.*, Rockbridge Publishing Company, Natural Bridge Station, Virginia, 1993

Yowell, Claude Lindsay, *A History of Madison County, Virginia*, Shenandoah Publishing House, Strasburg, Virginia, 1926

Newspapers
(Virginia unless otherwise noted)

(Clifton Forge) *Alleghany Tribune*
Alexandria Gazette
Baltimore Star (Maryland)
Baltimore American (Maryland)
Charlottesville Daily Progress
Clifton Forge Review
Covington Dispatch
Covington Virginian
(Winchester) *Evening Star*
Lexington Gazette
New York World (New York)
(Luray) *Page News & Courier*
Richmond Enquirer
Richmond Times
Staunton Vindicator
(Covington)*Virginian Review*
Washington Times (D. C.)

Unpublished Sources

Institutional Repositories

Alleghany County Circuit Court Clerk's Office, Covington, Virginia
    Deed and Plat Books
    Chancery Records
    Wills and Estates Settlements
    Birth, Death, Marriage Records
Alleghany Highlands Genealogical Society, Covington, Virginia
    Revercomb Family Scrap Book

City of Covington, Virginia, City Manager's Office
  Records of Cedar Hill Cemetery
Clarke County Historical Association, Berryville, Virginia
  Proceedings, Volume XV, 1963-1964
Clifton Forge Baptist Church, Clifton Forge, Virginia
  Minutes Book and Miscellaneous Papers 1876-1919
  The Road We Came, 1882-1965
Commonwealth of Virginia, Department of Health, Division of Vital Records, Richmond
  Birth Records, 1919
  Marriage Records, 1864
Covington Baptist Church, Covington, Virginia
  Minutes Book and Miscellaneous Papers 1841-1919
Duke University Rare Book, Manuscript, & Special Collections Library, Durham, North
  Carolina:
  John Singleton Mosby Papers
  John S. Russell Papers
Fauquier Bank, The, Warrenton, Virginia
  Eugene M. Sheel Map of Fauquier County, 1996
Fauquier County Circuit Court Clerk's Office, Warrenton, Virginia
  Deed Books
  Marriage Records
Fauquier Heritage Society, Marshall, Virginia
  The Elgin Family of Maryland and Virginia, Compiled by James G. Elgin,
    February, 1991
Fauquier Historical Society, Warrenton, Virginia
  John Mosby to Sam Chapman Letter, 1907
Genealogical Society of Page County, Page Public Library, Luray, Virginia
  The Hite Papers
  Works Progress Administration, Historical Inventory of Page County, Virginia, c.
    1935, printed March 1991
  Civil War Diary of George D. Buswell, Page County, Virginia
  Civil War Letters of Residents of Page County, Virginia
George Washington University Archives, Gilman Library, Department of Special
  Collections, Washington, D.C.:
  The George Washington University Through the Years, by G. David Anderson,
    University Archivist
Healing Springs Baptist Church, Healing Springs, Virginia
  Minutes Book 1882-1910
Library of Virginia (Formerly Virginia State Library), Richmond
  Minutes of Main Street Baptist Church, Luray, Virginia, Church Records,
    Miscellaneous Microfilm Reel No. 303
  Compiled Service Records of Confederate Soldiers who served in organizations
    from the State of Virginia
  Special Orders of the Adjutant and Inspector-General's Office, CSA, Rare Book
    Department

Records of Births, Deaths, Marriages 1820-1910
    City of Alexandria
    Counties of Alleghany, Fairfax, Fauquier, and Loudoun
    Personal Property Tax Lists for Alleghany County/Covington
    Personal Property Tax Lists for Staunton
    Pension Applications from Alleghany County under Confederate Pension
        Application Act of April 2, 1902, as Amended
Loving Funeral Home, Inc., Covington, Virginia
    Burial and Financial Records, 1919
Low Moor Presbyterian Church, Low Moor, Virginia
    (History of) *Low Moor Presbyterian Church* (Typed copy by Lucy Knighton,
        Historian, u.d., c. 1988)
Luray Baptist Church, Luray, Virginia
    Miscellaneous Papers and Records
Lutheran Theological Seminary, A. R. Wentz Library Archives, Gettysburg,
    Pennsylvania:
    Catalogs and Enrollments of Staunton Female Seminary for 1884-85 and 1885-86
Madison County Circuit Court Clerk's Office, Madison, Virginia
    Marriage Bonds
Museum of the Confederacy, Eleanor S. Brockenbrough Library, Richmond, Virginia
    J. Thomas Petty Diary
    Ledger of Reunions, Mosby's Command, kept by W. E. Grayson, Front Royal,
        Virginia
    William H. Chapman to Mrs. Ben Palmer, Letter, May 2, 1919
    McIlhany Papers
National Archives and Records Administration, Washington, D.C.
    4th U. S. Volunteer Infantry, Spanish War, Company Muster Rolls
    4th U. S. Volunteer Infantry, Spanish War, Regimental Returns
    Adjutant General's Office, U. S., *A Statistical Exhibit of Strength of Volunteer
        Forces, 1899*
    Adjutant General's Office, U. S., Spanish War, Miscellaneous Correspondence
    Adjutant General's Office, U. S., Spanish War, Regimental Register of Patients,
        4th U. S. Volunteer Infantry
    Adjutant and Inspector General's Office, Confederate States (Microfilm M-935)
    Compiled Service Records of Confederate General and Staff Officers and Non-
        regimental Enlisted Men who served in organizations from the State of
        Virginia
    Compiled Service Records of the Union and the Confederacy
    Compiled Service Records and Muster Rolls of Field, Staff and Band Officers
        who served in the U. S. Volunteer Forces in the Spanish War
    Division of Railway Mail Service/Rosters of Railway Postal Clerks, 1855-1897,
        (Record Group 028)
    General Records of the Department of Justice/Correspondence relating to Deputy
        Marshalls, 1897-1924 (Record Group 60)
    Official Register of the United States, 1877, 1881
    U. S. Postal Service, Postal Records, Roll 130

National Personnel Records Center, Civilian Personnel Branch, St. Louis, Missouri
    Records of Civilian Employees of the U. S. Postal Service after 1910
Official Register of the United States, Washington, D. C.
    Federal Employees Listings for the Period 1870-1880
Page Public Library, Luray, Virginia
    An Interim Report on Catherine Furnace, by Laura Rappleye, March 1981, n.p.
Rich Patch Union Church, Low Moor, Virginia
    Miscellaneous Papers
Sharon Baptist Church, Clifton Forge, Virginia
    Minutes Book, 1841-1910
United Daughters of the Confederacy, Alleghany Chapter, Covington, Virginia
    Mosby's Rangers/The 43rd Virginia Battalion, by Ella Lee Chapman, 1926
United States Bureau of the Census, Washington, D. C.
    Record of the Census for the State of Virginia, 1820-1910
        City of Alexandria
        Counties of Alleghany, Augusta, Fairfax, Fauquier, Loudoun, Madison,
        Middlesex, Page
University of Virginia, Alderman Library, Special Collections Branch, Charlottesville
    Jedediah Hotchkiss Papers
    John S. Mosby Papers
    John Warwick Daniel Papers
    Catherine Barbara Broun Diary/Family Events 1862-1865
    Scrapbooks of John S. Mosby, 1869-1915
Virginia Baptist Historical Society, University of Richmond, Richmond
    Catalogs of Richmond College for the 1858-59 and 1859-60 Sessions
    Index of Obituaries appearing in *Religious Herald*
    Minutes of Rappahannock Baptist Association of Virginia
    Religious Herald issues of January 16, 1873; September 30; 1875; March 23,
        1876; December 20, 1900; January, February, and March, 1902;
        July 3, 1919
    Reports of Augusta Baptist Association of Virginia, 1899-1907
    Reports of General Baptist Association of Virginia, 1882-1907
    Virginia Baptist Ministers Biographical Sheet for Reverend S. F. Chapman
Virginia Historical Society, Collections and Manuscripts Division, Richmond
    William H. Chapman Letters
    Frederick F. Bowen Papers
    Joseph Bryan Papers, 1866-1905
Washington and Lee University, Leyburn Library, Lexington, Virginia
    The Jedediah Hotchkiss Papers (60 Microfilm Reels)
Woodlawn Baptist Church, Alexandria, Virginia
    A Century of Growth 1869-1969

Private Collections and Interviews

Brown, Peter A. – Lexington, Virginia
Chapman, Mrs. David Coffman – Richmond, Virginia
Cockrell, Milton – Culpeper, Virginia
Crawford, Howard – Raleigh, North Carolina
Daly, Robert M. – Middleburg, Virginia
Gott, John K. – Arlington, Virginia
Hansen, Mrs. Archer – Winchester, Virginia
Hammond, Howard Revercomb – Greenville, South Carolina
Hudnall, George Revercomb – Covington, Virginia
Jackson, Mrs. Margaret Dressler – Covington, Virginia
Keen, Hugh – Tulsa, Oklahoma
Kincheloe, John T. – Fairfax, Virginia
Lacy, Jr., Paul B. – Covington, Virginia
Lewis, Mr. and Mrs. Charles – Buies Creek, North Carolina
Mays, Merrill S. – Covington, Virginia
Mewborn, Horace – Springfield, Virginia
Miller, Duane – Youngstown, Pennsylvania
Moyer, James M. – Vienna, Virginia
Revercomb, III, Horace A. – King George, Virginia
Russell, Mr. and Mrs. Chris – Millersville, Maryland
Stephenson, Mrs. Samuel Chapman – Richmond, Virginia
Wood, III, Oliver S. – Culpeper, Virginia

INDEX

ordination of 298
promotions of 47,134-135,192-193
receives advice from Willie Mosby 345-346
receives commission in U.S. Army 327
resigns Clifton Forge pastorate 314
resigns Covington pastorate 325
Chapman, William (great grandfather) 26
Chapman, William A. (grandfather) 26
Chapman, William Allen (father) 23,26,27
Chapman, William Allen "Willie" (son) 183,297
  311,319,321-323,333-337,343,348,350-354,357
Chapman, William Henry (brother)
  and Union assault at Second Manassas 67-69
  annihilates Berryville house burners 213
  appeals disbanding of artillery company 82
  assumes command on Northern Neck 273
  at disbandment of command 290
  attacks Gen. Duffie 187
  describes debacle at Loudoun Heights 142-144
  helps lead attack on Berryville wagon train 202
  helps raise artillery company 46
  in Southern Guards 46
  is described 235
  is elected captain of Company C 141
  is elected captain of Dixie Artillery 47
  is promoted to lt.-col. 265
  leads rout of Loudoun Rangers 243
  meets with Gen. Lee 272
  on success of Miskel Farm fight 112
  takes command of Rangers 270
Chapman's Battery (See Dixie Artillery)
Chappelier, James Pendleton 152
Charles City Court House (Va.) 11,
Charlestown (W. Va.) (now Charles Town) 146,
  154-156,188,207,209,210,215,217,218,256,
  257,266,285
Cheat Mountain 50
Chesapeake and Ohio Canal 107,179
Chester Gap (Road) 226-228,230
Chickahominy River 10,11,52,53,54,55,57
Churches:
  Bethel Baptist 296
  Broad Run Baptist 297
  Chantilly 94
  Clifton Forge Baptist 305,306,309-311,
    313-316,337
  Covington Baptist 302,303,305,310,311,321,
    323,325,339
  Cowpasture Union (see also Sharon) 306
  Ebenezer 297
  Healing Springs Baptist 313-316,318,323,333,
    337,339
  Laurel Hill Baptist 316
  Low Moor Union (Baptist) 303,307,309,310,
    315,318,323,325,333
  Luray Baptist 33

  Main Street (Luray) Baptist 33,34,62
    192, 295,296,297
  Menokin Baptist 281
  Mount Zion 181-183,297,335
  Mount Carmel 284
  North Fork 285
  Rich Patch 303,304,307,315,323,325,339
  Rich Patch Mines 307,325
  Sharon 303,304,306,309-311,313,315
  Woodlawn Baptist 298,299
Churchville (Va.) 30,37,49,50
Clifton Forge (Va.) 303-306,309-310,323,324
Cloyd's Mountain 170
Coats, Annie 299
Coffman family 27
Coffman, Jennie 27
Cole, Henry A. 142,144,148,149
Cole,Thomas 258,259
Coles Neck 279
Coles Point 279
Colquitt, Alfred 75
Columbian College 33,34,119
Confederate Adjutant and Inspector General
  (A&IG) 85,113,114,132
Confederate Congress 8,12,84,159
Conner, Lawrence L. 98
Conrad, Charles 101
Conscription Act 84,85
Copeland, J. F. 114
Corbin, Lemuel Armistead 273
Cornwell, John 147,148
Covington (Va.) 301-306,309-311,313,315,
  317-321,323-325,328,333,334,341,344-347,
  349-351,355,356
Covington Graded School 312,325
Covington Improvement Company 319-321
Cowpasture River 306
Crampton's Gap 75,76,77
Criglersville (Va.) 27
Criser, Perry (home) 227,230
Crook, George 162,169,170,216
Crowninshield, Casper 261
Cub Run 92,97,98,103
Culpeper County (Va.) 26
Culpeper Court House (Va.) 53,98,102,132
Custer, George Armstrong 211,212,228,229,
  231,232,238,252-255,257

D

Daniel, John Warwick 327,328,332,336,338,340,
  341,347
Danville (Va.) 337
Davis, Jefferson 83,100,272-274
Davis, John W. 191
Dearing, James (Dearing's Battalion) 114,
  131-134
Dearing's (Lynchburg) Battery 54

Front Royal (Va.) 41,45,54,164,171,217,225,
226,230,231,233,234,236,237,239,246,
251-255,343-345,356,358
Frying Pan (Va.) (now Floris) 95

G

Gaines' Mill, Battle of 54,55,56
Gains, Edmund (great grandfather) 26
Gains, Tabitha (great grandmother) 26
Gamble, William 270,286
Gansevoort, H. S. 222,223,244
Germantown (Va.) 94,95,220
Gibbons, Samuel 29
Gill, Jr., George Murray 285
Gilmer, Joseph 92,93,95,99
Gilmor, Harry 170-172
Glandell, John 118,119
Glascock, Alfred 186,202,209,213,235,241
Glascock, Jr., Aquilla 269,350
Glen Welby 289
Glendale (Frayser's Farm), Battle of 56,57,59,77
Gold Farm fight 217,218,220
Gooding's Tavern 140,141
Goose Creek 181,199,240
Gordonsville (Va.) 13,14,16,64,70,115,235,247,
270,285
Grant, Ulysses Simpson 153,158,161,162,169,
170,184,185,187,188,199,200,208,209,211,
237-239,249,265,276-278,283,286,289,295,
298,345
Grapewood Farm 129,132,139,149,189,254,260,
281,295,358
fight at 125-128
Gray, Robert 144
Green, Charles 126,128
Green, Henry 107,108
Greenback Raid 243,246,342
Greenwich (Va.) 123,126,129,154,192,356
Gregg, David M. 147
Gregg, Maxcy 79
Grogan, Charles Edward 250,251,253,259
Grove, Ben 130,131
Groveton (Va.) 68,69,72,93
Groveton Turnpike 66,69
Grubb, James W. 179,243,244
Guard Hill fight 165
Guilford Station (Va.) 150
Gunnell, George West 173,174
Gunnell, James N. 173,174

H

Hagerstown (Md.) 25,74,248
Hagerstown Road 75
Halleck, Henry Wager 61,185,188,239,241,249,
260,261,284,288
Hamilton's Crossing (Va.) 273,277,278
Hammond, John 139

Hampden Artillery (see also Caskie, William H.)
114,132,134
Hampton, Wade 76
hanging of Ranger Albert Willis 246

Hannon, Dr.Samuel L. 330
Hanover Court House (Va.) 11,13,14
Hanover Junction (Va.) 16
Harper's Ferry (W.Va.) 30,46,48,50,51,73-79,
141-143,148,157,162,176,177,179,180,184,
185,187,188,199-201,206,207,209,210,218,
219,224,236,243,244,252,266
Harris, Rev. W. O. 301,302,305
Harrison's Landing (Va.) 11,12,13,56,60,61
Hatcher, Henry A. "Harry" 106,110,114,186,
188,202,216,227,229,242,250,258
Hatcher's Mill 249
Hathaway, James 94,105
Havana, Cuba 326,331
Hawksbill Creek 23,25
Hayes, President 298
Haymarket (Va.) 125
Hearn, John W. 242
Heaton, Henry 142,143,184
Hefflebower, John N. 212
Heintzelman, S. P. 113,114
Herndon Station (Va.) 94,99,100,105-107
Herndon, John 192
Herndon, Rev. Thaddeus 192,358
Hibbs, William "Major" 101,103,119
Highland County (Va.) 53
Highlands 146
Hill, Ambrose Powell 62,72,78,79
Hill, Daniel Harvey 60,61,62,74,75,76
Hillsboro (Va.) 142,143
Hite, David 89
Hite, Isaac 59
Hobbs, J. J. 352,357
Hood, John Bell (Hood's Texans) 52,55,64,68,
69,75,76,78,118
Hooker, Joseph 75,114-116,120,123
Hopewell Gap 115,237
Hoskins, Bradford Smith 102,126-128,146
Hotchkiss, Jedediah 30-33,35,37,49-52,70
Huger, Benjamin 59,62
Hunter, Andrew 188
Hunter, David "Black Dave" 170-173,
185-188,199,200,211,238,261,301
Hunter, Robert W. 349
Hunter, William Lyle 98,112,114,148,152
Hunter's Mill 247

I

Iden, Benjamin 217,218
Immune Regiment (see also U.S. Volunteer
Infantry) 328,331
Ingalls, Rufus 140

Mann. William D. 125-128
Manzanillo. Cuba 329,330
Markham (Va.) 141,147
Marshal's Office (U.S.) 341,345
Martin, William H. "Willie" 119,182,193,205,
 215
Martinsburg (W.Va.) 73,74,81,162,169,176,188,
 189,199,200,236,248,249
Maryland Heights 74,77,184
Massanutten Mountain 23,25,29,53,54,74,225,
 238
Massaponax Creek (River) 273,278
Maurin's Battery 64
McClellan, George B. 7,9-13,15,16,50,52,
 55-57,59-62,64,70,73-75,78,79
McCobb, Joseph 149
McCormick, Province 212,213
McCue, John Willis 283
McDonough, Charles T. 257,258
McDowell, Battle of 53
McIlhany, Hugh Milton 341,342
McKim, Allen W. 353
McKinley, President 327,332,333
McLaws, Lafayette 74-78
McMaster, Charles 226-234
McNeill's Rangers 159,171
McVeigh, Richard Newton 286
Mechanicsville (Va.) 54
Merritt, Wesley 226,228,229,231,232,234,238,
 255,260,261,265,270,271
Merry's Store 304
Middleburg (Va.) 17,90,92,93,95,106,114,116,
 123,131,139,150,157,182,210,249,269,270
Middletown (Pa.) 331
Middletown (Va.) 74,171,172,210,237,241
Miles, Dixon S. 77
Milford (Va.) 225
Millwood (Va.) 156,163,208,209,265-267,
 288,289,291
Milroy, Robert H. 53,156
Minor, Albert G. "Ab" 227
Miskel Farm 107,108,111,113,114,119,122,
 152,181,189,193,250,317,358
Miss Beck 129,130,131,156,189,295,335,358
Monocacy (Md.) 74,184,186,197,198,209
Monteiro, Dr. Aristides 288,291,345
Montjoy, Richard P. 118,119,123-126,139,142,
 144,146,149,151,155,157,215,217,234,235,
 241,247,249,253,257,259,260
Montross (Va.) 273,279
Moon, ____ 198
Moore, Edwin 243
Moran, Richard Y. "Dick" 101,103,107-109,119
Morgan, W. L. 149

Mosby, John Singleton
 and first command 17
 and relationship with Willie Chapman 321
 captures Gen. Duffie 248
 captures Gen. Stoughton 96
 characterizes Sam Chapman 149
 communicates with Gen. Early 184
 concurs with Lee to execute Custer's
  men 252
 criticizes former ranger Hugh McIlhany 342
 criticizes former ranger Syd Ferguson 324
 death of 355
 defines Mosby's Confederacy 175
 destroys Union wagon train at Berryville
  204-206
 disbands command 290
 enlists in cavalry 5
 gives reasons for not attending reunions 345
 has command exempted from repeal of Partisan
  Ranger Act 159
 is captured 13
 is cause of retaliation upon citizenry 242
 is confined to jail 4
 is criticized by Gen. Lee 140
 is defeated at Grapewood Farm 126
 is defeated at Loudoun Heights 142-144
 is described 3
 is promoted 100,113,145,265
 is routed at Warrenton Junction 119
 is wounded 140,222,268
 loses artillery 244
 meets with Lee to reorganize command 265
 men ordered hung by Grant 208
 mourns death of Capt. Montjoy 259
 on Sam Chapman's wounding 128
 orders Dolly Richards to wipe out Blazer
  Scouts 257
 orders command to Northern Neck 271
 orders resignation of Walter Frankland 251
 organizes artillery company 197
 rebukes Sam Chapman 338,340
 recalls last raid 286
 relates contempt for former ranger Tom
  Richards 275
 resigns commission 9
 urges Sam Chapman to go to Philippines 332
Mosby, William H. "Willie" 197,340,345,347
Mosby's Command (see Viginia Cavalry)
Mosby's Confederacy 18,115,135,139,153,160
 236,260,261,267
Mosby's Light Artillery (Artillery Company)
 123,197,203,204,223,244,260
Moss, Thomas 227,229,230,233
Mossy Creek (Va.) 30-33,35,47,54,70
Mossy Creek Academy 31
Mossy Creek Ironworks 30,31